ECONOMIC REFORMS, GROWTH AND INEQUALITY IN LATIN AMERICA

Economic Reforms, Growth and Inequality in Latin America

Essays in Honor of Albert Berry

Edited by

GUSTAVO INDART
University of Toronto, Canada

ASHGATE

Published by
Ashgate Publishing Limited
Gower House
Croft Road
Aldershot
Hants GU11 3HR
England

Ashgate Publishing Company
Suite 420
101 Cherry Street
Burlington, VT 05401-4405
USA

Ashgate website: http://www.ashgate.com

British Library Cataloguing in Publication Data
Economic reforms, growth and inequality in Latin America :
essays in honor of Albert Berry
1.Income distribution - Latin America 2.Labor market -
Latin America 3.Latin America - Economic conditions - 20th
century 4.Latin America - Economic policy - 20th century
I.Berry, Albert II.Indart, Gustavo
338.9'8

Library of Congress Cataloging-in-Publication Data
Economic reforms, growth and inequality in Latin America : essays in honor of Albert Berry / [edited] by Gustavo Indart.
p. cm.
Includes index.
ISBN 0-7546-4217-8
1. Latin America--Economic conditions--1982- 2. Latin America--Economic conditions--1982---Regional disparities. 3. Latin America--Economic policy. I. Berry, R. Albert. II. Indart, Gustavo.

HC125.E3744 2004
330.98--dc22

2004010324

ISBN 0 7546 4217 8

Printed in Great Britain by Antony Rowe Ltd, Chippenham, Wiltshire

Contents

List of Figures

List of Tables

List of Contributors

Diana Alarcón is senior economist at INDES, the training institute of the Inter-American Development Bank. During a recent 2-year leave from the Bank, Dr. Alarcón worked at the Bureau for Development Policy in the UNDP, New York. She has worked previously as Professor of Economics at El Colegio de la Frontera Norte in Tijuana, Mexico (1988-95) and at the American University in Washington, D.C. (1996-97), and as labor economist at the International Labor Office in Geneva (1995-96). Dr. Alarcón specializes in issues related to poverty, income distribution and labor markets, with particular focus on Mexico. She is the author of *Changes in the Distribution of Income in Mexico and Trade Liberalization* (1994) and of numerous papers published in learned journals and specialized economic books. Dr. Alarcón holds a Ph.D. in Economics from the University of California at Riverside.

Oscar Altimir is Director of the *CEPAL Review* and consultant to ECLAC. He has previously held several positions at ECLAC including those of Adjunct Executive Secretary (1994-96), Director of the Division of Economic Development (1989-93), Director of the joint ECLAC/ONUDI Division of Industry and Technology (1984-88), and Director of the Division of Statistics and Quantitative Analysis, and has worked as a consultant to the World Bank (1973-75) and to the Ministry of Economy and Labour of Argentina (1971). His main areas of research interest include the analysis of income distribution and the incidence of poverty in Latin America. He has published extensively in these and other areas including a paper on "Income Distribution and Poverty through Crisis and Adjustment" in A. Berry, ed., *Poverty, Economic Reform and Income Distribution in Latin America* (Boulder: Lynne Rienner, 1998).

François Bourguignon is Chief Economist of the World Bank. Dr. Bourguignon has previously worked as Professor of Economics at the École des Hautes Etudes en Sciences Sociales (EHESS) in Paris, and has been honorary director of the Département et Laboratoire d'Economie Théorique et Appliquée (DELTA), an economic research center at EHESS. Dr. Bouguignon has also been Director of the Centre d'Economie Quantitative et Comparative at EHESS (1986-1987), Senior Researcher at the Laboratoire d'Economie Politique de l'École Normale Supérieure (1978-1985), and Assistant Professor of Economics at the University of Toronto (1975-1978). He has also worked as consultant to numerous international organizations including the PNUD, the ILO, the World Bank, and the OECD. His research focuses on income distribution, poverty, and economic development. Dr. Bourguignon has published more than 100 papers in learned journals and specialized economics books, and is the author or editor of 8 books.

Andrew S. Downes is Professor of Economics and Director of the Sir Arthur Lewis Institute of Social and Economic Studies (SALISES) at the University of the West Indies (UWI) in Barbados. Dr. Downes has a Ph.D. in Economics from the University of Manchester. His main research interests are in Applied Econometrics, Labor and Human Resource Economics, and Economics of Business Decisions. He is a former member of the Board of Directors of the Barbados Port Authority and the Central Bank of Barbados, and former Chairman of the Barbados National Productivity Board. Dr. Downes has worked as a consultant to several international organizations including the World Bank, the International Labor Organization, the Inter-American Development Bank, the Pan-American Health Organization, and the Caribbean Development Bank. He has published over 50 papers in learned journals and specialized economics books.

Fatma El-Hamidi is currently teaching at the Economics Department and at the Graduate School of Public and International Affairs (GSPIA) of University of Pittsburgh, and is a faculty practitioner at the University of Phoenix. Her research interests focus on economics of the labor market in the developing world. Dr. El-Hamidi is also working as a consultant with the World Bank in the area of labor markets in the Middle East.

Rafael Gómez is a Ph.D. graduate of the University of Toronto's Center for Industrial Relations. He is currently an Assistant Professor at the London School of Economics (LSE), Interdisciplinary Institute of Management. Dr. Gómez also holds joint appointments as Research Fellow at the Center for International Studies, Center for Industrial Relations, University of Toronto and Center for Economic Performance, London School of Economics. Over the past three years he has delivered lectures and taught courses in Human Resource Management, Labor Economics, and Comparative Industrial Relations. Rafael Gómez has been a recent speaker at several national and international conferences.

Morley Gunderson holds the CIBC Chair in Youth Employment at the University of Toronto, where he is a Professor at the Center for Industrial Relations (Director from 1985-97) and the Department of Economics. He is also a Research Associate of the Centre for International Studies, the Institute for Policy Analysis, the Institute for Human Development, Life Course and Aging, and the Institute for Work and Health. He has been a Visiting Scholar at the International Institute for Labor Research in Geneva, Switzerland, and the National Bureau of Economic Research, the North America Forum and the Hoover Institution at Stanford. He has authored 7 books, over 70 articles published in academic journals, and over 80 chapters in edited volumes on various topics including gender discrimination and pay equity; the aging workforce, pensions and mandatory retirement; youth employment; public sector wage determination; and the determinants and impact of immigration. In 2002, he received the Excellence in Education Award in Labour Economics from the Industrial Relations Research Association.

Gerry Helleiner is Professor Emeritus in Economics and Distinguished Research Fellow, Center for International Studies, University of Toronto, where he was on the faculty for over 30 years. His Ph.D. in economics is from Yale University where he subsequently held his first academic appointment. He is the author and editor of numerous books on aspects of international trade, international finance and development, the most recent of which was *Capital Account Regimes and the Developing Countries* (Macmillan). He has served and continues to serve on a number of editorial boards of journals of economics, politics and development. From 1990 until 1999, on a part-time basis, he was Research Director of the developing countries' Group of 24 at the IMF and World Bank. He has chaired the Boards of the North-South Institute in Ottawa and the International Food Policy Research Institute in Washington; at present he serves on the Executive Board of the African Capacity-Building Foundation in Harare. He has consulted for a wide range of international institutions and governments. Dr. Helleiner has recently been inducted into the Order of Canada.

Gustavo Indart is Lecturer of Economics, an associate member of the graduate faculty of the Department of Political Science, and an Associate Researcher at the Center for International Studies of the University of Toronto. He has a Ph.D. in Economics from the University of Toronto, and is the Coordinator of the Program on Latin America and the Caribbean at the Center for International Studies. Dr. Indart is interested in the Political Economy of Development with particular reference to Latin America, and has worked as consultant to the Inter-American Development Bank on poverty and income distribution in Paraguay and Nicaragua. As Coordinator of CIS's Program on Latin America and the Caribbean, Dr. Indart has participated on numerous research and capacity-building projects focusing on Latin America. He is the co-editor (with Albert Berry) of *Critical Issues in International Financial Reform* (Transaction Publishers, 2003).

Adriana Marshall is currently Career Researcher at the National Research Council of Argentina and Director of the Socio-Económicos Internacionales at the Instituto de Desarrollo Económico y Social, specialized in the interdisciplinary and comparative study of labour markets, and labour and social policies. Earlier she had been Researcher at the Netherlands School of Economics; Professor at the Facultad Latinoamericana de Ciencias Sociales; Research Associate at the Center for Latin American and Caribbean Studies of New York University; and Senior Research Officer at the International Institute for Labour Studies (ILO, Geneva). Dr. Marshall holds a Ph.D. from the Netherlands School of Economics and is the author of several books including *The Import of Labour - The Case of the Netherlands* (Rotterdam: Rotterdam University Press, 1973), *El Mercado de Trabajo en el Capitalismo Periférico - el caso de Argentina* (Santiago: PISPAL, CLACSO, 1978), *Políticas Sociales: El Modelo Neoliberal* (Buenos Aires: Legasa,

1988), and *Circumventing Labour Protection - Non Standard Employment in Argentina and Peru* (Geneva: International Institute for Labour Studies, 1992); and has published extensively in Argentinean and international journals.

Samuel A. Morley is presently Visiting Research Fellow at the International Food Policy Research Institute. Dr. Morley has a Ph.D. in Economics from the University of California at Berkeley. Previously he has been Professor of Economics at the University of Wisconsin (1968-76) and Vanderbilt University (1976-1993), Senior Advisor at the Inter-American Development Bank (1993-1997), and Expert on Poverty Alleviation at ECLAC (1998-99). His areas of research interest are labour market issues, income distribution, and poverty alleviation in developing countries. He is the author of several books and numerous papers published in specialized journals and economics books. Dr. Morley has worked as consultant to numerous international organizations including the World Bank, UNDP, ECLAC, IDB, the Ford Foundation and the International Food Policy Research Institute.

José Antonio Ocampo is currently Under-Secretary General of the Department of Economic and Social Affairs of the United Nations, New York. Previously he has held the position of Executive Secretary of the United Nations Economic Commission for Latin America and the Caribbean, and a number of posts in the Government of Colombia, including those of Minister of Finance and Public Credit, Director of the National Planning Department and Minister of Agriculture. He is the author of numerous books and articles on macroeconomic policy and theory, economic development, international trade and economic history. Dr. Ocampo obtained his Ph.D. in Economics from Yale University and has been honored with the Alejandro Angel Escobar National Science Award.

Gustav Ranis is the Frank Altschul Professor of International Economics at Yale University and the Henry R. Luce Director of the Yale Center for International and Area Studies. He was Assistant Administrator for Program and Policy for the Agency for International Development/Department of State, 1965-67, Director of the Economic Growth Center at Yale, 1967-75, and Director of the Pakistan Institute of Development Economics, 1958-61. He received an Honorary Degree from Brandeis University in 1982 and has been the subject of two Festschrift conferences. His publications include more than 20 books and 200 articles in professional journals.

Frances Stewart is professor of Development Economics, and Director of the International Development Centre, Queen Elizabeth House, University of Oxford. She has written widely on development issues. Her books include *Technology and Underdevelopment* (1977), *Planning to Meet Basic Needs* (1985), *Adjustment with a Human Face*, with G.A. Cornia and R. Jolly (1987); and *War and Underdevelopment*, with Valpy FitzGerald and Associates (2001). Prof. Stewart is a Board member of the International Food Policy Research Institute, the Overseas Development Institute, and of the Overseers of the Thomas Watson Institute for International Studies, Brown University. She is Chair of the Editorial Board of Oxford Development Studies.

Judith Teichman is Professor of Political Science at the University of Toronto. She is the author of *Policymaking in Mexico: From Boom to Crisis, Privatization and Political Change in Mexico* and *The Politics of Freeing Markets in Latin America: Chile, Argentina and Mexico,* along with numerous articles on the politics of economic policy making in Latin America, published in edited volumes and in scholarly journals. She is currently working on the politics of poverty alleviation programs in Mexico and Chile.

Jaime Tenjo was born in Bogota, Colombia. He did his undergraduate study at the Universidad Nacional de Colombia, and worked for several years at the Colombian Department of Planning. His first job at the Department of Planning was as research assistant of Albert Berry and Lauchlin Currie. In 1977 he traveled to Canada to pursue graduate studies. Dr. Tenjo obtained an MA in Economics at University of Toronto and later on a Ph.D. degree in the same university. After graduation he taught at Windsor University, Saint Mary's University and the University of Toronto. In 1996 he returned to Colombia to work at the Universidad de Los Andes, and since 1998 he has been Chair of the Department of Economics at Universidad Javeriana. Dr. Tenjo's research focuses on labor markets, inequality, unemployment and poverty.

Katherine Terrell is Professor of Corporate Strategy & International Business and Business Economics & Public Policy, at the Business School and the Gerald R. Ford School of Public Policy, the University of Michigan. She is also Research Director of Labour Markets and Human Resources at the William Davidson Institute. She publishes on issues of public policy and labour markets in emerging market and transition economies. Her research and teaching both focus on countries in the Central and Eastern European and Latin American regions, where the transition to the global market economy has been dramatic in the last decade. A number of her recent publications examine the impact of the transition and public policy on the labour markets of the Czech and Slovak Republics. She is currently working on the impact of globalization and minimum wages on employment and the distribution of income in Costa Rica. Professor Terrell is involved in teaching in the MBA (MPA) and Ph.D. programs of the Business School and the Ford School of Public Policy. She teaches Business Strategies in Latin America, Labour Markets and Public Policy in the Global Economy, and Development Economics.

Eduardo Zepeda is Professor of Economics and the Director of the Centro de Investigaciones Socioeconómicas of the Universidad Autónoma de Coahuila, Mexico. Dr. Zepeda has held several academic positions in Mexican universities, including the Universidad Autónoma Metropolitana and El Colegio de la Frontera Norte. His recent publications include a co-authored volume on *North American Integration: Theory and Practice* and various studies on labour market issues in Mexico.

Acknowledgements

Original versions of the papers included in this volume were presented at the conference on *Social and Economic Impacts of Liberalization and Globalization: Effects on Labor Markets and Income Distribution*, organized by the Center for International Studies of the University of Toronto in honor of Professor Albert Berry. The conference was funded by the International Development Research Centre (IDRC) and the Ford Foundation. The symposium focused on the analysis of income distribution, labor market, and trade issues in the Latin American context, the three areas to which Prof. Berry has paid most attention during his long and fruitful academic career.

Along with the International Development Research Center and the Ford Foundation, I would like to thank most particularly Gerry Helleiner and Sue Horton for their enthusiasm and dedication in the organization of the conference; Louis Pauly, Director of the Center for International Studies for his support for the conference and all other activities of the Center's Program on Latin America and the Caribbean; and Tina Lagopoulos and the Center's support team for their dedication in handling all the details of the conference. I would also like to express my appreciation to Rohinton Medhora, Vice President, Program, International Development Research Center, and Anthony Tillett, Program Officer, Community Development and National Philanthropy, at the Santiago office of the Ford Foundation, for their contribution towards the realization and success of the conference.

Gustavo Indart
Department of Economics
University of Toronto

Albert Berry

PART I

INTRODUCTION

Chapter 1

The Reform, Growth and Inequality Debate in Latin America

Gustavo Indart

Introduction

The debt crisis of the early 1980s triggered the demise of the income-substitution industrialization (ISI) strategy embraced by most Latin American countries in the post-war period. The Southern Cone countries – Argentina, Chile and Uruguay – had started this process even earlier, since the ISI model, as propeller of growth, had been showing signs of exhaustion by the early 1960s. For most other Latin American countries, however, it could be argued that the growth process was interrupted not so much because of loss of steam of the model itself, but rather as a result of the short-run impact of the debt crisis. Partly surrendering to international pressure but mostly due to lack of feasible short-run alternatives, most countries of the region came to abandon the ISI strategy *en masse* by the mid-1980s.

With some differences in both degree and timing, most countries introduced a series of structural reforms aimed at increasing the role of markets – and curtailing that of the State – in the attainment of economic and social objectives. These structural reforms were devised to facilitate the working of markets as mechanisms for the sectoral allocation of productive resources in the economy, as well as for the distribution of the added value thereby generated among the different income earners. As later summarized in the so-called 'Washington Consensus,' in most countries these reforms included the deregulation of domestic markets, the privatization of State-owned enterprises, the liberalization of trade and investment regimes, the liberalization of the financial sector, and the flexibilization of the labor market.[1] The outcome of this reform process was the substitution of the ISI

1 It is important to differentiate structural reform policies from stabilization policies since the two have different scopes and objectives. On the one hand, stabilization policies such as fiscal, monetary, and trade policies, are macroeconomic in nature and have the objective of stabilizing the economy to create the proper environment for sustainable economic growth to ensue. Structural reform policies, on the other hand, are microeconomic in nature and have the objective of altering the sectoral allocation of resources through changes in the relative prices of both goods and factors of production.

model of economic development by a more market- and outward-oriented economic model – the so-called *neoliberal model*. By the mid-1980s, the general consensus among both policy makers and mainstream economists was that the dismantling of the ISI model, and its substitution by the neoliberal model, would allow for the restoration of healthy economic growth in the region through a more efficient sectoral allocation of resources in line with each country's comparative advantages (Edwards, 1995; Burki and Perry, 1997). Interestingly, the theoretical underpinnings of this new model were based on traditional neoclassical theory – that is, on old theoretical premises considered in the past to be generally unsuited for developing economies and, therefore, long discarded by most development scholars.

A vast literature on the analysis of the economic and social impacts of structural reforms has accumulated over the last decade. On the economic front, particular attention has been directed to the study of the effects of the reforms on economic growth; on the social front, the focus has been on correlated changes in the distribution of income and in the incidence of poverty in the region. Three decades after the introduction of the first reforms in the Southern Cone countries, and close to two decades after their more rapid implementation in most of the other countries of the region, a rich body of statistical data has been gathered to allow for the analysis of the evolution of economic and social indicators in the period since the adoption of the neoliberal model. The raw data, however, does not speak for itself; instead, it speaks through the pen of the researcher and is therefore subject to the theoretical, methodological and ideological biases embedded in the researcher's interpretation. Not surprisingly, different studies have arrived at different conclusions regarding the economic and social impacts of the economic reforms. This book extends the debate by focusing on the effects of economic reforms on economic growth, social inequality, and labor market outcomes – three areas to which Professor Albert Berry has paid considerable attention during his long and fruitful academic career. The book aims to shed light on the question posed by Professor Berry in his influential *Poverty, Economic Reform and Income Distribution in Latin America*: 'Are the market-friendly economic reforms currently being widely adopted in the region promising for both growth and improved distribution? (Berry, 1998, 2).'

Structural Reforms and Economic Growth

Most early studies have shown that the impact of structural reforms on Latin American countries' growth failed to meet the initial high expectations of the early 1990s. This disappointment is especially evident when we compare the results of the 1990s – the region's per capita GDP growing by about 1.5 percent per annum – with those of the 1960s and 1970s, a period when Latin American income per capita was growing by about 3 percent per annum. However, a different conclusion is reached when we compare the economic performance of the region in the 1990s with that of the 1980s – when per capita GDP was contracting by about 1 percent per annum. It is the latter comparison that allows Fernández-Arias and Montiel (1997) to conclude that, in the late 1990s, Latin American per capita income would have been '12 percent lower, and the potential GDP growth in the future 1.9 percent lower, than their current averages' if not for the structural reforms of the past decade. These authors explain that the relatively slow growth of Latin American economies in the 1990s was mainly due to adverse international factors, and that higher long-term growth would be contingent on the deepening and broadening of the reform process itself. Easterly et al. (1997) express a similar view and, amid a series of qualifications, conclude that the 'response of economic growth to reforms … has not been disappointing' (p. 304). Barrera and Lora (1997) and Loayza et al. (2002) also find that the contribution of structural reforms to economic growth was positive when one compares growth performance in the 1990s with that of the 1980s. Even though growth materialized in the 1990s after a decade-long period of falling per capita income, proponents of the neoliberal model posit that this improvement is the outcome of the implementation of structural reforms. The challenge, however, is not only to determine whether the reforms have or have not been responsible for the restoration of growth in the region in the 1990s, but also to answer the pressing question of why growth has been so weak and volatile after a decade or more of reforms. Therefore, it could be argued that if the reforms are to be credited for the economic improvement of the 1990s, then they should also be held responsible for the flimsy growth performance. Neoliberal apologists, however, advance a plethora of justifications for the poor results, ranging from 'adverse external factors' to unfair comparison to the 'miracle economies of East Asia' to the always-handy 'insufficient depth of the reform process itself.'

Several studies have again recently focused on the effects of structural reforms on economic growth in the region (Escaith and Morley, 2000; Paunovic, 2000; Hofman, 2002; Correa, 2002; Bandeira and Garcia, 2002). This recent proliferation of research efforts was likely triggered by the work of Morley et al. (1999), which quantifies the process of structural reforms in 17 Latin American countries over 1970-95.[2] Morley et al.'s contribution is particularly important because it facilitates studies of the impact of structural reforms by comparing the reform period of the 1990s with that of the 1970s – rather than with that of the preceding 'lost decade.' These more recent studies have further fuelled the debate by failing to reach consensus regarding the effect of structural reforms on Latin American countries' economic growth in the 1990s.

---

2 Morley et al. (1999) extended the work initiated by Lora (1997), and Barrera and Lora (1997), who estimated structural reform indexes for the period 1985-95. Subsequently, Lora updated his own study in Lora (2001). Morley et al. estimate reform indexes for five main variables: trade reform, tax reform, capital account liberalization, privatization, and financial reform.

Comparing the growth rates in the 1990s with those in 1951-1980 for 17 Latin American countries, Paunovic (2000) reports lower average growth rates in the 1990s than in the base period – 3.4 and 4.9 percent, respectively – and finds that the best performers in the 1990s were those countries that 'have had a much better macroeconomic stabilization record and have adopted deeper and more comprehensive structural reforms' (p. 33) He also finds that these best performers had lower average growth rates in the base period, and low or negative growth rates in the period immediately before the reforms took place – which explains, in his view, why these countries embraced the reform process so wholeheartedly. In contrast, those countries that fared better in the base period had strong vested interests in maintaining the status quo, and were thus more reluctant to follow the reform path.

Hofman (2002) compares the 1990s growth performance of nine reforming countries[3] with their performance in pre-crisis periods and finds – like Paunovic – that the 1990s shows lower (simple) average growth rates than the pre-crisis period: 3.9 and 5.2 percent, respectively.[4] He also finds that high performers in the base-period were among the lowest performers in the post-crisis period, as well as the ones that experienced the highest inter-period growth deceleration. He argues, however, that the empirical results of the post-reform period are not so straightforward as to allow one to conclude that market-oriented structural reforms are conducive to the acceleration of long-run growth. Although the empirical evidence shows, on average, a positive correlation between the depth of the overall reform process and the growth performance of Latin American countries in the 1990s, it does not appear to support a causal link since reform index differentials among countries, as developed by Morley et al. (1999), are rather marginal: for instance, in Hoffman's sample of eight Latin American countries, all of them are reformers, with overall reforms indexes ranging from the low 0.8s (Brazil) to the high 0.8s (Argentina) in 1995.

The search for a causal link between the reforms and growth performance requires a more desaggregated analysis of the possible growth impact of the different structural reforms implemented in Latin American countries since the early 1980s. The work of Bandeira and Garcia (2002) falls into this category: they analyze the impact of the five reform areas identified by Morley et al. (1999) and find that all of them significantly affect the GDP. Moreover, in attempting to identify the mechanisms responsible for this impact, they report that the economic recovery of the late 1980s and the first half of the 1990s was attributable to the effects of the reforms on physical capital productivity.[5] But the authors add a

3 Hoffman includes Jamaica and eight Latin American countries in his sample of nine reforming countries.

4 The inter-period growth performance difference is even more striking when one considers weighted instead of simple average rates: 3.2 percent in the 1990s vs. 6.0 per cent in pre-crisis periods.

5 Barrera and Lora (1997), however, find that the impact of the reforms on growth was

caveat that questions their own results as well as those of others who had reached similar conclusions: 'It should be noted that these results, like those that appear in the empirical literature on economic growth in general, are conditioned by the econometric specifications and samples used, as well as the set of control variables selected' (p. 92).

Correa (2002) tests the robustness of the empirical evidence used to support the view that the structural reforms have had a positive impact on Latin American growth and finds that the evidence for the positive effects of structural reforms on that growth is far from conclusive; that in fact, it 'raises serious doubts about the effectiveness of the policy reforms' (p. 98). He also finds that the evidence contradicts 'the prevailing wisdom that the poor economic performance ... was due to adverse international environment' (p. 87) and concludes that 'the Washington Consensus policies are simply not working in Latin America' (p. 99).

Escaith and Morley (2000) – like Bandeira and Garcia (2002) later – question the conclusions of studies that support the view that reforms have a positive impact on growth. They argue that the explanatory power of the independent variables used in these studies is suspect since the results are sensitive to the choice of parameters or estimation procedures, thus 'rendering any precise quantification of the true contribution of the control variable to the total growth ... a futile exercise' (p. 29). Indeed, the positive impact of the reforms on growth was, at best, indirect, because 'the different individual components of the reform package have offsetting effects' (p. 31).[6]

Supporters of the neoliberal model are hard pressed in their attempts to gather empirical support for the existence of a positive link between the implementation of structural reforms and economic growth. But the evidence does not strongly support such a claim. Therefore, although the debate drags on, Rodrik's (2002) succinct conclusion seems justified:

> After more than two decades of application of neoliberal economic policies in the developing world, we are in a position to pass unequivocal judgment on their record. The picture is not pretty. Consider economic growth first. In Latin America, only three countries have grown faster during the 1990s than in the 1950-80 period. And one of these three was Argentina, a country whose hopes of economic salvation through financial integration with the world economy now lie in ruins.

This volume furthers the ongoing debate on the impact of structural reforms on economic growth in Latin America. In Chapter 3, José Antonio Ocampo provides

---

channelled particularly through the impact of the reforms on total factor productivity.

6 Rodríguez and Rodrik (1999) also cast doubts on the empirical results supporting a positive link between trade reforms and growth, saying that these results are highly sensitive both to the way trade reform is measured and to a number of other data problems, thus concluding that the positive link between trade reforms and growth is still unproven.

an overall evaluation of the reform process in Latin America and explains that, over time, the initial high expectations have led to significant frustration – that the benefits of reforms were overstated and their risks minimized. Ocampo recognizes that stabilization and structural reform policies were successful in many areas in reducing inflation, in creating credibility in the macroeconomic system, in generating export growth and diversification, and in attracting foreign investment. But he emphasizes that frustration resulted from low and volatile growth, increasing dualism/structural heterogeneity and, particularly, negative social outcomes. Ocampo points out that some of the basic assumptions of the reformers proved entirely wrong – particularly the assumptions that low inflation and more control on budget deficits would ensure stable access to international capital markets and dynamic growth, and that higher productivity in leading firms and sectors would automatically spread throughout the economy and lead to an acceleration of economic growth.

Ocampo challenges the two main explanations of the poor outcomes of reforms in Latin America: i) insufficient commitment to the original reform agenda; and ii) the need for 'second generation' reforms to complement the original 'Washington Consensus.' Both explanations share a linear view of the reform process, he says, and fail to recognize that the reforms themselves may have aggravated the problems Latin American economies face today. Ocampo – like Ffrench-Davis (2000) – proposes that it is essential to 'reform the reforms.' Three problematic areas of the reforms need to be addressed, he says: 1) the limited view of macroeconomic stability that has resulted in pro-cyclical macroeconomic policies that contribute to external sector volatility; 2) the failure to recognize that the emergence of dynamic comparative advantages is not necessarily a spontaneous outcome of market-oriented economies; and 3) the failure to bring the social dimension of the reform process to the foreground as an integral part of the process itself – and not as a complementary or residual issue, as in the present.

Focusing exclusively on the impact of reforms on growth could leave the reader with the impression that the concepts of economic growth and economic development are one and the same – but they are not. It is noted that there are two main reasons for focusing discussion on the effects of reforms on economic growth: one reason is, there exists a high degree of correlation between growth of per capita income and what most social scientists understand as development; a second reason is, economic growth is a *sine qua non* condition for economic development to materialize. But efforts are now being made to direct the attention to a broader set of issues that better describe the quest for economic development; accordingly, in Chapter 4, Gustav Ranis and Frances Stewart make an important contribution in this area. They argue that there is a strong case to be made for regarding 'human development' as the ultimate objective of human activity in place of economic growth, where human development is defined as enlarging people's choices in a way that enables them to lead longer, healthier and fuller lives. Chapter 4 focuses on a narrow subset of choices, those directed specifically at health and education, which are among the basic preconditions of choice in other dimensions. In a previous paper, the authors explored the links between human development and economic growth, both theoretically and empirically (Ranis et al., 2000). They described a dialectical relation between economic growth and human development: on the one hand, economic growth provides the resources to permit sustained improvements in human development; on the other, improvements in the quality of the labor force constitute an important contributor to economic growth. While these general connections are readily accepted, Ranis et al. emphasize that one needs to understand the links in more depth if this is to become useful to policy design. They argue that one needs to know whether a particular pattern of economic growth is more conducive to human development than another, and whether any specific type of human development is more conducive to growth than another. More important, the authors question whether human development should be promoted before, or after, economic growth is achieved. To answer these questions, they have explored the theoretical links and analyzed them empirically, drawing on cross-country data from all developing regions of the world. The exercise generated strong conclusions about the questions just posed.

Ranis and Stewart investigate how well their previous findings apply in the Latin American context, and what policy conclusions can be derived from the regional experience. They find that the Latin American region as a whole has been marked by relatively high levels of human development, but by lower performance on economic growth compared with that of the developing world's average during 1960-2000. This might have been the result of the region's much earlier political independence, they argue, and, consequently, of greater commitment to human development – particularly for the elite; this concept, however, appears at odds with Latin America being the region with the highest degree of inequality in income distribution. The authors report that the links from economic growth to human development are more variable in Latin America than on the world scene. The social expenditure ratio is satisfactory, but GDP growth has not translated in a significant way into human development improvement, indicating that country-specific circumstances could have affected the strength of the links. The links from human development to economic growth, on the other hand, are closer to the global results, with initial human development levels significantly affecting economic growth.

Ranis and Stewart's exploration of countries' behavior over time confirms the view that human development needs to be promoted in order to reach the virtuous cycle of growth and human development improvement. The authors find that, among all Latin American countries, only Ecuador has moved from an economic growth-lopsided position to a virtuous position. Regressions for Latin America tell the same story as for the global context: progress in human development led to economic growth improvement, but economic growth improvement did not systematically advance human development. Therefore, the authors' regional findings also contradict the usually recommended policy sequence – that is, that growth should be generated first, and that human development will naturally follow. On an optimistic note, Ranis and Stewart believe that the surge in social sector expenditures in Latin America in the 1990s may pave the way for improved economic growth – in contrast to the 1980s, when expenditure cuts handicapped growth and, therefore, human development.

Economic Reforms and Social Outcomes

Have the economic reforms of the last two decades contributed to poverty reduction and improved income distribution? Early analyses of evidence from the first half of the 1990s suggest otherwise. Certainly, the dismal growth performance of the 1980s and the weak growth of the early 1990s are neither propitious grounds for poverty reduction nor a bright light in the distribution front.

In an early comprehensive study on the impact of the economic reforms on poverty and income distribution in Latin America, Bulmer-Thomas (1996) doubts that the new model is capable of reversing the negative trends observed on these fronts in the 1980s (Altimir, 1994; Lustig, 1995). First, this author reveals an implicit problem of design in the outward-oriented, market-friendly model, indicating that its possible impact 'on income distribution and poverty was not a central consideration in its adoption throughout the region' (p. 296). Acknowledging that this impact might be ambiguous, Bulmer-Thomas speculates that 'a strong case could easily be made that full implementation [of the new model] will lead to an increase in both income inequality and poverty unless the NEW [New Economic Model] is associated with rapid economic growth' (p. 301). Indeed, any positive effects of the new model on income distribution and poverty would rest not only on the acceleration of export-led growth but also on the assumption that non-traditional Latin American exports are labor-intensive – leading to a tightening of the labor market and to higher real wages particularly at the lower end. Nevertheless, Bulmer-Thomas believes that even under these ideal circumstances, improvement in income distribution might require additional active redistributive government policy towards the bottom deciles. The disappointing results of the last decade lend strong support to Bulmer-Thomas' early speculations: accelerated growth has not materialized, and non-traditional exports have not been at the forefront in the use of unskilled labor; therefore, the impact on poverty reduction has been insufficient, while on income distribution it has been regressive.

In another comprehensive study, Berry (1998) discovers that distribution worsened significantly in the first half of the 1990s in most countries undertaking market-friendly economic reforms and, in line with Bulmer-Thomas, concludes that '[u]nless growth accelerates quickly in the next few years, and in some countries even if it does, it will once again be overoptimistic to assume that growth will prove an adequate antidote to poverty' (p. 33). Berry tells us that 'it appears likely the comparative advantage of the region does not lie in unskilled labor-intensive products' (p. 36), and therefore export-led growth might contribute little to poverty alleviation and much to greater inequality. He concludes that it is urgent to achieve a better combination of growth and distribution, and says this will require specific government action in regard to policy on education and training, SME support, and poverty redressal.

Morley (1997) draws a rather more optimistic picture than either Bulmer-Thomas or Berry. Despite worsening income distribution, he says, Latin America has made important inroads on poverty reduction in the 1990s, certainly in relative numbers and probably in absolute numbers as well – although not evenly across countries. According to Morley, the resumption of growth, together with the control of hyperinflation in Argentina and Peru, is the main reason for the decline in poverty in the region. The structural reforms adopted since 1985 have helped the poor, claims Morley, since poverty declined more in reforming countries than in late and reluctant reformers. Although any poverty reduction is good news indeed, one should not be over-complacent since, as Morley points out, 'we should remember that the poor still have not recovered [in 1997] from the losses they suffered from the debt crisis of the 1980s.'

Considering the foregoing, the question we should ask is not so much whether the present pattern of growth has promoted poverty reduction, but rather the more important one of how many years of sustained growth as presently experienced – that is, weak, and accompanied by worsening income distribution – are needed to make a significant dent on the incidence of poverty in the region? And the answer to the latter question is not promising, given the more recent data since 1997. Indeed, according to ECLAC (2003a), the percentage of the Latin American population below the poverty line has increased from 43.5 percent in 1997 to 44.4 percent in 2003,[7] which translates to 22.8 million more people joining the army of the poor. Data suggest that this poverty increase has been the result of weak growth-cum-income concentration in most countries of the region – since income distribution has become even more skewed since 1990. Indeed, income distribution worsened in 8 out of 13 countries over 1990-97, and it worsened further in another 8 out of 14 countries over 1997-2003, with only 2 countries experiencing improvements in distribution in each of these two periods (ECLAC, 2003a). Moreover, even the most successful poverty-reduction story of the 1990s merits qualifications. Poverty levels in Chile were reduced from 33 percent in 1990 to about 17 percent in 2000, prompting many observes to define this outcome as remarkable and to attribute it to the proper application of the market-friendly model in the Chilean context. While this reduction in poverty levels is commendable, one may wonder why poverty still remains at 17 percent of the total

---

7 Although higher than in 1997, the share of the poor in the total population was still lower in 2003 than in 1990 (48.3 percent). It must be noted that poverty incidence declined continuously during the 1990s, and only after 2000 was this trend reversed.

population after almost 15 years of economic growth at a rate of around 7 percent per annum (ECLAC, 2003b). These results raise important questions regarding the ability of market forces to alleviate structural poverty – an issue analyzed by Alarcón and Zepeda in Chapter 7.

In a recent study, Behrman et al. (2001) analyze the impact of trade and financial liberalizations on poverty levels and income distribution in Latin America during the 1990s. There is not a single case where income distribution might have clearly improved, say the authors, and only in three countries – Colombia, Dominican Republic and Paraguay – has the Gini coefficient shown a reduction, although not a statistically significant one. Given the lack of improvement in distribution, the authors conclude that economic growth alone was responsible for the decline in poverty. With respect to the role of trade and financial liberalizations on these outcomes, Behrman et al. find that trade liberalization likely has had no distinguishable effect on poverty and distribution, but that financial liberalization has had a significant effect on the increase in inequality and poverty. The authors conclude that the regressive effect of financial liberalization appears to be more important than the almost indistinguishable progressive effect of trade liberalization and, therefore, that the combined effect on poverty and distribution might have been regressive.

Several authors in this book contribute to this ongoing debate on the impact of economic reforms on poverty and inequality in Latin America. In Chapter 3, José Antonio Ocampo tells us that, although poverty declined as a percentage of the population over the period 1990-97, the number of poor people remained relatively constant at about 200 million. Moreover, while per capita GDP was about 6 percent higher in the late 1990s than in 1980, the poverty rate of the late 1990s was about 3 percentage points higher than that of 1980. Ocampo thinks economic growth is the most important factor determining the reduction of poverty levels in the 1990s, although several other elements also have had a positive effect on poverty: the end of hyperinflation (Argentina and Peru); an extensive system of social protection (Uruguay); targeted minimum pension policies (Brazil); and particularly minimum-wage policies. Further, in Chapter 11, El-Hamidi and Terrell will report that minimum wage legislation has aided in the reduction of poverty and inequality in Costa Rica.

Ocampo asserts that income distribution trends appear even less rosy, showing a general tendency to deteriorate over the decade. Distribution trends have been uneven across the region, with many countries experiencing greater inequality, and with just a few showing the opposite trend. More striking, in not a single country has inequality declined relative to the levels of the 1970s, while it has increased in many. Inequality is the outcome of many factors, Ocampo says, including education, demographics, employment, and the distribution of wealth. Progress has been made in education and demographics in the 1990s, but a clear deterioration has been experienced on the job front while little is known about wealth distribution. Ocampo acknowledges that the tendency towards greater income concentration could be attributed to different factors: structural reforms, the debt crisis, technological change, and other factors affecting wages and skill differentials.

In Chapter 5, Samuel Morley examines the distribution outcomes of the 1990s for 19 countries in the region, surveying the statistical and econometric evidence of the determinants of income distribution, and arguing that we should not automatically link the adoption of neoliberal reforms with the rising inequality observed over the decade in many countries of the region. The evidence shows, he says, that many cases do not fit this causal explanation. He argues that a number of reforming countries have not experienced a rise in inequality and that, in a number of others, the increase in inequality came in the late 1990s – well after the adoption of the reforms. Therefore, a wider focus on both the determinants of the distribution and some key case-study evidence would provide a clearer understanding of the distributional outcomes. Using regression analysis, Morley attempts to estimate a Kuznets curve augmented by several variables likely to affect the relationship between income and inequality – including measures of education, and the reform indexes developed by Morley et al. (1999). He finds an apparently robust and significant relationship between the distribution and the level of income – that is, he discovers the inverted U-shape curve predicted by Kuznets but non-existent in many recent studies. Further, Morley argues that the Kuznets curve has been shifting in a regressive direction over time, implying that growth has become less progressive recently. He concludes that neoliberal reforms appear to have a significant, but small, regressive effect on the distribution, where a 20 percent increase in the reform index – the approximate increase for the region over 1990-95 – would increase the average Gini coefficient by only 0.25 percent. Morley also notes that different economic reforms exercised different effects on the distribution: trade reform is regressive but not statistically significant; tax reform is regressive; liberalization of the capital account is progressive, while data on privatization and financial reform were insufficient to provide statistically meaningful results.

In Chapter 6, Oscar Altimir considers the impact of economic reforms on income distribution and poverty on the one hand, and on growth on the other, to be inter-dependent. This trend is clear in regard to growth and poverty, but less clear in regard to growth and income distribution. According to Altimir, the impact of economic reforms – particularly the opening up of the economy – on income distribution puts in motion opposite forces: it might favor unskilled labor through a Heckscher-Ohlin mechanism while, at the same time, weaken the traditional direct linkage between wages and demand of the ISI model; and more important, it might foster the adoption of new-age technologies, resulting in contradictory higher skill wage-differentials. Acknowledging that the initial impact of the economic reforms might have been an increase in inequality, the author speculates that the long-term economic expansion under the new model might eventually either correct this outcome, or aggravate inequality. He believes that the adoption of reforms has had considerable distributive cost implications and that, under the new economic order, centripetal and centrifugal forces will emerge, with some mainstream groups integrating in the global economy and others remaining excluded from the fruits of progress. Altimir concludes by raising the alarm that the present distributive polarization might eventually challenge the social cohesion of the developing world in general – and of Latin America in particular. Increasing inequality might put social integration into question, he says, segregating those sectors of the labor force rapidly converging to developed countries' wages from those participating in competitive domestic activities – and even further from those segments of the labor force remaining in low-productivity jobs.

In Chapter 7, Diana Alarcón and Eduardo Zepeda associate the persistence of poverty, income inequality, and poor employment outcomes in a context of regional growth and stability with a change in the basic relationship between economic growth and its impact on welfare. In the fast-growth period of the 1970s, poverty levels in Latin America fell dramatically from 45 percent of the total population in 1970 to 25 percent in 1982; however, the economic recession of the 1980s again increased poverty rates in the region. This inverse correlation between growth and poverty for the region as a whole was also evident in Mexico. The evidence from the 1970s and 1980s demonstrates that economic growth benefits the poor, while a stagnant economy benefits no one. But how does economic growth benefit the poor? The authors answer that empirical findings (e.g., de Janvry and Sadoulet, 1995 and 1999) indicate that the impact of economic growth on poverty is conditional on the level of inequality, being relatively low in countries with high income inequality – precisely the case in Latin America. Alarcón and Zepeda point out that inequality was countercyclical in the 1970s but, contrary to Morley's (1995) findings, procyclical in the recession periods of the early and mid 1980s. Distribution trends in Mexico were also similar to those of the region as a whole. As economic growth recovered in the 1990s, inequality continued to rise, thus showing procyclical behavior – not countercyclical as in the pre-crisis growth period. These findings are troubling, say the authors: in the last decade, Latin American growth has not only been weak but also correlated with higher inequality, thus diminishing the efficiency of growth as a mechanism to lower the high incidence of poverty. Therefore, the greatest new challenge facing the region in the new century is to find a way to improve the positive impact of growth on the lives of the poor. According to Alarcón and Zepeda, in highly urbanized Latin American societies, poverty reduction and better distribution of income will continue to be elusive goals unless formal employment opportunities are expanded to include larger segments of the population, and unless average wages – and especially those at the lower end – improve. This will require better policy design in general, and particularly better articulation between economic and social policies – a topic also addressed later in Chapter 9. Over the last 20 years, economic policy has focused on maintaining macroeconomic stability, fast growth, and rapid integration with the global economy, with little concern for the social costs of adjustment and structural change. Greater consistency is needed between the objectives of economic and social policies, between the short- and the long-run objectives, between stability and growth, and between rising productivity and overall welfare improvement.

As we have seen, there is growing recognition that market reforms have produced important contingents of winners and losers According to Judith Teichman – Chapter 8 – the big winners have been the domestic conglomerates and their foreign allies benefiting from their access to international financial markets, as well as from state largesse toward export subsidies and privatization schemes. The losers were the working poor and other vulnerable segments of society. Except in Chile, poverty reduction has remained elusive throughout the 1990s. Neither domestic market liberalizing elites, nor the multilateral lending institutions which were pressing so hard for market reform, attached much importance to the social implications of their reform agendas throughout the 1980s. However, concerns have shifted dramatically in recent years, says Teichman, with the World Bank and the Inter-American Development Bank having now poverty reduction as the overriding objective of their corporate missions, while the International Monetary Fund today provides a Poverty Reduction and Growth Facility. The failure of market reforms to deliver equitable prosperity is also reflected in the growing disillusionment of growing segments of Latin American societies with market reforms.

Teichman argues that, while changes in the international economic order are a prerequisite for the alleviation of inequality and poverty in Latin America, such changes are not sufficient: domestic power structures and domestic policy initiatives are equally important, she believes. Her argument is that, for an effective program that reduces poverty and inequality, three types of domestic coalitions supportive of such a goal are required. First, there must be a societal coalition – that is, a broad cross-section of society (big, small and medium business, labor, middle-sector groups, agriculturalists, grass roots organizations) that backs state pursuit of such an objective. Second, there must be an electoral coalition calling for poverty reduction and greater equity. This requirement is distinct from a societal coalition; electoral coalitions may be fleeting but are necessary in order to get policy change on the agenda and bolster a program's legitimacy in demonstrating broad and diffuse public support. And third, once the coalition assumes power, it must be possible to construct a third type of coalition: a governing coalition that can propel programs forward and help secure their implementation. The political challenges of equitable development in Latin America are substantial, notes Teichman; they involve a reduction in the policy influence of the extremely powerful winners of the last decades and an increase in policy access for those who have historically been disempowered – as well as those whose influence has been reduced in recent decades. While continued improvements in governance (regulations, mechanisms of accountability) are important, they alone cannot resolve issues of informal policy access and exclusion. Hence, once an equity coalition emerges, the establishment and maintenance of regular and effective channels of policy access must become an essential part of the process.

Economic Reforms and Social and Labor Policy

The impact of economic reforms – particularly trade liberalization – on the distribution of income comes from changes in the relative demand for labor of diverse skills, thereby causing changes in both relative wages and wage-differentials. For that reason, the conventional emphasis of the impact of trade liberalization – as well as of globalization – on labor markets is on the adjustment consequences pertaining to outcomes such as wages, employment, and wage inequality. Andrew Downes, Rafael Gómez and Morley Gunderson argue in Chapter 9 that these direct impacts of trade liberalization on labor market outcomes are important, but that more important are their *indirect* impacts on social and labor market policies. They reveal an ironic situation: the demand for social and labor market policy initiatives may be increasing in order to deal with the adjustment consequences of trade liberalization and economic integration, just at the time the ability of governments to supply such initiatives may be subjected to erosion by the forces of trade liberalization and globalization themselves. This perspective mirrors Alarcón and Zepeda's call in Chapter 7 for a better articulation between the design and formulation of economic and social policy. Downes et al. believe there is a need for a deeper understanding of the underlying causal mechanisms that link globalization and social policy, and the two-way interaction whereby social policies both affect and are affected by globalization. Well designed social and labor market policies are crucial to facilitate the adjustment to a more open and internationally integrated economy, contributing to an enhanced competitiveness of a country. At the same time, liberalization and globalization constrain the ability of nations to pursue their own independent labor and social policies. In the view of the authors, the latter will lead to downward harmonization to the lowest common denominator – not always a negative outcome since it might, in some instances, also stop governments from acting in a manner inconsistent with the best interests of their constituencies.

As Adriana Marshall contends in Chapter 10, studies on the causes of rising wage inequality in the 1990s have focused either on the employment and wage outcomes of trade liberalization or on the wage effects of changes in labor institutions. Only rarely were these two perspectives combined as in Berry (1998), who highlighted the role of both economic processes and labor institutions in the determination of wage inequality and, ultimately, income distribution trends. In most studies, however, the impacts of changes in union power, negotiation level, and minimum wages were analyzed only in reference to OECD countries. Marshall examines wage inequality trends in the Argentine manufacturing sector and their possible economic and institutional causes. The Argentine experience is a relevant case-study, given the far-reaching economic reforms implemented there in the early 1990s and their significant labor market implications. This process of reform included trade liberalization as well as important changes in wage setting institutions – for example, the state's withdrawal from the process of direct wage determination and the promotion of drastic modifications in bargaining structures.

Marshall finds that inter-industry wage dispersion and inequality increased in the 1990s, the coefficient of variation increasing from 0.26 in 1995 to 0.37 in 2000, and the Gini coefficient rising from 0.34 in 1996 to 0.38 in 2000. The evidence does not support the claim that larger dispersion of wage increases was correlated with greater dispersion of productivity growth rates. In her view, greater dispersion of wage increases has been the result of price stabilization and the subsequent replacement of the inflation rate as the common standard for wage negotiations by productivity and profitability parameters. The author concludes that greater wage inequality is the result of unemployment trends and their impact on trade union power, as well as of changes in bargaining strategies after the long period of high inflation and the reforms to labor regulation. Increases in demand for highly skilled workers as a result of technological innovation have a relatively small impact on wage inequality, says Marshall, since it is restricted to wage differentials between a small segment of professionals and all other manufacturing workers.

As Downes et al. postulate in Chapter 9, the unleashed forces of liberalization and globalization tend to limit the ability of national governments to implement independent labor and social policies, thus exerting pressure towards downward harmonization to the lowest common denominator. However, this apparently fatalistic view fails to acknowledge that all general tendencies breed countertendency forces as well. Therefore, it would be premature to surrender all national policy objectives to the mighty forces of liberalization and globalization. Globalization has changed the limits for national governments to maneuver, but there is still room for national policy within these new limits. Indeed, now more than ever should national governments pursue their own social and labor policies, albeit within the new more liberalized and globalized context. Minimum wage is but one of the social and labor market policies governments could pursue.

Minimum wage policies have always been controversial among scholars of economics and policy makers, and the debate has intensified recently. Supporters of minimum wages justify them as a way of improving the living conditions of the poor, unskilled, unorganized workers. Critics emphasize the efficiency losses associated with their use, and disqualify them as an adequate way of affecting inequality, saying that in developing countries, minimum wages are the principal source of labor market segmentation and unemployment. In Chapter 11, Fatma El-Hamidi and Katherine Terrell explore the effects of changes in the minimum wage on earnings inequality and the aggregate level of employment in Costa Rica's covered and uncovered sectors over the 1980-92 period. They examine whether changes in the minimum wage lead to a reallocation of labor between the covered and uncovered sector. The relatively high Costa Rican minimum wage has contributed to a declining trend in overall inequality, to lower inequality in the covered sector, and to more rapid decline in inequality in the covered sector as well, El-Hamidi and Terrell say. They conclude that minimum wage legislation has allowed the Costa Rican government to reduce wage inequality without decreasing the level of employment in the covered sector. Countering the traditional view, the authors announce that minimum wage legislation is assisting the reallocation of workers from the uncovered, traditional sectors to the covered, more modern ones.

National governments, therefore, can successfully implement their own social and labor policies despite the mighty forces of liberalization and globalization. Minimum wage legislation is just one example among a myriad of policy possibilities; national social security policy is another. As François Bourguignon elucidates in Chapter 12, the high macro-economic volatility in Latin American countries during the last 20 years, and the associated economic and social costs, have brought social insurance to the forefront of the current debate about necessary policy reforms in the region. Truly effective safety nets would indeed bring several major benefits. The example of industrial countries where social insurance developed on a large scale ever since the mid 1930s is encouraging. Bourguignon wonders, however, whether this means that Latin American and Caribbean countries should simply follow the same path. This is the basic question addressed in his chapter, and answers are not without ambiguity. The author concludes that recent policy initiatives undertaken in Latin America point to both an increasing demand for social protection and a capacity to respond to that demand through instruments adapted to existing constraints. These initiatives herald, perhaps, a genuine structural change in redistribution policy in the region. His analysis of two social programs – *Trabajar* in Argentina and *Progresa* in rural Mexico – suggests a strengthening of the belief that redistribution and social protection are important components of a development strategy, and increases the urgency to design instruments well adapted to the structural characteristics of the region.

*****

As indicated at the beginning of this chapter, this volume aims to strengthen the ongoing debate on the impact of economic reforms on economic growth, social inequality, and labor market outcomes – areas to which Professor Albert Berry has made significant contributions during his illustrious academic career. Each of the chapters that follows creates a substantial addition to this debate. But the aim of this volume is also to honor Professor Albert Berry for his outstanding scholarship over the years, bringing us a clearer understanding of these important issues. Therefore, this book represents a celebration of Professor Berry's life and work, and Chapter 2 gives us some candid insights in this regard.

References

Altimir, O. (1994), 'Income Distribution and Poverty through Crisis and Adjustment', CEPAL Review, No. 52.

Bandeira, A.C. and F. Garcia (2002), 'Reforms and Growth in Latin America', CEPAL Review, No. 77 (August), pp. 79-95.

Barrera, F. and E. Lora (1997), 'Structural Reforms in Latin America: Measurements and Growth Effects', Working Paper No. 350, Inter-American Development Bank, Washington, D.C.

Behrman, J., N. Birdsall and M. Székely (2001), 'Pobreza, Desigualdad y Liberalización Comercial y Financiera en América Latina', in E. Ganuza, R. Paes de Barros, L. Taylor and R. Vos (eds.), *Liberalización, Desigualdad y Pobreza: América Latina y el Caribe en los 90*, pp. 117-49, Eudeba for UNDP-ECLAC, Buenos Aires.

Berry, A. (ed.) (1998), *Poverty, Economic Reform, and Income Distribution in Latin America*, Lynne Rienner, Boulder, CO.

Bulmer-Thomas, V. (ed.) (1996), *The New Economic Model in Latin America and Its Impact on Income Distribution and Poverty*, St. Martin's Press, New York.

Burki, S.J. and G.E. Perry (eds.) (1997), *The Long March: A Reform Agenda for Latin America and the Caribbean in the Next Decade*, The World Bank, Washington, D.C.

Correa, R. (2002), 'Structural Reforms and Economic Growth in Latin America: A Sensitivity Analysis', *CEPAL Review*, No. 76 (April), pp. 87-104.

De Janvry, A. and E. Sadoulet (1995), 'Poverty Alleviation, Income Redistribution, and Growth during Adjustment', in N. Lustig (ed.), *Coping with Austerity: Poverty and Inequality in Latin America*, The Brookings Institution, Washington, D.C., pp. 101-145.

De Janvry, A. and E. Sadoulet (1999), 'Growth, Poverty and Inequality in Latin America: a Causal Analysis, 1970-94', University of California, mimeo.

Easterly, W., N. Loayza and P. Montiel (1997), 'Has Latin America's Post-Reform Growth Been Disappointing?', *Journal of International Economics*, Vol. 43, No. 3-4 (November), pp. 287-311.

ECLAC (Economic Commission for Latin America and the Caribbean) (2003a), *Panorama Social de América Latina – Síntesis*, ECLAC, Santiago.

ECLAC (Economic Commission for Latin America and the Caribbean) (2003b), *Anuario Estadístico de América Latina y el Caribe 2002*, ECLAC, Santiago.

Edwards, S. (1995), *Crisis and Reform in Latin America: From Despair to Hope*, Oxford University Press for the World Bank, Washington, D.C.

Escaith, H. and S. Morley (2000), 'The Impact of Structural Reforms on Growth in Latin America and the Caribbean: An Empirical Estimation', Serie Macroeconomía del Desarrollo No. 1, ECLAC, Santiago.

Fernández-Arias, E. and P. Montiel (1997), 'A Decade of Structural Reform: All Pain, No Gain?', Inter-American Development Bank, Washington, D.C.

Ffrench-Davis, R. (2000), *Reforming the Reforms in Latin America: Macroeconomics, Trade, Finance*, Macmillan and St. Martin's Press, London and New York.

Hofman, A.A. (2000), 'Economic Growth and Performance in Latin America', Serie Reformas Económicas No. 54, ECLAC, Santiago.

IDB (Inter-American Development Bank) (1997), *Latin America After a Decade of Reforms. Economic and Social Progress in Latin America 1997*, Inter-American Development Bank, Washington, D.C.

Loayza, N., P. Fajnzylber and C. Calderón (2002), 'Economic Growth in Latin America and the Caribbean: Stylized Facts, Explanations, and Forecasts', The World Bank, Washington, D.C.

Lora, E. (1997), 'A Decade of Structural Reforms in Latin America: What has been Reformed and How to Measure It,' Working Paper No. 348, Inter-American Development Bank, Washington, D.C.

Lora, E. (2001), 'Structural Reforms in Latin America: What Has Been Reformed and How to Measure It', Working Paper No. 466, Inter-American Development Bank, Washington, D.C.

Lustig, N. (ed.) (1995), *Coping with Austerity: Poverty and inequality in Latin*, Brookings Institution, Washington, D.C.

Morley, S. (1995), *Poverty and Inequality in Latin America: The Impact of Adjustment and Recovery in the 1980s*, The Johns Hopkins University Press, Baltimore.

Morley, S. (1997), 'Poverty during Recovery and Reform in Latin America: 1985-1995', Inter-American Development Bank, Washington, D.C.

Morley, S.A. (2000), 'The Effects of Growth and Economic Reform on Income Distribution in Latin America', *CEPAL Review*, No. 71 (August), pp. 23-40.

Morley, S. (2001), *The Income Distribution Problem in Latin America and the Caribbean*, ECLAC Books No. 65, ECLAC, Santiago.

Morley, S., R. Machado and S. Pettinato (1999), 'Indexes of Structural Reform in Latin America,' Serie Reformas Económicas No. 12, ECLAC, Santiago.

Paunovic, I. (2000), 'Growth and Reforms in Latin America and the Caribbean in the 1990s', Serie Reformas Económicas No. 70, ECLAC, Santiago.

Ranis, G., F. Stewart and A. Ramírez (2000), 'Economic Growth and Human Development', *World Development*, Vol. 28, No. 2 (February), pp. 197-220.

Rodrick, D. (2002), 'After Neoliberalism, What?', Kennedy School of Government, Harvard University, mimeo.

Rodríguez, F. and D. Rodrik (1999), 'Trade Policy and Economic Growth: A Skeptic's Guide to the Cross-National Evidence', Kennedy School of Government, Harvard University, mimeo.

Székely, M. (2001), 'The 1990s in Latin America: Another Decade of Persistent Inequality but with Somewhat Lower Poverty', Research Department Working Paper No. 454, Inter-American Development Bank, Washington, D.C.

Williamson, J. (1990), 'What Washington Means by Policy Reform', in J. Williamson (ed.), *Latin American Adjustment. How Much Has Happened?*, pp. 5-20, Institute for International Economics, Washington, D.C.

Chapter 2

Albert Berry: His Life and Work

Gerry Helleiner, Gustavo Indart, and Jaime Tenjo

R. Albert Berry's name is known in scholarly and developmental circles around the world. His research and writings have contributed significantly to our understanding of the sources of agricultural productivity; the roles and productivity not only of smallholders in the agricultural sector but also of small enterprises more generally; the functioning of labor markets; the determinants and the empirical record of changes in income distribution both at national and global levels; the roles of international trade and trade policies and of international migration in development; the returns to investment in education; the political economy of 'all of the above'; and a host of other issues.

Although his work is best known in Latin America, he has written and advised all around the world – in the Philippines, Pakistan and South Africa, among other places. Al Berry's work is characterized by a focus on critically important and challenging questions in the community of development scholars and practitioners; reliance upon but extreme care with the most relevant data; the caution of a true scholar in the interpretation of such data as are reliable; a willingness to challenge conventional thinking; and, above all, a deep humanitarian concern. No less important, Al Berry is known for his personal characteristics: his razor-sharp mind, lurking deceptively behind a quiet and self-effacing manner; his loyalty and willingness to go all out for his family, colleagues, students and friends; his unique responsiveness (some would say his constitutional inability to 'just say no') to requests for assistance or collaboration; his absolute reliability, albeit sometimes with a little delay because of the size of his 'in-tray' and the piles on his desk. He is a colleague's perfect colleague (except for those delays). And in personality and demeanor, he is quintessentially Canadian – or at least Canadian in the way in which internationally-minded Canadians 'of a certain age' like to see themselves.

Albert Berry was born and grew up in Southwestern Ontario, a fourth-generation child of Irish and Scottish ancestry. More important to his future career, he grew up on a smallish (125 acre, 50 hectare) mixed farm, five miles from the small town of St. Mary's, near the more famous Stratford of Shakespearean festival fame, in whose hospital he was born. His early years were spent in a close-knit and mutually supportive community, in which his extended family and neighbors had known one another through several generations. His first seven years of (primary) school (understandably, he skipped one grade) were spent in a small one-room schoolhouse, to which he walked about a mile from the farm every day, and in which Al and his brother at one time constituted forty percent of the total enrolment. The local church and community were important parts of life on a farm near St. Mary's. But the wider world was there too. Al's parents and relatives were well-informed and some were directly involved in public affairs; his extended family included two missionaries in China; and, as in so many other families of that period, poverty overseas was deployed by parents as a rationale for eating up one's dinner even if one didn't care for it. While Al was certainly not 'born with a silver spoon in his mouth', these were, in important respects, extremely rich beginnings; and he tells us that they had a profound impact upon his later worldview and his life. They must have done.

At the big (400 student) high school in St. Mary's, to which he thereafter traveled by bus, Al played basketball, did track, and gradually came to a decision for which we must all be thankful, that he would try economics at university, rather than agriculture or forestry, which had been the previous aspirations of choice. At the University of Western Ontario in London (Ontario), Al tells us that he did not do very well in his first test in economics. (That is so difficult to believe that we are unsure whether to believe him; but we haven't as yet been able to check the historical record.) In any case, with good professors, including Mark Inman, Grant Reuber and Ron Wonnacott, he persevered. At graduation he flirted with postgraduate studies in philosophy but, happily for us, he won fellowships from Princeton University and the Canada Council to pursue a doctorate in economics.

At Princeton, he studied – in a class numbering only eleven, and including the University of Toronto's own historian of economic thought, Sam Hollander, and Charles Frank (who later also became involved in development economics, and, later still, Vice-President of the European Bank for Reconstruction and Development) – under such greats of the economics profession as William Baumol, Richard Quandt, Oskar Morgenstern (whom Al remembers as a 'strange' lecturer), Jacob Viner and Fritz Machlup. Although mathematics was not as important in the economics programs of those times as it is today, Al found it easy. Its use in the elaboration of economic theory at that time was growing. Al says that he found pure economic theory 'aesthetically pleasing' and, naively as he now sees it, also thought it capable of direct application. Oddly, as it now also seems to us, Al's original proposal for a thesis topic involved the deployment of set theory in an attempt at the extension of some of Gerard Debreu's theorems. Although by this time he was already interested in 'applied' economics and in the real problems of poverty, Princeton had no professor who specialized in or knew much about economic development. The result was a thesis, principally supervised by Quandt, in micro-economic and welfare theory, taking off from some of Joan Robinson's writing on imperfect competition.

Development first became prominent in Al's career in 1962 (at the age of 25) when, for his first job, he accepted an offer, although his thesis had not yet been completed, from the newly created and Simon Kuznets-inspired Economic Growth Center at Yale University (in New Haven, Connecticut), originally led by Lloyd Reynolds with assistance from Gus Ranis. He was in the 'second cohort' of so-called 'country economists' at the Center, whose mandates were to undertake definitive statistically-based studies of the development of individual national economies in the developing world, while holding cross-appointments as professors in the Yale Department of Economics, then chaired by Raymond Powell. His colleagues in the cohort were Ron Soligo, Shane Hunt, Brian van Arkadie, Clark Reynolds and the late Steve Hymer. By the summer of 1963 Al was in Colombia which he had chosen for his country study, in part because Werner Baer (in the first cohort) had already appropriated the Brazilian one. He worked there for the next year and a half and, of course, repeatedly thereafter, first as Program Advisor for the Ford Foundation, subsequently as advisor to the Colombian Planning Commission, and since then as a visiting expert.

Albert first came to Colombia at a very important moment in its history: the country had managed to stabilize itself after a decade of political and economic difficulties and was in the midst of a period of relatively fast economic growth. An agrarian reform had been started, awareness of the need to look for new markets had resulted in important export promotion programs, and a series of institutional changes – that complemented an accelerated process of structural changes – were in the process of being implemented.

Very quickly Albert realized the need to develop a group of economists who had the necessary ability to do high quality research on the basis of which to make serious and well thought out policy recommendations. His vision was that such a group could also advise both the government and the private sector on different issues.

At the same time professor Lauchlin Currie had become the chair of the Economics Department at Universidad Nacional the most important public university in Colombia – and had started to introduce important changes to improve the academic standards and bring the theory taught in that program up to date. Albert did not hesitate to offer his support and that of the Ford Foundation, thanks to which many changes were implemented in the Department of Economics. The CID – Centro de Investigaciones del Desarrollo – was created and a number of professors and researchers were hired, including among others Francisco Thoumi, Humberto Camargo, Anthony Ternent, and Guillermo Calvo.

The association of the Foundation and the program of the Universidad Nacional, and more specifically that of Albert, was the beginning of one of the most interesting periods of intense academic debate in Colombia. The Universidad Nacional, as most public universities in Latin America in the sixties, had a very militant student movement strongly influenced by left wing ideologies. Marx, Engels, and Lenin were the intellectual heroes of a good number of students, and Fidel Castro, Che Guevara and Mao Tse Tung their political reference points.

Albert's arrival – and that of the newly hired professors – at Universidad Nacional opened a new chapter in the history of the Department of Economics by introducing the teaching of what we would now consider standard macro and micro theory at a level comparable with that of the undergraduate programs in North America. For many students it was the first time they had been exposed to a more or less rigorous treatment of these kinds of ideas, and for everybody it was a very stimulating change.

The new teachings gave rise to a period of intense academic debate among both the professors and the students. Many of the most important issues in economic theory were analyzed. For example, there was an intense discussion on the essence of value that confronted the classical economists' labor value theory with the marginalist analysis; another on-going debate was around the nature of economic development, another on free trade versus protectionism, etc. Professors and students organized 'study groups' to read the most important sources, and debated publicly their points of view.

Those debates were very formative for many of the students in the Department of Economics. Many of today's leaders in politics, government and research came from the group of students who either took classes with Albert or were influenced by the debates of those days. Among them one would mention Antonio Hernández, Gabriel Misas, César González, Alberto Corchuelo, Luis Eduardo Rosas, among others.

Albert's own research work on Colombia was truly a pioneer effort in many areas. He contributed significantly to the understanding of problems such as those of the agricultural sector, the development of the manufacturing sector, small-scale industry, income distribution, labor markets, demographic trends, rural-urban migration, international trade, macro policy and many others.

In those days researchers had little to work with compared with the resources available nowadays. The statistical information was of poor quality, covered very limited areas or sectors of the economy, changed constantly in its methodologies and classification criteria, and was published with long delays. Under those conditions researchers had to use a lot of creativity and intuition to use the information available and they were not always successful. Albert used to refer to a 'statistical leprechaun' who probably lived in the National Department of Statistics and made sure that researchers always missed one piece of information to complete any research task.

In spite of the leprechaun Albert managed to produce a series of articles, book chapters and books, some of which still are considered required reading for those who want to understand the development of Colombia. Some of the journals where Albert's work of those years was published include the *American Economic Review*, the *Journal of Political Economy*, and the *Journal of Economic Studies*.

As adviser to the Colombian Planning Commission, Albert participated in the design of a development plan named the Four Strategies (Housing Construction, Increased Agricultural Productivity, Export Promotion, and Income Distribution).

Albert Berry and Lauchlin Currie played a very active role in the design of the plan as a whole, and Albert was instrumental in the estimation of the impact of the housing construction program. This was the first (and perhaps the only) time that an economic plan was developed in Colombia in which the most important instrument was not government expenditures but the functioning of the market. The housing program was not one where the government would build houses directly, but one in which the necessary reforms were introduced to allow private financial institutions to channel resources into the housing construction industry. The program was so successful that 30 years later it is still in place, although with important changes.

Although Albert has not lived in Colombia for a prolonged period of time since the early 1970s, Colombia continued to be an important focus of his research and frequent visits kept him in contact with the issues and themes of the country's economic development. His 'Colombia Experience' in general has influenced a very important part of his research activity, of his publications, and of his life. Albert left a legacy in Colombia like no other foreign scholar has. His contributions to the understanding of economic problems are eclipsed by his kindness and his human quality. Colombians not only admire and respect him as a great economist and scholar: they also like him very much as a person.

As with so many other 'country studiers' at the Yale Economic Growth Center in its early period, the years Al spent there (while alternating with the years in Colombia) were extremely influential in the development of his interests and his future career. Excellent colleagues, exposure to all parts of the international development community, freedom to explore one's own emerging interests, and a rare collegiality and sense of purpose made the Growth Center an exciting and fruitful base from which to build expertise and experience in development economics. From 1966-68 and again from 1970-72 he was the Center's Assistant Director. Characteristically, when asked how he came into this job, Al replied that he guessed that he just didn't know how to say 'no.' He now recalls that he probably did too much administrative work at Yale and too little thereafter. At the same time, in various years, he taught undergraduate and graduate courses in principles of economics, statistics, macro-theory, international trade, and development. At that time Yale ran a special postgraduate program for junior – and middle – level overseas economists, mainly working in governments, in which Al also taught. Among his students were some who were to become among the most eminent of Latin American economists, such as Edmar Bacha and Guillermo Calvo. It was also, of course, during this period that he met another young economist – in Colombia – and soon married his loving life-partner, María Teresa, with whom he returned in 1969 to New Haven.

After staying on in New Haven a little longer than originally planned, to permit María Teresa to complete her own studies in economics, the Berry family returned to Canada in 1972. Al accepted a tenured appointment at his old alma mater, the University of Western Ontario, where he taught for the next two years and was able to see more of his parents again. By 1974, he was lured to the University of Toronto by another 'graduate' of the Yale Growth Center who wanted some company in development economics, and Lorie Tarshis, who was building a strong Economics Department in the Scarborough campus. Before moving there, however, he took a 14-month leave and spent it working with Mark Leiserson (another former 'Yalie') in the division on 'employment and agriculture' within the Research Department of the World Bank, which was then most ably directed by Hollis Chenery.

At the Bank Al worked principally on agriculture, employment and small enterprises. His colleagues included Richard Webb, Dipak Mazumdar (who subsequently came to Toronto), Richard Sabot and Lyn Squire. Al recollects that this was 'great experience' and, though he has not done much work with the Bank since those years, he learned its ways, its attributes and its problems.

In 1975, Al finally came to his base in Toronto to stay. There, he and María Teresa have raised their two wonderful daughters, Elizabeth and Marisa. At the University of Toronto he has been a pillar of the economics and development communities.

Al brought his interests in Latin America to the University of Toronto in the form of the Centre for International Studies' Program on Latin America and the Caribbean, which became formalized in 1992. Initial work (funded by the Ford Foundation) focused on the mechanisms and effects of trade, investment and technological change within the hemisphere. With a second Ford grant and a small but important grant from the Tinker Foundation, the focus shifted towards the effects of trade liberalization on income distribution and the performance of labor markets in a selected group of Latin American countries, areas of special interest to Al. A third research project funded by the Canadian Foundation for the Americas (FOCAL) and the IDRC was soon to follow in 1994. The FOCAL research project aimed to identify the implications of a changing hemispheric economic and trade regime for Canada and its LAC partners as well as to foster collaboration between researchers from Canada and the LAC region.

One important element of the Ford Foundation projects was the funding of short visits of Latin American researchers to the University of Toronto. Al has been pivotal in the development of strong linkages with researchers and their institutions through these visitors' programs. The visitors program allowed the creation of until then non-existent institutional linkages between the CIS and the participating LAC centers. Under Al's direction, these visits turned out to be an extremely rich arena for the exchange of ideas and experiences among Canadian and LAC scholars. Since 1994, more than 20 LAC researchers have spent 1-3 months at CIS under one or another of CIS' research projects in Latin America and the Caribbean. Several of the visitors have become life long collaborators, participating in many other CIS activities in Latin America and the Caribbean.

While continuing with its strong research focus, the Program on Latin America and the Caribbean had by 1996 started to engage as well in capacity-building activities in the region. Though the SPEAL Project funded by CIDA, economists from the University of Toronto and other Canadian universities delivered 29 short courses on specialized topics in four South American countries during the period 1996-2001. Al, of course, was the Canadian instructor in greatest demand to deliver these courses and, as always, he found the time to squeeze this extra activity into his busy schedule. The SPEAL Project was quite important in the sense that it allowed CIS to enhance its network of collaborators in both Canada and LAC countries. In Canada, the Program compiled a pool of possible collaborators consisting of more than 40 Canadian professors of economics who were bilingual in Spanish and English/French. An additional capacity-building project in Cuba followed in 1998, and Al once again participated actively delivering two courses in Havana and supervising the research of two Cuban visitors to the Centre for International Studies.

Under Al's direction, the Program on Latin America and the Caribbean has been a major success. A significant body of research was undertaken with modest financial resources. Three volumes have been published and another is in process, all edited by Al. The first book on *Poverty, Economic Reform, and Income Distribution in Latin America* (Lynne Rienner, 1998) included papers by several of the LAC visitors, and represented a major contribution towards our understanding of the social and economic impact of the economic reform process in Latin America, and as such it was selected by *Choice* magazine as an *Outstanding Academic Book* for 1998. The second volume on *Labor Market Policies in Canada and Latin America: Challenges for the New Millennium* (Kluwer, 2001) also provides an excellent indication of the kind of research carried out under Al's direction at CIS' Program on Latin America and the Caribbean; the third volume on *Critical Issues in International Financial Reform* (Transaction, 2003) presents a critical view of the prescriptions of the so-called Washington Consensus; and a fourth volume on financial crises is in the editing process.

Al has co-taught the core postgraduate course in development economics (usually with one or both of Sue Horton and Gerry Helleiner) for over twenty years and co-taught the course in the Political Economy of Development, with political science colleagues (Cranford Pratt and Dick Sandbrook), for about a decade. He has supervised, in a primary or secondary capacity, forty-eight PhD theses in economics, political science, history and forestry. In teaching, PhD thesis supervision, administrative and committee activity – quite apart from his own prodigious and continuing research and advisory work – it is difficult to imagine how things might have been at the University of Toronto without his inputs. He was one of the founders, with Rorke Bryan and Dick Sandbrook, of the enormously successful (and now nearly 15 year old) program in International Development Studies at Scarborough College. In 1997, Al's work was formally nationally recognized through his election as a Fellow of the Royal Society of Canada.

Albert Berry personifies what is best in the international community of scholars and practitioners of development. His sustained commitment, scrupulous honesty, and determination to engage productively in the key debates of the day have inspired, and continue to inspire, students and colleagues around the world. While celebrating Albert's life and work, and taking pride in our association with him, we express the hope that he will have many, many more years, after his formal retirement from academic life, to inspire even more.

PART II

REFORMS, GROWTH AND INCOME DISTRIBUTION

Chapter 3

Lights and Shadows in Latin American Structural Reforms[1]

José Antonio Ocampo

Introduction

No other region in the developing world embraced structural reforms earlier and more enthusiastically than did Latin America. The transition economies of Central and Eastern Europe did so, but somewhat later and as a result of radical political change. Structural conditionality since the 1980s is certainly part of the explanation but, in a strong sense, 'ownership' characterized the push towards a more liberal economic order in Latin America. Indeed, the wave of regional democratization that started in the mid-1980s progressively embraced structural reforms as part of its agenda. Furthermore, the 'Washington Consensus,' as presented by Williamson (1990), was largely based on Latin American debates and ongoing reforms.

The enthusiasm for reforms was associated with the dominance that orthodox economic thinking had acquired by the mid-1980s. The call for reforms was presented as an alternative to State-led industrialization, a development strategy that, according to orthodox analysts, had generated inefficient productive and State structures, as well as a bias against labor demand. In Latin America, the need to overcome the 'lost decade' of the 1980s also generated a very concrete source of support for reforms. It is now increasingly clear that the criticisms of State-led industrialization were simplistic[2] and the expectations generated by the

---

1. This is a revised version of a paper prepared for the Conference on Social and Economic Impacts of Liberalization and Globalization: Effects on Labor Markets and Income Distribution, organized by the Centre for International Studies of the University of Toronto in honor of Professor Albert Berry, April 2002. I am grateful to participants in the Conference, particularly Gustavo Indart, for their comments. I also thank Juan Martin and Jaime Ros for their useful suggestions, and María Angela Parra for excellent assistance.

2 For an alternative recent evaluation, see Cárdenas et al. (2000). The term 'State-led industrialization' is used to refer to the period that extends from the 1930s to the 1970s, rather than the widely used term 'import substitution industrialization,' which

reform process overstated. The advantages of previous development experience, in terms of productive development upon which new forms of structural transformation could be built, were ignored. The risks involved in the new strategy, amply elaborated by critics of the reform effort, were swept aside. Alternative reform agendas, such as ECLAC's 'Changing Production Patterns with Social Equity' (ECLAC, 1990), as well as early warnings about the damaging effects of capital account volatility and inadequate structural restructuring in the face of trade liberalization (ECLAC, 1994),[3] were also given insufficient attention.

As time went by, high expectations led to a significant degree of frustration. The return of moderate rates of economic growth in 1990-1997 generated positive evaluations of the reform effort (Edwards, 1995; IDB, 1997; and Burki and Perry, 1997), but the new 'lost half-decade' of 1998-2002 has brought these early assessments into question. Now, at the beginning of the twenty-first century, it is clear that the new development strategy has been effective in generating export dynamism, attracting foreign direct investment (FDI), and increasing productivity in leading firms and sectors. In most countries, inflation trends and budget deficits were effectively brought under control, and confidence in the macroeconomic authorities – including independent central banks – increased in most countries. Social spending rose and innovations were introduced in the way social policy was undertaken, with mixed results in the latter case. Increased social spending can also be explained by the wave of democratization that was simultaneously sweeping over the region. In parallel, and largely unrelated to the reform processes, advances were made in the sustainable development and gender equity agendas.

Nonetheless, these 'lights' were mixed with prominent 'shadows.' Economic growth was frustratingly low and volatile, and domestic savings and investment remained depressed in most countries. Overall productivity performance was poor, largely as a result of a growing underutilization of the available labor force. Increasing productive and labor market dualism became one of the most distinctive effects of the reform process, with the expansion of 'world class' firms – many of them subsidiaries of multinationals – coinciding with increasing unemployment and labor market informality. This, together with other factors – technological biases and changes in production structures that increased the relative demand for skilled labor – had adverse effects on an already poor income distribution record, weakening the effects of already-slow growth on poverty reduction.

There were obviously divergences in the nature of the reforms adopted in

inadequately captures the development patterns that characterized it.

3 This report was published in Spanish in 1995, and a revised Spanish version was published as ECLAC (1998b).

different countries. Other factors also influenced outcomes, particularly the social and power structures that accompany a skewed income distribution, lags in institution-building in several areas, and lagged effects of the debt crisis of the 1980s – for example, the weakening of State apparatuses. Diversity also resulted from significant differences among countries in terms of the size, structure and level of development, geographical position – particularly proximity to the United States market – and the strength or weakness of countries' economic, political, and social institutions.

This chapter provides an overall evaluation of the reform process in Latin America. It is based on wide-ranging research undertaken by the United Nations Economic Commission for Latin America and the Caribbean (ECLAC) in recent years, which provides the most comprehensive evaluation of the reform process available.[4] The chapter is divided into five sections, the first of which is this introduction. The next section looks at the characteristics of the reform process. The following two sections, which are the core of the paper, analyze in some detail the effects of reforms on economic performance and social trends. Finally, the last section draws some lessons for the future.

The Reform Process

The implementation of structural reforms aimed at opening up economies to foreign competition and increasing private-sector participation in development began in a few Latin American countries in the 1970s, particularly in the Southern Cone. The debt crisis led to some backtracking in the early 1980s, but the process gained significant momentum from the mid-1980s to the mid-1990s and rapidly extended to the whole region. It tended to level off in the second half of the 1990s, after reaching high levels of liberalization in most countries, with no major reversal during the turbulent macroeconomic events that started in 1998 (Figure 3.1).[5] Indeed, Venezuela, the country with the lowest level of liberalization in 2000 – according to ECLAC's indexes of structural reforms – still stood significantly above the regional average in 1990.

---

4 ECLAC (2003a) provides an overall assessment, which can be complemented with the analysis of social trends in ECLAC (2000a, 2000b and 2001), of issues associated with integration into the world economy in ECLAC (2002a and 2002b), and of sustainable development patterns in ECLAC/UNEP (2002). The results of a long-term ECLAC project on the impact of structural reform in Latin America and the Caribbean are summarized in Stallings and Peres (2000), Moguillansky and Bielschowsky (2001), Katz (2001), Morley (2001) and Weller (2001).

5 Figure 3.1 presents the evolution of ECLAC's indexes of structural reforms (see the methodology in Morley et al., 1999). The Inter-American Development Bank has designed an alternative index for 1985-2000 (see Lora, 2001).

Figure 3.1: Latin America, Indexes of Structural Reforms, 1970-2000

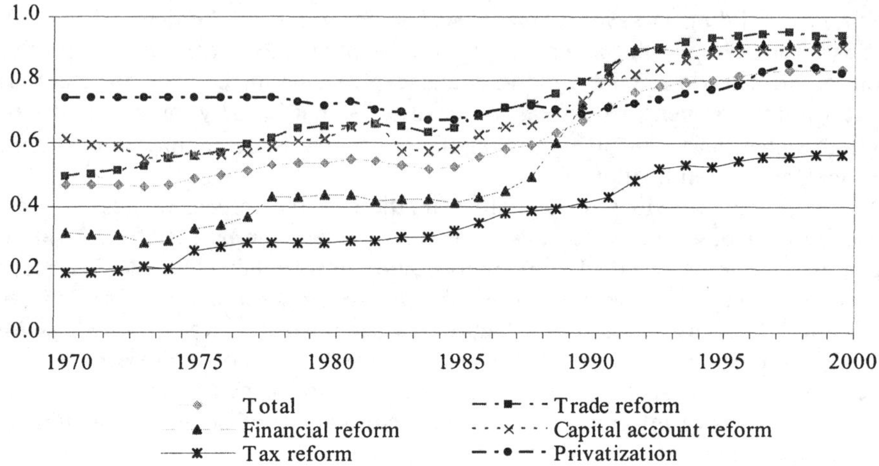

Source: ECLAC.

The reform effort was not uniform. Significant liberalization was evident in trade, external capital flows, and the domestic financial sector. In the tax area and, particularly, in privatization and labor markets, reforms were less ambitious.[6] This may seem counter-intuitive in the case of privatization, an area in which major efforts were undertaken. However, several firms accounting for large shares of GDP – particularly those operating in the mining and oil, electricity and water, and in some cases telecommunications sectors – remained State-owned in many countries. Also, in other areas, such as development banking, public sector involvement remained strong.

Reform strategies differed across the region. Stallings and Peres (2000), who studied nine countries, differentiate between 'aggressive' and 'cautious' reformers, with Argentina, Bolivia, Chile and Peru in the first category, and Brazil, Costa Rica, Colombia, Jamaica and Mexico in the second. The first group was characterized by comprehensive reforms undertaken over a short period, whereas a more gradual approach and uneven advance in different areas characterized the second. According to this classification, most Latin American countries should probably be placed in the second category. However, even the first group shows major exceptions in some areas; for example, Chile maintained its State-owned copper and oil companies, as well as both commercial and development public-sector banks, and relied significantly upon capital account

6 For labor reforms, see Lora (2001), as this is not included in ECLAC's reform indexes.

regulations throughout the 1990s.

A significant confusion in the debate has been generated by the tendency to mix *structural reforms* aimed at reducing the public sector's role in the economy and liberalizing markets with *macroeconomic stabilization* policies. Most aggressive reformers introduced liberalization together with major stabilization packages – for example, Chile in the mid-1970s, Bolivia in the mid-1980s, and Argentina and Peru in the early 1990s – but this pattern is far from universal. The difference is substantial because macroeconomic balances can be achieved with large differences in the degree of economic liberalization and, conversely, liberalized economies can maintain significant macroeconomic imbalances. Indeed, in several cases, macroeconomic strategies ran counter to the objectives of structural reforms, leading to currency overvaluation that negated the expected effects of trade reforms on exports, or to increased taxation to achieve fiscal balance. Furthermore, there is growing evidence that, whereas macroeconomic balances are essential for growth, links between structural reforms and growth are, at best, weak (Rodríguez and Rodrik, 2001). The latter statement is not inconsistent with the fact that some structural characteristics may affect economic growth – for example, the accumulation of human capital, improved infrastructure, openness and financial depth – because all of them may be achieved with quite different degrees of public-sector involvement. Thus, these structural *characteristics* should not be confused with structural *reforms* aimed at liberalization.[7]

Economic Performance

Macroeconomic Performance

The most salient economic advance in the 1990s was the increasing confidence in the region's macroeconomic authorities generated by improvements in fiscal conditions and reductions in inflation rates. On average, central-government budget deficits declined significantly in the second half of the 1980s, remained in an average range of between 1 and 2 percent of GDP through most of the 1990s, but have increased to levels of around 3 percent since 1999. This trend was not inconsistent with increased government spending – from a simple average of 17.4 percent of GDP in 1990 to 21.1 percent in 2001 – as government revenues simultaneously increased. Progress in this area has been uneven across the

7 This confusion is implicit in the otherwise excellent paper by Loayza et al. (2002), as these authors find that the accumulation of human capital, public-sector infrastructure, effective trade openness and financial depth have positive effects on growth. But all these factors – including openness – can be achieved with different degrees of public-sector intervention.

Figure 3.2: Net Resource Transfers to Latin America, 1970-2002

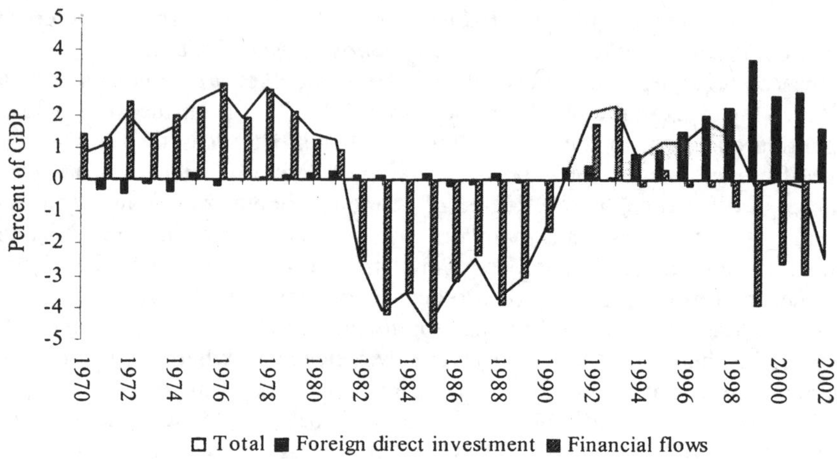

Source: ECLAC.

region, as reflected in the fiscal crises that some countries have experienced in recent years and the high public-sector debt ratios that continue to characterize several countries. Progress in the fight against inflation has been more uniform and long-lasting. Average inflation in Latin America fell steadily up to 2001, when it reached single digits in most countries. Setbacks in 2002, when average inflation increased for the first time in a decade, were concentrated in a few countries, particularly Argentina and Venezuela. Considering the major fiscal imbalances that had characterized the Latin American economies since the late 1970s, the long inflationary history of a number of them, especially in South America, and the hyperinflation that five of them – Argentina, Bolivia, Brazil, Nicaragua and Peru – experienced in the 1980s and early 1990s, these achievements are remarkable.

Nonetheless, the expectation that advances in the fiscal area and control of inflation would be reflected in access to stable external capital flows, high investment rates, and strong economic growth did not materialize. Renewed access to capital markets was evident in the early 1990s. As Figure 3.2 indicates, there was a sharp turn from negative to positive net resource transfers through the capital account in the early 1990s. Financial flows played the key role in the early part of this reversal. The most important event in this regard was the development of a dynamic market for Latin American bonds as a result of structural changes in industrial countries' capital markets, the inducement generated in the early 1990s by low U.S. interest rates, and the 1989 Brady Plan – which effectively created a secondary market for Latin American securities. In

Table 3.1: Recent Phases in Economic Growth in Latin America, Average Annual GDP Growth, 1986-2002

	1986-1990	1991-1994	1995-1997	1998-2002
Argentina	0.1	8.0	3.5	-3.3
Bolivia	2.3	4.0	4.7	2.2
Brazil	1.9	2.8	3.3	1.6
Chile	6.4	7.5	7.6	2.3
Colombia	4.8	4.1	3.4	0.4
Costa Rica	4.3	5.5	3.3	4.4
Cuba	-0.7	-9.7	5.1	4.2
Dominican Republic	2.8	4.1	6.7	5.8
Ecuador	1.8	3.7	3.1	0.8
El Salvador	2.1	5.6	4.1	2.7
Guatemala	2.9	4.2	4.1	3.3
Haiti	0.0	-6.0	4.6	0.4
Honduras	3.2	3.4	4.1	2.2
Mexico	1.9	3.5	2.0	3.2
Nicaragua	-3.4	1.0	5.0	4.3
Panama	-0.5	6.4	3.1	2.3
Paraguay	3.9	2.8	2.7	-0.4
Peru	-1.3	5.0	6.0	1.6
Uruguay	3.8	5.6	2.7	-3.1
Venezuela	2.8	3.4	4.3	-1.2

Source: ECLAC.

the second half of the 1990s, FDI became the leading source of net resource flows. The Asian crisis generated a return to large negative resource transfers through financial flows, indeed in magnitudes similar to those of the 1980s. FDI served as a compensatory factor up to 2001, but its sharp fall in 2002 generated a large negative overall net resource transfer for the first time in more than a decade.

Renewed growth had characterized only a handful of Latin American economies in the second half of the 1980s (Table 3.1). Thus, broad-based growth only started in the early 1990s and was, according to some analysts (e.g., IDB, 1997), a positive result of ongoing reform efforts. An alternative explanation, which is consistent with evidence presented below, relies on renewed capital flows. There were certainly links between these two processes: capital flows facilitated structural reforms and exchange-rate-based stabilization policies and, in turn, the boom in external financing was facilitated by reforms – through more liberal capital account regulations and privatization, which induced larger FDI flows, among other channels. However, the broad-based deceleration in growth that took place in 1995-1997, and, particularly in 1998-2002, indicates the prominent role of capital flows – particularly *financial flows* – as determinants of medium-term growth trends in Latin America. Thus, although trade and domestic

Table 3.2: Determinants of GDP Growth in Latin America

	Coefficient (t-statistics)				Mean (standard deviation)
Constant	0.0219 (1.06)	0.223 (2.21)	Fixed Effects	Fixed Effects	0.029 [a] (-0.027)
Inflation (log)					
Bounded at 40%	–0.011 (-0.47)		0.0195 (0.74)		0.1864 (0.1094)
Excess over 40%	-0.0114 (-2.48)	-0.011 (-2.63)	-0.0127 (-2.52)	-0.0097 (-2.02)	0.1668 (0.5011)
Net Resource Transfers (% of GDP)					
FDI	-0.5963 (-1.54)		-0.7972 (-1.89)		0.0054 (0.0103)
Financial Flows	0.5932 (5.7)	0.6321 (6.28)	0.5940 (6.03)	0.6379 (6.69)	-0.0051 (0.0247
Terms of Trade (Index)	-0.0083 (-0.88)		0.0005 (0.04)		1.0306 (0.2369)
Average Growth of Developed Countries' Imports	0.1217 (2.87)	0.1099 (2.61)	0.1250 (3.15)	0.1089 (2.75)	0.0343 (0.0558)
Total Reform Index					
Initial value	0.0427 (1.66)	0.1022 (0.90)	0.0741 (2.46)	0.021 (1.41)	0.6294 (0.1508)
Annual absolute change	0.0982 (0.81)	0.0183 (1.25)	0.1189 (1.0)	0.108 (1.0)	0.0128 (0.0201)
R-squared	0.5228	0.5013	0.6598	0.633	

[a] Mean and standard deviation of dependent variable.

Source: Panel data estimates for all Latin American countries for the periods 1976-1980, 1981-1985, 1986-1990, 1991-1994, 1995-1997, and 1998-2002, based on ECLAC data.

factors also played a role, fluctuations in the capital account became the major single determinant of the Latin American business cycle.

Indeed, this is what the econometric estimates of Table 3.2 indicate. This table presents panel data estimates for the determinants of economic growth since the mid-1970s, the period characterized by severe capital account instability. A very simple model, largely based on external variables, explains close to two thirds of the variance of economic growth, when country-specific factors – fixed effects – are taken into account. Financial flows and the growth of imports of industrialized countries exerted the strongest effects on growth performance, but the impact of the first of these factors would be twice as strong if the variance of the explanatory variable were taken into account. According to these results, the terms of trade and FDI did not have a statistically significant effect on growth. On the other hand, the ability to avoid an inflation of over 40 percent a year also had a strong effect, but moderate inflation – and thus its reduction to single-digit levels – did not generate a significant effect. Nor did the path taken by the reform process, as measured by ECLAC's indexes of reforms, have a consistent statistically significant effect on comparative growth performance, as reflected in the variability of the estimated coefficients and their generally weak statistical significance. This result is consistent with other analyses of the effects of structural reforms on economic growth (see below).

Macroeconomic policy management has been partly responsible for the sensitivity of economic growth to capital flows, for the propensity towards domestic financial crises, and for some features of the productive restructuring process, reflecting tensions between macroeconomic policies and reform objectives. In particular, the strong bias in favor of currency appreciation that characterized the periods marked by an abundance of external financing was partly responsible for the adjustment problems faced by tradable sectors in several countries, as well as for the speculative attacks and the increased risks of domestic financial crises that arose when there was a sudden stop in capital flows. Also, the tendency to adopt procyclical fiscal and, particularly, monetary and credit policies – which foster lending booms and drops in interest rates during periods of expansion, as well as marked monetary contraction and high interest rates during crises – has been an underlying cause of unstable economic growth and national financial crises. About half of the Latin American countries experienced domestic financial crises during the 1990s, absorbing considerable fiscal and quasi-fiscal resources and affecting, sometimes for extended periods, the very functioning of financial systems (ECLAC, 2002b, and 2003a, Chapter 3; Ffrench-Davis, 2003; Ocampo, 2002b).

Dependence on external financing was closely associated with some features of productive restructuring, which generated a structural deterioration in the trade balance/growth trade-off (see below) and a high degree of sensitivity in the trade balance to economic activity. The tendency to substitute foreign for domestic saving, which characterizes periods of intense capital inflows, played a similar role. More broadly, domestic savings remained depressed in the 1990s, making investment highly dependent on external savings at the margin. Investment rates experienced a partial recovery, particularly if the simple rather than the weighted average is considered, but this recovery has been cut short by the interruption of capital flows since the Asian crisis began (Figure 3.3).

Overall, long-term growth has been frustratingly low. For the period 1990-2002, the average growth rate of only 2.6 percent a year, or 1.0 percent per capita, was less than half the level experienced by Latin America between 1945 and 1980 – namely, average growth rate of 5.5 percent per year, or 2.7 percent per capita. The comparison of total rather than per capita growth rates is more

Figure 3.3: Fixed Investment in Latin America as a Percentage of GDP (1995 Prices)

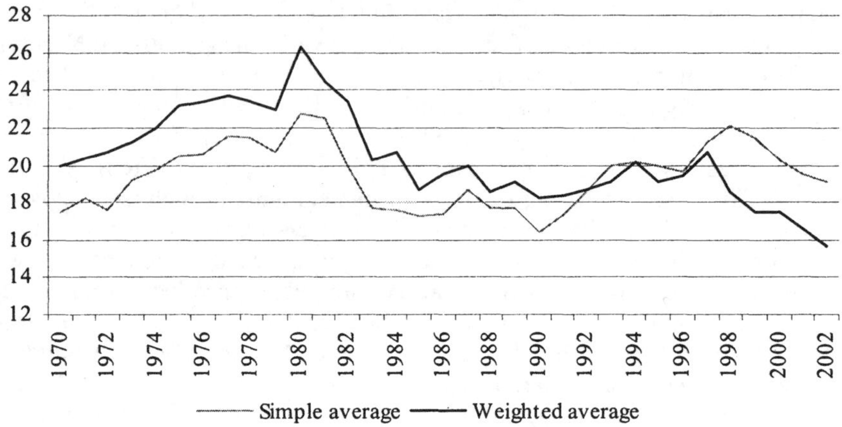

Source: ECLAC.

appropriate, as the demographic transition adversely affected per capita trends in the period of State-led industrialization, while the opposite was true in the 1990s, when the region benefited from a 'demographic bonus.' This is reflected in the fact that the labor force grew in the 1990s at rates quite similar to those that characterized the period 1945-1980. Moreover, the slowdown in long-term growth rates vis-à-vis 1945-1980 was a feature of most Latin American countries, the only major exceptions being Chile – which combined a poor record in 1945-1980 with rapid growth in 1990-2002, particularly up to 1998 – and the Dominican Republic – which grew rapidly in both periods. As discussed below, overall productivity performance was equally poor.

Integration into the World Economy

Dynamic export growth and FDI are the clearest signs of the significant progress made by the Latin American countries in their integration into the world economy. From 1990 to 2000, the region posted the fastest growth of export volumes in its history – close to 9 percent per year, higher than the rate achieved by world trade as a whole; then, the 2001-2002 world slowdown led to a sharp drop in real export growth to 2 percent per year. The strong growth of Mexican exports explains much of this strength in the 1990s. Indeed, in recent years Mexico has accounted for nearly half of Latin America's exports of goods. On the other hand, Brazil experienced export growth below both the regional average and its own historical performance since the 1960s; nonetheless,

Table 3.3: Composition of Latin American Exports, 1990 and 2000, Percent of Total Exports

			Manufactued products									
	Primary products		Based on natural resources		With low level of technology		With medium level of technology		With high level of technology		Non classified products	
	1990	2000	1990	2000	1990	2000	1990	2000	1990	2000	1990	2000
LAC	39.3	27.3	22.6	17.0	11.5	14.0	18.7	24.6	5.7	14.0	2.2	3.1
Mexico	29.4	11.7	9.4	5.8	10.6	14.7	31.8	38.5	14.9	25.3	3.9	3.9
Mercosur	36.5	34.7	23.6	24.1	14.8	11.0	20.7	21.2	3.2	6.6	1.1	2.4
Argentina	45.5	49.8	27.0	21.9	11.9	8.5	12.4	16.2	2.3	2.4	0.9	1.2
Brazil	32.0	27.1	23.3	25.5	14.9	11.6	24.9	24.3	3.8	8.9	1.1	2.5
Paraguay	78.0	57.4	12.8	14.5	6.6	8.7	1.8	0.8	0.1	0.7	0.7	17.9
Uruguay	36.4	36.7	14.3	20.5	36.1	22.0	8.4	13.6	1.2	2.8	3.6	4.4
Andean Community	58.1	59.5	30.0	24.5	5.6	6.3	4.4	6.4	0.3	0.9	1.5	2.4
Bolivia	61.7	56.0	21.2	24.7	6.4	13.4	1.0	1.1	0.3	1.0	9.3	3.8
Colombia	67.3	59.4	14.5	13.2	8.2	10.4	6.8	10.4	0.5	2.0	2.7	4.5
Ecuador	87.7	76.1	9.1	15.4	1.3	3.4	1.0	2.9	0.4	0.9	0.5	1.3
Peru	43.1	41.8	38.7	35.6	12.7	14.5	3.1	2.4	0.3	0.5	2.1	5.1
Venezuela	51.0	59.9	40.1	30.1	3.4	2.6	4.6	6.2	0.2	0.4	0.6	0.7
Central Am. Com. Mkt.	57.9	27.7	11.1	9.2	21.0	39.7	5.4	6.6	3.4	14.5	1.2	2.2
Costa Rica	56.9	29.1	7.0	8.5	25.5	17.1	6.1	8.3	3.5	34.3	1.0	2.8
El Salvador	46.4	13.4	11.4	9.8	24.9	62.7	8.2	5.9	8.2	6.4	0.9	1.8
Guatemala	53.0	36.1	16.9	12.4	20.5	39.9	5.0	7.4	3.6	2.5	1.0	1.7
Honduras	70.2	21.4	9.4	6.4	16.0	65.2	2.7	4.1	0.6	1.3	1.0	1.6
Nicaragua	70.9	46.9	15.1	8.8	3.9	36.7	4.6	2.5	0.9	0.3	4.5	4.7
Caricom	41.0	37.4	26.4	34.9	10.1	10.2	18.2	11.6	1.8	1.4	2.5	4.6
Others:												
Chile	41.9	40.3	49.4	48.6	2.4	3.0	3.5	5.7	0.3	0.7	2.4	1.7
Cuba	25.6	22.2	65.5	69.2	1.9	1.7	1.2	3.5	4.7	1.7	1.2	1.6
Haiti	11.0	8.9	4.3	2.9	67.0	85.2	8.4	1.0	6.3	0.3	2.9	1.6
Cayman Ils.	40.5	2.3	18.6	7.0	3.3	1.0	26.2	85.3	1.1	2.6	10.3	1.9
Panama	28.8	24.9	13.4	14.3	10.0	18.1	38.5	26.7	5.9	12.0	3.4	3.9
Dom. Rep.	12.7	4.9	11.6	8.6	49.6	62.7	18.5	17.5	1.6	3.5	6.0	2.9
Memo:												
S. Korea	3.2	1.7	7.4	12.0	41.7	16.9	25.9	29.2	20.5	38.4	1.3	1.8
China	14.6	4.7	8.2	6.9	53.6	47.6	15.4	17.3	7.3	22.4	0.8	1.1
Taiwan	4.4	1.3	6.7	4.8	38.8	21.8	25.2	25.0	23.8	45.5	1.1	1.5

Source: ECLAC.

contrary to the regional trend, Brazilian real export growth has increased in recent years. Most other countries experienced healthy real export growth of goods in the 1990s – close to 8 percent a year on average.

Export diversification progressed at different speeds in different countries and sub-regions. The most salient development was the rapid change in the composition of Mexican exports, though great diversification also took place in several Central American countries and in the Dominican Republic (Table 3.3). In the case of Mexico, a broad-based boom in manufacturing exports to the United States encompassed a wide range of products, including those resulting from in-bond assembly (*maquila*) activities. In the smaller countries, the diversification was more closely related to the development of assembly industries, again geared towards the United States market. Given the increased weight of assembly products in these countries, both the rate of growth and the degree of diversification of exports would be less pronounced if they were estimated in terms of value added – which is generally very small (ECLAC, 2003b, Chapter III). The change in the composition of exports was slower in Brazil, which also started out with a highly diversified export structure, and particularly in the rest of South America, where primary products and natural-resource-intensive manufactures – many of them also capital-intensive – still account for a large share of exports. Also, contrary to the pattern of Mexico and Central America, South American exports are less dependent on the United States market.

An important element in the expansion and diversification of exports was the significant progress of intra-regional trade associated with the strengthening of long-standing economic integration and free trade agreements and the creation of new ones. Between 1990 and 1997, trade growth within the two major South American integration processes – the Southern Common Market (Mercosur) and the Andean Community – was very rapid at 26 and 23 percent per year, respectively. It was slower but still dynamic at 17 percent a year in the Central American Common Market. A salient historical feature of intra-regional trade in Latin America – the preponderance of a diversified mix of non-traditional manufactures – continued to characterize this process. In fact, if such trade were excluded, the heavy concentration of South American exports in commodities would be even more apparent. The expansion of trade within the two South American integration blocks was abruptly interrupted in 1998, giving way to strong fluctuations in intra-regional trade and to a weakening commitment to regional integration.

Thus, Latin America has been generating two basic patterns of specialization that approximately follow a regional 'North-South' divide. The 'Northern' pattern is characterized by manufacturing exports with a high content of imported inputs – in its extreme form, *maquila* exports – mainly geared towards the United States market. This pattern goes hand in hand with traditional agricultural exports and agricultural export diversification in Central America, as well as the growth of tourism in Mexico and the Caribbean. The 'Southern' pattern is characterized by the combination of extra-regional exports of commodities and natural-resource-intensive manufactures and diversified intra-regional trade; as indicated, many of these goods are also capital-intensive. In the case of Brazil, this is mixed with some technology-intensive manufactures and services, and in Brazil and a number of other countries, with labor-intensive manufacturing exports. This implies that Mexico and some Central American and Caribbean countries have been participating to a greater extent in the more dynamic world markets for manufactures, whereas South America has focused on the less dynamic commodity markets. Nonetheless, a more detailed breakdown indicates that most Latin American countries specialize in goods that are not playing a dynamic role in world trade (ECLAC, 2002a and 2002c). There is also a third pattern of specialization, found in Panama and some small economies in the Caribbean Basin, in which service exports predominate – that is, financial, tourism and transport services. As discussed in the following section, specialization patterns have affected production patterns, particularly the dynamism of manufacturing production.

The boom in FDI was generated by both global and regional factors. The latter includes privatization, deregulation of natural-resource-intensive sectors, free trade agreements and preferential arrangements granted by more industrialized countries or regions – particularly the North American Free Trade Agreement (NAFTA) and the Caribbean Basin Initiative, and restructuring of production sectors in the framework of regional integration processes. Trade specialization and FDI patterns have been closely linked. Thus, whereas the 'Northern' specialization pattern has attracted multinationals actively involved in internationally integrated production systems, in South America investment in services, natural resources and production for regional integration processes is more prevalent.

FDI has included a large share of mergers and acquisitions of existing assets, first through participation in privatization processes and, more recently, through private mergers. It is estimated that in the late 1990s, mergers and acquisitions represented around two fifths of FDI in the region. A corollary of this process has been a rapid increase in the participation of foreign firms in production and sales, at the cost of public-sector firms in the first half of the 1990s and of both public and private firms in the second half.[8] A parallel development, smaller in magnitude, has been intra-regional direct investment, including mergers and acquisitions and a wave of strategic alliances between large domestic firms, in some cases as part of a transition towards sub-regional or regional multinational corporations.

The contrast between the dynamic internationalization of the Latin American economies and the weak GDP performance analyzed in the previous section is, undoubtedly, one of the paradoxical effects of structural reforms in the region. It reflects a considerable weakening of the links between international trade and domestic production, and thus GDP. This points to a reduction in the domestic production and technological linkages of export sectors, as well as the simultaneous destruction of the production linkages generated by previous import-substitution sectors unable to reconvert into export activities, or able to do so only through increased imports of intermediate goods and services. All these processes have been particularly intensive in manufacturing activities.

8 According to ECLAC estimates based on the sales of the largest thousand firms operating in the region, the share of foreign firms increased from 29.9 percent in 1990-1992 to 35.5 percent in 1994-1996, and to 41.6 percent in 1998-2000. The share of domestic private firms increased from 37.7 percent to 42.7 percent during the first half of the decade, but then fell to 41.3 percent; that of public-sector firms fell continuously from 32.5 to 17.1 percent.

Outsourcing by multinational firms, even in non-tradable sectors such as services, has further contributed to the weakening of their domestic linkages. In a very significant sense, many internationalized sectors have an increasing 'enclave' component: they participate actively in international transactions but very little in the generation of domestic value added. Indeed, the natural-resource-intensive sectors of the 'Southern' pattern of specialization may provide more opportunities for the formation of domestic production and technological linkages than the assembly activities characteristic of the 'Northern' pattern (ECLAC, 2003b, Chapter III, and de Ferranti et al., 2002).

Interestingly, despite the weaker linkages of internationalized sectors, there has been a strong cross-sectional correlation between export and GDP growth in Latin America. This correlation, together with the fact that rapid export growth did not lead to rapid GDP growth for the region as a whole, is closely associated with a third pattern, also regional in scope: the deterioration in the growth/trade deficit trade-off, which was reflected in an even more rapid growth of imports than that experienced by exports.[9] The trade deficit tended to widen in 1991-1997, reaching levels comparable to those of the 1970s but at growth rates that were close to 3 percentage points below those registered in that decade (Figure 3.4). This was the joint effect of *structural* changes in productive structures brought about by economic liberalization – including weaker domestic linkages of internationalized sectors – and the short-term *macroeconomic* policy bias towards real currency appreciation generated by booming capital inflows. Heavy dependence on volatile external financing was, in this regard, not only an effect but also a cause of this deterioration. Interestingly, this worsening of the growth/trade deficit trade-off would be even worse if the point of reference were the 1950s and 1960s, when rapid growth was consistent with small trade surpluses. This process worsened further during the recent 'lost half-decade' of 1998-2002, when the trade deficit remained stubbornly high despite very slow economic growth; indeed, the relevant point of reference is in this case the 1980s, when Latin America also grew very slowly but generated a large trade surplus.

It must be emphasized that, although there is a strong correlation between export and GDP growth, neither export nor overall GDP growth has been associated with particular export specialization patterns. Chile is the outstanding example of a country specializing in natural-resource-intensive exports that has also experienced rapid export and GDP growth. Ecuador and Venezuela are opposite cases. Mexico has extracted relatively slow GDP growth out of its exceptional export diversification and growth. In this regard, Costa Rica and El

9 See a similar analysis in UNCTAD (1999), which shows that this deterioration has occurred throughout the developing world, except in China and some other Asian economies.

Figure 3.4: Trade Balance, Net Resource Transfers and Economic Growth

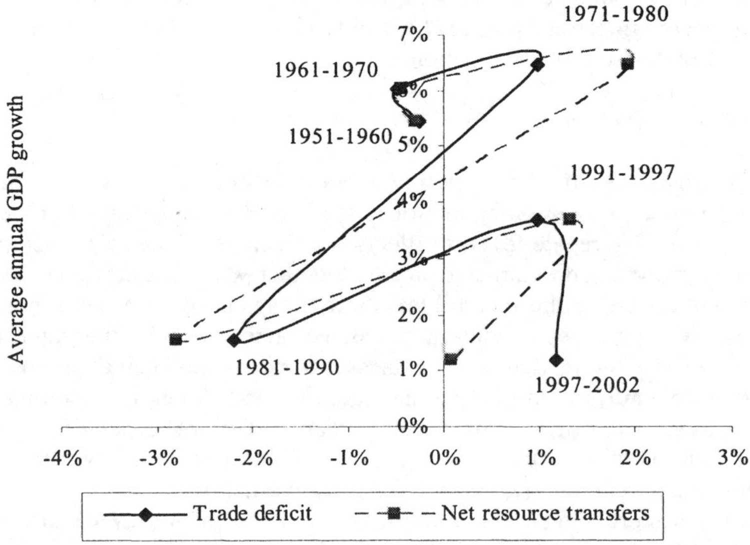

Source: ECLAC

Salvador, and particularly the Dominican Republic, have done better. As was indicated, the high import content of manufacturing exports and the tendency to specialize in the technologically simpler tasks within internationally integrated production systems may, indeed, result in natural-resource-intensive exports generating more domestic value added and linkages than manufacturing exports.

If specialization patterns are not part of the explanation, does the scope of reforms provide the clue to diverging GDP performance? Evidence coming from ECLAC research indicates that links between reforms and growth have been, at best, weak: some reforms have had positive effects on growth but others have had negative effects, and these impacts balance out to a statistically insignificant overall net effect; furthermore, even if their long-term effect were neutral or positive, their short-term impact was clearly negative (Escaith and Morley, 2001).[10] These results are consistent with parallel research on this link[11] and with

10 See also the recent sensitivity analysis of Correa (2002).

11 This is particularly true when the results of Lora and Barrera (1998) are compared with those of Lora and Panizza (2002), which used the Inter-American Development Bank reform indexes. Whereas the earlier paper estimated strong effects of reforms on growth, the latter only calculated weak temporary effects. Furthermore, a close inspection of the tables of this more recent paper indicates that this conclusion is not robust. Although Loayza et al. (2002) claim that reforms had significant effects on

the econometric estimates presented in the previous section. In any case, the best indication of the unclear effects of reforms on growth comes from the evaluation of macroeconomic trends since the 1990s vis-à-vis dynamic growth during the period of State-led industrialization.

Changing Production Patterns

The sluggishness of the region's average economic growth is a sign of macroeconomic, sectoral, and microeconomic problems. As noted in the previous section, at the aggregate level it reflects a worsening of the relationship between economic growth and external accounts, together with an insufficient recovery of investment ratios. At the sectoral level it is the result of the weak production and technological linkages of internationalized activities. At the microeconomic level, it reflects the tendency of businesses to adopt 'defensive' strategies – low-investment venturing, productive restructuring, and strategic marketing – as they try to adjust to the new context, rather than 'offensive' strategies – combining earlier restructuring efforts with substantial increases in investment in new equipment and technology, as well as strategic alliances.

At the sectoral level, some additional stylized facts may be discerned.[12] In many countries, a paradoxical effect of policies aimed at deeper integration into the world economy was the relative dynamism of tradable vs. non-tradable sectors. Transport, communications, energy and financial services, and construction were indeed dynamic, particularly during the expansionary phases of the regional business cycle. Among tradable sectors, manufacturing generally suffered the most compared with its own historical record prior to the debt crisis. This was especially true in the more traditional, labor-intensive industries like apparel, footwear, leather manufactures, and furniture, the exception being those industries associated with in-bond assembly (*maquila*) activities. The manufacturing sectors that performed better include *maquila* activities, the automobile industry – favored in Mexico by access to the United States market, and in South America by special protection mechanisms provided by current integration arrangements – some natural-resource-processing industries, and certain activities geared towards the domestic market during periods of booming demand, such as construction materials, beverages, and food processing.

---

long-term growth, they measure the effects of some long-term *characteristics* rather than *reforms*. Particularly, their results indicate strong long-term effects of human capital accumulation and infrastructure on economic growth. They also show somewhat weaker effects of trade openness and financial depth, but do *not* estimate those of trade and domestic financial *reforms*.

12 See ECLAC (2003a), chapters 4 and 5, Stallings and Peres (2000), Katz (2001), Moguillansky and Bielschowsky (2001) and, for agriculture, David (2000) and Ocampo (2000).

Agriculture also grew more slowly than it did before the debt crisis, with significant divergence in performance across the region. Moreover, some of the most dynamic activities in this sector followed long-term trends unrelated to the reform process – for example, the strong relative performance of soybeans or poultry production. Mining has tended to grow rapidly, but extraction activities have grown more rapidly than those that generate more value added – refining. Mining, like telecommunications and, to a lesser extent, energy, has benefited from institutional changes designed to open up opportunities for greater private-sector participation and FDI. In the case of mining resources, as well as FDI and intellectual property, an important feature of the reforms was stronger protection of property rights.

The mix between the growth of tradable and non-tradable sectors was diverse across the region through the 1990s and did not follow the Northern-Southern divide that characterized trade specialization patterns – although, as discussed below, employment trends did follow them. The association between specialization patterns and the relative dynamism of manufacturing was, on the other hand, quite strong. Economies specializing in manufacturing exports were characterized by the rapid relative growth of manufacturing production, while the opposite was true of economies that specialized in natural-resource-intensive exports. It is interesting to recall that the rising share of manufactures in GDP was a universal feature of Latin American countries during the period of State-led industrialization. During the reform period, this feature was found only in economies with a strong manufacturing export bias.

Slow GDP growth was associated with poor productivity performance, but the causal links involved must be carefully drawn. Even in manufacturing sectors – where productivity rose – the gap with the industrialized economies, particularly the United States, actually widened in many sectors in the 1990s. Indeed, in many countries and manufacturing activities, the productivity gap in relation to the United States narrowed more quickly during the 1970s and 1980s than during the 1990s, reflecting in part the slower pace of technological change in United States manufacturing during those previous decades. At the sub-sectoral level, the closing of the technology gap had more to do with the pace of economic growth in a particular sector and country than with patterns of technological catch-up induced by the reform process (Katz, 2001). Thus, for example, automobile production, for which selective instruments of protection were maintained, experienced productivity increases just as large as the natural-resource-intensive export activities, whereas import-competing sectors displaced by external competition did poorly in terms of productivity performance. Thus, the corresponding dynamics followed a Kaldor-Verdoorn pattern, in which growth determines productivity, rather than the opposite neo-classical causal link.

Agriculture also experienced a sustained increase in productivity, but this is a long-term trend that did not speed up to any significant extent during the 1990s (Dirven, 1997; Ocampo, 2000). Telecommunications, mining, and in some cases, energy are perhaps the sectors that most clearly demonstrate increases in productivity in the 1990s associated with the reform process as such, particularly privatizations and the growing role of multinational enterprises (ECLAC, 2003a, Chapters 4 and 5; Stallings and Peres, 2000).

In more general terms, productivity trends reflect a large discrepancy between the positive evolution of this variable in a group of successful firms and sectors and a poor performance at the aggregate level. Growth in total factor productivity (TFP) slowed down relative to its pre-debt crisis pace, even if recent years of low growth are excluded from the calculations: 1.7 percent a year in 1990-1998 vs. 2.0 percent in the era of State-led industrialization, or 0.8 percent vs. 1.0 percent for double-augmented TFP (Hofman, 2001). The slowdown was even sharper for labor productivity. Except for Chile, the Dominican Republic, and Uruguay, average labor productivity – measured as the ratio of GDP to the labor force – rose less in the region in 1990-2001 than in 1950-1980. Rising unemployment and, particularly, underemployment, largely due to poor overall economic growth, drove aggregate labor productivity. More broadly, overall productivity performance reflects the fact that labor, capital, technological capacity and, sometimes, land that were displaced from sectors and firms undergoing productive restructuring were not adequately reallocated to dynamic sectors. Again, the corresponding patterns followed a Kaldor-Verdoorn logic – that is, slow growth led to poor productivity performance – rather than the opposite neo-classical dynamic.

These patterns of productivity performance bring to light one of the main features of the productive restructuring processes that characterized the region during the reform period: the increased diversity of production sectors and agents within each economy – that is, increasing dualism, or 'structural heterogeneity,' using traditional ECLAC terminology. This indicates that the expectations that rising productivity in internationalized sectors would spread throughout the economy, thereby leading to rapid overall economic growth, turned out to be quite optimistic. Productivity *did* increase in dynamic firms and sectors, but external competition, FDI and privatization played an important role in that process. However, contrary to the expectations of reformers and the neo-classical links on which those expectations were based, positive productivity shocks did *not* spread out, but rather led to greater dispersion in relative productivity levels within these economies.

This is also an indication of the fact that restructuring was not 'neutral' in terms of its impact on different economic agents. The major winners were the multinational corporations and large national firms in sectors with static comparative advantages, but domestic firms in import-substitution sectors and, particularly, many small and medium-sized enterprises – both urban and rural – were unable to compete, and thus they experienced high mortality rates. The performance of small firms was closely tied to the dynamism of the sectors where they have a large share in production.[13]

The Changing Institutional Framework

Many of the changes in public policy that occurred during the reform period were aimed at redrawing the boundaries between public and private activity. The countries of the region faced the challenge of modernizing their public-sector institutions in terms both of their size and the rules of the game – policies, legal norms, and patterns of behavior. Both aspects proved to be crucial once the reforms began to mature. As shown by the experience of several countries, some of the institutional changes that were put in place – including the development of an adequate supervisory and regulatory framework in the domestic financial sector – played a crucial role in determining the balance between benefits and costs involved in the move towards economic liberalization.

Although this is a field in which most countries of the region still have a long way to go, progress has been made in some areas. At the macroeconomic level, a wide variety of discretionary oversight powers have been replaced by a few general rules that are not only more 'market-friendly' but also more stringent as far as compliance is concerned. By the same token, the distribution of functions – for example, between fiscal and monetary authorities – has been more clearly defined, making it possible to establish mutual accountability. In general, as discussed, these changes have strengthened the confidence of economic agents in macroeconomic authorities.

Other institutional and organizational changes originated in sectors in which new modalities of public and private operation played a key role. One of these was infrastructure services – particularly telecommunications, energy, and transportation, in which public action was increasingly geared towards promoting private investment and competition and, as a complement to this, controlling the distortionary effects of monopolies. As a result of these efforts, new institutional capacities were developed for promoting competition, regulating specific markets and, to a lesser extent, protecting consumers. Parallel to this development, the tasks that had formerly been melded in the operation of State-owned monopolies were split up, thus separating policy design from

13 See an extensive analysis of the issue of winners and losers in ECLAC (2003a), Stallings and Peres (2000), and Peres (1998), and of the dynamics of small firms in Peres and Stumpo (2000).

regulatory functions and service provision, even when the latter remained in State hands. Similar changes took place in the design of social policy – education, health, pensions and housing. In some cases, innovative schemes were developed for financing the services in question.

Although the institutions involved in all these areas have learned much from the process, the results achieved were modest compared with the magnitude of the challenge involved, and an active institutional learning process is still under way. Such lags have had significant economic effects. Thus, the more competitive climate and the opening up of opportunities for the private sector led to progress in terms of market efficiency and contestability, with potential benefits for consumers and resource allocation. However, a growing economic concentration created pressure in the opposite direction, even in tradable sectors. This tension had complex effects in infrastructure sectors, particularly when openness to private investment was not explicitly aimed at increasing competition or even led to the replacement – at least temporarily – of public monopolies by private ones and, more broadly, when the development of regulatory regimes lagged. Furthermore, where privatization processes were badly designed, with no prior regulation in place, the process gave rise to massive transfers of wealth. In social service delivery, other types of problems were involved (see below).

Fragility of Social Trends

Weakness of Labor Markets

The growing dualism among economic agents and sectors that characterized Latin America during the reform period has been reflected, in particular, in the performance of labor markets (ILO, 1999; ECLAC, 2002a, Chapter 10; Weller, 2001). Despite faster growth in relation to the 'lost decade' of the 1980s, open unemployment rose by almost 3 percentage points during the 1990s and increased abruptly in some countries – particularly during major external shocks. Indicators of deterioration in job quality are even more widespread, as shown by the relative increase in employment in low-productivity sectors. The share of urban-informal sector employment rose from 43.0 to 48.4 percent, generating seven out of ten new jobs between 1990 and 1999. This deterioration is also evident in an increase in temporary employment, in reduced coverage of social security systems, particularly for workers in small enterprises, and even in the number of individuals working without a written labor contract – the quintessential reflection of inadequate protection (Tokman and Martínez, 1999; ECLAC, 2002a, Chapter 10).

Figure 3.5: Variable Mixtures of Unemployment and Labor Informality, 1990-2000

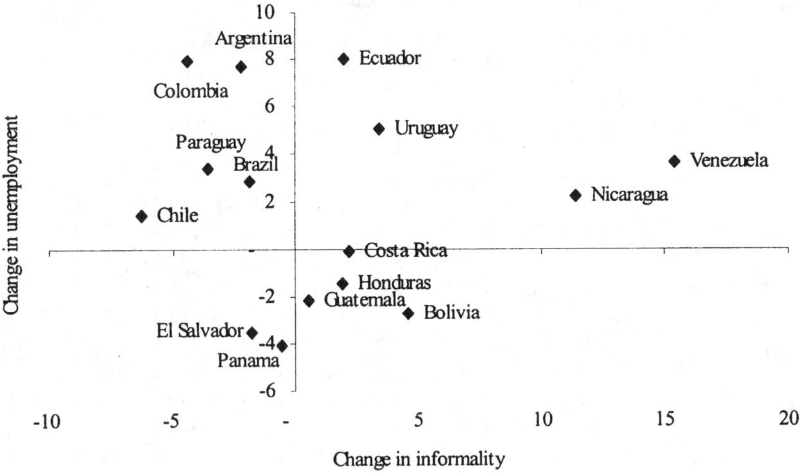

Source: ECLAC.

The mix between unemployment and informal-sector employment depended among other factors, on the patterns of economic growth, labor market policies, and international labor migration. In any case, most countries experienced deterioration in either one or the other of these dimensions or in both of them, indicating that these two mechanisms were complementary in terms of labor market adjustment (Figure 3.5). One specific factor that played a significant role in labor markets was the pattern of international specialization (ECLAC, 2002a, Chapter 10; Stallings and Weller, 2001). As Table 3.4 indicates, the 'Northern' pattern of specialization in manufactures – and some services – proved much more effective in generating employment, particularly wage-labor employment in tradable sectors, than 'Southern' specialization in natural-resource-intensive goods. Because employment did not follow specialization patterns in non-tradable sectors – particularly in relation to wage employment, whereas in tradable sectors it did, the growth of employment was more dynamic in the Northern part of the region. The better labor market performance of countries with the 'Northern' pattern of specialization is also reflected in Figure 3.5 in the more adverse informality-unemployment mix of most South American countries.

Weak job creation and its concentration in low-productivity activities indicate that Latin America has not been taking advantage of the opportunities that have opened up during the current stage of demographic transition, when the working-age population is growing rapidly and family dependency rates are dropping, facilitating the entry of more women into the labor market. This is reflected in the fact that while demographic growth fell from an annual rate of 2.7 percent in

Table 3.4: Patterns of Employment Generation and Labor Income Disparities, Annual Average Growth Rates and Wage Gap,[a] 1990 and 1999

	Total Employment			Wage Earner Employment			Private Sector Wage Gap [d]	
	Total	Tradable Sector [b]	Non-Tradable Sector [c]	Total	Tradable Sector [b]	Non-Tradable Sector [c]	c. 1990	c. 1999
Costa Rica	3.5	1.1 (1,9)	5.0 (3,6)	4.3	3.0 (2,7)	5.0 (3,3)	2.46	2.53
El Salvador	4.0	3.2 (3,8)	4.3 (1,9)	4.5	3.7 (5,0)	4.8 (3,4)	3.79	3.60
Guatemala	0.1	-1.2 (2,5)	2.1 (-1,1)	-0.7	-0.5 (0,9)	-0.8 (-3,6)	3.79	4.45
Honduras	4.9	3.9 (7,6)	6.2 (5,4)	4.0	3.3 (8,3)	4.4 (4,9)	5.13	3.34
Mexico	3.8	2.5 (4,8)	4.8 (5,4)	3.4	2.5 (4,2)	3.9 (4,7)	2.19	3.32
Nicaragua	6.5	7.1 (2,2)	5.9 (2,9)	6.6	10.7 (7,4)	4.5 (5,8)	2.53	2.76
Panama	3.2	-0.5 (3,2)	5.1 (2,4)	3.7	1.6 (3,2)	4.4 (2,2)	2.93	3.14
Regional ave.	*3.7*	*2.3 (4,0)*	*4.8 (2,8)*	*3.7*	*3.5 (4,8)*	*3.7 (2,9)*	*3.26*	*3.31*
Argentina	2.0	-2.4 (-2,7)	2.9 (3,8)	2.9	-2.6 (-3,0)	4.3 (4,3)	2.14	2.47
Bolivia	5.6	7.9 (8,4)	5.0 (0,2)	4.4	4.2 (5,4)	4.5 (2,4)	3.46	2.90
Brazil	1.6	-0.4 (-0,3)	2.8 (2,7)	1.8	-0.5 (-0,6)	2.9 (3,3)	6.58	5.46
Chile	2.4	-0.6 (-0.4)	4.0 (4,7)	3.0	-0.2 (-0,1)	4.7 (6,6)	4.05	4.87
Colombia	1.7	-0.3 (-0,7)	3.0 (3,3)	1.2	0.0 (-0,7)	1.9 (2,1)	2.59	3.82
Ecuador	4.2	2.7 (1,9)	4.6 (4,7)	4.0	2.1 (1,1)	4.7 (3,7)	2.85	3.72
Paraguay	3.7	3.6 (3,2)	3.8 (2,9)	4.4	4.3 (5,2)	4.4 (3,1)	2.75	3.62
Uruguay	1.1	-1.1 (-1,8)	1.8 (1,0)	1.5	-0.3 (-2,0)	2.0 (1,1)	2.45	3.14
Venezuela	3.8	1.8 (2,6)	4.5 (3,6)	2.6	1.2 (0,8)	3.1 (2,4)	2.12	3.32
Regional ave.	*2.9*	*1.2 (1,1)*	*3.6 (3,0)*	*2.9*	*0.9 (0,7)*	*3.6 (3,2)*	*3.22*	*3.70*
Total ave.	*3.3*	*1.7 (2,3)*	*4.1 (3,0)*	*3.2*	*2.0 (2,4)*	*3.7 (3,1)*	*3.24*	*3.53*

[a] The years used are 1990 and 1999, except for Bolivia, 1989 and 1999, Brazil 1993 and 1999, Chile 1990 and 1998, Colombia 1991 and 1999, Guatemala 1989 and 1998, Mexico 1989 and 1998, Nicaragua 1993 and 1998, Panama 1989 and 1999. For the following countries, geographical scope is: Argentina, Gran Buenos Aires; Bolivia, 8 main cities; Ecuador, El Salvador and Uruguay, urban zones; Paraguay, Asuncion and Departamento Central. [b] The data between parentheses correspond to manufacturing sector. [c] The data between parentheses correspond to government, social, community and personal services. [d] Ratio between average income of wage earners of 25 to 59 years old that work 20 or more hours weekly and have 17 or more years of education, and those who have between 6 and 9 years of education.

Source: ECLAC, on the basis of special tabulations of household surveys.

1950-1980 to 1.7 percent in the 1990s, the economically active population grew at a fairly steady rate – 2.7 percent in the earlier period and 2.6 percent in the 1990s. This increase should have made it possible to achieve a much higher growth in per capita output in the recent past than previously – just the opposite of the observed performance. It is clear, therefore, that this 'demographic bonus' is not captured automatically and, indeed, has not been captured in Latin America over the past two decades.

The considerable increase in the income gap between skilled and unskilled workers has been another widespread phenomenon (ECLAC, 1997; 2002a, Chapter 10). As Table 3.4 shows, only a few countries have been able to avoid this trend. Detailed analysis indicates that this development is the result of a widening income gap between college-educated and other workers (Morley, 2001). The widespread character of this trend indicates that divergent specialization patterns within the region are not part of the explanation; rather, technological change and the relative growth of sectors –particularly some services – with high demands for human capital seem to be the determining factors. Given these adverse trends, the greater participation of women in labor markets is the most positive pattern found across the region. In several countries, this pattern has been accompanied by a reduction in the still-large gender-income gap.

Social Spending and Restructuring of Social Services

If trends in labor markets have been the most adverse social trend in Latin America, the most favorable has been increased social-sector spending, which rose from 10.1 percent of GDP in 1990-1991 to 13.8 percent in 2000-2001 (Table 3.5), thus reaching the highest levels in the region's history (ECLAC, 2000a and 2000b). Moreover, the increase has been relatively faster in countries with lower per capita income, where social spending is also usually lower, as a reflection of their less developed social security systems. Uruguay and Brazil have strengthened their leadership in social spending, together with Argentina, Costa Rica and Panama. Colombia has been the only country moving from

Table 3.5: GDP per Capita and Social Expenditure, Latin American Countries, 1990-91 and 1998-99

	GDP per Capita (in 1995 US$)		Social Expenditure (% of GDP)	
	1990-91	1998-99	1990-91	1998-99
Argentina	5,916	7,762	17.7	20.5
Brazil	4,033	4,421	18.1	21.0
Chile	3,403	4,995	13.0	16.0
Colombia	2,032	2,210	8.0	15.0
Costa Rica	2,298	2,788	15.7	16.8
Guatemala	1,321	1,494	3.4	6.2
Honduras	686	710	7.9	7.4
Mexico	3,895	4,312	6.5	9.1
Nicaragua	447	463	10.8	12.7
Panama	2,422	3,001	18.6	19.4
Paraguay	1,644	1,576	3.1	7.4
Peru	2,202	2,717	3.3	6.8
Dominican Republic	1,472	2,013	4.3	6.6
Uruguay	4,779	6,111	16.8	22.8
Venezuela	2,985	2,998	9.0	8.6
Average	...	...	10.1	13.1

Source: ECLAC.

relatively low social spending to average levels relative to the pattern of spending by per capita income levels. In any case, regional disparities remain large, and in several countries, social spending continues to be clearly inadequate.

Increased spending has been accompanied by more selective allocation criteria, or targeting, which also accounts for some of the significant differences in the distributive impact of different types of spending (ECLAC, 2000a and 2000b). Changes have also been made in the way public resources are allocated, through the establishment of more decentralized systems. Nevertheless, the efficiency and quality of social services continue to be low. Also, the coverage of different services does not always reflect rising spending and improved targeting, or the demands generated by modernization and equity. Thus, despite improved coverage of secondary education – although the increase has been slower than that of competitors in East Asia – disparities in access between the top and bottom quartiles increased over the past decade (ECLAC, 2002a, Chapter 10). In addition, as indicated earlier, social security coverage has remained stagnant in most countries. Furthermore, problems relating to differences in the quality of services received by different social sectors are probably on the rise.

In some countries, increased spending has led to the development of arrangements for private-sector participation in the provision of certain social services, particularly social security and low-income housing. This trend may have brought progress in terms of efficiency, including the use of equivalence criteria for equating contributions paid into the social security system with benefits received from it, but strong evidence in this regard is not available. In some cases, however, this has gone hand in hand with a concentration of private service providers in the higher-income, lower-risk sectors and a weakening of the principles of universality and solidarity that should be honored by social security systems (ECLAC, 2000a). It should be noted, however, that, for the most part, these principles were also not properly applied in the region in the past, a fact reflected in the incomplete and segmented nature of social security coverage during the period of State-led industrialization, which included the proliferation of special arrangements that benefited certain social sectors.

Poverty and Income Distribution

Poverty rates shot up during the 'lost decade' from 40.5 to 48.3 percent of the total population, and fell (as growth recovered) to 43.5 percent in 1997, although the number of poor people stagnated at roughly 200 million. More important, the relationship between per capita GDP and poverty followed an asymmetric path over the past two decades, indicating that the debt crisis had adverse ratchet effects on poverty (Figure 3.6). Also, positive trends in poverty were sharply interrupted during the 'lost half-decade,' causing an additional 20 million people

Figure 3.6: Poverty and Per Capita GDP

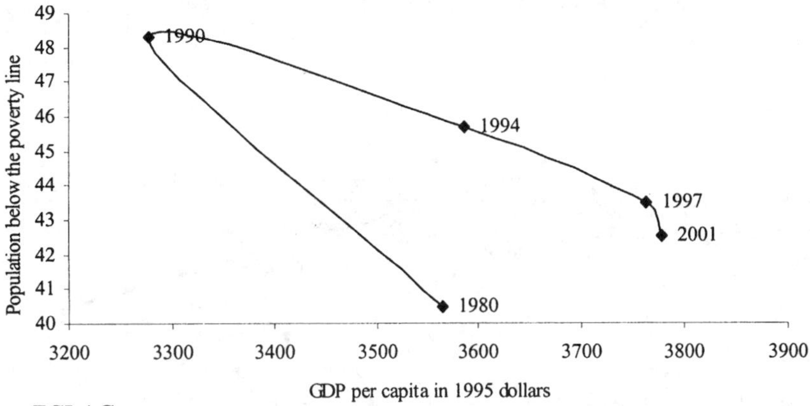

Source: ECLAC.

to fall below the poverty line. In recent years, whereas per capita GDP has exceeded 1980 levels by some 6 percent, poverty rates have remained 3 percentage points above pre-debt-crisis levels. Furthermore, hard-core poverty, particularly in rural areas, has represented a significant challenge in all countries.

Success in reducing poverty has varied across the region. There are a few countries – Venezuela being the most remarkable case – where poverty rates are still higher than in 1990 (Figure 3.7), and there is a larger group of countries that have not returned to pre-debt-crisis levels. Economic growth has been the most important factor in this regard. However, there are significant differences in performance relative to the average growth-poverty reduction pattern. Chile, which experienced the fastest rate of economic growth during the 1990s, also had a strong performance in terms of poverty reduction. Similarly, the good performance of Costa Rica and the poor performances of Colombia and Honduras can be attributed to differences in the rates of economic growth. Nonetheless, other countries show significant divergence from the average pattern: Uruguay and Brazil have done better than expected in terms of poverty reduction, whereas Argentina, Mexico and Venezuela have done much worse. Specific factors can explain deviations from the pattern, including the extensive system of social protection in Uruguay and the targeted minimum pension policies in Brazil. The end of hyperinflation also had a positive effect in all countries that had gone through that traumatic experience. Also, there is evidence that minimum-wage policies had a positive effect in this regard.[14]

Unlike poverty rates, income distribution trends have been uneven across the region but, on the whole, have shown a tendency to deteriorate. There are several

14 On the determinants of poverty, see ECLAC (1997, 2000a, 2000b, and 2001) and Morley (2001).

Figure 3.7: Poverty Reduction and Per Capita GDP Growth, Percentage Points, 1990-1999

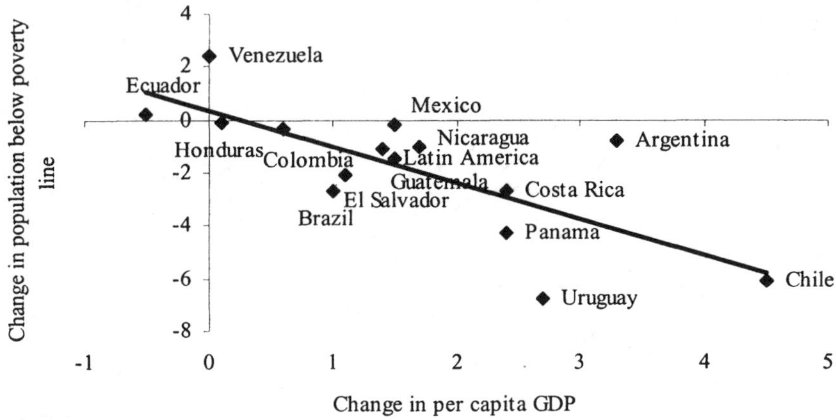

Source: ECLAC.

countries where income distribution, measured by either the Gini coefficient or relative poverty, displayed an adverse trend over the past decade but only a handful where the opposite is true (Table 3.6) – and some of these latter cases are debatable.[15] Although comparing data on income distribution over long periods is a complex matter, there is no country in the region where inequalities have declined relative to what they were three decades ago and, on the contrary, inequality has increased in many countries. Uruguay is perhaps the only country in the region where falling levels of poverty in the 1990s were accompanied by relatively equitable income distribution, but even there, distribution has not yet regained the favorable levels that the country enjoyed thirty years ago. Although comparable household surveys for Cuba are not available, this country probably has the most equitable income distribution in the region, although it deteriorated as a result of the dramatic economic crisis experienced in the early 1990s and the subsequent restructuring process, which was reflected in significant drops in per capita consumption.

ECLAC studies show that the inequalities are due to a combination of factors relating to education, demographics, employment, and the distribution of wealth. As regards the first two, some progress was made during the 1990s. As noted, educational coverage increased, but there are signs of growing dispersion in that

15 This is particularly the case in Honduras, where comparability of household surveys over time is a serious issue, as well as in Colombia, where income distribution has shown a clear deterioration in urban areas but has improved in rural zones. Intertemporal comparability of household surveys in Paraguay, where Table 3.6 indicates a sharp increase in inequality through the 1990s, also poses problems.

Table 3.6: Trends in Poverty and Income Distribution, c. 1990 and c. 1999

	Population below the Poverty Line		GINI Coefficient		Relative Poverty [c]	
	c. 1990	c. 1999	c. 1990	c. 1999	c. 1990	c. 1999
Argentina [a]	21.2	19.7	0.501	0.542	39.1	44.2
Bolivia [a]	53.1	48.8	0.538	0.586	44.1	45.5
Brazil	48.0	37.5	0.627	0.640	53.9	54.8
Chile	38.6	20.6	0.554	0.559	46.5	46.4
Colombia	56.1	54.9	0.601	0.572	48.9	46.6
Costa Rica	26.2	20.3	0.438	0.473	31.6	36.1
Ecuador [a]	62.1	63.6	0.461	0.521	33.8	42.0
El Salvador [b]	54.2	49.8	0.507	0.518	38.4	40.6
Guatemala	69.1	60.5	0.582	0.582	47.9	49.5
Honduras	80.5	79.7	0.615	0.564	52.3	46.4
Mexico	47.8	46.9	0.536	0.539	43.5	43.1
Nicaragua	73.6	69.9	0.582	0.584	45.9	45.9
Panama	42.8	30.2	0.560	0.557	46.4	46.4
Paraguay [a]	42.0	49.0	0.447	0.565	33.4	46.3
Uruguay [a]	17.8	9.4	0.492	0.440	36.8	32.2
Venezuela	40.0	49.4	0.471	0.498	35.5	38.6

[a] Urban area. [b] Initial year: 1995. [c] Percentage of population with per capita income below the 50% of the average income.

Source: ECLAC (2001).

coverage and, probably, in the quality of education among different groups of the population. Demographic dependence declined, but it remained an important factor in countries where there is a significant lag in the demographic transition. On the job front, however, there has been deterioration, as indicated earlier. The ongoing integration of women into the labor market is one of the few factors that have had a broad positive effect on income distribution in most countries in the region, as well as in other areas of development. Not much is known about what has happened in terms of wealth inequality, but it is quite possible that the situation has worsened in this area as well.

In view of the increasing educational requirements for all occupations, progress in education has been clearly insufficient in terms of improving employment opportunities and earning power. From the standpoint of the labor market, diminishing returns from education have meant that only 47 percent of young people in urban areas and 28 percent in rural areas have improved their occupational outlook by increasing their educational level – relative to their parents' – above the also-rising educational requirements in the job market. This result is consistent with household surveys, which show that only half of Latin America's youth believe that they will enjoy better opportunities than did their parents (ECLAC, 1998a and 2000b).

The increased demand for skilled labor has also defeated the favorable effects of the improved coverage of secondary education on income distribution. As noted, one sign of this is the growing income gap between college-educated and other workers. In some countries, there has been some narrowing of disparities between the incomes of workers who have received only primary education and those who have some secondary education, but this trend has been counterbalanced by greater dispersion of incomes among college-educated workers (Morley, 2001).

In broader analytical terms, there is considerable disagreement in the current literature as to why distribution has tended to deteriorate. Different studies focus on aspects such as structural reform, the debt crisis, or universal trends associated with technological change and other factors influencing wage and skill differentials (see above).[16] Berry (1998) is well known for his early emphasis on the adverse distributive effects of structural reforms, a hypothesis that has received increasing support in later research. Considering the analysis above, rising dualism is an important link between structural reforms and deterioration in income distribution, but other factors affecting income differentials – some of them worldwide in scope – have also played a role.

In any case, recent adverse trends have aggravated adverse distributive patterns that were already evident in Latin America in previous stages of development. Hence, the lack of equity is not just a characteristic of the recent reform period, but a pre-existing condition that reflects serious problems of social stratification handed down from generation to generation (ECLAC, 2000a, 2000b).

The Way Forward

As we look back at economic liberalization in Latin America, it becomes clear that the benefits of reforms were overstated and their risks overlooked. Reforms were successful in many areas, particularly in bringing down inflation and giving greater credibility to macroeconomic authorities, in inducing export growth and diversification, and in attracting FDI. But frustration also resulted from low and volatile growth, increasing dualism and, particularly, disappointing social outcomes. Some basic assumptions of reformers proved to be entirely wrong, particularly the assumptions that low inflation and better control of budget deficits would ensure stable access to international capital markets and dynamic growth, and that higher productivity in leading firms and sectors would automatically spread throughout the economy, leading to a broad acceleration of economic growth.

The interpretation of the poor outcomes of reforms remains highly

16 See, for example, Altimir (1997), Berry (1998), Morley (1995 and 2001), IDB (1997 and 1999), ECLAC (1997).

controversial. One view explains these results as the effect of an insufficient commitment to the original reform agenda, and thus, posits that the solution to the current frustrations is even more liberalization. An alternative view, much in vogue today, emphasizes that the original 'Washington Consensus' was an incomplete agenda, which must be complemented with a 'second generation' of reforms based on institutional and social development. Some proposals based on this line of reasoning are welcome (for example, Birdsall and de la Torre, 2001). Nonetheless, both approaches share a linear view of the reform process, failing to recognize that some of the basic assumptions of the liberalization process were in fact wrong and, thus, that the first generation of reforms may have created some of the problems we are facing today and that it is therefore essential to 'reform the reforms' (Ffrench-Davis, 2000; ECLAC, 2000a). Furthermore, the basic assumption of a unique 'recipe' ignores the essence of institutional development and democracy: diversity and learning. Indeed, as indicated above, there has been more diversity in the reform process than is commonly recognized.

A more promising approach, therefore, is to acknowledge that it is essential to build on the positive aspects of the reform process and on the new agenda of institutional and social reforms, and also to correct the basic problems that the first generation of reforms has already demonstrated. These problems lie in three basic areas: (1) the limited view of macroeconomic stability, which has resulted in pro-cyclical macroeconomic policies that heighten the effects of volatile external – particularly capital – markets, and thus, generate both an adverse investment climate and increased insecurity among social sectors; (2) the failure to realize that the emergence of dynamic economic activities is not necessarily a spontaneous outcome of the functioning of liberalized, open economies; and, even more, that production and technological linkages between dynamic firms and sectors and the rest of the economy are not automatic; and (3) the failure to recognize that the social dimension must be effectively mainstreamed into the reform process – particularly into macroeconomic, sectoral, and microeconomic policies, thus ensuring that successful social outcomes are not merely an issue of complementary – in many cases, residual – social policies. Moreover, it must be explicitly recognized that there are diverse solutions to all of these problems and that democracy must play an essential role in finding the appropriate policies for each particular context. This is the view advocated elsewhere by Rodrik (1999, 2001a, 2001b), by ECLAC (2000a) and by this author (Ocampo, 2002a), among others.

References

Altimir, O. (1997), 'Desigualdad, Empleo y Pobreza en América Latina: Efectos del Ajuste y del Cambio en el Estilo de Desarrollo', *Desarrollo Económico*, Vol. 37, No. 145 (April-June).

Berry, A. (1998), 'Confronting the Income Distribution Threat in Latin America', in A. Berry (ed.), *Poverty, Economic Reforms, and Income Distribution in Latin America*, Lynne Rienner, Boulder, CO, pp. 9-41.

Birdsall, N. and A. de la Torre, with R. Menezes (2001), *Washington Contentious: Economic Policies for Social Equity in Latin America*, Carnegie Endowment for International Peace and Inter-American Dialogue, Washington, D.C.

Burki, S.J. and G.E. Perry (eds.) (1997), *The Long March: A Reform Agenda for Latin America and the Caribbean in the Next Decade*, The World Bank, Washington, D.C.

Cárdenas, E., J.A. Ocampo and R. Thorp (eds.) (2000), *Industrialisation and the State in Latin America: The Post War Years. An Economic History of Twentieth Century Latin America*, Volume 3, Palgrave Press and St. Martins, New York.

Correa, R. (2002), 'Structural Reforms and Economic Growth in Latin America: A Sensitivity Analysis', *CEPAL Review*, No. 76 (April), pp. 87-104.

David, M.B. (2000), *Desarrollo Rural en América Latina y el Caribe: ¿La Construcción de un Nuevo Modelo?*, ECLAC/Alfaomega, Bogota.

De Ferranti, D., G.E. Perry, D. Lederman, and W.F. Maloney (eds.) (2002), *From Natural Resources to the Knowledge Economy: Trade and Job Quality*, The World Bank, Washington, D.C.

Dirven, M. (1997), 'El Empleo Agrícola en América Latina y el Caribe: Pasado Reciente y Perspectivas', Serie de Desarrollo Productivo, No. 43, ECLAC, Santiago.

ECLAC (Economic Commission for Latin America and the Caribbean) (1990), *Changing Production Patterns with Social Equity*, ECLAC, Santiago.

ECLAC (Economic Commission for Latin America and the Caribbean) (1994), *Latin America and the Caribbean: Policies to Improve Linkages with Global Economy*, ECLAC, Santiago.

ECLAC (Economic Commission for Latin America and the Caribbean) (1997), *The Equity Gap: Latin America, the Caribbean and the Social Summit*, ECLAC, Santiago.

ECLAC (Economic Commission for Latin America and the Caribbean) (1998a), *Social Panorama of Latin America, 1997*, ECLAC, Santiago.

ECLAC (Economic Commission for Latin America and the Caribbean) (1998b), *América Latina y el Caribe: Políticas para Mejorar la Inserción en la Economía Mundial*, second edition, Fondo de Cultura Económica, Santiago and Mexico City.

ECLAC (Economic Commission for Latin America and the Caribbean) (2000a), *Equity, Development and Citizenship*, ECLAC, Santiago.

ECLAC (Economic Commission for Latin America and the Caribbean) (2000b), *The Equity Gap, A Second Assessment*, ECLAC, Santiago.

ECLAC (Economic Commission for Latin America and the Caribbean) (2001), *Social Panorama of Latin America, 2000-2001*, ECLAC, Santiago.

ECLAC (Economic Commission for Latin America and the Caribbean) (2002a), *Globalization and Development*, ECLAC, Santiago.

ECLAC (Economic Commission for Latin America and the Caribbean) (2002b), *Growth with Stability: Financing for Development in the New International Context*, ECLAC Books No. 67, ECLAC, Santiago.

ECLAC (Economic Commission for Latin America and the Caribbean) (2002c), *Latin America and the Caribbean in the World Economy*, 2000-2001 Edition, ECLAC, Santiago.

ECLAC (Economic Commission for Latin America and the Caribbean) (2003a), *A Decade of Light and Shadow: Latin America and the Caribbean in the 90s*, ECLAC, Santiago.

ECLAC (Economic Commission for Latin America and the Caribbean) (2003b), *Latin America and the Caribbean in the World Economy*, 2001-2002 Edition, ECLAC, Santiago.

ECLAC/UNEP (Economic Commission for Latin America and the Caribbean/United Nations Environment Programme) (2002), *The Sustainability of Development in Latin America and the Caribbean: Challenges and Opportunities*, ECLAC Books No. 68, ECLAC, Santiago.

Edwards, S. (1995), *Crisis and Reform in Latin America: From Despair to Hope*, Oxford University Press for the World Bank, Washington, D.C.

Escaith, H. and S. Morley (2001), 'El Efecto de las Reformas Estructurales en el Crecimiento Económico de la América Latina y el Caribe. Una Estimación Empírica', *El Trimestre Económico*, Vol. 68, No. 272 (October-December).

Ffrench-Davis, R. (2000), *Reforming the Reforms in Latin America: Macroeconomics, Trade, Finance*, Macmillan and St. Martin's Press, London and New York.

Ffrench-Davis, R. (2003), 'Financial Crises and National Policy Issues: An Overview', in R. Ffrench-Davis and S. Griffith-Jones (eds.), *From Capital Surges to Drought: Seeking Stability for Emerging Markets*, Palgrave/Macmillan, London.

Hofman, A. (2001), 'Long-Run Economic Development in Latin America in a Comparative Perspective: Proximate and Ultimate Causes', Serie Macroeconomía del Desarrollo No. 8 (December), ECLAC, Santiago.

IDB (Inter-American Development Bank) (1997), *Latin America After a Decade of Reforms. Economic and Social Progress in Latin America 1997*, Inter-American Development Bank, Washington, D.C.

IDB (Inter-American Development Bank) (1999), *Facing Up to Inequality in Latin America, Economic and Social Progress in Latin America 1998-1999*, Inter-American Development Bank, Washington, D.C.

ILO (International Labour Organization) (1999), 'Trabajo Decente y Protección para Todos. Prioridad de las Américas', *Memoria del Director General*, fourteenth Regional Meeting of the Americas, Lima, August 24-27.

Katz, J. (2001), *Structural Reforms, Productivity and Technological Change in Latin America*, ECLAC Books No. 64, ECLAC, Santiago.

Loayza, N., P. Fajnzylber and C. Calderón (2002), 'Economic Growth in Latin America and the Caribbean: Stylized Facts, Explanations, and Forecasts', The World Bank, Washington, D.C.

Lora, E. (2001), 'Structural Reforms in Latin America: What Has Been Reformed and How to Measure It', Working Paper No. 466, Inter-American Development Bank, Washington, D.C.

Lora, E. and F. Barrera (1998), 'El Crecimiento Económico en América Latina después de una Década de Reformas Estructurales', *Pensamiento Iberoamericano*, Special Issue.

Lora, E. and U. Panizza (2002), 'Structural Reforms in Latin America Under Scrutiny', paper prepared for the seminar Reforming Reforms, Inter-American Development Bank Annual Meetings, Fortaleza, Brazil, March 11.

Moguillansky, G. and R. Bielschowsky (2001), *Investment and Economic Reform in Latin America*, ECLAC Books No. 63, ECLAC, Santiago.

Morley, S. (1995), *Poverty and Inequality in Latin America: the Impact of Adjustment and Recovery in the 1980s*, The Johns Hopkins University Press, Baltimore.

Morley, S. (2001), *The Income Distribution Problem in Latin America and the Caribbean*, ECLAC Books No. 65, ECLAC, Santiago.

Morley, S., R. Machado and S. Pettinato (1999), 'Indexes of structural reform in Latin America,' Serie Reformas Económicas No. 12, ECLAC, Santiago.

Ocampo, J.A. (2000), 'Agricultura y Desarrollo Rural en América Latina: Tendencias, Estrategias, Hipótesis', in ECLAC, *El Impacto de las Reformas Estructurales y las Políticas Macroeconómicas sobre el Sector Agropecuario de América Latina*, ECLAC/Alfaomega, Bogota.

Ocampo, J.A. (2002a), 'Rethinking the Development Agenda', *Cambridge Journal of Economics*, Vol. 26, No. 3 (May), pp. 393-407.

Ocampo, J.A. (2002b), 'Developing Countries' Anti-Cyclical Policies in a Globalized World', in A. Dutt and J. Ros (eds.), *Development Economics and Structuralist Macroeconomics: Essays in Honour of Lance Taylor*, Edward Elgar, Aldershot, U.K.

Peres, W. (ed.) (1998), *Grandes Empresas y Grupos Industriales Latinoamericanos: Expansión y Desafíos en la Era de la Apertura y la Globalización*, Siglo XXI Editores, Mexico City.

Peres, W. and G. Stumpo (2000), 'Small and Medium-Sized Manufacturing Enterprises in Latin America and the Caribbean under the New Economic Model', *World Development*, Vol. 28, No. 9 (September).

Rodríguez, F. and D. Rodrik (2001), 'Trade Policy and Economic Growth: A Skeptic's Guide to the Cross-National Evidence', in B.S. Bernanke and K. Rogoff (eds.), *NBER Macroeconomics Annual 2000*, Vol. 15, MIT Press, Cambridge, MA.

Rodrik, D. (1999), *Making Openness Work: The New Global Economy and the Developing Countries*, Overseas Development Council, Washington, D.C.

Rodrik, D. (2001a), 'Why is There So Much Economic Insecurity in Latin America?' CEPAL *Review*, No. 73 (April), pp. 7-29

Rodrik, D. (2001b), 'Development Strategies for the Next Century', in B. Pleskovic and N. Stern (eds.), *Annual World Bank Conference on Development Economics 2000*, Oxford University Press for the World Bank, New York.

Stallings, B. and W. Peres (2000), *Growth, Employment and Equity: the Impact of the Economic Reforms in Latin America and the Caribbean*, The Brookings Institution and ECLAC, Santiago.

Stallings, B. and J. Weller (2002), 'Job Creation in Latin America in the 1990s: The Foundation for Social Policy', *CEPAL Review*, No. 75.

Tokman, V.E. and D. Martínez (eds.) (1999), *Flexibilización en el Margen: La Reforma del Contrato de Trabajo*, ILO, Lima.

UNCTAD (United Nations Conference on Trade and Development) (1999), *Trade and Development Report, 1999*, UNCTAD/TDR/1999, United Nations, Geneva.

Williamson, J. (1990), 'What Washington Means by Policy Reform', in J. Williamson (ed.), *Latin American Adjustment. How Much Has Happened?*, Institute for International Economics, Washington, D.C., pp. 5-20.

Weller, J. (2001), Economic Reforms, Growth and Employment: Labor Markets in Latin America and the Caribbean, ECLAC Books No. 66, ECLAC, Santiago.

Chapter 4

Economic Growth and Human Development in Latin America[1]

Gustav Ranis and Frances Stewart

Introduction

A strong case can be made for regarding *human development* (HD) as the ultimate objective of human activity in place of *economic growth* (EG). HD has been defined as enlarging people's choices in a way which enables them to lead longer, healthier and fuller lives.[2] This is a very broad definition of HD, and can include a great variety of choices embracing, for example, political and cultural dimensions. This chapter focuses on a narrow subset of choices, those directed specifically at health and education, which are among the basic preconditions of choice in other dimensions. This paper conforms to the spirit of much of the work of Al Berry, whose major concern has been to move beyond growth of per capita incomes to a focus on their distribution, with the objective of improving the lives of the poor.[3]

In a previous paper (Ranis et al., 2000), we explored the links between HD – defined in this rather restricted fashion – and EG, both theoretically and empirically. Clearly, there exists a strong two-way connection between the two. On the one hand, EG provides the resources to permit sustained improvements in HD. On the other, improvements in the quality of the labor force constitute an important contributor to EG. While these general connections are readily accepted, one needs to understand the links in more depth for this relationship to be of much use to

---

1 A version of this paper was originally presented at the conference in honor of Professor Albert Berry on Social and Economic Impacts of Globalization and Liberalization: Effects on Labor Markets and Income Distribution, organized by the University of Toronto on April 19-20, 2002. A slightly modified version was published in *CEPAL Review*, No. 78, December 2002. We gratefully acknowledge the excellent research assistance of Tavneet Suri, as well as the help of Prateek Tandon.

2 The first UNDP Human Development Report stated that 'The basic objective of development is to create an enabling environment for people to enjoy long, healthy and creative lives' (UNDP, 1990, 9), and defined human development as 'a process of enlarging people's choices' (*Ibid.*, 10).

3 For an early example, see Berry and Urrutia (1976); for a more recent one, see Berry (1998).

policy. In particular, one needs to know whether any form of EG promotes HD, or particular patterns of EG are more conducive to HD; equally, whether any form of HD promotes EG, or whether there are specific types which are more conducive to promoting growth; and whether we can say anything useful about priorities if a choice is necessary – for example, should HD be promoted before EG, or can we delay the achievement of HD while promoting EG?

In order to answer these questions, in Ranis et al. (2000) we explored the theoretical links and then analyzed them empirically, drawing on cross-country data from all developing regions of the world. The exercise led to quite strong conclusions about the questions just posed. In this paper, we aim to investigate how well our general findings apply in the Latin American (LA) context, and what policy conclusions are to be derived from the LA experience.

The next section summarizes the findings of our earlier work. Some econometric estimates for LA, comparing them with the earlier global findings, are presented in the third section; the fourth section reports on some country cases in LA which have been particularly successful or unsuccessful. Finally, the fifth section presents brief conclusions.

HD and EG: Findings from the Previous Study

We view HD as the central objective of human activity and EG as a potentially very important instrument for advancing it. At the same time, achievements in HD themselves can make a critical contribution to economic growth. There are thus two distinct causal chains to be examined: one runs from EG to HD, as the resources from national income are allocated to activities contributing to HD; the other runs from HD to EG, indicating how, as well as being an overriding objective, HD helps increase national income. The two chains are pictured in Figure 4.1.

Chain A: From EG to HD

From a review of the literature on the determinants of HD, it appears that the main links in the chain from EG to HD relate to

1. The distribution of GDP between households and government, since each performs vital, if different, roles in generating conditions favorable for HD. Civil society, for example, through community organizations and other NGOs also plays a role. These organizations' share of national resources depends on the decisions of government and households on how much to allocate to them.
2. The distribution of income, because income going to poorer households is more likely to enhance our restricted concept of HD (education, health), since deficiencies are greatest among such households.

Figure 4.1: Human Development and Economic Growth

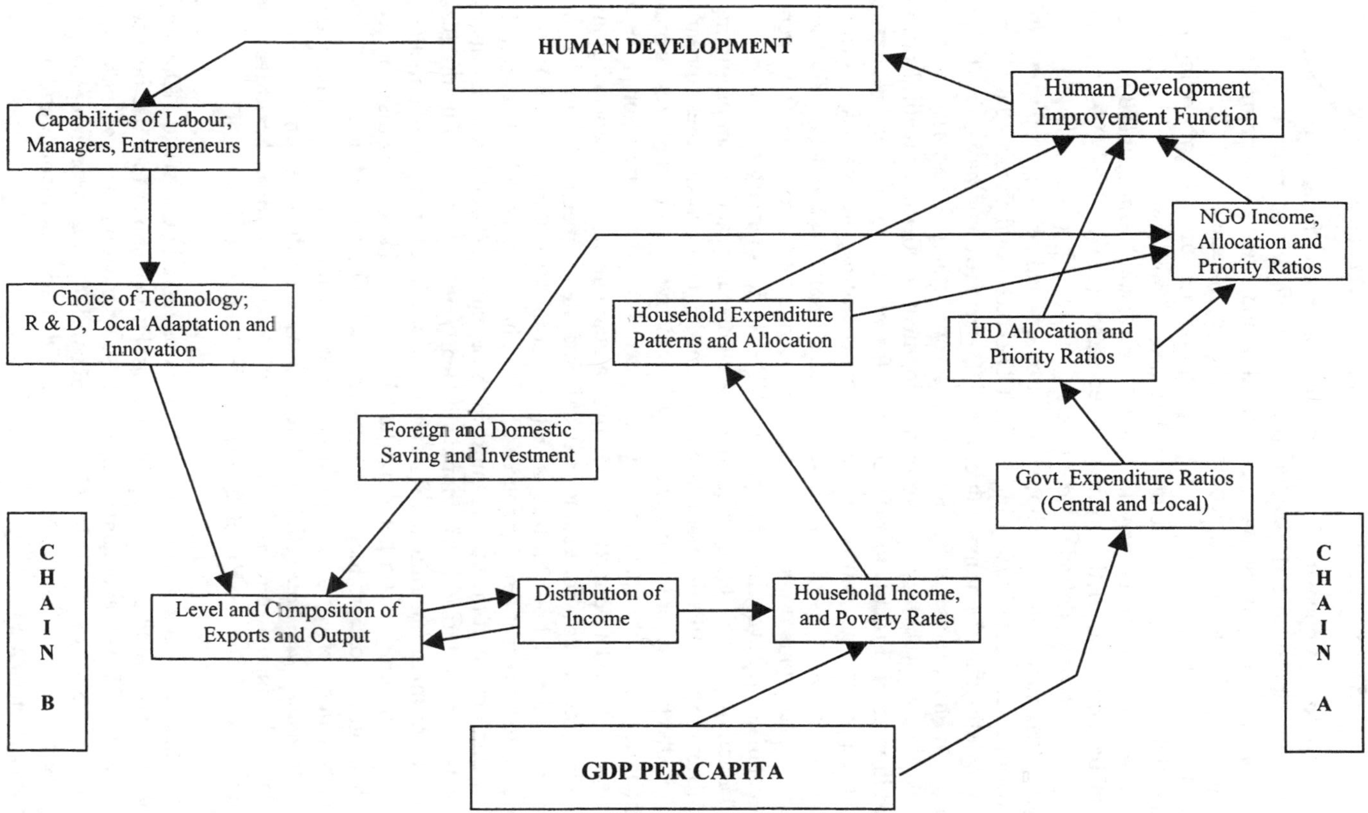

Source: Prepared by the authors.

3. Households' propensity to spend their after-tax income on items which contribute most directly to the promotion of HD in poor countries – for example, food, potable water, education and health. A major determinant appears to be the share of income controlled by females.
4. Turning to the government – the allocation of resources to improving HD as a function of total public sector expenditure, of how much of this flows to the HD sectors, and of the way in which it is allocated within these sectors. This can be expressed in the form of three ratios (see UNDP, 1991): the public expenditure ratio, defined as the proportion of GDP spent by the various levels of government; the HD-allocation ratio, defined as the proportion of total government expenditure going to the HD-sectors; and finally, the HD priority ratio, defined as the proportion of total HD-sector expenditure going to 'priority areas.' The precise definition of what constitutes a 'priority area' varies according to a country's stage of development, rendering this third ratio more arbitrary and difficult to measure than the other two. Within the health and education sectors, however, some expenditures are clearly much more productive in terms of achieving advances in HD than others – for example, basic education, especially at an early stage of development, is generally recognized to have a larger impact on HD than does tertiary education.
5. The activities of NGOs or other parts of civil society activity in promoting HD. Information on this is more scattered, but NGOs' expenditures appear to be typically heavily oriented towards HD objectives – for examples, generating incomes for the poor and directed towards schools, nutrition and health projects. In most contexts, NGOs play a supplemental or even marginal role, but in a few areas – for example, BRAC and the Grameen Bank in Bangladesh, the Harambee Schools in Kenya and the 'Comedores Populares' in Peru – they appear to represent a major source of HD-enhancement (Riddell et al., 1995).
6. The importance of the effectiveness of these various expenditures in raising HD levels. Expenditures on HD inputs are clearly not objectives in themselves, but rather constitute instruments for achieving advances in various dimensions of basic well-being. A further important link in Chain A concerns what type of provision is most productive at what level of development, and how different combinations effect a change in HD. We call this link in the chain the *HD improvement function* (HDIF); it resembles a production function in that it relates the inputs into HD, such as public expenditure on health services or potable water and the HD objective of achieving better health.

It is clear from this discussion of the various links in the EG to HD chain that, in general, we would expect important causal connections to exist between the economy and HD achievements, but that these connections are *not automatic*: the strength of the links in Chain A varies according to a large range of factors, including the structure of the economy, the distribution of income and assets, and the policy choices made.

Chain B: from HD to EG

Turning our attention to the second chain, from HD to EG, there is strong empirical support for the view that as people become healthier, better nourished and educated, they contribute more to economic growth. More specifically, both micro- and macro-level research show that

1. Extending primary education raises the productivity of both rural and urban workers. In agriculture, education raises productivity among farmers using modern technologies, with less impact, as might be expected, among those using traditional methods (Schultz, 1975; Welch, 1970; Rosenzweig, 1995; Foster and Rosenzweig, 1994). Education is also an important contributor to technological capability and technical change in industry.
2. Improved health and nutrition have direct effects on labor productivity, especially among poorer individuals (Behrman, 1993 and 1996). Morbidity has a negative impact on labor productivity, as shown, for example, by studies in Ghana and Côte d'Ivoire (Schultz and Tansel, 1993). In some contexts the evidence indicates even larger productivity effects arising from health and nutrition than from formal schooling, although the impact of education has been much more emphasized in the development literature.
3. Secondary education, including vocational, facilitates the acquisition of skills and managerial capacity.
4. Tertiary education supports the development of basic science, the appropriate selection of technology imports, their domestic adaptation and the development of indigenous technologies.
5. Secondary and tertiary education represent critical elements in the development of key institutions, government, law, and the financial system, among others, all essential for economic growth.
6. From a *macro*-perspective, the 'new growth theories' aim to endogenize technical progress by incorporating some of these same effects, emphasizing education as well as learning by doing and R & D. A number of empirical studies have shown the positive effect of education on economic growth at a macro level, with its size varying according to the measure of education and the particular macro-growth model adopted (e.g., Barro, 1991; Barro and Lee, 1993 and 1994).
7. Education affects the nature and growth of exports, which, in turn, affect the aggregate growth rate. It has been argued that even 'unskilled' workers in a modern factory normally need the literacy, numeracy and discipline which are acquired in primary and lower secondary school (Wood, 1994). Studies have shown a significant positive correlation between the growth of manufactured exports and the growth of GDP (e.g., Michaely, 1977; Krueger, 1978; Ram, 1985; Rana, 1988; Edwards, 1993).

8. Education can also affect per capita income growth via its impact on the denominator – that is, population growth. Many studies have shown a negative correlation between female schooling and fertility (Ainsworth et al., 1995).
9. Increasing basic education leads to a more equal income distribution (Psacharopolous et al., 1992, 48). In addition, recent studies suggest that a more equal distribution of assets and incomes has a positive effect on economic growth (Alesina and Rodrik, 1994; Alesina and Perotti, 1994; Persson and Tabellini, 1994; Birdsall et al., 1995).

As in Chain A, the strength of the various links in Chain B varies, and there is no *automatic* connection between an improved level of HD and increases in per capita GDP. Education, health and nutrition alone cannot transform an economy. The quantity and quality of investment, both domestic and foreign, together with the overall policy environment, represent other important determinants of economic performance. Income distribution again appears to be important in Chain B, as in Chain A.

Empirical Findings

Our earlier empirical work used cross-country regressions covering 35 to 76 developing countries, according to the availability of data for particular variables for 1960-1992. We tested the following hypotheses, derived from the analysis of Chain A, summarized above: HD improvement would be greater,

A1: the higher EG;
A2: the lower the proportion of the population below the poverty line; for a given level of GDP per capita, this means the more equally income is distributed;
A3: the more income households allocate to HD at a given income level; this may be related both to the level of female education and to the extent of female control over income within the household; and
A4: the higher the proportion of GDP devoted to social expenditure by the government.

With the change in HD – proxied by life expectancy shortfall reduction – over 1970-92 as the dependent variable,[4] for Chain A we found the following:

1. GDP per capita growth proved significant and quite strong in all of the equations, with higher growth of per capita income leading to better HD performance. According to one equation, a one percentage point increase in the average growth rate of GDP per capita was estimated to reduce life expectancy

4 Life expectancy shortfall represents how far a country's life expectancy falls below 85 years. The reduction in life expectancy shortfall measures the percentage change in this shortfall.

shortfall by more than 3 percentage points over the period.

2. The share of national resources going to social expenditure almost always proved significantly positive. For every percentage point increase in the average share of GDP invested in health and education (lagged), the life expectancy shortfall decreased by about 1.75 percentage points.
3. The initial female primary enrolment rate had a significant but small impact on the subsequent rate of improvement in life expectancy. We attributed this to the impact on household behavior of female income, knowledge, and control within the household.
4. Contrary to expectations, a more equal distribution of income did not seem to advance human development.
5. Both the African and Latin American dummies were negative and significant throughout, as we might have expected, given that the comparator was highly successful East Asia. In each case the coefficient was quite small.

For Chain B, we tested the following hypotheses: GDP growth would be higher,

B1: the higher HD;
B2: the higher the investment rate; and
B3: the more equal the distribution of income.

With annual growth of GDP per capita over 1970-92 as the dependent variable, for Chain B we found the following:

1. Measures of the initial level of HD invariably proved significant, although with low coefficients.
2. The change in life expectancy (1962-82) was positive and significant in all cases but one.
3. The domestic investment rate was always significant, except when the regional dummies were included.
4. Virtually all the lagged income distribution variables gave results with the expected sign – that is, a more equal income distribution is associated with higher economic growth; they were almost always significant, except when the regional dummies were included.
5. Regional dummies for Latin America were significantly negative in every case and, in one case, also for Africa.

In summary, the two chains, taken as a whole showed a significantly positive effect of EG on HD, and of HD on EG.

Virtuous and Vicious Cycles and Lop-Sided Development

The existence of two chains linking HD and EG was thus strongly supported by our results. This implies that an economy may be on a mutually reinforcing upward spiral, with high levels of HD leading to high growth, and high growth in turn promoting HD. Conversely, weak HD may result in low growth and, consequently, poor progress towards HD improvement.

Following this reasoning, we classified country performance into four categories: *virtuous*, *vicious,* and two types of *lop-sidedness* – that is lop-sided with strong HD/weak EG (called 'HD-lopsided'), and lop-sided with weak HD/strong EG ('EG-lopsided'). In the virtuous cycle case, good HD enhances growth, which in turn promotes HD, and so on. In the vicious cycle case, poor performance on HD tends to lead to poor growth performance, which in turn depresses HD achievements, and so on. The stronger the linkages in the two chains described above, the more pronounced the cycle of economic growth and HD, either in a positive or a dampening direction. Where linkages are weak, cases of lop-sided development may occur. On the one hand, good EG may not bring about good HD if, for example, there are weak linkages such as a low social expenditure ratio; on the other hand, a good HD performance may not generate good EG if there is a dearth of complementary resources such as low investment rates. Such cases of lop-sided development are, however, unlikely to persist. Either the weak partner in the cycle eventually acts as a brake on the other partner, leading to a vicious cycle case, or, if the linkages are strengthened over time, a virtuous cycle case results, possibly by policy change.

For the purpose of classifying country performance empirically, we compared the performance of each country with the average of all developing countries. It is important to explore how a country moves from one category to another over time. In our earlier work, both lop-sided categories proved very impermanent. The most interesting finding from this work indeed is that none of the countries that started as EG-lopsided were able to move from that category to the virtuous-cycle category: all fell back to the vicious-cycle (poor HD, poor EG) category. Thus, our previous global analysis suggested that it is not possible to move to a virtuous cycle via EG-lopsidedness, as this proved a dead end. In contrast, some countries which started as HD-lopsided did manage to move into the virtuous-cycle category.

Latin American Perspective

The global picture, now extended to 1960-2000, is presented in Figure 4.2, where the vertical dividing line represents the average HD shortfall reduction for the developing world as a whole, and the horizontal dividing line represents the average per capita GDP growth rate – both weighted by population. The measure

Figure 4.2: Classification of Developing Country Performance, 1960-2000

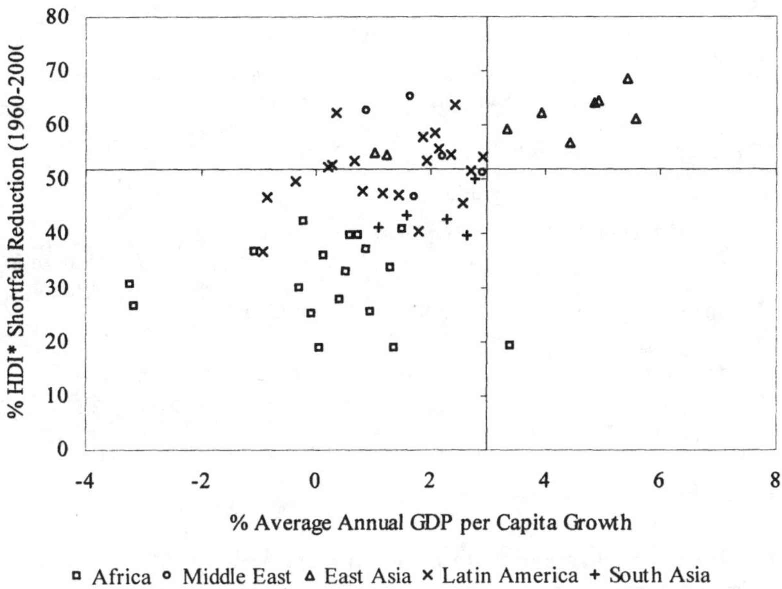

Source: Prepared by the authors.

of HD adopted, HDI*, is the same as the most recent formula for the Human Development Index of the UNDP, except that it excludes the income component – since we do not want income to appear as part of both HD and EG.[5]

The economic position of Latin America relative to that of other regions arises in part because of the particularly heavy impact of the 1980s debt crisis on the region – the so-called 'lost decade.' When we come to focus on the Latin American countries relative to each other – particularly for the 1980s – we mean that negative growth performance over that decade is the norm, and thus, countries with falling per capita income in the 1980s may nonetheless appear in the virtuous quadrant (e.g., Mexico).

Comparing countries across Latin America for 1960-2000, classified according

5 The UNDP's HDI includes life expectancy at birth, calculated as an index with a minimum of 25 years and a maximum of 85 years, an education component made up of adult literacy, a combined primary, secondary and tertiary gross enrolment rate, and a measure of real income weighted according to income level at PPP (UNDP, 2001). HDI* is a modified version of the UNDP's HDI, including only the non-income components, i.e., educational attainment as measured by a combination of adult literacy (2/3 weight) and mean years of schooling (1/3 weight), and longevity as measured by life expectancy at birth.

Figure 4.3: Classification of Country Performance in Latin America, 1960-2000

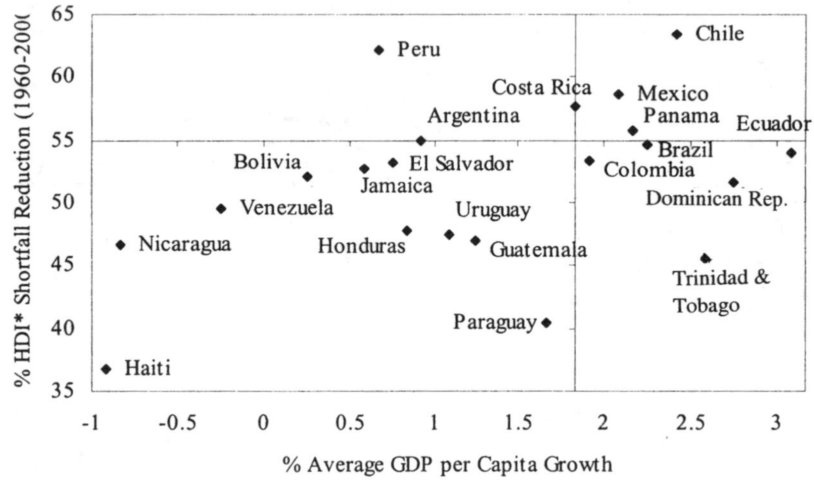

Source: Prepared by the authors.

to only the *region*'s average performance (Figure 4.3), we find that four countries appear in the virtuous category – Chile, Costa Rica, Mexico and Panama; the largest number of Latin American countries fall in the vicious category, with a small number in both the HD and EG-lopsided quadrants.

Again, it is enlightening to investigate country movements over time. Table 4.1 presents the positions of Latin American countries decade by decade. We classify countries in terms of growth and shortfall reduction of HDI* into vicious, virtuous, HD-lopsided and EG-lopsided quadrants, investigating how country-classification shifts over time. These transitions are based on how countries fare relative to the *Latin American* – not the *world* – average. We find that countries' positions fluctuate over time for a variety of both general and country-specific reasons. In contrast to movements in the global picture, Latin American countries move frequently in and out of the virtuous and vicious categories. This trend is due partly to the smaller number of countries but also to the economic uniformity of a single region, compared with diverse countries from around the globe. As a result, there is little difference between 'good' and 'poor' performance and quite small changes can lead to a switch in a country's classification. In addition, Latin America suffered particularly strong exogenous shocks associated with the debt crisis, which led to significant changes in countries' performance over the decades.

Most important, the Latin American analysis reinforces our earlier conclusion: it is highly unlikely for a country to be able to move from EG-lopsided to the virtuous category. In contrast, countries which are HD-lopsided are frequently seen to move into the virtuous category, while countries in the EG-lopsided quadrant

Table 4.1: Latin America, Country Classification According to Changes in Human Development (HD) and Economic Growth (EG), 1960-2000

Country	1960-1970	1970-1980	1980-1990	1990-2000
Argentina	HD-lopsided	HD-lopsided	HD-lopsided	Virtuous
Bolivia	Vicious	Vicious	Vicious	Vicious
Brazil	EG-lopsided	EG-lopsided	EG-lopsided	Vicious
Chile	HD-lopsided	HD-lopsided	Virtuous	Virtuous
Colombia	HD-lopsided	HD-lopsided	Virtuous	HD-lopsided
Costa Rica	HD-lopsided	HD-lopsided	Virtuous	Virtuous
Dominican Rep.	Vicious	EG-lopsided	EG-lopsided	EG-lopsided
Ecuador	Vicious	EG-lopsided	Virtuous	Virtuous
El Salvador	Vicious	Vicious	Vicious	EG-lopsided
Guatemala	Vicious	Vicious	Vicious	Vicious
Guyana	...	HD-lopsided	HD-lopsided	Virtuous
Haiti	Vicious	Vicious	Vicious	Vicious
Honduras	Vicious	Vicious	Vicious	Vicious
Jamaica	Virtuous	HD-lopsided	Virtuous	HD-lopsided
Mexico	Virtuous	Virtuous	Virtuous	Virtuous
Nicaragua	EG-lopsided	Vicious	Vicious	Vicious
Panama	Virtuous	HD-lopsided	HD-lopsided	Virtuous
Paraguay	HD-lopsided	Virtuous	Virtuous	HD-lopsided
Peru	Vicious	Vicious	Vicious	Virtuous
Trinidad & Tobago	Virtuous	Virtuous	HD-lopsided	Virtuous
Uruguay	HD-lopsided	HD-lopsided	Virtuous	Virtuous
Venezuela	HD-lopsided	HD-lopsided	HD-lopsided	HD-lopsided

Source: World Bank (2001).

tend to return to the vicious cycle. This has strong implications for the sequencing of policy, suggesting that, in contrast to the pattern often advocated, it is not possible to put growth first and worry about HD later because this will actually undermine both growth and human development. However, building up HD is a viable way of creating conditions for sustained growth and further improvements in HD.

It is instructive to investigate the extent to which our global econometric findings, summarized above, apply in the Latin American case, to identify the strength both of the overall two-way connections between HD and EG, and of the specific links which make up Chains A and B. In the Latin American case, we obviously have far fewer observations. Consequently, we used data for each decade, and for each country (i.e. pooling time series and cross-section). The results are presented in Tables 4.2 and 4.3.

For Chain A, we examined the shortfall reductions for both life expectancy and infant mortality as possible dependent variables – see columns (1) and (2) of Table 4.2. In column (1), we see a positive, although not significant, relationship between the growth rate and improved HDI over 1960-2000, where HD improvement is

Table 4.2: Chain A: Evidence from Latin American Experience, 1960-2000 OLS: Dependent Variable is Change in Human Development for a Decade [a, b]

Independent Variable	Dependent Variable	
	Life Expectancy Shortfall Reduction	Infant Mortality Shortfall Reduction
GDP per Capita Growth Rate, annual average over the decade x100	3.99 (0.83)	1.23 (0.15)
Public Expenditure on Education, as a % of GDP, annual average over the decade x 100	1.23 [d] (1.92)	-0.25 (0.22)
Gross Female Primary Enrolment Rate, annual average over the decade x 10000	1.42 (0.25)	0.17 [d] (1.74)
Dummy for 1970s x 100	0.90 (0.41)	9.80 [c] (2.54)
Dummy for 1980s x 100	3.22 (1.22)	12.07 [c] (2.63)
Dummy for 1990s x 100	-0.53 (0.23)	9.32 [c] (2.34)
Intercept x 100	8.89 [d] (1.71)	5.75 (0.63)
Number of Observations	76	76
R-squared	0.095	0.220

[a] For example, 1970-80. The 1970s is the omitted decade. [b] Figures in parentheses are absolute t-statistics. [c] Significant at the 5% level. [d] Significant at the 10% level.

Source: World Bank (various years), *World Development Indicators*.

measured by life expectancy shortfall reduction. Public expenditure on education[6] as a share of GDP at the beginning of each decade was positive and significantly related to life expectancy shortfall reduction. Female primary enrolment has a positive and significant effect on the infant mortality shortfall reduction in column (2). Although we would have liked to include a variable for income distribution, data limitations meant that this would have reduced the number of observations by three-quarters.

For Chain B, we found that two different measures of HD achievement at the beginning of each period (the literacy rate and log life expectancy) were positively and significantly related to growth in per capita income. It is noteworthy that in this chain we found that the dummy for the 1980s was negative and highly significant. This is a clear 'debt-crisis' effect, showing that HD achievements did not translate as well into growth in the 1980s as they did in other decades. The dummy for the 1990s was also significantly negative in the Chain B equations – presumably reflecting the continued impact of stabilization and adjustment on growth.

Taking the results as a whole, we find that Chain A appears to be weaker than

6 Used instead of education and health expenditure because of lack of data.

Table 4.3: Chain B: Evidence from Latin American Experience, 1960-2000 OLS: Dependent Variable is Growth of GDP per Capita Growth for a Decade [a, b]

Independent Variable	(1)	(2)
Literacy Rate, annual average over the decade	2.54 [d]	---
x 1000	(1.92)	---
Log Life Expectancy, annual average over the	---	3.94 [d]
decade x 10	---	(1.80)
Gross Domestic Investment, as a % of GDP,	4.20	4.54
annual average over the decade x 1000	(1.05)	(1.14)
Dummy for 1970s x 100	-0.45	-2.05
	(0.08)	(0.36)
Dummy for 1980s x 10	-3.39 [c]	-3.63 [c]
	(6.10)	(6.03)
Dummy for 1990s x 100	-8.57	-11.53 [d]
	(1.49)	(1.75)
Intercept x 10	-0.55	-14.80 [d]
	(0.53)	(1.72)
Number of Observations	84	84
R-squared	0.414	0.411

[a] For example, 1970-80. The 1970s is the omitted decade. [b] Figures in parentheses are absolute t-statistics. [c] Significant at the 1% level. [d] Significant at the 10% level.

Source: World Bank (various years), *World Development Indicators*.

Chain B in the Latin American context; that is, while better HD leads to higher growth in subsequent decades, growth rates in Latin America are not significantly related to changes in HD. This may be partly due to the importance of the debt crisis in Latin America and resulting adjustment requirements, which were often incurred at the expense of expenditures on human development when compared to our global results. In addition, it appears that variations in the policy setting, specifically in terms of priority ratios and factors determining the efficiency of the HD improvement function, were important in accounting for differences in HD performance. This indeed is supported by our account of specific country experiences, which follows.

Country Examples of Success and Failure on HD and EG

In this section we present thumbnail sketches of three of the good (virtuous-cycle) and three of the poor (vicious-cycle) performers. The aim is to identify specific circumstances and policies which appear to be responsible for such outcomes.

Chile is a country which managed good performance over the whole 40-year period, while undergoing dramatic changes in political regime and policy stance. Since the early 20th century Chile has had a strong commitment to HD. Already in

1930 three-quarters of the adult population was literate (Thorp, 1998). In the 1960s, and during the Allende period in the early 1970s, progress on HD was maintained through generous state expenditures on education and health. By the end of the 1960s social expenditure comprised 20 percent of GDP; registration in primary education covered 95 percent of 6-14 year olds, and 81 percent of births were delivered by professionals (Raczynski, 1988). Growth in income per capita was modest (1.6 percent per annum) and egalitarian relative to the region as a whole, yielding an HD-lopsided outcome.

Pinochet's political take-over in 1973 heralded dramatic changes in economic and social policy. Economic policy change involved a sharp move towards openness and a reduced role for the state. Over the first ten years this led – after an initial rise – to stagnant incomes and to rising unemployment, from 6 percent in the 1960s to more than 16 percent by the early 1980s. However, some of the ill-effects of this on HD were offset by major employment schemes. Income distribution worsened, with the urban Santiago Gini increasing from 0.47 in the 1960s to 0.52 in 1978-82 (Riveros, 1998).[7] After 1986 the economy grew rapidly (the highest growth in Latin America), fueled largely by expanding exports of non-traditional primary products.

Since the 1960s Chile had an extensive system of state-run welfare programs in the areas of social security, health, and education. In addition, it provided universal access to curative health care and programs of preventive care for all expectant mothers, infants, and children under six who did not have recourse to alternative health care. These programs were largely maintained despite sharp cuts in aggregate social expenditure, which fell from 4 to 2.5 percent of GDP between 1975 and 1990. Despite this reduction, Chile's HD continued to improve, mainly because of more effective targeting as a result of decentralization. In education, government spending focused on primary and secondary education and moved away from tertiary; indeed, expenditure on tertiary education declined from 38 percent of total government educational expenditure in 1980 to 19 percent in 1990. The government also developed a number of special programs and subsidies designed to protect the most vulnerable members of society, especially mothers and children. These included a family subsidy for those in extreme poverty, a supplementary feeding program for mothers and pre-school children and for children who fell below nutritional norms, and a school feeding program designed to help reduce dropouts and repetitions (Raczynski, 1988). Dropout rates in government schools declined from 7 percent in 1977 to 5 percent in 1984. The decentralization of health to municipalities focused the more restricted health budgets on disease prevention rather than curative medicine. Infant mortality fell from 73 per 1000 live births in 1972 to 17 in 1989.

The first ten years of the Pinochet period were thus not successful on EG, but

---

7 According to Berry (1998, 16) 'data on the distribution of consumption among greater Santiago households show one of the largest deteriorations ever recorded statistically in a developing country' between 1969 and 1978.

HD progress was maintained as a result of better targeting of the reduced social expenditures – that is, a greatly improved priority ratio leading to HD-lopsided development. The last few years of the Pinochet regime saw a resumption of economic growth and a move towards the virtuous category.

The resumption of democracy in 1990 led to a renewed expansion in social expenditures and to sustained and more egalitarian economic growth. During the 1990s, Chile's average per capita growth rate was 4.5 percent per annum, compared with 2.1 percent during the 1980s and 1.2 percent in the 1970s. Unemployment was reduced to low levels, and therefore the public employment schemes could be discontinued. A progressive tax reform was introduced which helped finance the rising social expenditures. Over 1990-99, expenditure on both education and health more than doubled. Thus, the 1990s saw Chile enter the virtuous category, with improved HD supported by increased growth and social expenditures; the sustained expansion in GDP per capita was, in turn, greatly facilitated by the combination of more effective economic policies and higher levels of HD.

Costa Rica, like Chile, has had a long historic commitment to HD. By 1950, Costa Rica's illiteracy rate was just one-fifth, whereas the overall Latin American rate was more than two-fifths (Thorp, 1998). A decision in 1948 to abolish the army released resources for social expenditures which had been consistently relatively high, although subject to cuts in the early 1980s. In 1988, half of government expenditure was again devoted to health and education, with nearly 30 percent going to priority areas.

In the 1960s and 1970s growth was fairly strong at 5-6 percent per annum. The extended welfare benefit system was nearly comprehensive in coverage. Costa Rica invested around 6 percent of its GDP in education. Universal primary school enrolment was achieved and secondary enrolments rose to around two-thirds, with 20 percent of individuals age 20-24 in higher education, and relatively equal female and male enrolments. Adult illiteracy dropped 8 percentage points in the 1960s. By 1980 only 13 percent of Costa Ricans over ten were illiterate, and the rate had dropped to 4.5 percent by 1999.

Improvements on health were rather slow in the 1960s, but then accelerated. About 3 percent of GDP was devoted to public health expenditure in Costa Rica in 1960 and this had risen to more than 5 percent by the end of the 1990s, much of this increase coming in the later part of the period. Life expectancy rates for Costa Rica were 67 years in 1960, reaching about 73 years by 1980, and 76 by 1995-2000. Infant mortality rates remained quite high throughout the 1960s, starting at 68 per 1000 live births in 1960, falling slightly to 62 by 1970. This was, however, followed by a significant improvement to 19 in 1980, and to 12 by 1999.

In Costa Rica, the social sector expenditure cuts of the first half of the 1980s fell most heavily on priority areas, with the share of the bottom 40 percent of households in educational expenditure falling from 42 percent in 1980 to 36 percent in 1986. However, social expenditure recovered in the second half of the decade. Moreover, the minimum wage was maintained, income distribution did not deteriorate, and HD progress resumed. As a consequence, a virtuous cycle could be maintained.

Mexico's progress on HD came much later than Chile's or Costa Rica's. In 1960 over a third of Mexico's adult population was still illiterate. Mexico falls into the virtuous category because of its improvements in HD and EG during 1960-1999. But the absolute standards attained were still significantly below those of Chile and Costa Rica. For example, by the end of the period life expectancy was 67 years, a little less than the Latin American average (69) and much lower than Chile's (75) and Costa Rica's (77) (Thorp, 1998).

Until 1970, during the presidency of Echeverría (1970-1976), Mexico enjoyed a classic 'growth with stability,' and advances were also made in HD. In the 1970s growth continued but it was supported by heavy borrowing and rising fiscal imbalances. Mexico's economic performance was strong throughout the late 1960s and 1970s when GDP growth averaged about 7 percent per annum (about 4 percent per capita), with manufacturing – the country's dominant growth sector – attracting considerable foreign investment. Absolute poverty declined from 76 percent in 1960 to 45 percent in 1981, with income distribution, however, remaining at unfavorable levels – Ginis between 0.5 and 0.6 (Maddison and Associates, 1992).

A central pillar of post-revolutionary government in Mexico has been a strong commitment to HD. In the 1960s this took the form of enhanced emphasis on land reform, health, sanitation, education and nutrition. Educational expenditures averaged around 18 percent of total government spending in the 1970s, while health expenditures averaged around 5 percent (IMF, various years). Good priority ratios also contributed, with primary education and vaccination programs receiving the bulk of public spending. As a result, HD improved significantly between 1960 and 1980; life expectancy rose from 59 to 66 years; infant mortality declined from 74 to 53 per 1000 live births; adult literacy rose from 66 to 83 percent; and gross educational enrolments almost doubled, going from 106 to 120 percent for primary enrolments, from 23 to 49 percent for secondary, and from 5 to 14 percent for tertiary.

The economic picture in the debt-ridden 1980s was different. In the 1980s, Mexico cut its expenditure ratio, with a corresponding decline in HD spending, which contracted by 6 percent per annum from 1983 to 1988. Real disposable income per capita fell 5 percent per annum during 1983-1988, and the country experienced rising unemployment and underemployment as well as greater poverty incidence. The share of education in total expenditure dropped by almost 30 percent, with most of the reduction absorbed by primary education (Friedmann et al., 1995). Teacher- and student-to-school ratios both declined between 1983 and 1988, while the per capita numbers of medical units, hospital beds and doctors fell. Despite the extremely poor performance on EG and HD, Mexico still did well relative to the rest of the region, though not well relative to global conditions.

After economic reforms initiated in the late 1980s, the economy performed better, bolstered by foreign investment, following the ratification of NAFTA. But financial crises in 1994 and 1998 were followed by economic contraction and social sector cutbacks. For the decade as a whole the average per capita growth rate was 1.25 percent per annum – following a negative average growth rate in the 1980s. In the early part of the 1990s there was an increase in the share of GDP going to the social sectors. Expenditures on education rose by 90 percent between 1989 and 1993, and health by 79 percent. There was a fall in general food subsidies, with a somewhat ineffective rise in targeting. A large program entitled PRONOSOL was established to make social expenditure more cost-effective and foster greater community involvement. *Solidaridad*, one of PRONOSOL's components, contained a wide range of social programs, including education and health, but has been accused of political manipulation by the then ruling party. The program was renamed and restructured in 1995, becoming less political.

In summary, Mexico's virtuous categorization for the 1960s and 1970s was achieved by economic growth and social expenditure. Another element supporting HD has been improved gender roles with the greater institutionalization of women's rights. For the 1990s, poorer performance on HD was probably due to inappropriate targeting, as well as cutbacks following the crises and the heritage of the 1980s.

Haiti was one of the worst performers in Latin America in the vicious cycle category. In 1960, the literacy rate was around 12 percent, by far the lowest across the continent. Although this had increased to nearly 50 percent by 2000, it was still lower than the literacy rates in most of Latin America in 1960. Life expectancy saw modest improvement over the four decades – from 42.4 to 53.2 years (with almost no improvement in the last decade), while infant mortality rates fell from 179 to 73 per thousand (still about twice the regional average) over the same period. Economic growth was negative for most of the four decades. Haiti's extremely weak performance on both HD and EG was due to political turbulence and an unequal economic and social structure. Political instability, at times involving serious violence and international embargoes, undermined economic performance, while HD improvements were weak not only because of poor economic performance, but also because of the high levels of inequality and lack of political commitment to the social sectors.

Francois Duvalier was elected president in 1957, following a rise of black nationalist sentiment. He was a repressive leader, who made himself president for life in 1964. After his death in 1971 his son succeeded him. The Duvalier regimes were highly corrupt and had little interest in social reforms. The regime collapsed in 1986, after strong internal dissent and pressure from donors. Over the next four years there were two coups, four presidents and severe political violence. Aristide, who was elected President at the end of 1990, attempted to introduce both political and social reforms. However, his government was overthrown in 1991, in a coup led by Raoul Cedras. Donors condemned this coup and sanctions were imposed by the international community. Following U.S. forces' occupation in 1994, Cedras went into exile, and in 1995 a coalition government was formed, but this proved unstable, owing to disputes about the liberalization reforms introduced. In 1999, parliament was dissolved, and in the elections of 2000, Aristide was again elected president, although he was not recognized by a coalition of opposing groups, which alleged that there had been substantial fraud in the elections. Since then, international assistance for the country has been frozen.

The political instability, sporadic violence, and economic sanctions had a severe adverse impact on economic growth, which was also held back by high levels of corruption leading to poor public investment decisions and a very weak HD situation. During the 1960s, growth averaged -1.5 percent per annum, compared to the Latin American average of about 2.1 percent. This improved markedly during the 1970s, but in the 1980s GDP fell by 2.3 percent per annum, worsening to -2.7 percent in the 1990s. Due to strong links poor growth translated into poor HD, and conversely, Haiti has found itself on a trajectory of low growth and poor human development for most of the past four decades. Income distribution has been extremely unequal throughout, with a small and corrupt elite taking a disproportionate share. While there is disagreement about the magnitude of inequality (Lundahl, 1996), it is clear that income was, and still is, concentrated within urban areas, while three-quarters of the population live in rural areas that have experienced declining agricultural production on a per capita basis since the 1970s (World Bank, 1991, 254). The consequence has been very high levels of poverty; in 2000, an estimated 65 percent of the population (80 percent of the rural population) was below the national poverty line, while the Human Poverty Index at 42.3 percent was equivalent to that of Bangladesh, double that of many other Latin American countries.

Haiti's weak tax system led to low expenditure ratios, with poor collection and a highly regressive structure. Public expenditures on education and health remained low throughout. In 1990, expenditure on health was 1.2 percent of GDP and on education 1.4 percent. By 2000 education had dropped to 1.1 percent of GDP while the health percentage had doubled. The priority ratios were, moreover, unfavorable, especially in the health sector. In the early 1990s it was estimated that over half of public sector physicians resided in the capital, leaving only 1.4 physicians per 10,000 people in rural areas (World Bank, 1993). The incidence of malnutrition and morbidity were high – about 30 percent of rural children and 48 percent of urban children were anemic, while 90 percent of deaths among 1-4 year old children were associated with malnutrition and intestinal diseases (*Ibid.*).

International sanctions are estimated to have had a significantly negative impact on nutrition and health. One study showed a rise in child malnutrition from 7 to 35 percent in the two years following the introduction of sanctions, while national measles coverage declined from 40 to 24 percent during this first year

(Hoskins, 1998).

Aristide attempted to introduce ambitious social programs, with a focus on promoting basic health and literacy, both in 1990 and 2000. However, the 1990 reforms were brought to an end first by the coup, and then after 2000 by lack of resources as well as by the increasing violence and volatile political climate.

In brief, political instability and its consequences have been a prime element in Haiti's abysmal performance, combined with a high degree of inequality and lack of commitment to the social sectors. The inequality and lack of social commitment not only help explain the poor HD achievements, but also contributed to political instability. The poor economic performance and weak HD achievements were mutually reinforcing such that Haiti's growth and HD record today resemble those of sub-Saharan African countries rather than those of its Caribbean neighbors.

Bolivia has also been a vicious cycle case, although less extreme than Haiti, with below average performance on both HD and EG. Historically poor levels of HD and high inequality put the country in a weak position to sustain economic growth. Life expectancy in 1960 was just 42.8 years, similar to that of Haiti at the time. However, by 2000, it had reached 62.6 – well above that of Haiti, but still below the regional average. Economic growth rates were quite poor throughout, but negative only in the 1980s. Bolivia's weak performance can be attributed to poor initial conditions, political instability, especially between the revolution of the 1950s and democratization in the 1980s, a period in which there was a succession of military coups but no serious violence, and to the impact of harsh adjustment programs which restored economic stability but failed to ignite economic growth, while affecting the social sectors adversely.

Bolivia has seen some major changes in economic direction. The revolution of the early 1950s introduced some fundamental changes including land reform, state-led development policies, and the nationalization of the mining industry. These policies were continued by successive governments until escalating inflation – which reached 24,000 percent at one point – and rising debt led to economic collapse in 1985, leading to radical IMF sponsored adjustment policies. The post revolutionary period saw greater emphasis on expanding the social sectors, but weak economic growth dampened the impact. The adjustment policies of the mid-1980s and 1990s were accompanied by a series of policies to protect the poor, including the Emergency Social Fund in the 1980s. In the 1990s, the economic reforms were accompanied by job programs, expansion of rural electricity, drinking water, and medical supplies. There was also radical decentralization of government programs. However, these programs were insufficient to achieve major social advance, given poor growth and employment. For example, the Emergency Social Fund failed to reach 95 percent of the rural population, 99 percent of the female poor and 90 percent of the unemployed, at a time when per capita incomes were falling by 2.0 percent per annum and rural poverty was estimated to have included almost all the rural population (Stewart and van der Geest, 1995).

After falling by 1.9 percent per annum in the 1980s, average annual per capita growth was only 1.4 percent in the 1990s. Until the 1990s, social expenditures were relatively low at 2.3 percent of GDP in education and 2.1 percent in health in 1980. There was, however, a significant rise in both in the 1990s – education to 5.5 percent of GDP in 2000, and health to 4.9 percent. Indeed, the latter half of the 1990s saw marked progress in some social indicators.

Marked rural/urban disparities are a major feature of Bolivia. Very high levels of rural poverty and poor rural services have held back both EG and HD. Most literacy programs have tended to be focused on urban areas and rural illiteracy has continued to be extremely high, especially among women. Countrywide, literacy rates were about 40 percent in 1960, then increasing, albeit slowly, to about 86 percent by 2000, with school attendance improving over the four decades.

In the health sector, public funding has been historically poor. The staff is poorly trained and the rural areas are once again much worse off, both in terms of access as well as efficiency. According to 2001 census data, about 80 percent of the rural population still has inadequate access to safe water and sanitation, compared to about 45 percent of the urban population.

Bolivia's fairly poor HD performance to a large extent reflects its poor EG performance – which in turn is partly due to the weak levels of achievement on HD historically – and partly to political instability and poor economic policies which held back investment, plus harsh adjustment programs which brought about stabilization but not sustained economic growth. Some serious attempts to promote HD – for example, through social funds and decentralization – have not been enough to counter the impact of poor economic performance.

Nicaragua's experience falls into three distinct periods: the Somoza era, covering the 1960s and 1970s; the Sandinista revolution and subsequent government, which was accompanied by continuous civil war; and the post-war period of the 1990s. Nicaragua was one of the last countries in Latin America to make any substantial progress on HD. Over half the adult population was illiterate in 1960, and life expectancy was only 47 years (Thorp, 1998).

During the Somoza period there were high rates of growth, but growth was very unequally distributed. The Somozas themselves owned or controlled 60 percent of national economic activity. There was low social expenditure, which was also unequally distributed. By the late 1970s only 65 percent of primary school age children were enrolled in school, and only 22 percent completed the full six years of primary education. Three-quarters of the rural population was illiterate. Infant mortality rates were around 100 per 1,000 live births. Between 1965 and 1975 the number of children under five suffering from malnutrition doubled, at a time when GDP also doubled.

Economic growth was sharply disrupted by the revolution of 1979, with GDP shrinking by a quarter in that year. The Sandinistas had a strong commitment to expanding social expenditures and improving the distribution of assets and incomes. In the early years of their regime, in 1980 and 1981, GDP jumped by 5 percent, and there was a big expansion in social expenditure and social service coverage. The proportion of GDP spent on primary and secondary education doubled, and adult illiteracy declined from 50 percent to 23 percent. The health sector expanded greatly, with an emphasis on preventive and primary care, targeting the principal causes of infant, child and maternal mortality, providing broader coverage, and eliciting higher levels of community participation. In both health and education, therefore, there were favorable priority ratios. Both health and education outcomes showed improvements: Nicaragua's life expectancy in 1980 was about 59 years (compared with 47 years in 1960), and gross primary enrolment was about 94 percent (compared with 66 percent in 1960). However, GDP dropped every year from 1984 to1990 – with a cumulative drop of over 40 percent for the decade – as a consequence of the war, the U.S. trade embargo, and the reluctance of foreign banks to invest. Inflation spiraled. The situation was aggravated by natural disasters, including hurricanes and drought. By 1990 per capita income was below that of the 1970s. GDP per capita fell on average by 4.1 percent per annum over the 1980s.

The economic collapse and disruptions caused by the war eventually undermined the social sectors – despite the Sandinistas' efforts. The literacy rate, for example, declined to the levels of the late 1970s. The infant mortality rate, which had declined to 63 per 1000 during the early Sandinista years, began to rise again, reaching 72 per 1000 in 1989.

The post-war era of the 1990s was dominated by debt and adjustment problems, as well as by a drought and hurricane and other natural disasters. Economic recovery never really got under way, and social expenditures were subject to cuts. In the 1990s, growth rates of GDP per capita were just barely positive, at an average of 0.3 percent per annum over 1990-1999.

In summary, the Somoza years illustrate how good economic growth can fail to translate into HD when it is badly distributed, with unequal income and asset distribution and low social expenditures accompanied by poor priority ratios. In contrast, the Sandinista period greatly improved HD initially by better distributed and higher levels of social expenditure, but this benefit was negated by the effects of wars, the embargo, and natural disasters. The post-war era exhibited the problems of war debt, inadequate finance, and stringent adjustment policies.

Some Conclusions

The Latin American region as a whole has been marked by relatively high levels of, and improvements in, HD, but by lower performance on EG compared with that of the developing world's average during 1960-2000. Latin American life expectancy at the start of our period, in 1960, was substantially longer than in the rest of the developing world. This trend may well be due to the region's much earlier political independence and, consequently, greater commitment to HD – particularly for the elite. Latin America was also the region with the highest degree of inequality in income distribution (Berry, 1998).

Our efforts to estimate the strengths of various links in Chains A and B indicate, on the one hand, that the links from EG to HD (i.e., Chain A) are more variable in Latin America than those on the world scene. The social expenditure ratio has held up well, but GDP growth did not systematically translate into HD improvement in a significant way, indicating that there were country-specific circumstances which affected the strength of the Chain. The links in Chain B, running from HD to EG, on the other hand, showed themselves to be closer to the global results, with initial HD levels significantly affecting EG. For both chains, we were constrained in what we could test because of the more limited country data availability for some variables, and fewer country observations.

Our country cases illustrate how specific circumstances influenced the strength of various links in Chains A and B. We covered three countries which fell in the virtuous quadrant over the period taken as a whole – Chile, Costa Rica and Mexico – and three which fell into the vicious quadrant – Haiti, Bolivia and Nicaragua.

With respect to the three success cases, high growth accompanied by high social expenditure ratios translated into HD improvements – that is, Mexico in the 1960s and 1970s, and Chile in the 1960s. An alternative path to success, illustrated by Costa Rica, is moderate and relatively well distributed growth, accompanied by very high social expenditure ratios, with good priority ratios. Chile in the middle period (1975-1990) has illustrated a third path to success, characterized by very well targeted social expenditures, with uneven growth for much of the period and only moderate social expenditure ratios. Later, Chile fell into the high growth and good social expenditure ratio category.

There are clearly also many paths to failure. Growth accompanied by very poor distribution of both private income and social services served to weaken Chain A substantially in the case of Nicaragua during the Somoza period and generally in Haiti. Severe economic shocks and a failure to protect social sectors during adjustment accounted for the relative failure of HD in Bolivia in the 1980s, and in Nicaragua during the 1990s. Political instability also undermined economic growth and consequently HD, for example, during the 1960s in Bolivia, and in Haiti in recent decades, while war and a trade embargo were important elements undermining HD improvement in Nicaragua in the 1980s. External sanctions also affected Haiti adversely in the 1990s. In Nicaragua, natural disasters were a significant negative feature in every decade. Heavy external debt, accumulated as a result of war in the case of Nicaragua, also stymied HD efforts in Bolivia and post-war Nicaragua.

The exploration of how countries behaved decade by decade (Table 4.1) confirms the view, reached earlier on a global basis, that one needs to promote HD if one is to reach a virtuous cycle of growth and HD improvement. Only one Latin American country moved from an EG-lopsided position to a virtuous position (Ecuador, but only barely and probably not sustainable as shown in the long-run picture of Figure 4.3). Our regressions for Latin America tell the same story: HD improvements do lead to EG improvements, although in this case EG improvements did not systematically generate HD improvements. Our regional findings therefore also contradict the usually recommended policy sequence – that is, that growth should be generated first and HD will naturally follow. On a final optimistic note, the recent surge in social sector expenditures in Latin America in the 1990s may well pave the way for improved growth in this decade, in contrast to the cuts of the 1980s which handicapped both growth and, therefore, HD earlier on.

References

Ainsworth, M., K. Beegle and A. Nyamete (1995), 'The Impact of Female Schooling on Fertility and Contraceptive Use: A Study of Fourteen Sub-Saharan African Countries', LSMS Working Papers No. 110, The World Bank, Washington, D.C.

Alesina, A. and D. Rodrik (1994), 'Distributive Politics and Economic Growth', *Quarterly Journal of Economics*, Vol. 109, No. 2 (May), pp. 465-90.

Alesina, A. and R. Perotti (1994), 'The Political Economy of Growth: A Critical Survey of the Recent Literature', *The World Bank Economic Review*, Vol. 8, No. 3.

Barro, R. (1991), 'Economic Growth in a Cross-section of Countries', *Quarterly Journal of Economics*, Vol. 106, No. 2 (May), pp. 407-43.

Barro, R.J. and J.-W. Lee (1993), 'International Comparison of Educational Attainment', *Journal of Monetary Economics*, Vol. 32, No. 3 (December), pp. 363-94.

Barro, R. J. and J.-W. Lee (1994), 'Losers and Winners in Economic Growth', Proceedings of the 1993 World Bank Annual Conference on Development Economics, The World Bank, Washington, D.C.

Behrman, J.R. (1993), 'The Economic Rationale for Investing in Nutrition in Developing Countries', *World Development,* Vol. 21, No. 11 (November), pp. 1749-71.

Behrman, J.R. (1996), 'Impact of Health and Nutrition on Education', *World Bank Research Observer*, Vol. 11, No. 1 (February), pp. 23-37.

Berry, A. and M. Urrutia (1976), *Income Distribution in Colombia*, Yale University Press, New Haven.

Berry, A. (1998), 'Confronting the Income Distribution Threat in Latin America', in A. Berry (ed.), *Poverty, Economic Reform and Income Distribution in Latin America*, pp. 9-41, Lynne Rienner Publishers, Boulder, CO.

Birdsall, N., D. Ross and R. Sabot (1995), 'Inequality and Growth Reconsidered: Lessons from East Asia', *World Bank Economic Review*, Vol. 9, No. 3, pp. 477-508.

Edwards, S. (1993), 'Openness, Trade Liberalization, and Growth in Developing Countries', *Journal of Economic Literature*, Vol. 31, No.3 (September), pp. 1358-93.

Foster, A.D. and M.R. Rosenzweig (1994), 'Technical Change and Human Resources and Investments: Consequences of the Green Revolution', University of Pennsylvania, mimeo.

Friedmann, S., N. Lustig and A. Legovini (1995), 'Mexico: Social Spending and Food Subsidies During Adjustment in the 1980s', in N. Lustig (ed.), *Coping with Austerity: Poverty and Inequality in Latin America*, Brookings Institution, Washington, D.C.

Hoskins, E. (1998), 'The Impact of Sanctions: A Study of UNICEF'S Perspective', Working Paper Series, UNICEF Office of Emergency Programmes, UNICEF, New York.

IMF (International Monetary Fund) (various years), *Government Financial Statistics Yearbook*, IMF, Washington, D.C.

Krueger, A. (1978), *Foreign Trade Regimes and Economic Development: Liberalization Attempts and Consequences*, Ballinger, Cambridge, MA.

Lundahl, M. (1996), 'Income and Land Distribution in Haiti: Some Remarks on Available Statistics', *Journal of Interamerican Studies and World Affairs*, Vol. 38, No. 2-3 (Summer-all), pp. 109-26.

Maddison, A. and Associates (1992), *The Political Economy of Poverty, Equity and Growth: Brazil and Mexico*, The World Bank, Washington, D.C.

Michaely, M. (1977), 'Exports and Growth: An Empirical Investigation', *Journal of Development Economics*, Vol. 4, No. 1, pp. 49-53.

Persson, T. and G. Tabellini (1994), 'Is Inequality Harmful for Growth?' *American Economic Review*, Vol. 84, No. 3 (June), pp. 600-21.

Psacharopolous, G., S. Morley, A. Fiszbein, H. Lee and B. Wood (1992), *Poverty and Income Distribution in Latin America: The Story of the 1980s*, The World Bank, Washington, D.C.

Raczynski, D. (1988), 'Social Policy, Poverty and Vulnerable Groups: Children in Chile', in G.A.Cornia, R. Jolly and F. Stewart (eds.), *Adjustment with a Human Face*, Vol. 2, Oxford University Press, Oxford.

Ram, R. (1985), 'Exports and Economic Growth: Some Additional Evidence', *Economic Development and Cultural Change*, Vol. 33, No. 2 (January), pp. 415-25.

Rana, P. (1988), 'Exports, Policy Changes and Economic Growth in Developing Countries after the 1973 Oil Shock', *Journal of Development Economics*, Vol. 28, No. 2 (March), pp. 261-64.

Ranis, G., F. Stewart and A. Ramírez (2000), 'Economic Growth and Human Development', *World Development*, Vol. 28, No. 2 (February), pp. 197-220.

Riddell, R., M. Robinson, J. de Coninck, A. Muir and S. White (1995), *Non-governmental Organizations and Rural Poverty Alleviation*, Oxford University Press, New York.

Riveros, L. (1998), 'Chile's Structural Adjustment: Relevant Policy Lessons for Latin America', in A. Berry (ed.), *Poverty, Economic Reform and Income Distribution in Latin America*, pp. 111-36, Lynne Rienner Publishers, Boulder, CO.

Rosenzweig, M.R. (1995), 'Why Are There Returns in Schooling?' *American Economic Review*, Vol. 85, No. 2 (May), pp. 153-58.

Schultz, T.P. and A. Tansel (1993), 'Measurement of Returns to Adult Health', LSMS Working Paper No. 95, The World Bank, Washington, D.C.

Schultz, T.W. (1975), 'The Value of the Ability to Deal with Disequilibria', *Journal of Economic Literature*, Vol. 13, No. 3 (September), pp. 827-77.

Stewart, F. and W. van der Geest (1995), 'Adjustment and Social Funds: Political Panacea or Effective Poverty Reduction?', in F. Stewart, *Adjustment and Poverty: Options and Choices*, Routledge, London.

Thorp, R. (1998), *Progress, Poverty and Exclusion: An Economic History of Latin America in the 20th Century*, John Hopkins for the Inter-American Development Bank, Baltimore.

UNDP (United Nations Development Program) (1990), *Human Development Report 1990*, Oxford University Press, New York.
UNDP (United Nations Development Program) (1991), *Human Development Report 1991*, Oxford University Press, New York.
UNDP (United Nations Development Program) (2001), *Human Development Report 2001*, Oxford University Press, New York.
Welch, F. (1970), 'Education in Production', *Journal of Political Economy*, Vol. 78, No. 2 (March-April), pp. 33-59.
Wood, A. (1994), 'North-South Trade, Employment and Inequality: Changing Fortunes in a Skill-Driven World', *IDS Development Studies Series*, Oxford University Press, Oxford.
World Bank (1991), *Trends in Developing Economies*, The World Bank, Washington, D.C.
World Bank (1993), *Caribbean Region: Access, Quality and Efficiency in Education*, The World Bank, Washington, D.C.
World Bank (various years), *World Bank Development Indicators*, The World Bank, Washington, D.C.

Chapter 5

Reform, Macroeconomic Instability and the Distribution of Income in Latin America in the 1990s

Samuel A. Morley

Introduction

Latin America has the highest level of income inequality in the world. Recent evidence shows that, in many countries, inequality has risen even further in the 1990s, particularly since 1995. Since this increase has occurred not long after the widespread adoption of the neoliberal reforms, it is tempting to link the one with the other. But a closer look at the evidence reveals the existence of a large number of cases that do not fit very well this causal explanation. On the one hand, a number of reforming countries have not experienced a rise in inequality; and, on the other hand, the increase in inequality came in a number of countries in the late 1990s, well after the adoption of the reforms. Therefore, we think that a wider focus on both the determinants of the distribution and some key case-study evidence will help us understand what is taking place and why.

The chapter is organized as follows. In the next section we present a conceptual framework to approach the analysis of income distribution and of the factors that influence distribution both in the short- and the long-run. The third section shows the distribution evidence from the 1990s for 19 countries in the region, and the fourth presents quantitative reform indexes and some econometric evidence on the determinants of inequality. The fifth section takes up complementary case-study evidence in countries that have experienced sudden changes in inequality or where inequality has remained roughly constant for long periods. The final section summarizes the conclusions.

Determinants of the Distribution

From an economist's perspective, the examination of the distribution of income is approached in two parts: first, the distribution of earnings among active participants in the economy, and second, the distribution of income across all the individuals or the households in the society. The distribution across the workers and the owners of capital and land, the *primary* distribution, should be mainly determined by market forces. The second distribution – across all the households or the individuals in the society – is the one that most people care about because it determines the distribution of welfare and the level of poverty in society. The second distribution is derived from the first, but it is also affected by demographic factors such as the dependency ratio and the extent to which high-wage earners have high- or low-wage mates. These demographic factors change in the long-run, but probably not much in the short-run.

Our main focus here will be on the elements that affect the primary distribution, assuming that whatever changes that distribution will have an equivalent impact on the household distribution. We will assume as a useful abstraction that the primary distribution is determined in a set of markets for the various factors of production. These markets are not a physical location, but rather a network of contracts, pricing arrangements and understandings that determine the prices of each of the factors of production. For simplicity, we will consider only three factors of production: physical capital, human capital or skilled labor, and unskilled labor. In reality, of course, there are many different kinds of physical capital – each with a different return, and many graduations of skilled labor.

As in other economic markets, factor prices are determined by the interaction of the supply of each factor and the demand for each factor service. Markets clear at a price at which someone is willing to use the available supply of each of the factors. This set of market-clearing factor prices determines the relative price of skilled and unskilled labor and the rate of return on capital. In the labor market, it may well be the case that demand is so low that many are forced to work part time in the informal sector, or become unemployed altogether if the legally prescribed minimum wage in the formal sector exceeds the value of the marginal product of a fully employed labor force.

On the demand side, economic growth and expansionary macroeconomic policy increase the demand for each factor of production, thus raising their prices. What happens to relative factor prices depends on the nature of the growth process. If growth is skill-intensive, skill-differentials widen; if it is led by unskilled labor-intensive sectors such as agriculture, the reverse occurs. Structural reforms change the composition of output by shifting factors of production toward certain sectors and away from others. That is, the demand side determines the position of factor demand curves, which one would expect to depend negatively on the prices of complements, and positively on the prices of substitutes.

The supply side is critical to the understanding of the dynamics of the process. In the short-run, the supply of factors of production is fixed because each of the factors is a stock that produces a flow of services. That stock can change, but the change takes time. We are artificially dividing time into periods short enough for us to consider the stocks as being constant. In each of these time periods there is a fixed stock of factors determined by past investment decisions, and a set of factor demand curves. Together, the two determine the short-run set of factor prices.

While this process sets the valuation of the factors of production, one needs to know the distribution of ownership of the factors of production in order to determine the primary earnings distribution, since it is the owner that receives the payment for the factor services. The primary distribution in the short-run is thus determined jointly by the relative factor prices that come from the factor market and by the pattern of ownership of the factors of production.

The dynamics of the process comes from the growth of factor supply. Investment increases the stock of physical capital, while the education system produces graduates who enter the labor force and change the supply of both skilled and unskilled labor. Training and experience also increase the stock of skilled labor – or human capital. Migration also changes the position of factor supply curves, both for unskilled and skilled labor.

It is important to remember that investment takes time and that the amount that can be added to the stock of any of the factors is relatively small over a short period. Thus, in any period as short as say a year, it is impossible to shift the factor supply curves out by more than 3-5 percent. That means that in the short-run, it is changes coming from the demand side that will most likely explain observed changes in the primary distribution.

If we artificially divide time into periods in which the stock of factors of production is fixed, we get a short-run distribution. But as factor supplies change over time, so does the primary distribution change. But since the demand for factors is likely to change over time as well, the factor prices that we observe over time reflect changes in both supply and demand. That is why we may be unable to detect any apparent historical relationship between changes in the stock of human capital and relative wages, or between the growth rate and the primary distribution.

Another important feature of the distribution process is the dynamic feedback between factor prices and changes in factor supplies through investment. Relative wages and returns on physical capital determined in the factor markets affect investment and education decisions. If there is a rise in the rate of return on capital, investment in physical capital increases. Similarly, if there is an increase in the wage differential between skilled and unskilled labor, or between university and high school graduates, that increase will tend to enhance the demand for university education. Fewer people will enter the labor force after high school, and more people will enter university. Over time, those trends will increase the share of educated labor in the total labor force. If there were no changes on the demand side, this increase in the supply of skilled or educated labor would reduce the skill-differential. One could thus think of the initial rise in the skill-differential or in the return to capital as a dynamic signal that sets in motion an investment process that eventually adjusts factor supplies and relative factor prices to a long-run equilibrium. By definition, that equilibrium is one in which additions to supply are just sufficient to offset changes in the demand for factor services coming from economic growth and technological change.

From the point of view of the primary distribution, a rising skill-differential that tends to increase inequality in the short-run is also a signal of an expanding supply of educated labor or physical capital in the long-run. These long-run changes on the supply side may well reverse the short-run rise in inequality that induced them since they tend to drive down the rate of return to capital, both human and non-human. And one must bear in mind that the expansion in the supply of the well educated implies a rise in upward mobility for the young, more of whom will enter the labor market with university education instead of secondary or primary.

Thus, an important distinction can be made between the short- and the long-run meaning of a rise in the skill differential or in the rate of return to capital. In the short-run, an increase in either of these two is almost surely regressive. But in the long-run, so long as the supply side reacts positively to these changes in the rate of return, the change could be progressive either because of upward mobility, or because the increase in physical capital drives down the rate of return and raises the productivity and the average wage of workers.

The ambiguity being discussed here is a specific example of the dual function of income in a market system. On the one hand, relative income determines the distribution at each point in time. Any relative increase in the income of the rich is regressive. But on the other hand, income is the signal or incentive by which economic agents are encouraged to change their behavior. A rise in the skill-differential induces socially desirable education investment. Similarly, a rise in profits induces investment and a shift of productive resources from less desirable to more desirable uses. One makes a serious error of interpretation if one concentrates only on the short-run regressive effect of changing factor returns without taking into account progressive long-run supply responses.

To summarize, in both the short- and the long-run the primary distribution will be determined by the returns to the different factors of production and by who owns them. In the short-run, changes in the demand for factors caused by fluctuations in macroeconomic conditions – for example, recession, inflation or minimum wage policy – will drive the distribution. In the short-run, factor supply is roughly constant but, in the long-run, changes on the supply side will be an important additional influence on the observed distribution. If one thinks of the long-run as meaning that an economy is on its production frontier and growth path and not in a cyclical downturn or boom, one would expect that the distribution would be less volatile in the long-run than in the short. That trend will be relevant when we look at the behavior of the observed distribution during recessions or in the period immediately after a significant change in conditions – such as the period of implementation of neoliberal reforms.

In thinking about what might happen to the distribution over time when an economy is growing, we must keep another element in mind – the growth process. The general relationship between growth and distribution has been studied for a very long time. In a classic article, Simon Kuznets analyzed empirically the relationship between growth and equity using the historical experience of England and the United States (Kuznets, 1955). He found that throughout the19th century inequality rose as both countries grew, but then, around the beginning of the 20th century, the trend reversed and inequality began to decline. This non-linear, inverted U-shaped relationship between output per capita and inequality – the Kuznets curve – has been the subject of a vast literature that has looked for similar relationships in other countries and in cross-sections between countries.[1] We will test the Kuznets curve hypothesis later; here, however, we will concentrate on a key part of the Kuznets insight – the notion of linkages.

Kuznets' rationale for the relationship is based on the idea that the growth process is specific rather than universal. It starts somewhere specific, either in a sector, a region, or a city. From that starting point its effects spread by a variety of linkages to the rest of the economy. In the first stages of this process inequality rises; later, as the effect of the growth stimulus spreads in the population, inequality begins to decline.

Linkages are a key aspect of the relationship between growth and inequality; they determine the 'spread effect' of growth in the economy. The stronger they are, the faster and further the benefits of growth expand and the more equitable the growth becomes. This notion can be applied in a variety of important ways in Latin America. In some economies there are large backward regions or indigenous populations only weakly or marginally connected to the modern, dynamic sector where growth is occurring. The Northeast and North of Brazil, the Andean region of Peru, and the indigenous areas of Southern Mexico are powerful and tragic examples of what we are discussing because in these three areas, and in many more besides, linkages are weak. The areas themselves have a significant proportion of the nation's population, meaning their relative income levels have a noticeable effect on inequality. But for reasons not entirely understood, growth in the dynamic sectors does not induce much forward or backward linkage activity in these areas. As a result, when these countries grow, there is only a small spread effect to their backward or poor regions. Growth under these conditions tends to be inequitable. One could conclude that in these countries, growth increases inequality in the sense that if the entire country were to remain in the same conditions as its backward regions, inequality would be lower. Here, growth leaves behind significant proportions of the population; growth always leaves people behind if one accepts the idea that growth starts in a particular sector or area of the

1 Kuznets (1955) hypothesized that the inverted U-shaped relationship between income and the distribution can be explained mainly by the movement of population from the low-income rural economy to the higher-income urban economy.

country. The key aspect is that if the linkages are weak and the areas left behind are large, then there will be little movement toward the Kuznets turning point. The interval in which growth is inequitable is likely to be a long one.

Sectoral characteristics of growth are also important. If the growth process is led by an advanced industrial sector and if agriculture lags behind, inequality will expand, especially in countries with a large rural population. Conversely, if growth is led by unskilled labor-intensive sectors such as construction or agriculture, inequality contracts as the economy grows. Sectoral disturbances also can have an important short-run effect. Agriculture in particular is subject to quite severe short-run shocks such as crop failures, drought, El Niño, and falling terms of trade, all likely to have significant effects on the observed distribution of income in the short-run.

An Overview of the Distribution Evidence

Interpreting the Historical Evidence

There has been a widespread increase in inequality in the 1990s. One of our concerns is whether or not the neo-liberal reforms caused the increase in inequality; and if not, then what did. Using the historical evidence as a basis for linking the adoption of reforms to the change in inequality presents at least two serious difficulties. First, we have to assume that all the other factors that could have influenced the distribution changed only a little over the period. But such was not the case in many of the countries in the sample: Brazil, Argentina, Peru, and Mexico all stopped high levels of inflation during the reform process. That was bound to have an effect on real wages and the wage differential and, through that, on the distribution of earnings. Argentina, Ecuador, Jamaica, Paraguay and Venezuela had serious recessions. Others had large real currency appreciations that negatively affected the relative income of the rural sector. All of these disturbances likely affected the distribution and could, in fact, be the main reason for the observed movements in distribution over the period. Those changes themselves could have been caused by the adoption of reforms – but they might not have been. In any case, because the 1990s was such a turbulent decade, it is especially difficult to assign the observed changes in the distribution to any one cause.

The second issue that is relevant in any policy impact analysis is the analytical distinction between the short- and long-run. Presumably, it takes time to adjust to any change in structural conditions. Distribution observations made during the period when economic agents are adjusting to the change are likely to be quite different from those made in the long-run after the adjustment is complete. The longer the adjustment period is, the more likely other exogenous changes in conditions will occur whose effects will be easily confused with the reforms one is attempting to study. One of the most obvious of such other events is recession. If one is going to measure impact by comparing distribution observations before and after the adoption of reforms, one should have the economy on its long-run supply curve for both observations. But, in fact, many of the economies in the region have been in recession for much of the period since 1995, in particular for the most recent observations listed in Table 5.1, a list that includes Argentina, Paraguay, Colombia, Honduras, Ecuador, Peru, Venezuela and Jamaica. For these countries, we really cannot use the latest observed distribution data to determine what the long-run impact of the reforms will be, even though these observations were made well after the adoption of the reforms. These economies are not on their long-run supply curves.

Another problem with historical distribution data is the choice of dates for the comparison. In most countries, household surveys are not conducted every year, or even every second or third year. It is therefore quite easy to get a significant change in trend and in interpretation based on the end points one chooses for comparison. Mexico is a good example of this difficulty: there was a very big increase in inequality there between 1984 and 1989, but very little change thereafter. If one starts the comparison in 1989 – as we did in Table 5.1 – one finds little change in the distribution. However, if one starts the comparison in 1984, one discovers that Mexico shows a large jump in inequality. Another example is Argentina, which in 1989 experienced a severe hyperinflation and a big rise in inequality. Its Gini coefficient rose from .44 to .53 between 1986 and 1989, and then fell back to the mid .40s between 1990 and 1993 after inflation was brought under control (World Bank, 1995). Most of the reform program of interest to us here was adopted under the Menem government after 1989. Choosing 1989 as a starting point for the before and after distribution comparison, reforms were followed by a reduction in inequality. Using instead 1986 as the starting point, reforms were followed by an increase in inequality that was partially offset by stopping hyperinflation in 1990 and 1991.

Finally, there is the question of the accuracy of the data itself. Despite significant improvements in survey techniques in the region, many problems persist, one of the most serious being underreporting of income, particularly from profits. In no country is profit income accurately captured. Indeed, more to the point, what is reported is the distribution of labor income and transfers rather than total household income.[2] ECLAC attempted to correct for this source of underreporting by adjusting upward the income from profits of the top 20 percent of households by the estimated percent of underreporting. Other researchers have not made this correction, partly explaining the difference between their estimations and those of ECLAC.

2 Honduras and Nicaragua report only labor income.

Table 5.1: Changes in the Distribution of Household Income per Capita in Latin America during the 1990s [a]

Country	1989	1990	1991	1992	1993	1994	1995	1996	1997	1998	1999	2000	Source
Argentina		0.4200		0.4100		0.4390				0.4390			ECLAC
Bolivia		0.5449			0.5323		0.5274	0.5877	0.5890		0.6014		Székely
Brazil	0.6400	0.6200		0.5800	0.6000		0.6000	0.6000	0.6000	0.6000	0.600		Barros
Chile		0.5470		0.5220		0.5558		0.5638		0.5587			Székely
Colombia			0.5670		0.6038		0.5697		0.5758	0.5679	0.5620		Székely
Costa Rica	0.4595		0.4598		0.4549		0.4571		0.4589	0.4612			Székely
Dom. Rep.				0.4820						0.4560			Aristy
Ecuador							0.5600			0.5616			Székely
El Salvador				0.5310	0.5230	0.5300	0.5000						M&V
El Salvador							0.5052		0.5195	0.5589	0.5455		Székely
Guatemala	0.4980									0.4850			ECLAC
Honduras	0.5704			0.5489				0.5284	0.5908	0.5852	0.5843		Székely
Jamaica	0.4360				0.3820			0.3690					K&H
Nicaragua					0.5670					0.6024			Székely
Mexico	0.5309			0.5341		0.5361		0.5276		0.5377			Székely
Panama			0.5625				0.5602		0.5756	0.5652	0.5631		Székely
Paraguay							0.5700			0.5692	0.5942		Székely
Peru			0.4643			0.4832		0.4762	0.5065				Székely
Peru			0.4670			0.4580		0.4350				0.4933	S&D
Uruguay	0.4064			0.4319			0.4209		0.4300	0.4338			Székely
Venezuela	0.4396				0.4288		0.4669		0.4863	0.4706	0.4675		Székely

[a] All the series are national household income per capita with the exception of Jamaica which is household expenditure per capita, and Argentina and Uruguay which are urban distributions, not national. Note that in Peru, the S&D distribution uses the same areas for 1994 and 1996 that were surveyed in 1991. This may explain the differences with the Székely estimates. The Aristy estimates are preliminary results made available to the author.

Sources: ECLAC – Social Panorama of Latin America and the Caribbean (various years). *Székely* – Székely (2001). *Barros* – Barros *et al.* (2000). *Aristy* – Aristy (2001). *M&V* – Mejía and Vos (1997). *K&H* – King and Handa (2001). *S&D* – Saavedra and Díaz (1999).

This is only a specific example of the general problem of underreporting of income. Székely and Hilgert (1999) have investigated the problem and demonstrated its importance. They assert that inequality is grossly underestimated both because the rich are underrepresented in the survey and because their income is underreported. In several countries the total income of the highest ten individuals in the survey is similar to the wage of the average manager. In ten of the countries they examined, the average wage of the manager is actually higher than the income of the ten highest households (*ibid.*, 13). There are important differences in the degree of underreporting across countries, and perhaps over time as well, making comparisons either across countries or over time suspect.

All these data problems cause large and inexplicable differences between the estimates of the distribution derived by different researchers. If those differences were confined only to the level of inequality at a point in time, but not to changes over time, one could still speak with some confidence about inequality trends. However, there are large and significant differences both in the levels and the trends reported, not only by individual researchers but also by official institutions in the region – in particular, the Inter-American Development Bank and ECLAC who base their distribution estimates on the same household surveys.

Consider Figure 5.1, where we compare the change in the distribution in nine

Figure 5.1: Comparison of Changes in the Gini Coefficient over the 1990s, Selected Latin American Countries, Percentage Points

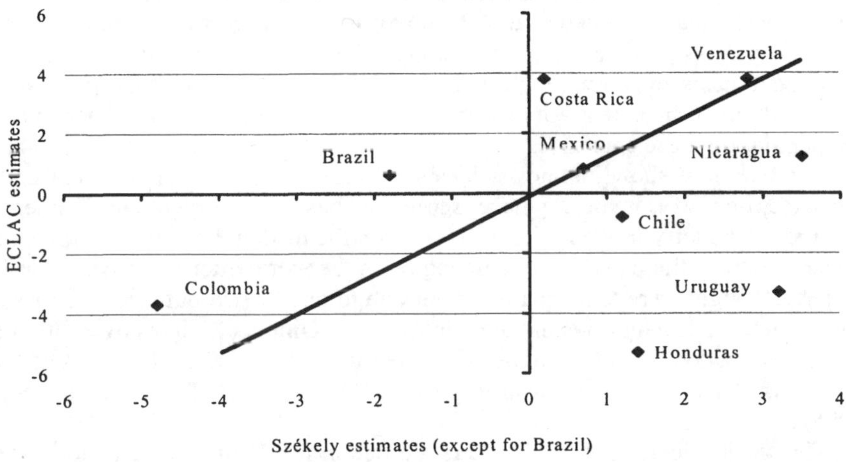

Sources: ECLAC's *2001 Social Panorama*. The Székely series from Székely (2001) using the years closest to those in the ECLAC data, except for Brazil for which we used Gini coefficients reported in Barros et al. (2000).

countries for which data is available over the 1990s as reported in Székely (2001) and in ECLAC (2001). The data show that in Chile, Uruguay, Brazil, and Honduras the two sources disagree as to the sign of the change. Regarding Costa Rica, both Székely and local Costa Rican researchers assert that the distribution remained virtually unchanged over the 1990s. ECLAC claims it increased by 4 percentage points – a very large increase indeed. In fact, in only three countries – Mexico, Colombia and Venezuela – are the two sources in basic agreement over what happened.

If assertions are to be made about inequality, reforms, and growth, there must be at least an agreement on what the changes in inequality were. In fact, ECLAC and the IDB would be providing a great service were they to compare estimates and resolve these apparently quite significant differences in many countries.

Changes in the Distribution in the 1990s

Given the foregoing data problems, Table 5.1 presents the best available distribution evidence for the 1990s. Wherever possible, we have used Székely's (2001) series because he systematically attempted to adjust surveys from different countries and different years to account for variations in income definition and reporting. For each country, we have presented reasonably comparable estimates at different points in the 1990s. For several countries, no single series covers the entire decade, but there is an overlapping year that permits a fairly accurate estimate of what the overall distribution trend was. In such cases, we have shown both series. Finally, Ecuador and Paraguay have a large rural population where national surveys have been only recently taken; so for those countries, we can make statements only for the period after 1995. Argentina and Uruguay surveys cover only the urban areas – a reasonable result, given the high urban percentage of the population these countries.

The data first show just how widespread high inequality is in the region. With the exception of Jamaica, whose survey is based on expenditure rather than income, no country in the region reaches even the median level of the Gini of Sub-Saharan Africa, the most inequitable region in the world after Latin America. Latin America's high average inequality is not due to one or two outlying countries. No less than 11 of 19 countries in the table have had Gini coefficients over .50 in their latest observation, which is higher than the maximum Gini in all but 14 of the 88 non-Latin American countries in the World Bank data set (Deininger and Squire, 1996).

The second feature of Table 5.1 is the rise in inequality in the majority of the countries in the region since 1990, or between the earliest and latest observations in the table. All but 5 of the 19 countries had such an increase, and in 6 of them the increase was more than 2 percentage points – a most unwelcome feature of the post-reform world. More to the point, given the questions raised at the beginning of

Table 5.2: Changes in the Distribution of Income in Latin America during the 1990s

Countries and periods with significant increases in inequality:		
Argentina (1992-1998)	Nicaragua (1993-1998)	
Bolivia (1995-1999)	Paraguay (1995-1999)	
Colombia (1991-1993)	Peru (1996-2000)	
El Salvador (1997-1999)	Uruguay (1989-1992)	
Honduras (1996-1999)	Venezuela (1992-1997)	
Countries and periods with roughly constant inequality:		
Brazil	Panama	Ecuador
Chile	Costa Rica	Uruguay (1992-1997)
Mexico	Guatemala	
Countries and periods with falling inequality:		
Colombia (1993-1999)	Peru (1991-1996)	
Dominican Republic (1992-1998)	Bolivia (1990-1995)	
Jamaica (1990-1996)	Honduras (1989-1996)	

Source: Table 5.1.

this chapter, it is critical to date the increases more specifically. That is, when did these increases in inequality occur? Looking at the table with this in mind, one sees that in most countries the increase came in the second half of the decade; indeed, in several cases it came even after a reduction in inequality before 1995. A rough calculation reveals ten cases of significant increases in inequality over the 1990s (Table 5.2). Eight of those took place after 1995, and two – Colombia and Uruguay – before. In Peru, El Salvador, Honduras, and Bolivia there was some leveling of the distribution between 1990 and 1995, but the improvements have been reversed since 1995. This matter of dating the changes in inequality becomes important when we ask whether or not the increases were due to the adoption of reforms. If the bulk of the reforms took place in the 1980s, it would be hard to conclude that they caused an increase in inequality in the late 1990s, particularly if that increase was preceded by a fall in inequality in the early 1990s.

Not all the distribution evidence is negative. In Costa Rica and Uruguay, inequality has fallen to levels found in developed countries. Inequality is unlikely to fall much further in these two countries, not because growth is inequitable but because there are lower limits to income inequality in any society. Finally, the Dominican Republic and Jamaica experienced a decline in inequality. However, the decline in Jamaica was the result of a severe and lengthy recession in which the rich lost more than did the poor – whose expenditure and income could not decrease much because they live nearly at the subsistence level.

Thus, inequality is either rising or stuck at a very high level in almost every country in the region. Even in relatively equitable countries like Argentina, Uruguay, and Venezuela the distribution is now much less progressive than it was at the beginning of the decade. Only the Dominican Republic and Costa Rica have low or declining inequality and an adequate growth rate. Such is the reality and the core of the distribution problem in the region.

In Table 5.2 we have separated a group of countries where the distribution was roughly constant – changed by less than 1 percentage point over the decade or a significant part of the decade. That group comprises Brazil, Chile, Colombia, Mexico, Guatemala, and Panama, where inequality has risen sharply in the past and is now stuck at a very high level. This apparent inertia or lack of trend in the distribution is significant, particularly since, in many cases, it started well before the 1990s and continued for many years after the adoption of reforms. For example, Brazil's Gini was .58 in 1972, rose to .60 by 1976 and, except for some years in the early 1980s, has stayed at that level ever since – despite recession, hyperinflation, and recurrent debt crises. In Chile, the national distribution has varied between .57 and .55 ever since 1987, the date of the first national survey comparable with later observations. Costa Rica's Gini has been virtually constant since 1987, as has Mexico's since 1989.

The distribution patterns in Table 5.2 are dramatically different from those of just five years ago. If we had made a comparable table for around 1995, we would have found that eight countries had no trend in their distribution: Colombia, Argentina, Brazil, Chile, Mexico, Panama, Costa Rica, and Guatemala; that six countries had falling inequality: Bolivia, the Dominican Republic, El Salvador, Honduras, Jamaica, and Peru; and that only three had registered a significant increase in inequality: Venezuela, Uruguay, and possibly Nicaragua.[3]

The difference between the situations at the middle and at the end of the 1990s is significant for assessing the impact of the reforms. As we shall see, the bulk of the neoliberal reform package was adopted in most countries by the early 1990s at the latest. Thus, the fact that there was no significant increase in inequality in the first years under the reforms suggests that the reforms are not the reason for the observed rise in inequality over the entire decade. Rather, something must have occurred after 1995 that made the whole inequality picture worse in most countries. There could have been a delayed reaction to the reforms – but that explanation is not too plausible for most countries.

Econometric Evidence on the Determinants of the Distribution

The most obvious way to estimate the separate impact of policy reforms and other variables while avoiding the pitfalls of 'before and after' historical comparisons is by a regression that includes, in addition to some sort of quantification of the policy reforms, all other variables that could potentially affect the distribution. These other variables are interesting in their own right. Since there are not enough observations in any particular country to make a straight time-series feasible, one is forced to use a combined cross-section-time-series instead.

3 We would not have had information on Paraguay and Ecuador in 1995.

Clearly there are serious econometric difficulties in attempting to use pooled cross-section-time-series evidence to capture a time-series relationship for a single country. Essentially, one is assuming that the relationship between distribution and income in today's high-income countries is similar to what the less developed countries can expect when they reach the current income level of more advanced countries. In other words, unknown country-specific effects do not affect the relationship between income and the distribution. There are many factors that vary across countries that can have an impact on the distribution or on its responsiveness to changes in income, and these need to be included in the model. In addition, we use a fixed-effects model with country-specific constants to capture any unknown country-specific factors affecting the distribution relationship.

Some of the surveys are based on the distribution of family income; others, on the distribution of per capita family income. Most of the surveys are based on income, but some use expenditure data instead because this data is measured with significantly less error than is income, and because it is a better indicator of permanent income. Another important aspect is the distinction between urban and national surveys. Both Fields (1994) and Deininger and Squire (1996) have argued that one should use only national surveys in any analysis of the distribution of income. But in Bolivia, Ecuador and Paraguay, urban surveys were the only ones available until recently, and in both Argentina and Uruguay they are still the only ones available. One therefore has the choice of either excluding these countries from any analytical work or attempting to control for systematic differences between urban and national surveys using dummy variables. We have chosen the latter strategy. Not only does this approach expand substantially the size of our sample, but it also permits us to see whether there is any systematic difference in reaction in income or income growth between the urban and the national surveys. The final sample used for the regression analysis consists of 261 observations in 16 countries from 1960 to 1997. No country was included in the survey unless it produced at least four separate observations.

Indexes of Reforms

In order to do an econometric study that included the reforms, it was essential to develop a quantifiable index that would allow comparing the extent of the reforms between countries, or the progress of the reforms over time in a single country. Our attempt to do this is described in detail in Morley et al. (1999), which is an extension of work initiated by Eduardo Lora at the IDB (Lora, 1998). The indexes also help to identify when the bulk of the reforms took place, facilitating the interpretation of the historical distribution evidence.

Our index is a simple average of reform indexes in five areas: trade, finance, tax, privatization, and capital account. In each area we tried to choose indicators such as tariffs or tax rates that reflect government policies – rather than proxies for those policies such as openness to trade or the government deficit. Each index is normalized to be between zero and 100. The 100 is assigned to the country and to the year in which the sector was reformed the most or was free from distortion or government intervention, and the zero to the country and year with the greatest degree of intervention.[4] We do not imply by this procedure that a high value for an index is better than a low one, but only that the high-value sector is closer to a pure, non-government market solution.

The trade reform index is the average of two subcomponents: the average level and the dispersion of tariffs. We were unable to obtain a satisfactory measure of non-tariff restrictions, signifying a weakness of the index because in some cases – for example Brazil – it significantly affected the timing of trade reform. Domestic financial reform is the average of three sub-indexes: the control of bank-borrowing and bank-lending rates, and the reserves to deposit ratio. Tax reform has four subcomponents: the maximum marginal tax rate on corporate and person incomes, the value added tax rate, and the efficiency of the VAT. Our index for privatization is 100 minus the share of value-added in state-owned enterprises in non-agricultural GDP. Capital account reform is the average of four subcomponents reflecting the extent of government control of foreign investment: limits on profit and interest repatriation, controls on external borrowing, and capital outflows. Unlike the other indexes, the capital account index is based on a subjective interpretation of the descriptions in the IMF's annual *Balance of Payments Arrangements* publication.

In this definition of reform, we make a clear distinction between what we call *structural reforms* and *macroeconomic policy reforms*, examples of the latter being government deficit reduction, inflation control and exchange rate management that could be called stabilization reforms. In many countries, the two types of reforms were adopted simultaneously in the face of balance of payments or hyperinflation crises. Here, we are explicitly studying the structural reforms only. However, the impact of stabilization reforms will be captured through their effect on inflation and the level of income.

To some extent, the choice of what to include in our measurement of structural reform was arbitrary. Two important excluded reforms were those in the labor market and financial market regulation. We excluded the former because, in Lora's work, the labor reform index by country changed little between 1985 and 1995, and because Lora's measure would not have captured the important changes that occurred in the Southern Cone countries in the 1970s. We excluded financial market regulation because of the lack of an adequate measure for it. Elimination of price subsidies is another reform not included, though that reform probably had

4 Formally each sub-index is defined as $I_{it} = (IR_{it} - Min)/(Max - Min)$, where IR_{it} is the raw value of the index in country *i*, year *t*, and *Max* and *Min* are the maximum and minimum values of the raw index for all countries over the period 1970-95.

Figure 5.2: Indexes of Structural Reforms in Latin America, 1970-1995

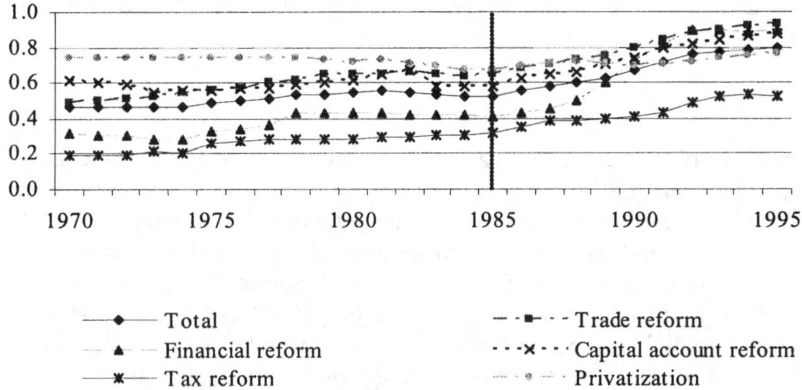

Source: Morley et al. (1999).

important effects in some countries.

Figure 5.2 is a graphic presentation of the region-wide averages for each of our reform indexes. It gives a quick picture of what has been reformed most and when the process has occurred. Note that these indexes are non-weighted, simple arithmetic averages of the values of the respective indexes for each of the countries. Note also that although most of the countries in the region made most of their reforms in the period between 1985 and 1990, other countries such as the Dominican Republic, Peru, Ecuador, Honduras, and Venezuela started the process later – the last three still remaining among the least reformed countries in the region. These are the countries where one would expect the distributional impact of the reforms to be felt in the period after 1995; yet, inequality remained roughly constant in Ecuador, increased in Honduras and Venezuela, and decreased in the Dominican Republic – a big reformer – during the period when it was reforming the most. Peru seems to be the only country where rising inequality followed directly a period of rapid reform. In most of the other countries in the region, reforms in the 1980s or early 1990s were followed by a period of either falling or constant inequality. It was only after 1995 that this trend reversed in some of these countries.

Lora (2001) has recently updated his reform indexes to cover the period up to 1999 and has identified Bolivia, Brazil, the Dominican Republic, El Salvador, Guatemala and Jamaica as the countries that made significant reforms (raised the index by over 10 percent) between 1995 and 1999. The cases of Bolivia and El Salvador are consistent with the regressive reform hypothesis, but those of the other four countries are not. And to make a convincing case for these two countries, as well as for Peru, one would have to explain how they managed to achieve rapid reform and falling inequality before 1995 and, then, further reform and rising inequality afterward.

Regression Results

Many previous efforts have been made to econometrically estimate models of the relationship between the level or growth rate of income and the distribution of income. Most have been estimations of the Kuznets relationship using cross-country distribution and income data (Ahluwalia, 1976; Anand and Kanbur, 1993; Bruno et al., 1996; Clarke, 1995; Deininger and Squire, 1996; de Janvry and Sadoulet, 1999; Fields, 1994; Ravallion and Chen, 1997). All but the last of these studies use a worldwide sample of countries. The difficulty with that approach, as Fields points out, is that since Latin America is a middle-income region and has the highest inequality in the world, one can get an apparent inverse U-shaped Kuznets curve simply by choice of the sample. Fields found that if he included a dummy for the Latin observations, the supposed relationship between income and inequality disappears. Deininger and Squire (1996) found exactly the same thing. Using data from 63 surveys covering 44 countries, Bruno et al. (1996) tested the Kuznets hypothesis for both levels and changes over time. In no case could they find evidence of an inverted U-shape, and in no case was the relationship between the distribution and income significantly different from zero. Ravallion and Chen (1997) regressed changes in the Gini coefficient against changes in mean real consumption using data covering 67 countries. They found a negative and significant relationship between the two in the full sample. However when they excluded the observations from Eastern Europe and Central Asia, the relationship disappeared. We follow in the same line, estimating a Kuznets curve augmented by several other variables, like the reform indexes and measures of education, that are likely to affect the relationship between income and inequality.

The details of the econometric results are reported at length in Morley (2000 and 2001b). Table 5.3 displays several of the estimated equations for a sample including both national and urban data. The equations include dummies for various sample characteristics, such as whether it is urban or national (*URBAN*); whether it is based on a household income or a household income per capita distribution (*HHLD*); whether it is based on expenditure or income (*EXPEND*); and whether the survey was adjusted for underreporting by ECLAC. Our discussion is drawn from the equation with fixed effects, cross-section weights, and trend variables (equation 3).

We drew three main conclusions from the econometrics. First, there appears to be a robust and significant relationship between the distribution and income. It has the inverted U-shape that Kuznets predicted. Both the coefficients on income and

Table 5.3: Regression Analysis, Combined Sample Results

Variable	Fixed Effects						Single Intercept	
	Pooled LS		Cross-Section Wts					
	(1)		(2)		(3)		(4)	
	Coeff.	t-Stat.	Coeff.	t-Stat.	*Coeff.*	t-Stat.	Coeff.	t-Stat.
INCOME	-0.0001	-7.0504	-0.0001	-7.3174	-0.0001	-7.9707	-0.0001	-5.2978
1/INCOME	-260.3067	-2.9407	-208.7411	-2.8671	-336.4263	-4.0021	-69.3106	-1.1264
URBAN	-0.0336	-5.3983	-0.0333	-6.9739	-0.0320	-6.7043	-0.0278	-3.7291
ECLAC	-0.0522	-8.3100	-0.0510	-9.2131	-0.0530	-9.4478	-0.0568	-6.8944
EXPEND	-0.0874	-4.6603	-0.0875	-2.9325	-0.0838	-2.8620	-0.1109	-9.4870
INFLATION	0.0114	1.2774	0.0112	1.3838	0.0138	1.7027	0.0510	3.8580
HHLD	-0.0089	-1.5645	-0.0118	-2.3858	-0.0154	-3.0176	-0.0144	-1.8140
HIGH	-0.0065	-2.8047	-0.0082	-3.2362	-0.0039	-1.3811	-0.0080	-5.4828
PRIMARY	0.2482	3.1068	0.1965	2.7995	0.2311	3.2581	0.0167	0.3300
TREND*INC	0.0000	6.0880	0.0000	6.2408	0.0000	7.1460	0.0000	4.6505
REFORM	0.0261	1.2573	0.0303	1.6333	0.0633	2.8999	-0.0095	-0.3703
TREND					-0.0030	-3.1760	-0.0015	-1.4856
LANDLIST							0.0364	4.5922
CONSTANT							0.7387	8.2049
R-squared	0.8620		0.9756		0.9755		0.9341	
Adjusted R-sq.	0.8468		0.9729		0.9726		0.9306	
Durbin-Wats	1.5275		1.6061		1.6065		0.6725	
F-statistic	146.8103		940.4532		845.5984		270.2431	
D.F.	261		261		261		261	

Variable Definitions:
INCOME – Income per capita in year and country of the sample observation.
URBAN – Dummy, equal one for urban sample.
ECLAC – Dummy for samples with adjustment for underreporting done by ECLAC.
EXPEND – Dummy for samples based on expenditure rather than income.
INFLATION – Dummy for observations taken when rate of inflation was over 1000% per year.
HHLD – Dummy equals one for samples based on the distribution of household income rather than household income per capita.
HIGH – Percentage of adult population with university education.
PRIMARY – Percentage of adult population with no more than primary education.
TREND – Trend variable, equals one in 1970.
REFORM – Average reform index for country and year from Morley *et al.* (1999).
LANDLIST – Dummy variable equal to one for countries with highly unequal land distribution.

Source: Morley (2001b).

the inverse of income are negative, and highly significant. But the Kuznets curve has been shifting in a regressive direction over time; that is, growth is now less progressive than it used to be. We obtained this result by introducing a trend term in the regressions, both in the constant and as an interaction term with income. Both terms are highly significant. The constant term (*TREND*) is negative, suggesting a gradual improvement in inequality over time, other things being equal. But the interaction term (*TREND*INC*) tells a different story. It is positive and significant in all of the regressions, including the one with the common constant and those for the urban and national samples considered separately. That says that the slope of the Kuznets curve changes over time. That the coefficient is positive means that to the left of the inflection point where the curve itself is upward sloping, the slope is getting gradually steeper. To the right of the inflection point where the slope itself is negative, the slope gradually becomes flatter. In addition, the interaction term makes the inflection point itself shift gradually to the right over time, extending the range over which growth is regressive.

Thus, the trend terms tell two opposing stories. The trend term on the intercept is progressive: it shifts the Kuznets curve down. But the interaction term is regressive. The positive interaction means that growth has become systematically less progressive than what it was. We believe that this trend mainly reflects the increasing skill-intensity of growth and the rising premium accorded to education and skill. Further, the time term in the regressions helps to explain the apparent lack of trend in the observed distributions over time. Indeed, rather than moving down a stationary Kuznets curve where one might expect falling inequality, observations at different points in time are on different Kuznets curves, with later curves flatter than earlier ones.

Generally speaking, the neoliberal reforms appear to have a regressive effect on the distribution; but while significant, this effect is small. Increasing the reform index by 20 percent – approximately the increase for the region between 1990 and 1995 – would increase the average Gini coefficient by only .25 percent. Reforms in different areas produce differing effects on equity. Trade reform is regressive as suggested by Berry (1998), Robbins (1995) and others, but it is not very robust statistically.[5] Tax reform is clearly regressive, while opening up the capital account is clearly progressive. For the other two reforms – privatization and financial – the data were not good enough to give statistically meaningful results.[6]

Education is an important qualifier to our discussion of the Kuznets curve. We included two education variables in the model: the percentage of workers with no more than primary school (*PRIMARY*), and the percentage with university education (*HIGH*). A high percentage of poorly educated workers produces a large

---

5 The econometric estimates for each of the individual reforms are not reported here, but can be found in Morley (2000).

6 Behrman et al. (2001) did a cross-section panel analysis similar to ours using data from the 1980s and 1990s. They found that commercial reform had an insignificant but progressive effect on inequality while financial reform was regressive and significant, just the opposite of our findings. There are at least three explanations for this difference in findings. First, they used a four-year lag between the reform index and the inequality measure, while we had no lag. Second, they excluded many variables, particularly income, that might have a relationship to inequality. Indeed, if the excluded variables are correlated with the reforms, they will affect the sign of the relationship between the reforms and inequality. And third, they used the ratio of income of the rich and the poor rather than the Gini to measure inequality.

and regressive effect on the distribution. In Argentina, for example, the share of adults with no more than primary school education has fallen from 81 percent in 1974 to 64 percent in 1996.[7] According to regression (3) in Table 5.3, this improvement alone should have lowered the Gini coefficient by about 4 percentage points (.23*.17). At the same time, the negative coefficient on *HIGH* tells us that increasing the share of university graduates in the adult population is progressive – that is, it shifts the Kuznets curve down. Note that the absolute size of the effect of expanding the share of university graduate is much smaller than the effect of reducing the share of the poorly educated, suggesting that one gets a bigger distribution bang by spending money to reduce the size of the group with primary or less education than by expanding the coverage of high school and university education.

Case-Study Evidence

The econometric evidence from the previous section shows an average relationship between different variables. But it leaves out a great deal of the country-specific factors which may have a great effect both on the level and the rate of change of inequality in particular countries at particular times or in particular circumstances. As Professor Berry has often shown, one gets a much deeper understanding of how the distribution process works by taking a closer look at case-study evidence. Three different cases are of interest. First, cases where inequality rose or fell significantly in the 1990s to help understand the troubling recent increase in inequality. Second, cases where there was a sudden sharp increase in inequality before the 1990s are also of interest. Finally, of interest are the countries where inequality has been essentially constant over long periods in spite of quite large changes in conditions.

Changes in Inequality in the 1990s

As shown in Table 5.1, inequality has been rising in a large number of countries during the second half of the 1990s exactly in sync with a generalized slowdown in the growth rate in most countries in the region. So, did the slowdown in growth have anything to do with the increase in inequality? To answer this question, we plotted the changes in the distribution against the changes in income for those countries that had a significant change in inequality over the 1990s (Table 5.2). To avoid clutter, we left out the countries where the distribution was more or less constant over the decade. The results are displayed in Figure 5.3. Overall, there is

7 This finding is consistent with the results from other cross-section studies (Bruno et al., 1996).

Figure 5.3: Changes in Gini and GDP, Selected Latin American Countries and Periods, Percentage Points

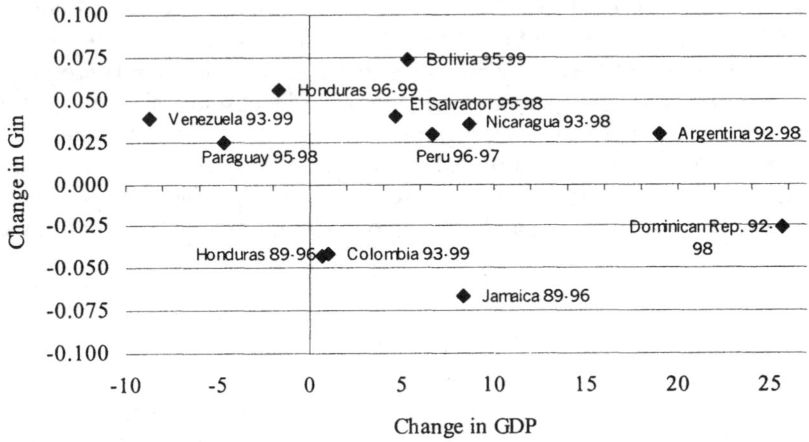

Sources: Table 5.1 and ECLAC.

no relationship between the two variables: five countries are in the NE quadrant where there is income growth and rising inequality; four countries are experiencing growth and falling inequality; and another three, are undergoing recession and rising inequality. This pattern is quite different from that of the 1980s when recessions were very often associated with rising inequality and recoveries with either constant or falling inequality (Morley, 1995, Table 2.2). For the 1990s, no clear relationship exists between the slowdown in the economy and the changes in the distribution.

In the calculations used for Figure 5.3 we compared incomes for the first and the last years of the period. But it may be argued that if a country is growing rapidly at the beginning of a period and then experiences an extended slowdown towards the end, it may suffer from the same conditions as does a country whose per capita income has actually declined, particularly if there has been a big increase in unemployment, even if its per capita income is higher at the end of the period than at the beginning. That scenario developed in both Argentina and Bolivia among the countries in the NE quadrant of Figure 5.2. Both had income growth, while their unemployment rates doubled at the same time. Sharp increases in unemployment also help explain the increase in inequality in Venezuela and Paraguay. But Colombia also had a big increase in unemployment in the late 1990s, and yet its inequality fell by 4 percentage points after peaking in 1993.

For a better understanding of the sectoral dimension of growth and inequality, one should consider the relative performance of agriculture when examining

Table 5.4: Average and Minimum Wages in Latin America in the 1990s

Country / Period	Average Wage First Yr.	Average Wage Last Yr.	Minimum Wage First Yr.	Minimum Wage Last Yr.	Wage Index (Base=1) Avg. Wage	Wage Index (Base=1) Min. Wage	Avg/Min
Argentina 92-98	101.7	99.0	57.9	98.4	0.973	1.699	0.5728
Bolivia 95-99	100.0	117.0	100.0	123.2	1.170	1.232	0.9497
El Salv. 95-98			100.0	95.3		0.953	
Honduras 96-99			96.0	105.8		1.102	
Nicarag. 93-98	93.3	100.7			1.079		
Paraguay 95-99	100.0	98.6	100.0	101.5	0.986	1.015	0.9714
Peru 96-97	95.2	94.5	103.2	181.2	0.993	1.756	0.5653
Venez. 93-99	124.4	96.8	95.3	82.3	0.778	0.864	0.9010
Colombia 93-99	97.9	105.9	102.1	103.7	1.082	1.016	1.0650
Dom. R. 92-98			98.4	106.3		1.080	
Jamaica 89-96	100.0	112.0	100.0	92.0	1.120	0.920	1.2174
Honduras 89-96			111.6	96.0		0.860	
Colombia 91-93	92.4	97.9	104.6	102.1	1.060	0.976	1.0855

Sources: Wage data are from ECLAC (2002). Jamaica's wages are skilled and unskilled and are taken from King and Handa (2001).

historical trends. If the growth of agriculture falls far behind that of the other sectors, an increase in inequality will likely result. Such an event was obviously a key factor in Honduras where hurricane Mitch caused a 15 percent contraction in agricultural output between 1997 and 1999, and a 4 percentage-point reduction in the agricultural share.

The same pattern of falling agricultural share is evident in several other countries – for example, in Peru between 1996 and 1997, El Salvador over 1995-99, and Colombia over 1991-93. The agricultural share rose in Paraguay, but this was because of the performance of the modern export-oriented soy and grain sector. *Campesino* agriculture is in crisis in Paraguay; its cash crop – cotton – has been devastated by disease, pests and falling prices. As a result, cotton exports have fallen by over two thirds since 1995, and rural poverty has risen by 20 percent (Morley, 2001a). Thus, Paraguay is another country where agricultural performance would help elucidate the problem of inequality. Jamaica, however, presents the opposite picture: agriculture was a leading sector helping to reduce inequality even in the face of fairly slow growth.

Wages and wage differentials are another important determinant of the distribution. Table 5.4 presents the available information for those countries that exhibit in Table 5.2 large changes in inequality. Minimum wages rose in real terms in 7 of the 12 countries whose data were studied. In some countries, notably Argentina and Bolivia, the increase occurred in spite of economic recession. In two others, the Dominican Republic and Colombia (1993-99), minimum wages rose and inequality fell. But other than in these two cases, increases in minimum wages are not helpful in explaining inequality trends except, possibly, in El Salvador and Venezuela. The evidence thus suggests that changing the minimum wage without considering the demand for unskilled labor and the amount of unemployment will have little effect on inequality – and the tactic could make the situation even worse for those at the bottom of the income pyramid if it forces workers into unemployment or the informal sector.

Table 5.4 also illustrates movements in relative wages. The last column on the right shows the ratio of the average and minimum wage indexes in the final year of the comparison for each country – the initial year being the base year with an index value of 1. Therefore, a number greater than 1 means a widening of the skill-differential. With that in mind, a glance at the table suggests that the relative wage evidence is not well correlated with the observed changes in inequality. One might expect that a rise in the skill-differential would be observed in countries where inequality also increased. However, the skill-differential fell in Argentina, Bolivia, Paraguay, Peru and Venezuela, while inequality increased in all of them. In Colombia and Jamaica, the differential increased in both periods; yet, in two of these three cases, inequality fell.

While there is no relationship between changes in income and changes in inequality, there exists a weak relationship between changes in inequality and the reforms. Those countries with higher reform indexes tended to have larger increases in inequality over the 1990s – after controlling for growth. The relationship is significant, and consistent with our more complete econometric study of the evidence from 1970-95.

Two other patterns in the distribution data are indeed puzzling. The first is the inertia or rigidity of the distribution observed in many countries in spite of fairly large changes in conditions and policies. The second is the irreversible nature of many of the observed increases in inequality.

Examples of Large, Irreversible Increases in Inequality

There are a number of countries that have had a large, one-time increase in inequality, often associated with some sort of policy intervention or macro-shock. Most of these increases have led to a permanent increase in inequality – even after the shock had disappeared. Those who thought that reversing the shock would reverse the increase in inequality have been disappointed to find that this has not happened.

Five cases stand out: Mexico between 1984 and 1989, Chile and Argentina during the 1970s, and Brazil during the 1960s. In each of these cases the Gini coefficient rose by around 5 percentage points or more, moving the countries to new and permanently higher levels of inequality. Many other countries have experienced large increases in inequality, but in each of these cases a subsequent reversal occurred. What can explain these apparently permanent shifts, and do they have anything to do with the neoliberal reforms?

Recall that both Argentina and Chile implemented a significant part of their reform programs prior to the mid-1980s. For Chile, our aggregate reform index rose from .32 in 1973 to .72 in 1987, making Chile the second most reformed country in the region – after Uruguay. Argentina achieved less, but still, its index rose from .41 in 1976 when the reforms started, to .61 in 1986, and .81 in 1990 (Morley et al., 1999). In both countries, commercial, financial and tax reforms were the central components of the early reform program. Mexico exhibited a different result; it began trade and financial reforms during 1985-87 by eliminating quantitative import restrictions and narrowing tariff differentials, but the changes it implemented were far less dramatic than those in the Southern Cone, partly because Mexico had always had lower tariffs than had Argentina and Uruguay (Ros and Bouillon, 2001). This policy change took place in Mexico during the long downturn that followed the 1982 debt crisis, a period in which there was a contraction of real wages, a sharp increase in inflation followed by stabilization, a widening of the skill-differential, and a shift in the primary distribution toward profits (Székely, 1998, 64-67; Ros and Bouillon, 2001, Table 2).[8]

A factor common to all these three countries is macro-instability and inflation during the periods under consideration. Chile suffered through two severe recessions between 1973 and 1987, and Argentina had three between 1976 and 1990 – none quite as severe as the 1982-83 downturn in Chile. Mexico also had high inflation and a deep recession during 1984-89, when output per capita decreased by 6 percent. Brazil experienced an increase in inflation during 1960-63 – incidentally, a factor partly responsible for the overthrow of the civilian government by the military. The military there imposed an orthodox stabilization program in 1964 that led to an intermittent three-year recession and a sharp reduction in minimum wages.

A factor that characterizes Chile, Brazil, and Argentina, but not Mexico, is the effect of a regime change on the labor market. The three countries were controlled by bureaucratic-authoritarian military regimes that intervened dramatically in the labor markets in an effort to control inflation and civil unrest. The three military governments effectively curtailed unions, increased labor market flexibility, and generally reduced the bargaining power of labor vis-à-vis management (Ffrench-Davis and Raczynski, 1990; and Morley, 1982). In Chile, the government reduced the coverage of the minimum wage, relaxed conditions for dismissal of workers, suspended labor unions, closed the labor courts, limited the permissible activities of labor unions, and encouraged the organization of competitive labor unions within enterprises (Ffrench-Davis and Raczynski, 1990, 8). In Argentina, under the military regimes between 1976 and 1983, union activities were prohibited, and

8 Székely (1998, 69) also points out that there was a sharp decline in the guaranteed price for corn and beans, and that per-hectare yield fell by 25 percent between 1984 and 1989.

wage increases were set by the government. The actions of this new regime, coupled with inflation and the drastic recession after 1982, led to a sharp decline in real wages between 1976 and 1983 (Beccaria, 1991; and Altimir and Beccaria, 1999). These two cases seem somewhat similar to that of Brazil during 1963-80. Brazil had a reforming military government that sharply curtailed labor bargaining power in the context of a successful inflation control program and a first round of tariff reductions. The result was a long period of rapid growth, wage stagnation, and a one-time upward shift in inequality, which has not yet been reversed.

It is impossible at this level to determine what role each of these three factors played, but the combination of recurrent recession, commercial liberalization, and the regime change in the treatment of labor are the best explanations we can find for the one-time upward shift in inequality in these countries. Common to all of them was a fall in the real value of the minimum wage, a rise in the skill-differential, and a reduction in the inflation rate.

Mexico is the other interesting case that experienced a permanent jump in inequality. The timing of this jump is critical; it occurred between 1984 and 1989. Many critics of the reform model have used the observed rise in inequality in Mexico as evidence that the reforms were regressive (Alarcón and McKinley, 1998; Ros and Bouillon, 2001). However, according to the reform indexes in Morley et al. (1999), the main reforms took place under the Salinas administration – that is, after 1989. Therefore, not all the reforms can be blamed for the increase in inequality. Trade reform, however, did start earlier and could be an important factor in rising inequality between 1984 and 1989. But it seems more likely that this increase in inequality was the result of inflation and of government attempts to control it. There was a dramatic spike in inflation during 1987 and 1988, and then a very sharp decline in 1989. Between 1984 and 1989 the real value of the minimum wage fell 31 percent. The increase in inequality, therefore, appears to have been partly due to the increase in the inflation rate, and partly a result of government control over minimum wage adjustments to assist in the fight against inflation. But average wages were roughly constant, consistent with the widening of the skill-differential observed over the period.[9] The rising wage differentials and falling minimum wage increased the dispersion of labor earnings at the same time that it increased the share of profits in total income. As a result, the income share of the top decile rose from 36 percent to 42.5 percent, but all other deciles lost ground between 1984 and 1989. The Gini coefficient rose from .474 to .537, a rise in inequality that has been, so far, permanent.

---

9 Note that Székely (1998) finds a reduction in wage inequality in his recent study, which is inconsistent with the findings of de la Torre (2000). Székely shows that during this period, average real wages were compressed downward for all but the top education class. Wage inequality fell but, at the same time, the gap between those with university education and everyone else widened considerably (*ibid.*, 66).

Inertia in the Distribution

As shown in Table 5.2, income inequality has remained essentially unchanged over the 1990s in a significant number of countries in the region, and in several cases, for even longer periods. In Mexico, Chile, Brazil, and Panama, inequality took a large one-time jump in the 1980s or earlier, and then stayed about constant at the higher level. In Costa Rica and Guatemala, comparable observations are only available from near the end of the 1980s, so we cannot be sure whether inequality had been also constant earlier – and the same is true for Ecuador from 1995 on. But in all these cases, it is significant that the distribution has fluctuated relatively little over fairly long periods.

Of particular interest in all the cases in Table 5.2 where the distribution was constant, or roughly constant, is that the countries were not in severe recession when either the first or the last observation of inequality was made over the 1990s. Such is also the case for Brazil from the 1970s to the 1990s. Thus, these countries must have been close to, or on, their long-run supply curves or production frontiers; therefore, what we are likely observing is the behavior of inequality over the long-run.

Most of the countries in the group had an increase in the skill-differential, and yet, they did not experience an increase in income inequality. How could that situation have developed? When one looks behind the aggregate numbers in different countries, as we did in Morley (2001b), one sees a number of different patterns.[10] In Costa Rica and Brazil, the gain in relative income was at the top. In these countries, the increase in wage gaps at the top tends to widen inequality, a trend just about offset by a reduction in wage gaps at the bottom. In other countries such as Chile, the gains in wages at the top are offset by the increases in the size of the group at the top. All these cases exhibit a rough equivalence between various inequality-increasing and inequality-reducing factors.

This result should not be surprising. First, changes in relative factor prices should be moderate in countries on their long-run growth paths, because demand and supply patterns change slowly in the absence of short-run macro shocks or market interventions – such as those observed in the Southern Cone in the 1960s and 1970s. Second, the econometric results summarized earlier make a strong case that there is some regressive factor that tends to make the distribution more unequal over time. We hypothesized that the regressive factor is skill-intensive growth. This regressive factor partially or totally offsets the positive effects of changes in the education structure that have been occurring at the same time. Countries have reduced the variance in earnings of their poorest members and, in some cases, of their richest members – a progressive stance. But, at the same time,

---

10 See in particular the decomposition of the Theil index of inequality in Morley (2001, Chapter 6).

there has been a widening in the differences in average earnings between education groups – and this is regressive.

Conclusions

We draw the following conclusions from this survey of the experience and the econometric evidence on the determinants of the distribution:

1. For countries on their long-run growth path, there will likely be no big improvements in the distribution of income without the imposition of significant changes in growth strategy. High inequality reflects the region's concentrated ownership of human capital, the relative scarcity of skilled workers, and skill-intensive growth. These trends reflect the characteristics of the growth process and education decisions made in the past. Most countries in the region are now making a concerted effort to raise the education level of young cohorts just entering the labor force. But that process is slow and does little more than just offset the effect of skill-intensive growth. High levels of inequality are likely to continue to be a feature of growth in the region.
2. Macroeconomic conditions or government interventions in the labor market, such as those that occurred in the Southern Cone in the 1960s and 70s, can have an important short- and long-run effect on the distribution. Recessions accompanied by either rising unemployment or falling minimum wages will increase inequality. Very high inflation also likely increased inequality in various countries, mainly, we surmise, through its effect on the real value of the minimum wage and the profit share. The policy implication for Latin America is the emphasis on the importance of getting to, and staying on, a long-run sustainable growth path.
3. The neoliberal reforms seem to have had a slightly regressive effect on inequality, but the effect is small and could even be reversed in the long-run – according to the results of Behrman et al. (2001). There are some cases where inequality increased immediately after the adoption of the reforms, but many more where inequality was constant, or where it declined before rising in the late 1990s.
4. The sectoral characteristics of growth also affect inequality trends. Countries with large backward regions or sectors with weak linkage to leading sectors will have a particularly difficult time reducing inequality as they grow. Governments can help to offset this tendency by supporting construction and agriculture, two sectors that are heavy users of unskilled labor.
5. Our econometric results confirm that investment in education is progressive. But the impact is likely to be small in the short-run, and could easily be completely offset if growth is as skill-intensive as it has been in many countries in the region.

References

Ahluwalia, M. (1976), 'Inequality, Poverty and Development', *Journal of Development Economics*, Vol. 3, pp. 307-42.

Alarcón, D. and T. McKinley (1998), 'Increasing Wage Inequality and Trade Liberalization in Mexico', in A. Berry (ed.), *Poverty, Economic Reform, and Income Distribution in Latin America*, pp. 137-153, Lynne Rienner, Boulder, CO.

Altimir, O. and L. Beccaria (1999), 'Distribución del Ingreso en la Argentina', Serie Reformas Económicas No. 40, ECLAC, Santiago.

Anand, S. and S.M.R. Kanbur (1993), 'The Kuznets Process and the Inequality-Development Relationship', *Journal of Development Economics*, Vol. 40, No. 1 (February), pp. 25-52.

Aristy, J. (2001), 'Liberalización de la Balanza de Pagos: Efectos sobre el Crecimiento, el Empleo y el Bienestar. El Caso de la República Dominicana', in E. Ganuza, R. Paes de Barros, L. Taylor and R. Vos (eds.), *Liberalización, Desigualdad y Pobreza*, Eudeba for UNDP-ECLAC, Santiago.

Barros, R. Paes de, R. Henriques and R. Mendonca (2000), 'A Estabilidade Inaceitavel: Desigualdade e Pobreza no Brasil', in R. Henriques (ed.), *Desigualdade e Pobreza no Brasil*, IPEA, Rio de Janeiro.

Beccaria, L.A (1991), 'Distribucíon del Ingreso en la Argentina: Explorando lo Sucedido desde Mediados de los Setenta', *Desarrollo Económico*, Vol. 31, pp. 320-38.

Behrman, J., N. Birdsall and M. Székely (2001), 'Pobreza, Desigualdad y Liberalización Comercial', in E. Ganuza, R. Paes de Barros, L. Taylor and R. Vos (eds.), *Liberalización, Desigualdad y Pobreza*, Eudeba for UNDP-ECLAC, Santiago.

Berry, A. (ed.) (1998), *Poverty, Economic Reform, and Income Distribution in Latin America*, Lynne Rienner, Boulder, CO.

Bruno, M., M. Ravallion and L. Squire (1996), 'Equity and Growth in Developing Countries: Old and New Perspectives on the Policy Issues', Policy Research Working Paper No. 1563, World Bank, Washington, D.C.

Clarke, G.R.G. (1995), 'More Evidence on Income Distribution and Growth', *Journal of Development Economics*, Vol. 47, No. 2 (August), pp. 403-427.

Deininger, K. and L. Squire (1996), 'A New Data Set Measuring Income Inequality', *World Bank Economic Review*, Vol. 10, No. 3, pp. 565-91.

De Janvry, A. and E. Sadoulet (1999), 'Growth, Poverty and Inequality in Latin America: a Causal Analysis, 1970-94', University of California, mimeo.

De la Torre, R. (2000), 'La Distribución Factorial del Ingreso en el Nuevo Modelo Económico en México', Serie Reformas Económicas No. 58, ECLAC, Santiago.

ECLAC (Economic Commission for Latin America and the Caribbean) (1998), *The Equity Gap: Latin America, the Caribbean and the Social Summit*, ECLAC, Santiago.

ECLAC (Economic Commission for Latin America and the Caribbean) (2001), *Una Década de Luces y Sombras: América Latina y el Caribe en los Años Noventa*, Alfaomega, Bogota.

ECLAC (Economic Commission for Latin America and the Caribbean) (2002), *Economic Survey of Latin America and the Caribbean, 2000-2001*, ECLAC, Santiago.

ECLAC (Economic Commission for Latin America and the Caribbean) (various years), *Social Panorama of Latin America and the Caribbean*, ECLAC, Santiago.

Fields, G. (1994), 'Data for measuring poverty and inequality changes in the developing countries', *Journal of Development Economics*, Vol. 44, No. 1 (June), pp. 87-102.

Ffrench-Davis, R. and D. Raczynski (1990), 'The Impact of Global Recession and National Policies on Living Standards: Chile, 1973-89', CIEPLAN Technical Note No. 97, third edition, CIEPLAN, Santiago.

King, D. and S. Handa (2001), 'Liberalización de la Balanza de Pagos, Pobreza y Distribucíon en Jamaica', in E. Ganuza, R. Paes de Barros, L. Taylor and R. Vos (eds.), *Liberalización, Desigualdad y Pobreza*, Eudeba for UNDP-ECLAC, Santiago.

Kuznets, S. (1955), 'Economic Growth and Income Inequality', *American Economic Review*, Vol. 45, No. 1, pp. 1-28.

Londoño, J.L. and M. Székely (1997), 'Sorpresas Distributivas después de una Década de Reformas: América Latina en los Noventa', Research Department Working Paper No. 352, Inter-American Development Bank, Washington, D.C.

Lora, E. (1998), 'Una Década de Reformas Estructurales en América Latina: Qué se Ha Reformado y Cómo Medirlo', *Pensamiento Iberoamericano*, special issue.

Lora, E. (2001), 'Las Reformas Estructurales en América Latina: Qué se Ha Reformado y Cómo Medirlo', Research Department Working Paper No. 462, Inter-American Development Bank, Washington, D.C.

Mejía, J.A. and R. Vos (1997), 'Poverty in Latin America and the Caribbean: An Inventory, 1980-95', Integration and Regional Programs Department Working Paper No. 1-4, Inter-American Development Bank, Washington, D.C.

Morley, S.A. (1982), *Labor Markets and Inequitable Growth: the Case of Authoritarian Capitalism in Brazil*, Cambridge University Press, New York.

Morley, S.A. (1995), *Poverty and Inequality in Latin America*, Johns Hopkins, Baltimore.

Morley, S.A. (2000), 'The Effects of Growth and Economic Reform on Income Distribution in Latin America', *CEPAL Review*, No. 71 (August), pp. 23-40.

Morley, S.A. (2001a), 'Rural Poverty in Paraguay', Report prepared for the World Bank poverty assessment, mimeo.

Morley, S.A. (2001b), *The Distribution Problem in Latin America*, ECLAC, Santiago.

Morley, S.A., R. Machado and S. Pettinato (1999), 'Indexes of Structural Reform in Latin America', Serie Reformas Económicas No. 12, ECLAC, Santiago.

Ravallion, M. and S. Chen (1997), 'What Can New Survey Data Tell Us about Recent Changes in Distribution and Poverty?' *World Bank Economic Review*, Vol. 11, No. 2, pp. 357-82.

Robbins, D. (1995), 'Trade, Trade Liberalization and Inequality in Latin America and East Asia: Synthesis of Seven Country Studies', Harvard Institute for International Development, mimeo.

Ros, J. and C. Bouillon (2001), 'La Liberalización de la Balanza de Pagos en México: Efectos en el Crecimiento, la Desigualdad y la Pobreza', in E. Ganuza, R. Paes de Barros, L. Taylor and R. Vos (eds.), *Liberalización, Desigualdad y Pobreza*, Eudeba for UNDP-ECLAC, Santiago.

Saavedra, J. and J.J. Díaz (1999), 'Desigualidad del Ingreso y del Gasto en el Perú antes y después de las Reformas Estructurales', Serie Reformas Económicas No. 34, ECLAC, Santiago.

Székely, M. (1998), *The Economics of Poverty, Inequality and Wealth Accumulation in Mexico*, St. Martins Press, New York.

Székely, M. (2001), 'The 1990s in Latin America: Another Decade of Persistent Inequality but with Somewhat Lower Poverty', Research Department Working Paper No. 454, Inter-American Development Bank, Washington, D.C.

Székely, M. and M. Hilgert (1999), 'The 1990s in Latin America: Another Decade of Persistent Inequality', Research Department Working Paper No. 410, Inter-American Development Bank, Washington, D.C.

World Bank (1995), *Argentina's Poor: A Profile*, World Bank Report No. 3318-AR, The World Bank, Washington, D.C.

Chapter 6

Distributive Tensions under the New Economic Order[1]

Oscar Altimir

Introduction

The emerging world order may evolve in such a way as to foster the social and economic advancement of the populations of Latin America. However, current social structures suggest that the path to a rosy economic future may be fraught with tensions inherent in distributive polarization that challenge social cohesion in the region.

Why concern ourselves with income inequality in the midst of absolute poverty? The demand for equity is increasing, partly driven by the ongoing process of globalization. This demand for greater equity not only focuses on the elevation of the poor to the threshold of dignity, but also on their greater inclusion in society, social mobility, equal opportunity, and a reduction in unsavory social distances. This greater demand for equity is also encouraged by cross-section studies showing that long-term inequality is detrimental to investment and growth (Alesina and Perotti, 1996; Alesina and Rodrik, 1994; Birdsall et al., 1996; Aghion et al., 1999).

Latin America has traditionally been a land of inequality. The countries of the region are among the most socially unequal in the world, the majority of them having income-concentration indexes well above the world average and much higher than those in industrialized countries, Eastern Europe, and Asia (IDB, 1999). This chapter, however, is concerned only with those Latin American countries that became semi-industrialized or substantially modernized during the post-war period, including the less-inegalitarian countries of Argentina, Costa Rica and Uruguay. The opinions and concerns expressed here reflect a perception that the roots of inequality and the conditions for integration into the global economy are different for these countries than for other Latin American countries, less industrialized and with inequality and poverty rooted in ancient agrarian conditions.

---

1 This paper was presented at the conference in honor of Albert Berry organized by the University of Toronto in April 2002. The author wishes to express his recognition to an anonymous commentator for many helpful comments.

Although the evolution of inequality has followed different paths in all of these countries, none of them has led to lesser inequality. In all these countries, the distributive effects of post-war development, of the crises of the eighties, and of liberalization and reform, are discernible, though not always apparent. These trends in the distribution of income, combined with the different growth records, have determined different long-term paths of absolute poverty. The next section provides evidence of the evolution of both the distributive and the deprivation dimensions of that inequality using two indexes: the Gini coefficient of the distribution of current income for social inequality, and the incidence of income poverty for human deprivation. The evidence, however, is taken from household surveys which neither capture the whole range of incomes from production, nor capital gains or the real income effects of abrupt changes in prices, nor the effects of in-kind social expenditure.

Ascertaining the effects of economic reforms on income distribution is a difficult task, especially if we fail to specify the types of effects under consideration, namely: (i) the proximate impacts of the adoption of reforms; (ii) the effects during the transitional period from the old order to the new; or (iii) the change to a new and relatively stable distributive pattern under the conditions of the new economic order. The third section reviews some outstanding exercises that attempt to measure what may transpire to be (i) and (ii). The fourth section speculates about possible relevant distributive trends that may prevail under the conditions of the evolving process of globalization. The fifth and last section explores challenges to social cohesion emerging from income-distribution tensions in countries subject to the new economic order, and strategic choices open to public policy with the aim of compensating losers and helping winners to live harmoniously in the globalized world of tomorrow.

It is tempting to declare the imminent demise of globalization at times of growing skepticism over it, and focus again on national strategies for development. The latter are central, but to be effective they must still be designed for a context of increasing globalization; they must heed not the globalization panacea of the enthusiast, but the ever growing importance of global networks and arenas and the progressive fading of national borders.

The Long-Term Evolution of Inequality and Poverty

Country Trends of Inequality

Inequality in each of the countries considered has passed through different phases but, over the last half century, has tended to increase in a convergent way since the more egalitarian countries – Argentina, Costa Rica, and Uruguay – grew more

Figure 6.1: Probable Evolution of Inequality in Latin America, Income Per Capita Gini, Selected Countries, 1950-2000

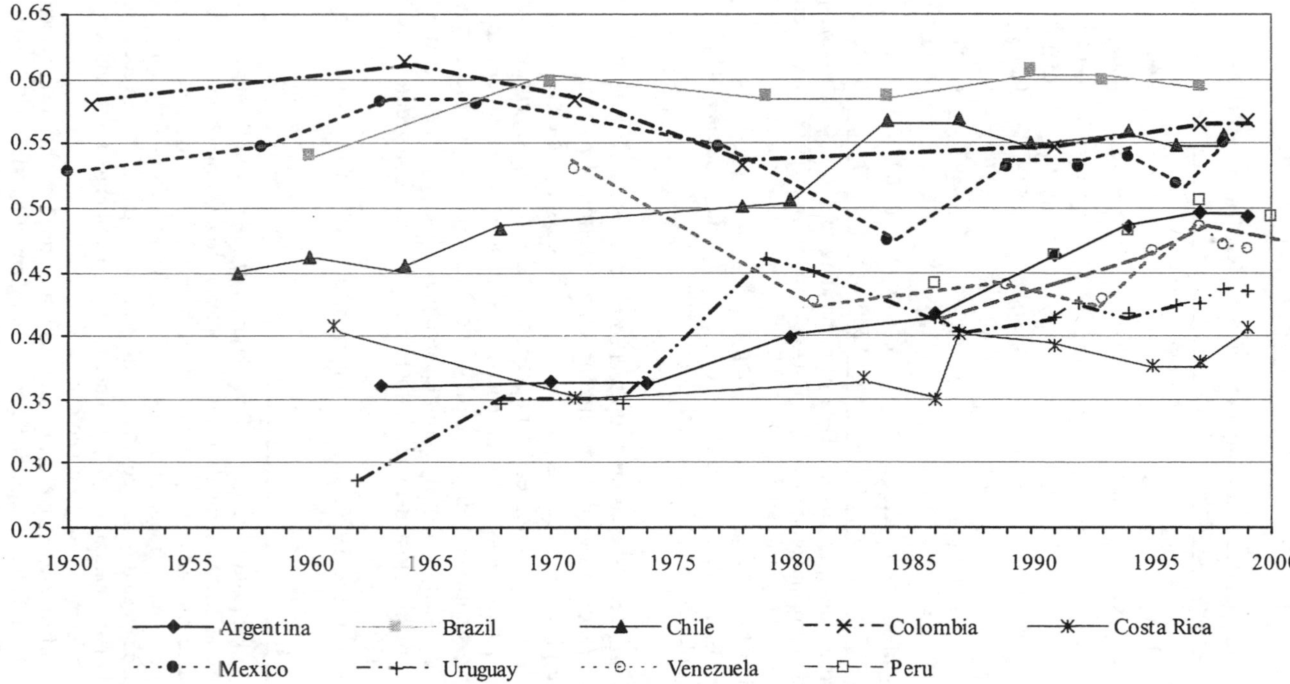

Source: Author's estimates, based on chaining selected pairs of comparable measurements (see Table 7.1).

Table 6.1: Comparative Inequality in Latin America, Gini Coefficient, Selected Countries

Country	First observation		1980	1991	1999
	Year	Value			
Argentina (Urban)	1963	0.361	0.398	0.463	0.494
Brazil	1960	0.541	0.587 [a]	0.607 [b]	0.595 [c]
Chile	1957	0.450	0.506	0.550 [b]	0.556 [d]
Colombia	1951	0.580	0.533 [e]	0.548	0.567
Costa Rica	1961	0.408	0.367 [f]	0.392	0.407
Mexico	1950	0.529	0.548 [g]	0.531 [h]	0.550 [d]
Peru	1986	0.442	...	0.464	0.493 [i]
Uruguay (Urban)	1962	0.286	0.460 [a]	0.415	0.435
Venezuela	1971	0.530	0.427 [j]	0.440	0.468

[a] Data corresponding to 1979. [b] Data corresponding to 1990. [c] Data corresponding to 1997. [d] Data corresponding to 1998. [e] Data corresponding to 1978. [f] Data corresponding to 1983. [g] Data corresponding to 1977. [h] Data corresponding to 1989. [i] Data corresponding to 2000. [j] Data corresponding to 1981.

Sources: For Brazil, Chile, Costa Rica, Peru, Uruguay and Venezuela: Altimir (1997); for Argentina, Colombia and Mexico: Altimir (1996).

unequal (Figure 6.1).[2] Evolution up to 1980 had been heterogeneous: unequalizing growth in Brazil and Chile; an encouraging inverted-U pattern in Colombia and Mexico; a phase of decreasing inequality in Costa Rica and Venezuela; and increased inequality after early liberalizing reforms in Argentina and Uruguay. During the 1980s, inequality increased in almost all countries of the region, the only clear exceptions being Uruguay and Mexico.[3] While the concentration of income had been generally counter-cyclical (Morley, 1995), most countries emerged from the 'lost decade' with levels of inequality greater than in the pre-crisis period (Table 6.1).

Evolution in the 1990s did not improve the picture. In Argentina, Colombia,

2 Trends in inequality are assessed on the basis of the data in Figure 6.1 and Table 6.1. These are author's estimates, obtained for each country by chaining selected pairs of comparable measurements considered of acceptable quality, and linking them to a benchmark measurement of inequality in the distribution of per capita income. Years have been selected, when possible, corresponding to periods when the economies were close to their potential output, in order to appreciate long-term trends, devoid as far as possible of significant cyclical components.

3 The case of Mexico, however, is not easily interpretable. The measurement for 1984 – just in the middle of the stabilization program after the debt crisis – reveals a significantly lower inequality than in 1977, while in 1989 –after four years of falling real incomes – the distribution appears to have deteriorated almost to the level of the late 1970s (Altimir, 1994).

Table 6.2: Long-Term Evolution of Poverty in 4 Latin American Countries

Year	Indexes of poverty incidence: Constant PL [a]	Indexes of poverty incidence: Shifting PL [b]	P(0) (% households): Constant PL [a]	P(0) (% households): Shifting PL [b]
	Argentina (Urban) (Index 1980 = 100)			
1953	17	...	2	...
1961	18	...	2	...
1963	23	...	3	...
1970	55	...	4	...
1975	43	...	3	...
1980	100	...	7	...
1986	171	...	12	...
1994	171	...	12	...
1997	214	...	15	...
	Colombia (National) (Index 1988 = 100)			
1938	169	151	86	77
1951	157	141	80	72
1964	149	135	76	69
1971	124	112	63	57
1978	108	192	55	52
1988	100	100	51	51
1993	84	...	43	...
1994	92	96	47	49
1997	88	100	45	51

Year	Indexes of poverty incidence: Constant PL [a]	Indexes of poverty incidence: Shifting PL [b]	P(0) (% households): Constant PL [a]	P(0) (% households): Shifting PL [b]
	Chile (Urban) (Index 1987 = 100)			
1957	136	96	47	36
1960	125	91	43	35
1968	76	61	26	23
1978	131	113	45	43
1980	108	97	37	37
1987	100	100	38	38
1990	87	...	33	...
1992	73	87	28	33
1994	58	...	23	...
1996	50	...	19	...
1998	45	...	17	...
	Mexico (National) (Index 1984 =100)			
1950	212	157	72	53
1963	177	137	60	47
1967	148	118	50	40
1977	112	100	38	34
1984	100	100	34	34
1994	114	...	36	...
1998	116	...	38	...

[a] ECLAC poverty lines for 1988 updated for price changes. [b] Poverty lines were shifted according to a 0.5 elasticity with respect to real GDP per capita, except for periods of recession, when constancy (i.e. zero elasticity) was assumed.

Source: Altimir (2001).

Peru,[4] and Venezuela, social equity continued to deteriorate; in Brazil, Chile, and Costa Rica, inequality remained approximately at the high levels already attained in their respective historical trends; and in Mexico and Uruguay, social inequality began to increase again.

4 Data available for Peru does not allow for estimating a series of comparable measurements farther back than 1986.

Poverty Trends

In the long-run, despite phases of enhanced inequality, the incidence of absolute poverty tended to decline in most countries as a by-product of growth – except in Argentina, where the effect of rising inequality prevailed, spreading poverty in a society previously almost poverty-free (Table 6.2). However, a caveat should be applied against invariant absolute poverty lines for long periods, heedless of the fact that the rise in incomes changes lifestyles, the latter being the context for poverty norms (Altimir, 2001). Taking this fact into consideration, the application of an income elasticity to poverty lines makes poverty reductions appear less spectacular but still significant. In Chile, the trend towards poverty abatement, interrupted in the 1980s, was restored in the 1990s, reducing poverty incidence to unprecedented levels. In Colombia and Mexico, post-war economic growth and U-shaped evolution of inequality halved the pervasive poverty of the 1950s, although progress did not continue into the 1990s.

Current ECLAC estimates show increased poverty resulting from the recession and inflation of the 1980s, particularly in the urban areas where an additional 5 to 10 percent of households became poor. Estimates also show contrasting performances on the poverty front in the 1990s: abatement to unprecedented levels in Brazil, Chile, Costa Rica, Peru, and Uruguay; smaller reductions in Argentina, Colombia and Mexico; and continuing grave poverty in Venezuela (Table 6.3).

Effects of Liberalization and Reforms on Income Distribution and Poverty

Globalization and the Change of Development Style in Latin America

The post-World War II style of development[5] prevailing in Latin America was characterized by a growth dynamic based on (i) the export of natural resources in which these countries had traditionally enjoyed comparative advantages; (ii) industrialization protected from external competition and oriented to the domestic market; (iii) expansion and diversification of consumption; and (iv) the sustained

---

5 The notion of 'style of development' is used here in its positive sense, as the stylized configuration of actual processes of growth and change systemically interrelated in a given society – as used by Pinto (1976) and Altimir (1990) – and not in the normative sense in which it has been sometimes used – for example, by Wolfe (1976) – referring to the characteristics of development 'preferred' by different social groups and representing optative patterns of development and types of society attainable by means of appropriate strategies and policies. On the other hand, 'style of development,' in that positive and factual sense, is preferred here to the related notion (blueprint) of 'development model' because of its wider – societal beyond the economic – focus, its more empirical than paradigmatic characterization and, thereby, its more open-ended implications.

Table 6.3: Poverty Incidence in Latin America, Selected Countries, c. 1980s and 1990s, Percent of Households

		Households below the poverty line [a]					Households below the indigence line				
			Urban areas					Urban areas			
Country	Year	Country total	Total	Metrop. area	Other urban	Rural areas	Country total	Total	Metrop. area	Other urban	Rural areas
Argentina	1980	9	7	5	9	16	2	2	1	2	4
	1990	...	...	16	...	...	...	...	4	...	...
	1999	...	16	13	21	...	...	4	3	6	...
Brazil [b]	1979	39	30	21	34	62	17	10	6	12	35
	1990	41	36	...	...	64	18	13	...	...	38
	1999	30	26	...	...	45	10	7	...	...	21
Chile [c]	1987	39	38	33	41	45	14	14	11	15	17
	1990	33	33	28	37	34	11	10	8	11	12
	1998	18	17	12	19	23	5	4	3	5	7
Colombia	1980	...	36	30	37	45	...	13	10	14	22
	1991 [d]	50	47	39	50	55	23	17	14	18	31
	1999 [d]	49	45	38	47	56	23	19	17	19	31
Costa Rica	1981	22	16	15	17	28	6	5	5	6	8
	1990	24	22	20	25	25	10	7	5	9	12
	1999	18	16	15	17	21	8	5	5	6	9
Mexico	1984	34	28	... [e]	... [e]	45	11	7	... [e]	... [e]	20
	1989	39	34	...	...	49	14	9	...	...	23
	1998	38	31	...	...	49	13	7	...	...	24

Table 6.3 (cont.): Poverty Incidence in Latin America, Selected Countries, c. 1980s and 1990s, Percent of Households

		Households below the poverty line [a]					Households below the indigence line				
			Urban areas					Urban areas			
Country	Year	Country total	Total	Metrop. area	Other urban	Rural areas	Country total	Total	Metrop. area	Other urban	Rural areas
Peru	1979	46	35	29	41	65	21	12	9	15	37
	1986	52	45	37	53	64	25	16	11	22	39
	1997 [f]	37	25	...	...	61	18	7	...	...	41
Uruguay	1981	11	9	6	13	21	3	2	1	3	7
	1990	...	12	7	17	...	...	2	1	3	...
	1999	...	6	6	5	...	...	1	1	1	...
Venezuela	1981	22	18	12	20	35	7	5	3	6	15
	1990	34	33	25	36	38	12	11	7	12	17
	1999	44	...	...	...	...	19	...	...	...	...
Latin America [g]	1980	35	25	...	...	54	15	9	...	...	28
	1990	41	35	...	...	58	18	12	...	...	34
	1999	35	30	...	...	54	14	9	...	...	31

[a] Includes households below the indigence line or in extreme poverty. [b] Average of the figures for Rio de Janeiro and Sao Paulo. [c] Calculations based on national social-economics surveys (CASEN) from 1987, 1990 and 1998. [d] From 1993, sample one the geographic cover of the survey to include the totality of the urban population of the country and the rural population. [e] The sample is too small to make estimates for the Federal District. [f] Figure provided by the National Institute of Statistics and Informatics (INEI), based on the National Household Survey (ENAHO) for the fourth quarter of 1995. [g] Estimate for 19 countries of the region.

Source: ECLAC, Social Panorama (various years).

growth of public expenditure aimed at progressively establishing *sui generis* systems of social protection and financing overall strategic investments. In doing so, an extensive bureaucracy was established to facilitate relevant state activism and absorb an increasing middle-class population that the expanding private sector could not fully incorporate.

Public indebtedness, the challenges of deepening industrialization, increasing overall resistance to the inward-looking-state-centered strategy, and the triple external shock – terms of trade deterioration, higher international interest rates, and capital-flow reversal – that precipitated the payment crisis of the 1980s, all ended by knocking off the post-war style of development and by favoring the adoption of reforms to move the economic order towards unregulated markets, private investment, and more integration into the international economy. At the same time, ongoing globalization processes and the changing rules of international trade also put into question the post-war development strategy and favored regime change.

Multiple Effects of Reforms

Numerous contributions have identified the effects of economic reforms – or merely trade liberalization – on growth, but few have considered the effects of the reforms on income distribution and poverty. However, the two research approaches are inter-dependent. Reforms aim to build a new economic order and, hence, setting them up implies overhauling the mechanisms of income generation, income appropriation, and capital accumulation, bringing about abrupt changes in relative prices and changes in taxation and subsidies. On the other hand, reforms are intended to enhance growth by a more efficient allocation of resources and, therefore – other things being equal – to mitigate income poverty. The expectations concerning the effects of reforms on income distribution are less clear: on the one hand, opening up the economy favors unskilled labor through a Heckscher-Ohlin mechanism; on the other, it weakens the old ISI linkage between wages and demand, replacing it with an adverse linkage between export-led growth and wages. Moreover, the adoption of new-age technologies may create higher skill wage-differentials until education and training substantially shift the supply of higher skills – and provided that the demand for lower skills does not fall enough to offset this improvement.

An ambitious multi-year project was undertaken by ECLAC, with the collaboration of local researchers, to analyze structural reforms and their multiple impacts on nine Latin American economies (Stallings and Peres, 2000). A comparison of data from the pre- (1950-80) and post-crisis (1990s) periods reveals mixed achievements in these economies (Table 6.4). By the end of the 1990s, all these economies had recovered the levels of investment and productivity lost in the 1980s, some economies now performing even better than before the crisis. However, new and efficient investments were concentrated in a few technologically-matured sectors facing falling terms of trade, and whose rates of

Table 6.4: Relationship between Reforms and Outcomes in the 1990s, Selected Latin American Countries

Country	Reforms	Investment [a]	Productivity [b]	Growth [c]	Employment [d]	Equity [e]
Argentina	Aggressive	=	+	+	–	–
Brazil	Cautious	–	–	–	–	+
Chile	Aggressive	+	+	+	+	+
Colombia	Cautious	+	–	–	–	–
Costa Rica	Cautious	+	–	–	+	+
Mexico	Cautious	=	–	–	+	–
Peru	Aggressive	=	+	+	–	+

[a] Investment: + means that a country had a higher investment coefficient in the 1990s than in the base period (1950–80); – means that it had a lower coefficient; = means there was little change. [b] Productivity: + means that growth of total factor productivity was higher in the 1990s than in the base period (1950–80); – means that it was lower; = means there was little change. [c] Growth: + means that a country grew faster in the 1990s than in the base period (1950–80); – means that it grew more slowly. [d] Employment: + means that the country ranked high on the labor market index; – means than it ranked low; = means that there was little change. [e] Equity: + means that primary income distribution in the latest available year was more equal than the pre-reform period; – means that it was less equal; = means that there was little change.

Source: Stallings and Peres (2000).

return are expected to be lower than before the reforms. Given these facts, a significant increase in growth in the near future is not likely and, therefore, unemployment rates might remain high, aggravating inequality.

Hurdles in Method of Assessment

Difficulties are anticipated in properly assessing the income-distribution impact of the reforms and of the first phase of operation of the economy under the new economic order. A clear distinction is required with respect to (i) the distributive impact during the period immediately after the adoption of the reforms; (ii) distributive changes during the transitional phase from the old to the new paradigm, which may be represented as a 'disruption' lasting several years; and (iii) the distributive structure that may prevail under the new economic order.

Next, an appropriate measurement system must be adopted, the most accessible being the 'before and after' (the reforms) analysis at the country level. This approach requires the identification of 'normal' years so as to disentangle the most patent cyclical – possibly transient – disturbances.[6] However, this approach does

6 It should be noted that, in addition to cyclical fluctuations, income distributions obtained from continuous surveys usually fluctuate around the cycle on a monthly basis, in what

not allow for the controlling of other variables, which can only be observed in parallel, in a 'proto-econometric' way.

Econometric modeling is impractical at the country level, because of insufficient observations; if feasible, it would require considering explicitly the change of regime implicit in the adoption of the new economic order. Econometric modeling at the regional – or even world – level, pooling countries and periods, overcomes the limitation of insufficient observations. However, in the extreme case, different-quality data may be pooled. On the other hand, if the econometric model at the regional or world level does not properly identify relevant periods, the impact of the entire change of regime may be smoothed out.

Computable general equilibrium models can be an appropriate tool for capturing the complete effects of reforms. However, the estimation of functions depends too much on past performance, and calibrating procedures depend too much on hypotheses, for that approach to be effective.

Micro-simulation techniques, country-wise, are a new tool for quantifying the effect of changes in employment, or personal variables, on income distribution. However, a problem is envisaged in tracing back the origin of those changes to policy or institutional changes.

Studies on the Impact of Reforms on Income Distribution

In a pioneering project, Berry (1998) analyzed the accumulating evidence showing that the shift towards a market-friendly economic model is 'systematically associated with an abrupt and significant deterioration in income distribution' (p. 9). After reviewing the distribution record of the region and the evidence from 10 countries, Berry concluded that, by the mid-1990s, (i) distribution had worsened significantly in most countries undertaking market-friendly reforms; (ii) beyond this close association, no definitive conclusions could be derived by simply comparing countries' experiences concerning what drives this increase in inequality; (iii) 'neither theory nor the record has provided much evidence on how lasting the negative distributional effects would turn out to be' (p. 36); and (iv) the urgency for achieving better combinations of growth and distribution.

Complementing these findings, Altimir (1994) examined the changes in income distribution and poverty in the 1980s and early 1990s in ten Latin American countries, as well as macroeconomic and labor market conditions, in a 'proto-econometric' attempt to catalogue the association of distributive changes with the processes of adjustment and policy reform in each country. He explored different macroeconomic phases on the assumption that different relationships could prevail between distributive changes and macroeconomic variables during instability and inflation, recession, and recovery and growth close to the production frontier. The

may be a random walk that introduces some uncertainty associated with the period of the year selected for analysis.

analysis concluded that, while income concentration has been countercyclical during the lost decade of the 1980s as noted by Morley (1995), (i) the phase of external adjustment produced more inequality in some cases than in others; (ii) the phase of recovery after external adjustment in most cases did not bring improvement in the distribution; and (iii) the positive effects of disinflation and recovery were not as intense as the negative effects of high inflation and recession. As a consequence, in most countries that completed recovery after the adoption of economic reforms in the early 1990s, and that initiated growth along a path close to potential output, income inequality was higher than at the start of the 1980s (Altimir, 1997).

Londoño and Székely (1997) studied pooled national data for the region from 1970 to 1995 and concluded that (i) in spite of recovery and stability, poverty and inequality had not declined significantly in the 1990s in the region as a whole; and (ii) with a common stable macroeconomic environment, inequality and poverty was sharply reduced in the 1970s, while the reforming period did not exhibit distributive progress.

Further, Robbins (1996) has presented evidence that trade liberalization has contributed to more skill wage-differentials in Argentina, Chile, Costa Rica, and some Asian countries. Spilimbergo et al. (1997) postulated that the effects of trade openness on inequality depend on factor endowments in a manner inconsistent with the simple Heckscher-Ohlin framework since, for a given endowment of factors, trade openness is associated with greater inequality.

Morley (2000) proposed a model for the distribution of household income in Latin America as a function of the following: income; a vector of distributional relevant variables, such as education or land distribution; a vector index of economic reforms;[7] a vector of dummies reflecting sample characteristics; and a trend.[8] Based on 261 observations in 16 countries between 1960 and 1997,[9] the estimates of the model reveal a regressive – albeit not significant – effect of reforms on income distribution. However, Morley's model accounts for only the direct impact of reforms on inequality, ignoring their contributions to enhanced growth and inflation abatement, as happened in instances in the early 1990s.[10] On

7 Developed by Lora and Barrera (1997) and modified and extended by Morley et al. (1999).

8 The specification of the model allows for the representation of a Kuznets relationship between inequality and income, and for testing whether that relationship shifts over time.

9 However, only 57 observations correspond to the 1960s and 1970s, so the results are mostly representative of the 1980s and 1990s. It should also be noted that pooling data provided by different authors from the same survey enhances the importance of that survey, and of its eventual bias, on the sample, while pooling Ginis for different concepts of income artificially increases the variance.

10 Escaith and Morley (2001) have estimated the effect of the same reforms on economic growth, showing that the average reform index did not have a significant effect on the

the other hand, different reforms produce various offsetting effects on the distribution; in particular, trade and tax reforms have statistically significant regressive effects, while capital account liberalization is judged to be progressive. These results are robust, whereas those for privatization and domestic financial liberalization are either ambiguous or not significant.

Behrman, Birdsall, and Székely (2000) estimated the impact of economic reforms on wage differentials by education level, based on 79 observations in 18 Latin American countries during 1980-98, using the same index of reforms as Morley's. They devised a strategy that yields direct estimates on whether the impact of reforms is a function of education, and incorporated the timing of reforms by experimenting with the independent variables alternatively lagged from 1 to 8 years. The impact of the overall reform effort on wage differentials was found to be regressive and statistically significant for both the difference between university and secondary education and that between university and primary, but the magnitude of the impact declines as the lags of the reform variable increase. However, the explanatory power of this unique model is low, though the explanation of the variance improves (close to R-square 0.2) when the five different reform indexes are considered separately. Capital account liberalization and tax reform have strong, statistically significant, regressive impacts; the impact of liberalization decreases with time, while the effect of tax reform does not decrease when lagged. The authors interpret that 'trade liberalization *per se* has not widened wage gaps. On the contrary, trade reform reduces wage gaps with some lag (although not significantly).' However, their results are ambiguous: trade openness weakly increases the high/secondary education gap, an impact that decreases when lagged; it reduces (also weakly) the high/primary education gap, an effect that also tends to decrease and disappear when lagged.

An ambitious ECLAC/UNDP project of comparative analysis of the post-liberalization performance of 17 Latin American and Caribbean countries approached the problem from multiple sides: 'before and after' country analysis, decomposition of aggregate demand, employment and productivity, some counterfactual policy simulations in CGE models, and micro-simulations to assess the impact of labor market changes on income distribution (Ganuza, Paes de Barros, Taylor and Vos, 2001). The focus of the analysis was the effects of liberalization of the balance of payments on inequality – although the effects of other reforms were also considered in the country studies.

Following is a summary – for the countries considered here – of the main findings of a complex and rich set of analyses:

---

growth rate, because the various components of the reform package had different and sometimes opposing effects. In particular, trade liberalization and openness tend to negatively affect the rate of growth, holding all other factors constant, although this result is neither statistically significant nor robust to alternative specifications.

(i) The dominant macroeconomic feature of reforms in the 1990s has been the stop-and-go cycles caused by the massive inflow of capital and its eventual slowdown. In Chile and Costa Rica, exports provided an engine of growth. In Chile, Mexico, and Brazil, investment also contributed to demand expansion. In the other countries, aggregate demand was driven – up or down – by private consumption or debt-financed government spending (Taylor and Vos, 2001, Table 3).

(ii) With the exception of Argentina, the 'before and after' analysis shows that liberalization has brought about only modest aggregate productivity increases, although greater in traded than in non-traded goods sectors. These aggregate outcomes have been largely determined by within-sector productivity shifts and output growth, little influenced by shifts from low-productivity to high-productivity activities (Vos, 2002).[11]

(iii) Inequality of primary incomes increased in almost all countries in most spells during the 1990s (Taylor and Vos, 2001, Table 1).

(iv) Skill income-differentials increased in almost all countries and periods.[12]

(v) The effects of trade liberalization on inequality were approximated by means of a micro-simulation approach, assuming that all changes in labor market conditions are a consequence of trade liberalization.[13] Only in Brazil and Chile has the simulated effect of liberalization reduced inequality, while in Argentina, Colombia, Costa Rica, Mexico, and Uruguay, liberalization enhanced it.[14] On the other hand, of the different labor market variables considered, changes in remuneration is the most influential in most countries (Ganuza, Paes de Barros and Vos, 2001).[15]

(vi) Sectoral adjustment has promoted the adoption of more skill-intensive

---

11 In fact, the most significant employment reallocation effects have been in the other direction, towards low productivity agriculture – as in Mexico – or the urban informal sector.

12 Only in Chile (1992-97), Brazil (1994-97), and Uruguay (1986-90) did skills income-differentials narrow (Taylor and Vos, 2001, Table 1).

13 Thus, if simulating the impact of changes in participation rates, unemployment, employment structure, remuneration structure and remuneration levels on inequality at the household level results in smaller inequality than the observed one, the inference would be that liberalization has produced greater inequality than the one that would have emerged without the reforms (or conversely).

14 However, the magnitude of the difference between simulated values and observed values is, in many cases, smaller than 3 percent and, in a number of instances, smaller than 1 percent. Although no interpretation can be ascribed to the magnitude of the difference (beyond the estimation of confidence intervals), it becomes clear that the effect of trade liberalization itself might have been smaller than that of other reforms, as shown by Morley (2000).

15 However, similar analysis for Argentina reveals that the main variable pushing for higher inequality of earnings in 1990-94 is the extension of unemployment (Altimir et al., 2002).

technologies in many instances, unskilled workers being forced into unemployment or the informal sector (Vos, 2002).

Inequality and Poverty under the New Economic Order

Institutional reforms do not represent a simple change of the game rules by the authorities, nor merely a shift in official strategy. Reforms constitute a realignment of the economic order in which societies function and advance. Therefore, the adoption of reforms affects how the new economic order functions, as well as the forces that mold the distribution of income. But the time required for these changes to play themselves out is long and the outcome is uncertain. Although the adoption of reforms may be swift and sweeping, consolidating a new development style – not necessarily the blueprint envisaged by the reformers – will take considerable time and may even require complex negotiation at cross-roads.[16]

These considerations favor a long-term view and help sort out which forces will represent strong distributive tensions to the emerging development model tied to globalization. Those tensions will emerge from hard-to-change structural features of these more developed Latin American economies.

Even though the introduction of reforms might have had an unequalizing effect, the normal functioning and long-term expansion of the economies in the new economic order may, perhaps, correct that outcome, or alternatively may aggravate inequality. The change of regime negates the extrapolation of past trends; therefore, we must to some extent speculate about possible distributive consequences of emerging changes or, at the very least, about identifying strong structural tensions on the distributive front. Only Chile, where the economic order was reformed a quarter of a century ago, stands out as a peculiar case study, for which the global insertion has nevertheless changed.

It is possible that integration of the more advanced Latin American countries into the global economy offers the prospect of accelerating growth and the creation of good jobs. Let us, therefore, first look at the long-term picture of convergence-divergence with respect to the developed world, the recent changes in the patterns of specialization, the record of productivity and technical change under the new economic order, and the picture of productive heterogeneity within our economies, with the purpose to looking at these issues in the context of technological progress in the global arena.

---

16 That is clearly the case of Argentina's present predicament, a decade after the adoption of reforms. Chile may have achieved such a consolidation, when the first democratic government ratified the economic reforms adopted by the authoritarian regime a decade and a half earlier, while managing at the same time to inject additional resources into social policy. In the case of Brazil, the introduction of reforms has been more gradual and has proceeded via a constitutional mandate to enhance social expenditure.

Table 6.5: Relative Levels of per Capita GDP, 1950-1998, International 1990 Dollars, U.S. = 100

	1950	1973	1990	1998
Argentina	52	48	28	34
Brazil	17	23	21	20
Chile	40	31	28	36
Colombia	23	21	21	19
Mexico	25	29	26	24
Peru	24	24	13	13
Venezuela	78	64	36	33
Korea	8	17	37	49
Taiwan	10	25	43	58
Spain	25	52	53	52
France	55	79	78	72
Germany	41	72	69	65
Netherlands	63	78	74	74
Japan	20	69	81	75
UK	72	72	71	68
USA	100	100	100	100

Source: Maddison (2001).

Lack of Convergence

One way to evaluate the long-term economic performance of developing countries is to see whether their *per capita* income – or the productivity on which it is based – *converges* to the income levels of developed countries.[17] This view is particularly germane to the appraisal of the benefits of globalization, since they are expected on the basis of neoclassical predictions.

Since 1950, growth rates in Latin America have been lower than those in South East Asia and Western Europe and close to those of the United States and the United Kingdom, which were the 'laggards' of the developed world, having the highest per capita income by the end of World War II. As a consequence, Latin America's growth shows, on average, neither convergence nor divergence compared with that of the richest countries of the world, although even the best performers of the region trailed the European countries, which were catching up to the U.S. and the U.K. at the time. However, growth in Brazil and Mexico significantly converged between 1950 and the 1970s, while in Chile, it diverged in the same period; subsequently, the whole region declined in the 1980s, and only Chile and Argentina reconverged in the 1990s (Table 6.5) – though Argentina later

17 This notion of convergence corresponds to that of the *absolute convergence* of capital/labor of poor countries to rich countries, and not to that of the *conditional convergence* of countries to their steady-state equilibrium.

plunged into a recession still affecting the economy in 2003.

The gaps in productivity with respect to developed countries – as measured by GDP per hour worked – were slightly smaller because of demographic factors – e.g., lower rates of working-age population, of female participation in the labor force, and of employment – and lower labor inputs per capita, but they followed approximately the same pattern of long-term lack of convergence, and in Argentina, Peru, and Venezuela, even divergence in the second half of the 20th century.

Factor Endowment and Factor Mobility

Globalization is enhancing the mobility of productive factors and the size of product markets. However, the international mobility of different factors is developing at different speeds: financial capital has become extremely mobile; physical capital is mobile to the extent that transnational corporations' overseas direct investment changes geographical localization more easily; and even technology flows faster, becoming increasingly mobile within proprietary bounds – depending on countries' absorptive capacities and skilled labor supply. Unskilled labor is still immobile internationally, although it increasingly pushes the immigration barriers raised by developed countries, and natural resources keep immobile beyond transboundary operations.

The more developed Latin American countries are richer in natural resources than in unskilled labor. Moreover, the opening up of China to international trade has shifted comparative advantages away from unskilled labor in the rest of the world. Therefore, these countries' static comparative advantages have moved further towards natural resources, while any advantages based on medium- and high-skill labor have yet to be developed (Katz and Stumpo, 2001).

Increasing integration into the global economy meant access to trade and capital, both financial and greenfield FDI. The long-term effects of these strategic reforms are still uncertain – in size more than their being positive – and are therefore debated (Rodríguez and Rodrik, 1999).[18] But their short-term consequences have been notoriously destructive. Dismantling the protected industries before implementing another industrial policy has destroyed productive capacity and erased technological capabilities developed previously (Katz, 2001). Short-term and otherwise volatile capital has hardly served the intended financing of investment, and has instead translated into financial and property bubbles as well as into consumption sprees – thus contributing to short-term expansion, to

18 On the other hand, opening up to capital flows provides the developing country with new activities linked to global markets and technology, in the case of greenfield FDI, but also with highly volatile financial flows, which may contribute little to long-term growth if the financial system has not developed the appropriate market segments or instruments to efficiently channel resources to investment.

financed pro-cyclical fiscal policies, and to exchange rate appreciation. However, the capital has been as quick to flee in the face of the reversal of such patterns, aggravating the crises. Capital attracted by the privatization of monopolies and other take-over operations may not behave very differently. On the contrary, most FDI by TNCs may make significant contributions to long-term growth, depending on their own strategies (Mortimore and Peres, 2001), without such negative short-term consequences.

Patterns of Specialization and Industrialization

The composition of Latin American exports has changed much since the 1970s. The predominance of primary exports has receded before the advance of

Table 6.6: Latin America (14 Countries),[a] Composition of Exports by Destination, 1970-74 and 1995, Percents

	Intra-Latin America		World	
	1970-74	1995	1970-74	1995
A. Primary commodities	*51.0*	*19.7*	*53.6*	*32.2*
1. Agricultural products	11.7	10.3	29.9	16.0
2. Mining products	1.0	2.4	6.2	4.0
3. Energy products	38.3	7.0	17.6	12.2
B. Industrialized products	*48.8*	*79.7*	*46.0*	*65.6*
1. Semi-manufactures	23.3	29.9	33.6	30.5
1.1 Based on agric. and labor-intensive	7.5	10.3	9.5	11.9
1.2 Based on agric. and capital-intensive	3.1	4.8	6.0	5.2
1.3 Based on minerals	6.4	8.4	9.2	9.1
1.4 Based on energy	6.2	6.5	8.9	4.4
2. Manufactured goods	25.5	49.8	12.4	35.1
2.1 Traditional industries	7.2	12.4	5.2	8.4
2.2 Basic-input industries	4.8	10.2	1.9	7.2
2.3 New labor-intensive	7.0	10.7	3.0	8.3
a) Medium technological content	4.1	6.3	1.6	4.5
b) High technological content	3.0	4.4	1.4	3.8
2.4 New capital-intensive	6.5	16.6	2.3	11.2
a) Medium technological content	5.0	14.7	1.7	10.1
b) High technological content	1.5	2.0	0.6	1.2
C. Other	*0.2*	*0.5*	*0.4*	*2.2*
Total	100	100	100	100

[a] Argentina, Bolivia, Brazil, Chile, Colombia, Costa Rica, Ecuador, Guatemala, Honduras, Mexico (excluding maquila), Paraguay, Peru, Uruguay and Venezuela. Exports with low technological content are summed-up with traditional industries.

Source: ECLAC (1998), Table III.9, on the basis of official data.

manufactures, with semi-manufactured goods maintaining traditional importance. Manufactured goods now amount to more than a third of the region's exports and most of the increase corresponds to new industries, mainly of medium technological content (Table 6.6).

Latin America has been the main arena for this diversification, constituting the biggest market for Chilean and Colombian manufactures of all kinds, and the almost exclusive market for exports of new industries from Argentina, Uruguay, and Costa Rica. It is also the main market for new Brazilian industries, whose export markets are otherwise diversified. But, except for border trade, Latin America is not a relevant market for Mexico, which trades mainly with the U.S. Thus, intra-regional trade provides a dynamic context for technological apprenticeship and international competition (Agosin and Ffrench-Davis, 2002).

Two different patterns of industrialization have been emerging from restructuring in Latin America in the 1980s and 1990s. One of them, dominant in most South American countries, is based on a shift towards industrial commodities tied to the processing of natural resources in highly automated, capital-intensive plants. These are technologically mature industries in which engineering efforts are concentrated on improving processes and production. The other pattern is dominant in Mexico, Central America, and some Caribbean economies, where labor-intensive assembly industries are rapidly increasing their share of total manufacturing, most of them operating as *maquiladoras* for the U.S. market. They use the latest technology but pay wages to semi-skilled workers that are a small fraction of those paid in the U.S. On the other hand, the automotive industry has continued to be preferentially treated in the bigger countries of the region (Katz, 2001).

The combination of these patterns of industrialization with primary commodities and emerging exports of services constitutes a pattern of specialization such that only 18 percent of exports involves increasing shares of dynamic product markets, while another 3 percent represents decreasing shares in such markets. Thus, almost 80 percent of Latin American exports consist of products that do not have a dynamic market, and more than a third of these exports represent a decreasing share of even those slow-growing markets (ECLAC, 2001).

Productivity and Technical Change

The lack of convergence of Latin American economies with the developed ones, in welfare and labor productivity, is the result of a complex combination of some activities lagging, and others catching up with, the international production frontier – represented here by the U.S.

Commercial agriculture in recent years has shown some remarkable successes: Argentina and Brazil became the world's leading exporters of soybean and soybean products; and increasing demand for protein- and vitamin-rich food stimulated production and exports of meat, fruits and vegetables in most of these

Table 6.7: Labor Productivity Gap in Latin American Manufacturing; Nine Countries; 1970, 1980, 1990 and 1996; U.S. = 1.00

	1970	1980	1990	1996
Argentina	0.42	0.41	0.55	0.67
Brazil	0.28	0.26	0.29	0.37
Chile [a]	0.25	0.24	0.23	0.20
Colombia [b]	0.29	0.25	0.37	0.34
Costa Rica [b]	...	...	0.15	0.14
Mexico [c]	0.32	0.30	0.44	0.38
Peru	0.33	0.25	0.16	0.15
Uruguay [a]	0.35	0.22	0.20	0.22

[a] Data only up to 1995. [b] Data only up to 1992. [c] Data only up to 1994.

Source: Katz (2000).

countries, to yearly rates of expansion of 4 to 8 percent. In all these successes, technological innovation has played an essential role, fostered by TNCs or their interaction with public research institutions.[19] On the contrary, traditional crop production was adversely affected by sluggish demand and little technological change.[20]

In general, the bigger the producers, the better they managed to restructure and take advantage of the new production technologies. Small producers relied on traditional crops and technologies, and competed with imports. Agriculture as a whole generates little employment;[21] therefore, it is the additional income provided by increased productivity – beyond price fluctuations – that has an impact on income distribution.

Fundamental changes to property rights in the mining sector brought significant flows of FDI into the mining sectors of Chile, Argentina, and Peru, triggering a major transformation of the industrial technology and organization (Katz, 2001). This resulted in an overall expansion of labor productivity of more than 50 percent over 1991-98. Most of the improvement in mining techniques occurred in big firms, mostly capital-intensive TNCs that generate little employment.

Reform in telecommunications was driven by different approaches: privatization temporarily maintaining the monopoly in Argentina and Mexico,

19 In the case of soybean, technology was developed by the interaction of private firms with the state institutes for research and diffusion of agricultural technology: INTA in Argentina, and EMBRAPA in Brazil.

20 In the case of tropical crops, this is the consequence of the little interest shown by agro-industrial TNCs and Northern research institutions in these crops and the decrease of public research on them (Perry, 2002).

21 In Costa Rica, agricultural employment expanded at 0.9 percent a year in the 1990s; in Chile, Mexico, and Colombia at 0.5 percent or less; in Argentina and Uruguay it was stagnant; and it decreased in Venezuela and Brazil at -0.8 and -1.4 percent a year respectively (ECLAC/IICA, 2001).

Table 6.8: Labor Productivity Indicators in Manufacturing, Nine Latin American Countries and the United States, 1970-1996 and 1990-1996, Average Annual Rates of Change

	1970-1996			1990-1996		
	Industrial product	Employment	Labor productivity	Industrial product	Employment	Labor productivity
Argentina	1.18	-2.62	3.80	4.87	-3.15	8.02
Brazil	2.81	0.95	1.86	2.26	-6.41	8.67
Chile	2.76	1.51	1.25	6.40	3.49	2.91
Colombia	3.98	1.24	2.74	3.52	-0.22	3.74
Costa Rica [a]	4.39	4.83	-0.44	...	...	...
Mexico	3.79	0.91	2.88	2.27	-0.03	2.30
Peru	1.17	2.85	-1.68	5.09	1.97	3.12
Uruguay	0.61	0.37	0.24	-1.46	-8.58	7.12
United States	2.39	0.35	2.04	5.04	0.30	4.74

[a] Data only up to 1992.

Sources: PADI data base of the ECLAC Division of Production, Productivity and Management; Katz (2000).

privatization and deregulation in Chile; and modernization of the state enterprise in Costa Rica and Uruguay. Although with varying consequences for welfare, all strategies raised productivity – from about half the productivity in the U.S. in 1988 to virtual equality in 1996 (Walter and Senén González, 1998).

During 1970-90, only in Argentina, Colombia, and Mexico did labor productivity in the manufacturing sector converge towards that of the U.S. (Table 6.7). Between 1990 and 1996, dramatic increases of productivity occurred in Argentina, Brazil, and Uruguay, narrowing the gap with U.S. manufacturing (Table 6.8). However, this outcome was at the expense of employment, with technical change mainly in the organization of production.

Moreover, only a few industries in each country achieved sufficient long-term technological progress to double in 1996 their productivity of 1970; in the 1990s only the automotive industry and industries based on natural resources reduced significantly their productivity gap vis-à-vis the U.S. in the region (Katz, 2000).

Significantly, Chile – the older reformer in the region – enhanced manufacturing productivity in the three decades at a slower pace than did Argentina, Mexico, or Brazil, allowing for a greater employment. Technical change in the 1990s was also less intensive in Chile than in those countries, causing its manufacture to diverge from the international frontier and its manufacturing employment to grow (Table 6.8).

Structural Heterogeneity and Income Disparities

Sectoral differences in productivity and proportions of the labor force involved are normal: in the region as a whole, labor productivity in manufactures is about 40 percent higher than in services and almost double that in agriculture, while output per worker in utilities doubles productivity in manufacturing and productivity in mining more than triples it. However, average sectoral productivities smooth out the real picture: within each sector, or even an activity, segments of high-productivity firms coexist with ample segments of low productivity units. This structural heterogeneity (Pinto, 1965) may be present in any economy, but its pervasiveness, permanence, and segmentation make it a critical feature of Latin America.

Productivity differentials in mining and agriculture vary by country; in 1980, output per person in agriculture compared with manufacture ranged from 0.62 in Argentina to 0.15 in Mexico. The lower these averages are, the greater the importance of low-productivity segments, beyond commercial agriculture, representing a classical example of abundant unskilled labor reserve (de Janvry and Sadoulet, 1999). An indirect quantification of these segments can be obtained by the proportions of occupied people living in poverty in the rural areas: in Brazil, Colombia, Mexico, and Venezuela, they amount to about half the rural labor force, while in Chile and Costa Rica they represent less than 20 percent of it (ECLAC, 2001).

In most countries, small – excluding micro enterprises – and medium-sized units employ about a half of the labor force in the manufacturing sector. The productivity gap between this segment and large firms is large: never less than 40 percent[22] and, in the case of Peru and Venezuela, more than 75 percent (Table 6.9). However, the performance of SMEs as a whole in the first half of the 1990s has been positive: its production has kept pace with that of large firms and, in Argentina and Mexico, gained ground up to 1993, narrowing the productivity gap. Macroeconomic conditions have strongly determined the performance of SMEs, and trade liberalization has had mixed effects: clearly negative in Brazil and Uruguay, and towards sectoral specialization within the segment in the other countries, where some SME activities suffered in the face of competing imports but others strengthened their competitive advantages in serving domestic markets (Peres and Stumpo, 2000).[23]

In the urban areas, between a third of the labor force in Chile, and half in Brazil

22 The relative productivity figures for Brazil in Table 6.9 are higher because of the greater size of enterprises defined as medium-sized.

23 Regarding the heterogeneity of the SME sector, it must be noted that this sector includes medium-sized units performing not very differently from some of the less dynamic large firms, as well as small units whose circumstances may be closer to that of micro enterprises.

Table 6.9: Relative Performance of Latin American Manufacturing SMEs, Selected Countries

	Employment (%)	Relative Productivity (large firms = 100)	Production increase (%)		
			Period	Large firms	SMEs
Argentina	44.6	56.6	1984-1993	4.1	47.7
Brazil	66.8	77.2	1985-1997	38.0	11.4
Chile	22.1	37.6	1990-1996	39.9	55.6
Colombia	52.5	45.2	1991-1996	15.2	16.2
Mexico	44.6	56.1	1988-1993	14.5	48.6
Peru	52.5	25.4	1992-1994	28.3	16.8
Uruguay	57.9	47.8	1988-1995	-14.8	2.5
Venezuela	39.5	24.5	1990-1995	-22.6	-5.2

Source: Peres and Stumpo (2000).

and Venezuela, is engaged in low-productivity occupational categories,[24] earning on average 20 percent to 45 percent less than the average earnings of the entire urban labor force (Table 6.10). Again, looking at the incidence of poverty among the urban labor force, the data show that between a third and a half of the workers in these low-productivity categories earned incomes 'below the poverty line' in Brazil, Colombia, Mexico and Venezuela, while less than 20 percent in these categories lived in poverty in Argentina, Chile, Costa Rica, and Uruguay in the late 1990s (Table 6.11).

Working in low productivity jobs represents exclusion from the mainstream of society, as does being out of work. Traditionally, open unemployment was not high because under-employment in the informal and public sectors – but also in formal low-productivity activities – cushioned that social risk. Structural reforms – particularly trade liberalization and privatization, along with the pursuance of fiscal austerity – diminished those cushioning capacities and, in some instances, induced productive changes leading to significant lay-offs (ECLAC, 2000). Be that as it may, in Argentina, Colombia,[25] Uruguay, and Venezuela the urban unemployment rate increased by 5 to 10 percentage points in the 1990s – reaching rates of between 15 and 20 percent of the urban labor force – while informal employment

24 Low-productivity occupational categories include wage earners in establishments employing up to 5 workers, domestic employees, and non-professional or technical own-account workers. This being an *a priori* characterization, it is likely to include a proportion of people working in not-so-low productivity jobs. This is clearly the case of Argentina, where non-professional own-account workers have average incomes greater than the average earnings of the entire labor force (Table 6.10).

25 Unemployment in Colombia is not strictly comparable with that of the other countries, since it includes hidden unemployment – inactive persons willing to work. These, however, represent no more than 10 percent of the combined total unemployed.

Table 6.10: Composition and Relative Incomes of the Employed Population by Occupational Category, Urban Areas, Selected Latin American Countries, 1999, Percents

	Argentina		Brazil		Chile [a]		Colombia		Costa Rica		Mexico [b]		Uruguay		Venezuela	
	%L [d]	Yme [c]	%L [d]	Yme [c]	%L [d]	Yme [c]	%L [d]	Yme [c]	%L [d]	Yme [c]	%L [d]	Yme [c]	%L [d]	Yme [c]	%L [d]	Yme [c]
Employers	*4.4*	*3.44*	*4.7*	*3.34*	*3.9*	*4.96*	*4.3*	*2.88*	*8.0*	*1.73*	*4.8*	*4.44*	*4.0*	*2.61*	*5.1*	*2.63*
Wage-earners	*72.7*	*0.80*	*66.6*	*0.93*	*76.4*	*0.75*	*57.4*	*1.12*	*72.7*	*0.98*	*72.9*	*0.85*	*72.4*	*0.98*	*57.9*	*0.91*
Public Sector	15.6	0.97	13.0	1.50	10.9	0.96	8.7	1.91	17.2	1.47	14.2	1.29	16.2	1.24	14.9	1.06
Private Sector	57.1	0.75	53.6	0.80	65.5	0.71	48.7	0.97	55.5	0.85	58.7	0.76	56.2	0.91	43	0.83
Professionals and technicians	9.1	1.33	11.0	1.57	11.6	1.65	5.7	2.06	8.9	1.62	6.6	1.68	6.5	2.07	4.9	1.83
Establishments of > 5 workers	28.5	0.77	25.7	0.73	38.7	0.56	37.8	0.85	29.7	0.80	33.1	0.76	31.8	0.91	24.0	0.83
Establishments of 5 workers	13.7	0.53	8.4	0.48	9.1	0.43	...	...	11.8	0.60	14.9	0.46	10.4	0.59	12.1	0.57
Domestic employment	5.8	0.33	8.5	0.32	6.1	0.29	5.2	0.64	5.1	0.28	4.1	0.32	7.5	0.39	2.0	0.40
Own account workers [e]	*23*	*1.23*	*28.6*	*0.73*	*19.7*	*1.22*	*38.3*	*0.67*	*19.2*	*0.73*	*22.4*	*0.73*	*23.6*	*0.76*	*36.9*	*0.91*
Professionals and technicians	4.4	1.65	2.1	1.87	3.6	2.47	2.6	1.90	2.0	1.20	1.9	1.80	3.0	1.40	1.6	2.02
Others	18.6	1.13	26.5	0.64	16.1	0.94	35.7	0.58	17.2	0.67	20.5	0.63	20.6	0.67	35.3	0.86
Employed in low productivity categories	42.2	0.89	47.3	0.68	34.4	0.80	40.9	0.61	41.6	0.75	44.3	0.76	41.5	0.69	53.7	0.89

[a] 1996. [b] 1998. [c] Mean income relative to the average. [d] Percentage of the employed population. [e] Including unpaid family workers.

Source: ECLAC (2001).

Table 6.11: Incidence of Poverty in Selected Occupational Categories, Selected Latin American Countries, Urban Areas, 1999, Percents

	Argentina	Brazil	Chile [a]	Colombia	Costa Rica	Mexico [b]	Uruguay	Venezuela
Total population	20	33	22	51	18	39	9	49
Total employed	10	24	15	38	10	31	5	35
Public sector wage earners	6	14	7	12	3	12	2	28
Private sector wage earners								
Establishments of > 5 workers	9	26	18	38 [c]	9	36	5	37
Establishments of 5 workers	17	32	24 [d]	…	14	49	9	52
Domestic employment	22	39	20	35	27	57	12	50
Own account workers in nonprofessional, non technical occupations								
Manufacturing and construction	14	33	10	60	17	39	12	33
Agricultural, forestry and fisheries	8	27	10	54	16	30	9	34

[a] 1996. [b] 1998. [c] Includes wage earners in establishments employing up to five persons. [d] This category includes establishments employing up to four persons only.

Source: ECLAC (2001).

Table 6.12: Unemployment Rates, Selected Latin American Countries, 1980-2000, Percent of the Labor Force

	1980-90	1994	1997	2000[a]
Latin America	6.6	6.3	7.3	8.4
Argentina [b]	5.5	11.5	14.9	15.1
Brazil [b]	5.3	5.1	5.7	7.1
Chile [c]	11.9	7.8	6.1	9.2
Colombia [b d]	11.2	8.9	12.4	20.2
Costa Rica [b]	6.8	4.3	5.9	5.3
Mexico [b]	4.3	3.7	3.7	2.2
Peru [b]	7.4	8.8	9.2	8.5
Uruguay [b]	8.9	9.2	11.5	13.6
Venezuela [c]	9.3	8.7	11.4	13.9

[a] Preliminary figures. [b] Urban areas. [c] Total nationwide. [d] Includes hidden unemployment.

Source: ECLAC, on the basis of official country statistics.

continued to increase except in Argentina (ILO, 2002). On the contrary, unemployment did not significantly increase until recently in Brazil, Costa Rica, Chile, and Mexico, cushioned in the first two cases by the continuing expansion of informal employment (Table 6.12).

Indeed, unemployment hit laborers of different skills with similar intensity. In those countries where open unemployment doubled or tripled, it did so among workers with all levels of education (Table 6.13). Since technical change promoted by structural adjustment has been in generally biased toward higher skills, such evenness must be an indication that reforms tended to demolish some preserves for the educated segments.

The Wage Gap

Job creation in the 1990s involved a restructuring of labor demand towards the highest educational levels – except in Peru. New employment was more intense for wage-earners in Argentina, Colombia, Chile, and Costa Rica, and for own-account workers in Brazil and Peru. Moreover, there has been an increase in new job openings in wage employment for those with medium and high levels of education, and in independent employment for those with low levels. This demand by firms for educated workers signifies either that technology-based industry needs educated workers or that a surplus of these workers makes it affordable to hire them.[26] On the other hand, the highly-skilled self-employed substantially increased their share among the new jobs (Weller, 2001).

26 The latter implies either a short-run 'devaluation of credentials' or, if made permanent, an upgrading of requirements in anticipation of coming technical change.

Table 6.13: Open Unemployment by Years of Schooling in Urban Areas, Selected Countries, 1990 and 1999, Percents

	Year	Years of schooling				
		Total	0 -5	6 - 9	10 - 12	13
Argentina [a]	1990	5.9	6.8	5.9	3.0	...
	1999	14.7	17.0	17.4	14.5	10.2
Brazil	1990	4.5	4.2	6.2	4.5	1.8
	1999	11.4	9.9	15.6	12.2	5.2
Chile	1990	8.7	9.3	10.1	9.2	6.3
	1999	10.1	12.8	12.2	10.2	7.1
Colombia	1990	9.3	6.6	11.3	12.4	7.4
	1999	19.2	15.3	23.2	23.2	14.1
Costa Rica	1990	5.3	6.4	6.0	5.7	3.0
	1999	6.1	9.2	7.8	4.7	2.8
Mexico	1990	3.3	1.3	4.3	3.8	2.4
	1999	3.2	2.1	2.6	3.7	3.9
Uruguay	1990	8.9	5.6	10.2	10.0	5.9
	1999	11.2	8.9	13.1	11.4	6.3
Venezuela	1990	10.2	9.7	12.1	9.3	6.1
	1999	14.5	11.7	15.5	16.2	12.7

[a] In 1990, the levels of schooling which have data entered correspond to 0-6 years, 7-9 years and 10 years or more, respectively.

Source: ECLAC (2001).

Given the workplace bias towards the educated, it is not surprising that the wage gap widened in most countries. The income of university graduates, relative both to average income and the income of workers with poor education, rose significantly in Chile, Colombia, Mexico, and Peru, but only modestly in Argentina; on the contrary, those income differentials remained unchanged in Brazil and Costa Rica (Table 6.14).

Macroeconomic Volatility

Latin American economies have been traditionally plagued by macroeconomic volatility: the average standard deviation of growth rates since 1970 has been approximately twice the dispersion in industrial economies (Gavin and Hausmann, 1996); more important, even when the high volatility of the 1980s is reduced in the 1990s, it remains historically high (Rodrik, 2001). On the other hand, the instability in private capital flows was the main determinant of macroeconomic volatility in the 1990s.[27]

27 Rodrik (2001) has regressed averages of GNP volatility for each Latin American country in the 1980s and the 1990s on a number of determinants: the volatility of terms of trade, volatility of private capital flows, volatility of monetary conditions, financial depth, per capita income and a dummy for the 1990s. The volatility of private capital

Table 6.14: Wage Differentials by Educational Level,[a] Selected Latin American Countries, 1990s, Percents

	University graduates vs. average wage		University graduates vs. 7-9 years of education	
	Initial year [b]	Final year [b]	Initial year [b]	Final year [b]
Argentina (1991–97)	164.3	169.6	218.3	227.9
Brazil (1992–97)	380.2	383.5	553.2	553.3
Chile (1990–96)	231.6	247.9	366.1	448.6
Colombia (1988–95)	222.2	261.6	276.7	327.2
Costa Rica (1990–96)	285.0	273.2	323.1	316.7
Mexico (1991–97)	182.1	232.1	160.1	302.2
Peru (1991–97)	220.7	275.0	321.0	403.1
Median	226.9	267.4	298.9	365.2

[a] Ratio of average wages of specified groups. [b] Initial and final year of period indicated for each country.

Source: Weller (2000, p. 167).

Morley (1995) has estimated that in Latin America, for every 1 percent decline in growth, the incidence of poverty rises by 2 percent. From another point of view, had Latin American countries experienced degrees of variability of growth rates similar to those of industrial countries, 25 percent of the poor in the region would have been freed from poverty (IDB, 1999). In a more telling commentary on the asymmetry of the sensitivity of poverty incidence to changes in growth rates, de Janvry and Sadoulet (1999) estimate that each 1-percent decline in per capita income during the recession years of the 1980s offset the poverty decline of the 1970s corresponding to income per capita increases of 3.7 percent in urban areas, and of 2 percent in rural areas.

The Conditions for Technological Progress in the Global Context

The following quotation (U.K., 1996, p.10) deftly outlines the need for systemic competitiveness at the national level:

> Improving competitiveness is central to raising the underlying growth of the economy and enhancing living standards. Achieving this means removing the impediments to investment in machines, people and ideas and improving the efficiency with which resources are used throughout the economy, not just in those sectors directly involved in international trade.... The need to improve our competitiveness is not imposed by Government, but by changes in the world economy. Improving competitiveness is not about driving down living standards. It is about creating a high skills, high productivity

---

flows emerges as the most important and highly significant correlate of GNP volatility in the model.

and therefore high wage economy where enterprise can flourish and where we can find opportunities rather than threats in changes we cannot avoid.

The challenge for developing countries is far more exacting than described in that quotation if the goal is to close the productivity gap with developed countries. Attaining and maintaining international competitiveness in the long-run requires (i) the strengthening of the national innovation system and (ii) the pursuance of dynamic competitiveness.

The creation or adoption of technology, with the corresponding acquisition of technological capabilities, is an interactive process, involving linkages not only within the production system itself but also with the educational, training, basic research and technology, and even financial systems. It also requires market incentives and the development of appropriate non-market rules and strategies. This set of agents, institutions, norms and implicit externalities is the national innovation system (NIS) supporting and conditioning the incorporation of technology into the national productive system (Nelson and Rosenberg, 1993; ECLAC, 1996).

Meanwhile, to attain and maintain international competitiveness in the medium- and long-run implies pursuing it dynamically. Static competitiveness, based on inherited resources, represents the starting point for expanding exports; but in the long-run, it is eroded in international markets – along both the price and demand dimensions – by technological change and increasing incomes. Such an erosion does not materialize if competitiveness is pursued dynamically, with cost advantages continually emerging as the result of permanent restructuring internally to more complex processes and products, as well as from industries of low value added to others of higher value added (Lall and Mortimore, 2000).

In the global arena, the emergence of the new technological paradigm is transforming productive systems. This process has the potential for rapidly increasing productivity and, therefore, for enhancing incomes, employment, and welfare. At the same time, it is changing the opportunities for the location of production and innovation and the national patterns of comparative advantage. Advantages based on knowledge and technology are gaining pre-eminence, while advantages based on the inherited resource endowment are becoming less significant.

Advances in communications and transport are shrinking economic space and facilitating the constitution of global or international 'integrated production systems' (IPSs) within which functions are spread world-wide to take advantage of differences in cost, skills, technological capabilities, or logistics. Within IPSs, investment, technology, and skills are increasingly mobile, and all segments of the system have to operate with the same blueprints and standards. At the same time, intra-IPSs trade is the most dynamic segment of intra-trade within TNCs, which represents 40 percent of their total trade, itself about 65 percent of world trade (Lall, 2000).

This world is far from the model world of constant returns to scale. Production within IPSs means increasing returns to scale compared with production within the 'national' firm. Particularly, the accumulation of knowledge is an activity with increasing returns, which is why investment, technology and skills – though increasingly mobile – are concentrated by company and country.

Latin American countries, striving for progress in productivity to close the gap with the international frontier and the internal gap of the excluded relative to the included, have several options:

(i) Put unskilled labor in *maquila*-type activities that can be detached from IPSs, and try to grow whatever few linkages could be established from the assembly activity to the NIS.
(ii) Attract intra-IPSs activities into the country, either through FDI or through incorporating national companies into a global IPS. This implies that the corresponding segment of the national productive system virtually jumps to the international frontier. This strategy, however, is focused on the linkages with the global IPSs, not on internal linkages that may not be 'up to the task.'
(iii) Develop clusters of activities around the exploitation of a natural resource, or an already-acquired technological capability, which has competitive advantages in the world market. The focus of this strategy is on maximizing the linkages between the resource and the NIS by adding value and knowledge to the original resource.
(iv) Put the linkages of the NIS at the center of a strategy to enhance the competitiveness of promising domestic industries in order to create quality jobs at all levels.

These guidelines are intended to be a stylization of alternative but not mutually exclusive strategies, each with a different focus, with a different degree of difficulty in a globalized context, and with a different possible outcome in terms of productive structure and income distribution. The ordering of desirable outcomes in terms of equity is the reverse of the one in which the alternatives are presented. The final suggestion could maximize opportunities for human capital formation and higher wage potential through the multiplication of competitive links and the expansion and densification of the NIS. The third strategy has similar implications, but within a more limited scope, since it attempts to maximize competitive linkages, but only around exports. The integration of a national segment into an IPS implies the upgrading of a segment of the productive apparatus and the labor force to the international frontier, delinking it from the remaining domestic segments. The *maquila* strategy is more fragile and rests more on low wages than on developing local technological capabilities.

The Challenges to Social Cohesion

Inclusion and Exclusion

According to the analyses reviewed above, the adoption of reforms to change the economic order has had considerable distributive costs, compounded in some cases by costs of recurrent crises. We dealt above with whether the normal functioning of Latin American economies under the new economic order would enhance or narrow income disparities. In a nutshell, the answer is that there will be both centripetal and centrifugal forces in action, with some mainstream groups integrated into the global economy, but others excluded from the fruits of progress – perhaps putting social integration into question.

The picture is neither one of immiserizing growth nor one of upward mobility for all participants, but of further segmentation, with some groups reaching international frontiers of productivity, and others lagging behind. Globalization of productive systems is a force towards convergence of the component parts, since all parts should operate at the technological frontier, with increasing returns to scale. On the other hand, production outside IPSs should strive for international competitiveness on its own merits and on the basis of externalities originating in the national innovation system, or fall behind if the NIS is weak. The development of clusters around advantageous natural resources shares both challenges: the basic resource may already be part of a global chain, but the possibility of adding value depends on the localization of other functions of the chain, and the potential for developing a cluster of activities depends on constituting an appropriate innovation system and building the necessary infrastructure.

Public policy can foster international competitiveness based on the acquisition and accumulation of knowledge on all fronts: first, to leverage FDI in order to acquire strategic segments of IPSs and maximize technological linkages with the NIS and, second, to densify the NIS and complete and upgrade the Information and Communications Technologies (ICT) platform to facilitate digitalization of the domestic productive system. But these policies are (i) costly, requiring fiscal resources or other appropriate financing; (ii) knowledge-intensive, requiring investment in human capital in anticipation of demand; and (iii) selective – against the grain of conventional wisdom.

The trends outlined in this chapter have complex distributive consequences difficult to ponder, impossible to quantify, and which compound a panorama of long-term expansion with the prospect of increasing segmentation and differentiation. According to this hypothesis, those segments of the skilled or semi-skilled labor force that are part of IPSs or global chains would increase their relative incomes, converging to developed-country wage levels, widening skill differentials at the upper echelons of the local spectrum but, at the same time, differentiating their newly acquired technological skills from those with similar educational level – outside global chains – where incomes would lag. Among these, workers in any activity attaining international competitiveness through the NIS, or in clusters around globalized natural resources, would find themselves in an intermediate situation, their incomes slowly converging to developed country levels. For the less skilled workers – whose level of education would be increasing – the Heckscher-Ohlin possibility of rising wages at the expense of unskilled workers in developed countries would represent lagging incomes relative to the converging ones.

The above speculation refers to formal employment and the associated incomes. It does not assess the proportions of the labor force in different segments, nor how job-creating competitive growth could be. Neither does it take into consideration the effects on employment and incomes of recession-induced macroeconomic volatility characterizing these economies under the new economic order.

In summary, social polarization would increase, between those included in international systems, either by participating in them or by attaining international competitiveness, those who lag behind in other non-competitive – and therefore insecure – formal employment, and those suffering from exclusion in unemployment or low-productivity jobs.

The Demand for Social Protection and Investment

Rodrik (1997) noted that the welfare-state reforms in continental Europe were undertaken when the countries there opened up to international competitiveness and integrated with the international economy – before the need to compensate losers and provide social protection. Latin America faces a similar economic situation, although some aspects of the globalization processes make the position appear more dramatic.

The many forms of exclusion induced by poverty, unemployment, and low productivity call for public redressing. Until recently, the political weakness of the poor made the undertaking dependent on the perceptions of the ethical imperatives or the negative externalities of poverty by the privileged or the middle classes (O'Donnell, 1998). Today, the Latin American poor increasingly mobilize in emergencies, demanding assistance.

But globalization processes tend to exacerbate demands for social protection and services among all social strata. In the globalization of values and consumption fostered by the global media and telecommunications, Latin Americans are aspiring to standards of education and health similar to those attained in developed countries. People become aware of expensive, technology-intensive treatments for their illnesses and of educational opportunities enjoyed in the developed world.

On the other hand, investment in human capital is essential for a development strategy centered on attaining and maintaining international competitiveness based on the acquisition of technological capabilities, as the one outlined to take full advantage of the opportunities offered by globalization.

Table 6.15: Social Expenditure in Latin American and OECD Countries, 1980-81, 1990-91 and 1998-99

	Social Expenditure per Capita (International Dollars, 1997)			Social Expenditure (% GDP)		
	1980-81	1990-91	1998-99	1980-81	1990-91	1998-99
Argentina	2,092	1,821	2,537	16.8	17.7	20.5
Brazil	...	1,130	1,453	...	18.1	21.0
Chile	848	744	1,399	17.7	13.0	16.0
Colombia	287	363	875	7.8	8.0	15.0
Costa Rica	744	920	1,202	15.2	15.7	16.8
Mexico	642	476	739	8.6	6.5	9.1
Peru	204	132	368	4.5	3.3	6.8
Uruguay	979	1,181	2,046	14.9	16.8	22.8
Venezuela	761	538	499	11.5	9.0	8.6
	1981	1991	1997	1981	1991	1997
France	5,248	7,188	...	30.6	34.9	...
Germany	6,678	7,950	8,232 [a]	33.7	29.4	36.8 [a]
Italy	4,232	5,024 [b]	...	26.4	26.9 [b]	...
Spain	2,960 [c]	2,828	4,107	27.2 [c]	19.7	26.0
Sweden	4,619	5,828	5,463	26.3	28.5	25.8
United Kingdom	3,827	5,427	6,124	26.4	29.5	29.3
United States	4,265	6,108	7,142	19.4	22.8	23.6

[a] 1996. [b] 1988. [c] 1982.

Sources: Latin American countries: ECLAC, *Social Panorama* (various issues). OECD countries: IMF, *Government Finance Statistics Yearbook* (various issues), *EUROSTAT* (various issues), and *International Financial Statistics Yearbook* (2001).

The protection of old age with pensions is also suffering by the impact of the increasing numbers of seniors and the informality of work on contributive systems in both pay-as-you-go and individual capitalization pillars, while retirees also share the general aspiration to greater wealth (Uthoff, 2002).

The perception of need emerging from all corners will increasingly represent a pressure to raise social expenditure. Real per-capita social spending[28] in the more developed Latin American countries has been expanding, significantly in some cases: Argentina and Uruguay spend about half as much as Spain, and less than a third that of the U.S.; Brazil, Chile, and Costa Rica spend a fifth of the U.S.'s level; while Colombia and Mexico spend little more than a tenth of that level (Table 6.15).

Per capita expenditure on health in countries like Germany and the U.S. is about 2000 international dollars of 1997. In most of the more developed Latin American countries, the comparable level of expenditure is about 250 dollars

28 Including pensions, which represent sizeable portions of the total (Tables 6.15 and 6.16).

Table 6.16: Public Expenditure per Capita in Health, Education, and Social Security; Latin American and OECD Countries, International 1997 Dollars

	Expenditure per capita in health			Expenditure per capita in education			Expenditure per capita in social security		
L. American countries	1980-81	1990-91	1998-99	1980-81	1990-91	1998-99	1980-81	1990-91	1998-99
Argentina	565	408	572	417	340	576	939	856	1,081
Brazil	...	223	234	...	231	269	...	504	796
Chile	128	117	245	63	147	342	355	398	658
Colombia	42	53	239	108	142	276	112	138	303
Costa Rica	329	290	350	272	222	315	96	286	417
Mexico	267	219	171	250	191	307	...	20	189
Peru	49	29	73	139	54	119	1	44	153
Uruguay	66	203	249	126	173	290	771	784	1,464
Venezuela	109	91	78	324	206	223	172	142	150
OECD Countries	1981	1991	1997	1981	1991	1997	1981	1991	1997
France	720	1,467	...	1,042	993	...	3,192	4,204	...
Germany	1,586	1,854	1,971 [a]	870	920	978 [a]	3,807	4,631	4,810 [a]
Italy	847	978 [b]	...	708	716 [b]	...	2,628	3,280 [b]	...
Spain	580 [c]	655	857	216 [c]	234	671	2,125 [c]	1,912	2,299
Sweden	...	...	...	577	638	510	3,457	4,540	4,470
United Kingdom	788	975	1,160	830	949	969	1,855	3,069	3,680
United States	896	1,592	2,194	1,118	1,978	2,180	2,034	2,291	2,531

[a] 1996. [b] 1988. [c] 1982.

Sources: Latin American countries: ECLAC, *Social Panorama* (various years). OECD countries: IMF, *Government Finance Statistics Yearbook* (various issues) and *International Financial Statistics Yearbook* (2001); *EUROSTAT* (various issues).

(Table 6.16).[29] Except for Argentina, which spends as much on education as does Spain, most of the countries spend less than a third of the per capita expenditure enjoyed by Germany or the United Kingdom. Pension expenditure in most of Latin America has improved greatly from comparatively low levels which contributed to situations of exclusion in the past; in Argentina and Uruguay, these expenditures are half the per capita level of that in Spain and a third of that in the U.K., while in Brazil and Chile they represent a fifth of this level, and even less in the other countries.

On the other hand, unemployment schemes are nonexistent or incipient in Latin America, while they constitute a central part of the social arrangements in the OECD countries. Likewise, welfare programs are of recent vintage in Latin America and represent minor budget commitments, being financed in many cases by loans from international institutions. In this area, the social pressures do not call for improving the existing services, but for incorporating into the social protection arrangements safety nets to deal with these major social risks.

Fiscal capacity to finance increasing social expenditure is limited by efficiency considerations, and by one aspect of globalization: the desire to attract FDI, so necessary for participating in ISPs, induces governments to cap the tax rates which fund social benefits and to compete with other nations in offering low tax rates or exemptions (Avi-Yonah, 2001).

Social Cohesion under the Tensions of Globalization

To take advantage of the opportunities provided by globalization processes for development, Latin American countries should participate as much as possible in global chains and international production systems, thereby attracting FDI and developing clusters around advantageous natural resources. At the same time, a major strategy for strengthening the national innovation system is needed not only to maximize internal linkages to those global chains, but also to foster systemic competitiveness in domestic activities – with particular attention to SMEs.

Such participation would cause tension over social integration, and tend to segregate those segments of the labor force rapidly converging to developed economies' wages from those participating in competitive domestic activities, which will, in turn, tend to fare better than the labor force remaining in low-productivity jobs. As long as the domestic productive system remains low-keyed through a dense network in the national innovation system, it will not converge to the productivity of developed countries. Even so, it will maintain or enlarge the mass of the excluded: the unemployed, those employed in low-productivity jobs, and subsistence farmers.

In those circumstances, the demand for social protection will expand, not only

---

29 Argentina spends more than double that level, probably harboring more inefficiency, or as a result of the use of inappropriate deflators.

from the mostly silent excluded, but also from middle- and low-strata of the included, who will demand 'developed country' services, as well as protection from the risk of being excluded. Further, social expenditure will be subject to the pressure to 'converge' to developed country standards.

Macroeconomic stability would require the tax burden to grow significantly in order to sustain expanding social expenditure. But that would be under the tension of domestic activities striving for international competitiveness by cutting costs, and of the globalization-induced competence to cap the tax burden so as to attract FDI and participate in international production systems.

References

Aghion, P., E. Caroli and C. García-Peñalosa (1999), 'Inequality and Economic Growth: The Perspective of the New Growth Theories,' *Journal of Economic Literature*, Vol. 37, No. 4 (December), pp. 1615-60.

Agosin, M. and R. Ffrench-Davis (2002), 'Trade, Specialization and Economic Growth in Latin America', paper presented at the Seminar on Globalization, ECLAC and the World Bank, Santiago, March 6-8.

Alesina, A. and R. Perotti (1996), 'Income Distribution, Political Instability, and Investment,' *European Economic Review*, Vol. 40, No. 6 (June), pp. 1203-209.

Alesina, A. and D. Rodrik (1994), 'Distributive Politics and Economic Growth: A Critique of Recent Literature,' *The Quarterly Journal of Economics*, Vol. 109, No. 2 (May), pp. 465-90.

Altimir, O. (1990), 'Development, Crisis and Equity', *CEPAL Review*, No. 40 (April).

Altimir, O. (1994), 'Income Distribution and Poverty through Crisis and Adjustment', *CEPAL Review*, No. 52 (April).

Altimir, O. (1996) 'The Long-term Evolution of Inequality and Poverty in Argentina, Colombia and Mexico', background paper for R. Thorp (1998), *Progress, Poverty and Exclusion. An Economic History of Latin America in the 20th Century*, Johns Hopkins University Press for the Inter-American Development Bank.

Altimir, O. (1997), 'Desigualdad, Empleo y Pobreza en América Latina: Efectos del Ajuste y del Cambio en el Estilo de Desarrollo', *Desarrollo Económico*, Vol. 37, No. 145 (April-June).

Altimir, O. (2001), 'Long-Term Trends of Poverty in Latin American Countries,' *Estudios de Economía*, Vol. 28, No. 1 (June), pp. 115-55.

Altimir, O., L. Beccaria and M. González Rozada (2002), 'Income Distribution in Argentina, 1974-2000', *CEPAL Review*, No. 78 (December).

Avi-Yonah, R. (2001), 'Globalization and Tax Competition: Implications for Developing Countries, *CEPAL Review*, No. 74 (August), pp. 59-66.

Behrman, J.R, N. Birdsall and M. Székely (2000), 'Economics Reform and Wage Differentials in Latin America', Working Paper No. 435, Research Department, Inter-American Development Bank, Washington D.C.

Berry, A. (1998), 'Confronting the Income Distribution Threat in Latin America' in A. Berry (ed.), *Poverty, Economic Reforms, and Income Distribution in Latin America*, pp. 9-41, Lynne Rienner, Boulder, Colorado.

Birdsall, N., D. Ross and R. Sabot (1996), 'La Desigualdad como Limitación del Crecimiento en América Latina', *Gestión y Política Pública*, Vol. 5, No.74 (first semester).

de Janvry, A. and E. Sadoulet (1999), 'How Effective Has Aggregate Income Growth Been in Reducing Poverty and Inequality in Latin America?', in N. Lustig (ed.), *Adverse Shocks and Social Protection: Policies Issues for the Developing World*, Inter-American Development Bank and Brookings Institution Press, Washington, D.C.

ECLAC (Economic Commission for Latin America and the Caribbean) (various years), *Social Panorama of Latin America*, Social Development Division and Statistics and Economic Projections Division, ECLAC, Santiago.

ECLAC (Economic Commission for Latin America and the Caribbean) (1996), *Strengthening Development: The Interplay of Macro- and Microecomics*, ECLAC, Santiago.

ECLAC (Economic Commission for Latin America and the Caribbean) (1998), *América Latina y el Caribe: Políticas para Mejorar la Inserción en la Economía Mundial*, revised second edition, Fondo de Cultura Económica/ECLAC, Santiago.

ECLAC (Economic Commission for Latin America and the Caribbean) (2000), *The Equity Gap: A Second Assessment*, ECLAC, Santiago.

ECLAC (Economic Commission for Latin America and the Caribbean) (2001), *Una Década de Luces y Sombras, América Latina y el Caribe en los Años Noventa*, ECLAC/Alfaomega, Bogota.

ECLAC-IICA (Economic Commission for Latin America and the Caribbean – Inter-American Institute for Cooperation on Agriculture) (2001), *Panorama of Agriculture in Latin America and the Caribbean, 1990-2000*, ECLAC and IICA, Santiago.

EUROSTAT (various issues), *L' Europe en chiffres*, Paris.

Escaith, H. and S. Morley (2001), 'The Impact of Structural Reforms on Growth in Latin America and the Caribbean: An Empirical Estimation', Serie Macroeconomía del Desarrollo No. 1, ECLAC, Santiago.

Ganuza, E., R. Paes de Barros, L. Taylor and R. Vos (2001), *Liberalización, Desigualdad y Pobreza: América Latina y el Caribe en los 90*, Eudeba for UNDP-ECLAC, Santiago .

Ganuza, E., R. Paes de Barros and R. Vos (2001), 'Efectos de la Liberalización sobre la Pobreza y la Desigualdad', in E. Ganuza, R. Paes de Barros, L. Taylor and R. Vos (eds.), *Liberalización, Desigualdad y Pobreza: América Latina y el Caribe en los 90*, Eudeba for UNDP-ECLAC, Santiago.

Gavin, M. and R. Hausmann (1996), 'Securing Stability and Growth in a Shock Prone Region: The Policy Challenge for Latin America', Working Paper No. 315, Inter-American Development Bank, Washington, D.C.

IDB (Inter-American Development Bank) (1999), *Facing Up to Inequality in Latin America. Economic and Social Progress in Latin America 1998-1999*, Inter-American Development Bank, Washington, D.C.

ILO (International Labour Organization) (2002), *Panorama Laboral 2002*, International Labour Organization, Regional Office for Latin America and the Caribbean, Lima.

IMF (International Monetary Fund) (various years), *Government Finance Statistics Yearbook*, International Monetary Fund, Washington, D.C.

IMF (International Monetary Fund) (2001), *International Financial Statistics Yearbook*, International Monetary Fund, Washington, D.C.

Katz, J. (2000), 'Structural Changes and Productivity in Latin American Industry, 1970-1996', *CEPAL Review*, No. 71 (August), pp. 63-80.

Katz, J. (2001), *Structural Reforms, Productivity and Technological Change in Latin America*. ECLAC Books No. 64, ECLAC, Santiago.

Katz, J. and G. Stumpo (2001), 'Sectoral Regimes, Productivity and international Competitiveness', *CEPAL Review,* No. 75 (December), pp. 131-52.

Lall, S. (2000), 'Export Performance, Technological Upgrading and Foreign Direct Investment Strategies in the Asian Newly Industrializing Economies, Serie Desarrollo Productivo No. 88, ECLAC, Santiago.

Lall, S. and M. Mortimore (2000), 'Competitiveness, Restructuring and FDI: An Analytical Framework' in UNCTAD (ed.), *The Competitiveness Challenge: Transnational Corporations and Industrial Restructuring in Developing Countries*, United Nations Conference on Trade and Development, New York.

Londoño, J.L. and M. Székely (1997), 'Persistent Poverty and Excess Inequality: Latin America, 1970-1995', Working Paper No. 357, Inter-American Development Bank, Office of the Chief Economist, Washington, D.C.

Lora, E. and F. Barrera (1997), 'A Decade of Structural Reform in Latin America: Growth, Productivity and Investment Are Not What They Used to Be', Working Paper No. 350, Research Department, Inter-American Development Bank, Office of the Chief Economist, Washington, D.C.

Maddison, A. (2001), *The World Economy: A Millennial Perspective*, Development Centre Studies, OECD, Paris.

Morley, S.A. (1995), *Poverty and Inequality in Latin America: The Impact of Adjustment and Recovery in the 1980s*, Johns Hopkins University Press, Baltimore.

Morley, S.A. (2000), 'The Effects of Growth and Economic Reform on Income Distribution in Latin America', *CEPAL Review,* No. 71 (August), pp. 23-40.

Morley, S.A., R. Machado, and S. Pettinato (1999), 'Indexes of Structural Reform in Latin America', Serie Reformas Económicas No. 12, ECLAC, Santiago.

Mortimore, M. and W. Peres (2001), 'Corporate Competitiveness in Latin America and the Caribbean', *CEPAL Review,* No. 74, pp. 35-57.

Nelson, R. and N. Rosenberg (1993), 'Technical Innovation and National Systems' in R. Nelson (ed.), *National Innovation Systems: A Comparative Analysis*, Oxford University Press, New York and Oxford.

O'Donnell, G. (1998), 'Poverty and Inequality in Latin America: Some Political Reflections' in V. Tokman and G. O'Donnell (eds.), *Poverty and Inequality in Latin America: Issues and New Challenges*, University of Notre Dame Press, Notre Dame, Indiana.

Peres, W. and G. Stumpo (2000), 'Small and Medium-Sized Manufacturing Enterprises in Latin America and the Caribbean under the New Economic Model', *World Development*, Vol. 28, No. 9 (September), pp. 1643-55.

Pinto, A. (1965), 'Concentración del Progreso Técnico y de sus Frutos en el Desarrollo Latinoamericano', *El Trimestre Económico*, Vol. 32, No. 125 (July-September).

Pinto, A. (1976), 'Notas sobre Estilos de Desarrollo en América Latina', *Revista de la CEPAL*, first semester.

Robbins, D. (1996), 'HOS Hits Facts, Facts Win: Evidence on Trade and Wages in the Developing World', Harvard Institute for International Development, Cambridge, Massachusetts.

Rodríguez, F. and D. Rodrik. (1999), 'Trade Policy and Economic Growth: A Skeptic's Guide to the Cross-National Literature', NBER Working Paper 7081, National Bureau of Economic Research, Cambridge, Massachussets.

Rodrik, D. (1997), *Has Globalization Gone Too Far?*, Institute for International Economics, Washington, D.C.

Rodrik, D. (2001), 'Why Is There so Much Economic Insecurity in Latin America?,' *CEPAL Review,* No. 73 (April), pp. 7-29.

Spilimbergo, A., J.L. Londoño and M. Székely (1997), 'Income Distribution, Factor Endowments and Trade Openness', Working Paper No. 356, Inter-American Development Bank, Office of the Chief Economist, Washington, D.C.

Stallings, B. and W. Peres (2000), *Crecimiento, Empleo y Equidad: El Impacto de las Reformas Económicas en América Latina y el Caribe*, ECLAC/Fondo de Cultura Económica, Santiago.

Taylor, L. and R. Vos (2001), 'Liberalización de la Balanza de Pagos en América Latina. Efectos sobre el Crecimiento, la Distribución y la Pobreza' in E. Ganuza, R. Paes de Barros, L. Taylor and R. Vos (eds.), *Liberalización, Desigualdad y Pobreza: América Latina y el Caribe en los 90*, Eudeba for UNDP-ECLAC, Santiago.

U.K. (United Kingdom Cabinet Office) (1996), *Competitiveness: Creating the Enterprise Centre of Europe*, Her Majesty's Stationery Office, London.

Uthoff, A. (2002), 'Mercados de Trabajo y Sistema de Pensiones', *CEPAL Review*, No.78 (December), pp. 39-52.

Vos, R. (2002), 'Globalization and Rising Labor Inequality in Latin America', paper presented at the Seminar on Globalization, ECLAC and World Bank, Santiago, March 6-8.

Walter, J. and C. Senén González (1998), *La Privatización de las Telecomunicaciones en América Latina: Empresas y Sindicatos ante los Desafíos de la Reestructuración*, Editorial Universitaria de Buenos Aires (EUDEBA), Buenos Aires.

Weller, J. (2001), *Economic Reforms, Growth and Employment. Labour Markets in Latin America and the Caribbean*, ECLAC Books No. 66. Santiago: ECLAC.

Wolfe, M. (1976), *El Desarrollo Esquivo. Exploraciones en la Política Social y la Realidad Socio-Política*, ECLAC/Fondo de Cultura Económica, Mexico, D.F.

Chapter 7

Economic Reform or Social Development? The Challenges of a Period of Reform in Latin America: Case Study of Mexico[1]

Diana Alarcón and Eduardo Zepeda

Introduction

Latin American countries have gone through a long and socially costly period of transition since the onset of the debt crisis in 1982. Following the painful recession of the early 1980s, deep structural changes were implemented in the economies of the region in an attempt to re-establish basic macroeconomic equilibrium in a context of more open, export-oriented economies. Latin America recovered macroeconomic stability in the 1990s, but sustained growth still remained elusive. More important, this struggle against low and unstable growth does not appear to be over yet, as shown by the deep Argentine recession and the low levels of growth elsewhere in the region.

The social cost of recession, stabilization and reform has been substantial. Poverty, income distribution and employment indicators all worsened sharply during the 1980s and failed to recover with the re-ignition of growth in the 1990s, thus revealing a lack of connection between economic growth and improvement in the living conditions of large segments of the population. Judging by some of the most standard welfare indicators, renewed growth in Latin American economies has not yielded parallel improvements in the distribution of income, the incidence of poverty, or employment opportunities.

1 The views expressed in this paper are those of the authors and do not represent the official view of the institutions where they work. We want to thank Gustavo Indart and Albert Berry for comments on a previous version of this paper. A slightly modified version of this paper appeared first in the *Oxford Development Studies*, Vol. 32, No. 1, 2004 (http://www.tandf.co.uk/journals/carfax/13600818.html).

Adding to these puzzling outcomes, the low levels of social expenditure of the 1980s failed to bring about a worsening of social outcomes in the region. Despite the general recession that followed the debt crisis, a number of social indicators – particularly those related to health and education – continued to improve throughout the last two decades of the 20th century. This lack of synchronicity between current social expenditure and outcomes is explained to a large extent by the delayed effects of previous social investment in the form of a more educated and healthier population. But precisely how long these lags between social investment and outcomes are, and how systematic their relationship is, are still questions in search of answers.

The improved social outcomes of the 1990s can be seen as the result of social-sector reforms and greater investment in health and education. All countries of the region made an important effort to recover, and even surpass, the levels of social investment that prevailed prior to the debt crisis, but higher social expenditure in education and health, and only slightly less in housing and pensions has not been enough to generate less social inequality, less poverty, and better employment opportunities.

In this chapter we provide empirical evidence to support the view that the persistence of poverty, income inequality, and poor employment outcomes in a context of regional growth and stability may be associated with a change in the basic relationship between economic growth and its impact on welfare. We first review cross-country comparable economic and social information to assess the impact of economic reforms on the social sector of Latin American countries. We then turn to the case-study of Mexico to examine the missing link between renewed growth and social investment on the one hand, and poverty, income distribution and employment on the other. Our analysis of employment trends in the Mexican manufacturing sector reveals that the successes of reducing inflation, of reorienting the structure of production towards exports, and of restoring moderate economic growth have not translated into equivalent successes regarding the expansion of employment opportunities and improvements in living conditions. In highly urbanized Latin American societies, it appears that poverty reduction and better distribution of income will continue to be elusive goals unless formal employment opportunities are expanded to include larger segments of the population and unless average wages – and especially those at the lower end – improve.

Adjustment, Growth and Social Progress in Latin America

Latin America has experienced economic instability and low levels of economic growth since the early 1980s. Despite a significant reduction in the rate of population growth, income per capita in the early 1990s was lower than in 1980,[2] thus contributing to the concept of the 'lost decade.'[3]

The region's rapid growth period of the 1970s was followed by a sharp contraction in output in the early 1980s and by a modest recovery thereafter. It was not until 1994 that Latin American GDP per capita recovered its 1980 peak level, and then growth continued at a very slow pace, averaging about 1.1 percent per annum during 1994-2000. Mexico, a fast growing country during the 1970s, was badly hit by the debt crisis of the early 1980s, and has endured since then a long period of slow and unstable growth. Mexico did not recover its growth potential until the 1990s, and had to wait until 1998 to return to its 1981 level of per capita GDP.

Factors singled out as responsible, at least in the short-run, for the crisis and subsequent poor economic performance of the region were the accumulation of large external public debts and the emergence of large fiscal deficits, resulting in high rates of inflation. But the explosive impact of the external debt was actually manifested when the sharp contraction of the economies of the region increased the weight of the external debt relative to GDP; afterwards, countries were forced to continue borrowing just to meet their liabilities due to the sharp reversal in net external transfers of funds. Although the restructuring of the external debt and the economic recovery of the region decreased the debt burden during the 1990s, poor economic performance still translated into a debt-GDP ratio significantly larger than the average ratio of the 1970s.

Mexico, one of the large borrowers of the 1970s, was a leading country in Latin America in the 1980s in terms of debt management and adjustment. The conjunction of reduced oil prices, high interest rates, and short-term external financing of current account deficits all contributed to the worsening of Mexico's debt indicators, and thus, became largely responsible for the eruption of the debt crisis in 1982. Henceforth, debt negotiations and the inflow of fresh funds gradually started to improve debt indicators, particularly after 1989.

During the 1980s, large debt burdens cum economic contraction caused Latin American governments' finances to deteriorate further and, not surprisingly, the rates of inflation to skyrocket. Although Latin America has been an inflation-prone region since the early 1960s, rates of price increases grew significantly in the 1980s (Table 7.1). At some point during that decade, several countries in the region experienced inflation rates in the hundreds and even thousands percent. Mexico, a traditional low-inflation country by Latin American standards, had rates

---

2 Most of the information presented in this section comes from data compiled by Molina *et al.* (2000). Although not the most recent for each country, this is the only data series fully comparable across Latin American countries over the period 1970-99. Most data for Mexico comes, however, from national sources.

3 For the sake of accuracy, it must be pointed out that the 'lost decade' actually comprised a 'decade and a half of lost production.'

Table 7.1: Annual Rates of Inflation in Latin America; Selected Countries; 1970-81, 1982-89 and 1990-99

	Average			Maximum		
	1970-81	1982-89	1990-99	1970-81	1982-89	1990-99
Argentina	128	338	24	444	3,080	2,314
Brazil	102	172	609	102	1,431	2,948
Colombia	21	21	22	33	28	30
Costa Rica	13	30	17	37	90	29
Dominican Republic	10	17	11	17	45	50
Guatemala	9	13	12	16	37	41
Honduras	8	5	19	18	10	34
Mexico	17	84	20	29	132	35
Nicaragua	19	317	339	48	10,205	7,485
Panama	7	2	1	16	4	2
Paraguay	12	20	14	28	32	38
Peru	33	102	66	75	3,399	7,482
Uruguay	58	56	42	97	80	113
Venezuela	9	13	48	22	84	100
Mathematical average	32	85	89	47	928	1,472

Source: Molina et al., 2000.

near or above the 100-percent mark for several years; most countries experienced inflation rates several times higher than those registered in the 1970s. It has been suggested, therefore, that servicing the external debt strained deficits and monetary policy to the point where inflation was difficult to control; to that extent, inflation was debt-driven. In the early 1990s, governments' efforts to align fiscal balances, restructure the external debt, and renew financial inflows succeeded in reducing inflation rates in the region and restoring positive – albeit low – average rates of economic growth.

The social impact of the 'lost 15-year decade' will be examined next. The economic contraction, high rates of inflation, and fiscal constraints on government expenditures were all expected to have a negative impact on social indicators. However, while poverty and inequality worsened in the region during the 1980s and 1990s, other social indicators surprisingly were not negatively affected.

Income Poverty

The data show that, *ceteris paribus*, a negative correlation exists between economic growth and the incidence of income poverty in Latin America. Economic growth has significantly influenced reductions in the incidence of poverty in the region. In 1970, almost 45 percent of the Latin American population was considered poor; a decade later, in 1982, the incidence of poverty was restricted to less than 25 percent of the population – a remarkable reduction in a short period (Figure 7.1). However, the economic recession of the 1980s again

Figure 7.1: Poverty Incidence and GDP Per Capita in Latin America, 1970-1999

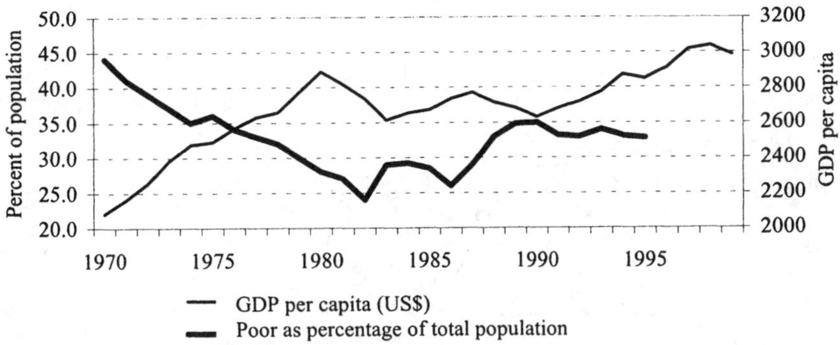

Source: Londoño and Székely (1997).

increased poverty rates in the region.[4] A similar inverse correlation between economic growth and poverty was evident in Mexico: the incidence of poverty fell in the 1970s and increased sharply in the 1980s (Table 7.2).

This economic picture leads to a simple and straightforward conclusion: economic growth benefits the poor; lack of economic growth benefits no one – neither the poor nor the rich. In a period of expanding productive activity, economic growth normally increases employment opportunities and helps raise average incomes, generating the conditions for improvement in overall standards of living.

An interesting related issue has recently been addressed in the literature: how does economic growth benefit the poor? Empirical findings suggest that the impact of economic growth on poverty is conditional on the level of inequality. It has been shown that the impact of growth on the incidence of poverty is low in countries with high income inequality (de Janvry and Sadoulet, 1995) – precisely the case in Latin America. Measured by the Gini coefficient,[5] income inequality in Latin America was fairly high in 1970 (0.58), declined slightly during the period of fast economic growth in the 1970s, and then decreased further during the recessions of

4 It was not until 1997 that the proportions of households below both the poverty and extreme poverty lines returned to their 1980 level, where these poverty lines are defined as incomes of at least two dollars and one dollar a day (PPP), respectively. The decline in poverty rates has not been, however, strong enough to reduce the absolute number of those considered poor or extremely poor. Londoño and Székely (1998) estimate that 23 million poor people have been added to the pool of the extremely poor over the last 25 years – in 1970 there were 51.4 million extremely poor people in the region, and by 1995 the number had increased to 74.5 million.

5 Gini coefficients take values from 0 to 1, with 1 representing maximum inequality.

Figure 7.2: Income Distribution in Latin America as Measured by Gini Coefficient, 1970-1995

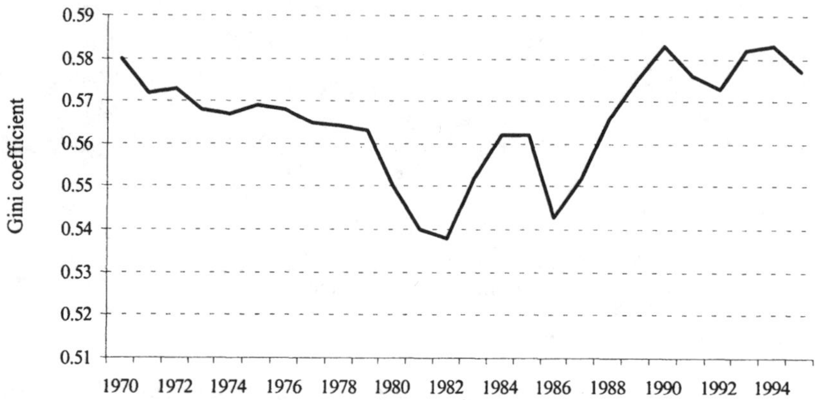

Source: Molinas et al. (2000).

1982 and 1986 when the contraction of the economy made many individuals poorer simultaneously (Figure 7.2). A more troubling trend became evident in the early years of recovery when the region's modest economic growth appeared to generate rapidly rising inequality. Mexico followed this same pattern; income inequality there steadily declined from 1963 to 1977, and fell further during the crisis years of the early 1980s (Table 7.2). Later, as economic growth recovered in the 1990s, inequality also began to increase.

These broad patterns suggest the presence of deep underlying forces changing the nature of the relation between growth and poverty. During the 1990s, an important shift was perceived in the relation between growth and poverty. Increases in income inequality weakened the potential positive effect of growth in per capita income on the incidence of poverty. Indeed, the region's growth elasticity of poverty has decreased from 1.9 in 1982 to 1.3 in the 1990s (Londoño and Székely, 1998) – that is, a 1 percent increase in per capita consumption led to only a 1.3 percent decrease in poverty in the 1990s, as opposed to an almost 2 percent decline in the 1980s.[6]

6 The growth elasticity of poverty is the ratio of the percentage change in the FGT poverty index to the percentage change in consumption per capita that induces it. The FGT poverty index developed by Foster *et al.* (1984) represents a family of poverty indexes where the change of one parameter yields three poverty estimates: i) the proportion of people whose income is below a given poverty line (poverty rate); ii) the distance between the average income of the poor in relation to the poverty line (poverty gap); and iii) a measure of inequality in the distribution of income among the poor (also known as

Table 7.2: Inequality, Poverty and Growth in Mexico, Percents, 1963-2000

Year	Gini index	Poverty incidence [a]	Inter-period annual rate of growth		
			Gini	Poverty	GDP
1963	0.606	60.9	...	...	...
1968	0.586	40.8	-0.67	-7.70	7.89
1977	0.518	30.4	-1.36	-3.22	5.20
1984	0.501	40.9	-0.48	4.33	4.38
1989	0.549	41.3	1.85	0.20	1.22
1992	0.543	31.4	-0.37	-8.73	4.31
1994	0.528	31.2	-1.39	-0.32	3.19
1996	0.534	40.1	0.57	13.37	-0.70
1998	0.570	32.8	3.32	-9.56	5.84
2000	0.564	30.8	-0.53	-3.10	5.18

[a] The incidence of poverty is based on an estimated extreme poverty line.

Source: Authors' calculations based on Hernández and Velásquez (2002) and INEGI.

These findings are troubling: not only has Latin America taken a long time to recover its growth potential, but economic growth now takes place in a context of higher income inequality, diminishing the efficiency of growth as a mechanism to lower the high incidence of poverty. This discovery presents one of the greatest challenges faced by the region in the 21st century: how can we improve the positive impact of economic growth on the living conditions of large segments of the population presently marginalized from the benefits of expanding economies.

Other Dimensions of Welfare

Income poverty is only one measure of household welfare; another way of estimating poverty and deprivation is by observing the satisfaction of basic needs by individuals and households. This section examines Latin American trends in social expenditure and selected social sector outcomes for which we have comparable information across countries for the period from 1970 to the late 1990s.

Social public expenditure – that is, the aggregate of reported public expenditures in education, health, housing and social security (pensions) – decreased in the region during the recession of the 1980s both as a percentage of GDP and in absolute terms. Although social expenditure as a share of GDP was slightly higher in the mid 1980s compared with the 1980 figure, in a context of declining real GDP per capita it actually implied a decrease in per capita resources allocated to the social sector. Allocation of resources to the social sector became a more important priority after 1990, social expenditure increasing in most countries both as a percentage of GDP and in per capita terms, being led in particular by

the FGT index).

Table 7.3: Selected Social Indicators for Latin America, 1960-2000

	1960	1970	1980	1990	1995	1997
Average Years of Schooling	2.8	3.4	3.9	4.7	4.9	...
Infant Mortality (per thousand)	...	83.7	60.4	41.0	...	31.7
Access to Drinking Water (percent)	...	54.0	71.1	78.8	75.3	...

Source: Molina et al. (2000).

greater expenditures in education and health. Despite contraction of per capita social expenditure during recession years, a systematic improvement in basic social indicators was observed across the region. Measured by average years of schooling and literacy rates, education improved continuously throughout 1960-90. Similarly, health indicators showed continuous improvements – for example, trends in infant mortality and life expectancy steadily improved (Table 7.3). Accessibility to drinking water has been less uniform across the region. While the pace of improvement slowed down in most countries in the 1990s, Mexico continued showing progress in most social indicators until the end of the century.

These apparently contradictory trends – declining social expenditures and improving social indicators – may be explained on the basis of a specific category of social investments: those investments whose social impact is usually perceived several years later. Positive social outcomes observed in the late 1980s and in the 1990s could thus be attributed to expenditures incurred in the late 1970s, when social expenditure was on the rise. This reasoning is also consistent with the observed slowdown in improved access to drinking water in the region during the 1980s, a social investment with no significant time lag between the actual expenditure and its social impact.

It appears, therefore, that the real per capita decline in social expenditure of the 1980s should slow down progress in the different dimensions of welfare in following years, unless important efficiency gains were made in the use of resources. Latin America, however, has not been particularly efficient in allocating social expenditure. A rough comparison of expenditures and achievements in education and health in Latin American and Asian countries reveals striking differences. Relative to Latin American countries, Asian countries with similar – or lower – levels of income per capita spend proportionally similar – or less – resources in education and health – but with much better results than those achieved in Latin America (Tables 7.4 and 7.5). Even the Philippines, often referred to as the 'Latin American country' of Asia, has achieved better results in education than has any Latin American country, and has done so with significantly less resources.

It becomes apparent that welfare improvements in the region require not only greater social expenditures, but also greater efficiency and equity in the use of available resources. Londoño and Székely (1998) found that average schooling in

Table 7.4: Public Expenditure on Education and Outcomes in Latin America and Asia, 1980 and 1990s, Selected Countries

	Real GDP per Capita (PPP)		Expenditure in Education (% GDP)		Average Schooling (years)		Completed Primary School (%)	
	1980	1997	1980	1996	1980	1990s	1980	1990s
Brazil	3,680	6,480	3.6	5.5	3.2	3.8	20	30
Ecuador	2,730	4,940	5.6	3.5	6.1	5.9	67	63
Guatemala	2,500	4,100	1.8	1.7	2.7	3.0	40	36
Mexico	4,600	8,370	4.7	4.9	4.8	6.7	66	73
Nicaragua	1,520	1,950	3.4	3.7	3.2	3.7	38	43
Paraguay	2,250	3,980	1.5	3.9	5.1	5.0	53	60
Venezuela	5,690	8,860	4.4	5.2	5.5	5.0	70	86
Sri Lanka	830	2,490	2.7	3.4	5.6	6.0	...	97
Philippines	2,090	3,520	1.7	2.2	6.5	6.9	...	70
China	450	3,130	2.5	2.3	4.8	5.9	...	85
Korea	2,470	13,590	3.7	3.7	7.9	9.9	...	99
Thailand	1,480	6,690	3.4	4.1	4.4	5.6	...	87

Source: Molina et al. (2000).

Latin America in 1995 was 2 years less than would be expected given the region's level of development, and 4 years less than in Southeast Asian countries with similar levels of development. Moreover, lower levels of education produced, in turn, greater inequality in educational opportunities in the region (Londoño and Székely, 1997). During the 1990s social expenditures increased in the region and profound reforms in the social sectors focused explicitly on improving efficiency in the use of resources. Unfortunately, similar efforts were not directed to improving access to, and equity in, basic social services.

During recessions, as indicated above, apparently contradictory results between the economic impact of recession and performance indicators of welfare can be observed for the region. The lack of consistency between economic and social policies in the region remains a controversial issue, and might help to explain the absence of significant improvements in poverty, income distribution, and employment indicators. Indeed, economic policy objectives focus on macroeconomic stability and show little concern for the promotion of broad-based growth with positive social impacts. Similarly, social policy – concerned particularly with designing safety nets to counteract the negative impact of economic policy – has probably alleviated extreme forms of poverty but has failed substantially to provide even basic improvement in labor productivity through greater investment in education and health, nor has it provided the basis for expanding access to productive assets for large segments of the population to improve their standard of living and stimulate economic growth. This lack of consistency between economic and social policy objectives has reinforced structural inequalities in the region and increased the volatility of growth, thus

Table 7.5: Public Expenditure on Health and Outcomes in Latin America and Asia, 1980 and 1997, Selected Countries

	Real GNP per Capita (PPP)		Expenditure in Health (% of GDP)		Infant Mortality (per 1,000 life births)		Life Expectancy (years)	
	1980	1997	1980	1990	1980	1997	1980	1997
Brazil	3,680	6,480	0.6	2.7	70	34	63	67
Ecuador	2,730	4,940	0.4	2.0	74	33	63	70
Guatemala	2,500	4,100	0.6	0.9	84	43	57	64
Mexico	4,600	8,370	1.9	1.6	51	31	67	72
Nicaragua	1,520	1,950	0.4	6.7	84	43	59	68
Paraguay	2,250	3,980	0.5	1.2	50	23	67	70
Venezuela	5,690	8,860	2.6	2.0	36	21	68	73
Sri Lanka	830	2,490	2.0	1.8	34	14	68	73
Philippines	2,090	3,520	0.4	1.0	52	35	61	68
China	450	3,130	1.3	1.8	42	32	67	70
Korea	2,470	13,590	0.2	2.7	26	9	67	72
Thailand	1,480	6,690	0.4	1.1	49	33	64	69

Source: Molina et al. (2000).

failing to provide a broader base for expanding growth in the region.

In the next section we illustrate one aspect of the inconsistencies between economic and social policies by first discussing regional employment trends, then evaluating more deeply employment outcomes in Mexico – a country where economic reforms have failed to expand job opportunities and improve living conditions in general. This discussion illustrates the failure of economic reforms to generate suitable employment for large segments of an increasingly urban population. Poor labor market performance has been an important factor behind the continuing high incidence of income poverty and relatively weak improvements in welfare indicators.

Economic Restructuring and Employment Trends in Latin America

Employment trends are probably the best indicators of the impact of economic growth on development. Not surprisingly, poor labor market outcomes represent some of the main concerns of Latin Americans. A survey by Corporación Latinobarómetro indicated unemployment, wage deterioration and employment instability as the top preoccupations of respondents – much greater than concerns about lack of opportunities in education, or issues of social security, or even poverty in general.[7] In highly urban economies like those in most Latin American

---

7 Corporación Latinobarómetro carries out annual public opinion surveys in 17 Latin American countries; they can be accessed at www.latinobarometro.org.

Table 7.6: Average Annual Rate of Unemployment in Latin America; Selected Countries; 1985, 1990 and 2000

	1985	1990	2000
Argentina	6.1	7.5	15.1
Bolivia	5.7	7.2	7.4
Brazil	5.3	4.3	7.1
Chile	17.0	7.4	9.2
Colombia	13.8	10.5	17.2
Costa Rica	7.2	5.4	5.3
Ecuador	10.4	6.1	14.1
El Salvador	...	10.0	6.6
Honduras	11.7	6.9	...
Mexico	4.4	2.8	2.2
Nicaragua	3.2	7.6	9.8
Panama	15.7	20.0	15.3
Paraguay	5.1	6.6	10.0
Peru	10.1	8.3	7.0
Dominican Republic [a]	...	19.6	13.9
Uruguay	13.1	9.2	13.6
Venezuela	14.3	11.0	13.9
Latin America	9.5	8.2	10.5

[a] The 1990 figure corresponds to 1991.

Source: ILO (2001, Table 1-A).

countries, the most important source of income for large segments of the population is labor earnings. In general, economic growth that expands job opportunities translates into better living conditions. In turn, better housing conditions and improved health and education – factors that facilitate access to job opportunities – require implementation of social policies that promote a more equal distribution of public resources and expanding opportunities for citizens.

The poor performance of Latin American labor markets is symptomatic of a disconnection between the objectives of narrowly defined economic policies and their social impact. The analysis of Mexico will serve to illustrate how apparently successful restructuring policies aimed at reestablishing positive net flows of foreign direct investment and increasing exports have failed to generate good employment opportunities overall. Such a disconnection between general macroeconomic objectives and their impact on everyday living conditions puts into question the traditional wisdom of narrowly defined economic policies. The review of employment trends in Mexico during the period of reform and restructuring provides evidence of the need to make the macroeconomic objective of achieving healthy growing economies consistent with the social objective of expanding the opportunities for people to improve their living conditions.

Employment conditions deteriorated throughout the region in the 1990s – unemployment increased, labor absorption fell, informality increased

Table 7.7: Informal Labor Force as Percentage of Non-Agricultural Employment in Latin America, 1990 and 2000

	1990	2000
Argentina [a]	52.0	49.3
Brasil[2]	40.6	47.1
Chile	37.9	38.0
Colombia	45.7	55.6
Costa Rica	41.2	45.2
Ecuador	55.6	51.6
Honduras [b]	57.6	60.7
Mexico	38.4	39.2
Panama [c]	36.0	37.3
Peru	52.7	59.2
Uruguay [c]	39.1	43.1
Venezuela	38.6	50.6
Latin America	42.8	46.9

[a] Figures are for 1991 and 1998. [b] Second figure is for 1999. [c] First figure is for 1991.

Source: ILO (2001, Table 6-A).

systematically, and wage differentials grew. Poor labor market outcomes were not the result of a fast-growing labor force because its rate of growth decreased from 3.1 percent in 1980 to 2.5 percent in 1990. But employment creation decreased markedly in all countries of the region during 1991-96 relative to 1985-90, the only exception being the Dominican Republic. Despite the lack of unemployment insurance in most countries of the region, open unemployment gradually increased throughout the 1990s. According to ILO estimates, the Latin American average unemployment rate increased from 8.2 percent in 1990 to 10.5 percent in 2000 (Table 7.6), and the rate of visible underemployment – the proportion of the employed population willing to work more hours – also increased.

In a region where unemployment insurance barely exists, unemployment rates do not necessarily reflect the real state of employment. Workers without formal-sector jobs engage in all kinds of unregulated, low-productivity activities in the informal sector, which has led to a rapid increase in the share of informal employment in the region from 40 percent in 1980 to 42.8 percent in 1990, and to 46.9 percent in 2000 (Table 7.7).[8] It has been estimated that the informal sector generates 7 of every 10 new non-agricultural jobs in the region, predominantly micro enterprises and independent workers (ECLAC, 2002b, 48). Although wages increased throughout the 1990s, only in 2000 did they surpass the 1980 levels. Wage changes over the 1990s varied across countries. Average industrial wages increased by 1.8 percent per annum, particularly as a result of annual wage

8 Informal sector workers are those occupied in non-agricultural activities and are either self-employed, or working in micro enterprises or in domestic services.

Table 7.8: Latin America Real Industrial Wage Index, 1980, 1990 and 2000 (1980 = 100)

	1990	2000	Average Annual Growth (Percent)
Argentina	75.0	77.4	0.3
Bolivia	86.7	93.3	0.7
Brazil	96.7	128.8	2.9
Chile	105.8	155.5	3.9
Colombia	114.8	136.1	1.7
Costa Rica	109.7	136.3	2.2
Ecuador	74.1	97.8	2.8
Honduras [a]	73.4	87.7	...
Mexico	59.6	59.5	0.0
Panama [b]	97.8	135.3	3.7
Paraguay	102.4	98.3	-0.4
Peru	34.4	42.4	2.1
Uruguay	110.8	117.5	0.6
Venezuela	57.0	48.0	-1.7
Average [c]	84.7	103.3	1.8

[a] Figure for 2000 corresponds to 1999. [b] Figure for 1990 corresponds to 1991. [c] Weighted average (excluding Honduras).

Source: ILO (2001, Table 9-A).

increases of more than 3 percent in Chile, Costa Rica, and Panama. In Paraguay and Venezuela, however, average wages decreased, and in Mexico they remained unchanged (Table 7.8).

Changes in real wages have varied not only across countries but also across sectors within countries. Returns to different levels of education have moved in different directions – returns to primary, and especially secondary, education decreased significantly, while returns to higher education increased rapidly. With the exception of Costa Rica, wage differentials increased during 1990-95, and high wage inequality has generated high income inequality.

This disappointing employment record has not helped reduce the level of poverty in Latin America, and simple demographic expansion has enlarged the pool of poor people. High and – at times – rising unemployment levels, high and increasing numbers of workers occupied in informal activities, and stagnant or decreasing wages at the low end of the distribution all have contributed to break the historical link between economic growth and poverty reduction. Indeed, within different occupational categories, the proportion of people earning incomes below the poverty line increased over the 1990s, particularly in the informal sector. In three categories typical of informal urban markets in Latin America, the incidence of poverty increased or remained relatively unchanged in about half the cases in a

Table 7.9: Incidence of Poverty by Occupational Category in Latin America, 1990 and 2000, Selected Countries, Percents

	Formal Activities						Informal Activities					
	(1)		(2)		(3)		(4)		(5)		(6)	
	1990	2000	1990	2000	1990	2000	1990	2000	1990	2000	1990	2000
Argentina	0	6	12	9	15	17	21	22	6	14	8	8
Bolivia	0	23	42	41	53	53	31	27	46	66	40	43
Brazil	0	14	30	26	48	32	49	39	40	33	36	27
Chile	0	6	30	16	38	22	37	17	28	14	23	12
Colombia	27	12	45	38	0	0	38	35	54	60	53	54
Costa Rica	0	3	15	9	22	14	28	27	28	17	24	16
Ecuador	33	30	50	55	60	70	56	61	70	68	61	62
El Salvador	14	9	35	26	50	44	32	41	50	43	41	35
Guatemala	20	19	47	41	61	53	42	46	48	51	35	46
Honduras	29	41	60	64	76	81	51	58	81	80	73	72
Mexico	0	11	37	26	0	44	60	38	32	34	28	24
Nicaragua	47	0	54	54	64	68	74	74	60	59	45	52
Panama	12	5	24	12	38	24	31	20	42	24	38	26
Paraguay	23	11	40	27	49	40	29	27	41	42	31	31
Peru	14	14	20	21	28	32	16	23	36	52	33	36
Uruguay	8	2	10	5	17	9	25	12	21	12	14	9
Venezuela	20	28	24	37	34	52	33	50	25	33	22	34

(1) Wage employees public sector; (2) Waged employees private sector, 6 or more employees; (3) Wage employees private sector, 5 or less employees; (4) Domestic workers; (5) Own account construction workers; (6) Own account trade and services workers.

Source: ECLAC (2002a. Annex Table 16).

17-country sample.[9] Poverty increased in 40 percent of the cases involving workers of private micro enterprises. Moreover, the proportion of poor in formal sector occupations remained unchanged or increased slightly in more than 40 percent of the cases (Table 7.9). The evidence thus shows that the expansion of employment as a result of the economic recovery of the 1990s has not been sufficient to release people from poverty.

The causes of poor labor market performance are not clear, and a vast volume of literature has examined trends in employment conditions and wages in an attempt to single out the factors determining poor labor market outcomes. Several hypotheses have been advanced in these studies to explain topics such as the impact of liberalization on employment and wages, technological change, the impact of exchange rate fluctuations, inflation, stabilization policies, greater market volatility, short- vs. long-term effects, minimum wage policies, etc. While we do not intend to elaborate further on the plausible explanations set forth, it appears that, with so many factors at play, no single factor can be responsible for such a complex set of interactions. But one thing is clear: the long process of stabilization and structural adjustment in Latin America has not lived up to expectations.

9 The three categories are domestic workers, own account workers in construction, and own account workers in trade and services.

Economic Restructuring and Employment Trends in Mexico

Mexico went through a long period of stabilization and structural adjustment, as did most countries in the region.[10] The prevailing policies proved successful in promoting greater inflows of foreign direct investment and in achieving macroeconomic stability and good export performance, but also had negative outcomes such as slow rates of economic growth, persistent overvaluation of the domestic currency, and increasing vulnerability to international financial flows. More important, social outcomes such as poverty, and changes in income inequality, proved far less favorable than did economic ones. In this regard, the analysis of labor market performance becomes central to our understanding of social outcomes. Low productivity activities and precarious occupations are two compelling causes of stagnating incomes among the poor. Focusing our attention on labor market trends will help us understand the worrisome inconsistency between relatively successful macroeconomic policies and poor social outcomes.

Over the last twenty years, Mexico has faced the challenge of creating sufficient jobs for more than one million new workers every year. Past high rates of population growth are mostly responsible for today's rapidly growing labor force, but the large numbers of women joining the labor force has also contributed to this expansion – female employment becoming a survival strategy to compensate for falling family incomes and unstable jobs (Cortés, 2000), as well as a reflection of deeper social changes. These two factors explain the rapid growth of labor supply, and the employment performance of the Mexican economy since the mid-1980s has not been strong enough to provide sufficient employment opportunities for this growing supply of labor.[11] Few good jobs have been created for those joining the workforce, while labor conditions for much of the working population have stagnated or worsened. Precarious occupations such as street vending and different forms of self-employment have mushroomed in large cities, worsening the already deficient conditions of urban labor markets. Poverty and inequality, not surprisingly, have remained high in Mexico as in many other Latin America countries.

10 For a critical view of Mexico's economic strategy, see Dornbusch and Werner (1994), Edwards (1997), Krugman (1995), Ros (1994), and Sachs *et al.* (1995). For an analysis of structural reforms at the regional level, see Clavijo and Valdivieso (2000), Morley *et al.* (1999), and Stallings and Peres (2000).

11 Mexico is a mid Latin American performer in terms of employment creation in general, and wage employment creation in particular. See Graph IV.I and Table IV.4 in Weller (2001).

Employment Trends in the Manufacturing Sector

Overall employment growth in manufacturing has been uneven. Economic census data show that the total number of workers in manufacturing establishments increased from 2.7 to 4.2 million throughout 1988-98 – an average growth of 4.6 percent per annum.[12] But micro manufacturing firms – an important component of the informal sector – were responsible for the creation of 46.3 percent of these 1.5 million new jobs. Employment in the formal manufacturing sector – that is, excluding micro establishments – grew at an annual average rate of only 3.1 percent; meanwhile, employment in large manufacturing units grew at a discouraging average rate of 0.8 percent per annum.[13]

Employment Performance of Large Plants The disappointing employment-creation record of large manufacturing plants – other than those in the maquiladora program[14] – has been mostly responsible for the slow growth in manufacturing jobs and urban employment generally. This development represents a serious setback for a country characterized by an economic base historically structured along import substitution industrialization lines, where the creation of 'good' urban jobs largely depends on the employment-creation performance of large manufacturing firms. On the brighter side, manufacturing exports have increased over the last two decades at an impressive annual average rate of 15 percent, but the bulk of these exports was produced in only two sectors dominated by relatively few large firms.[15] In any case, the fast export growth in manufactures has not been sufficient to generate an equivalent fast growth in employment in an export sector dominated by large firms with poor employment-creation potential.

The job-creation performance of large manufacturing plants has been indeed discouraging. The level of total employment in these plants decreased at an annual

12 These figures correspond to manufacturing activities carried out in 'fixed location' establishments, including maquiladoras, as defined by INEGI. Therefore, these figures do not include those manufacturing activities realized *in situ* by self-employed workers.

13 Micro manufacturing establishments are taken here as those that have a fixed location and employ less than 16 workers. Large manufacturing units are those with 251 and more employees.

14 The maquiladora program was started in the 1960s to facilitate the processing of duty-free imports for re-exporting under more liberal investment rules. Plants subscribing to this program initially engaged in mostly simple assembly operations but, over time, the program came to include more sophisticated manufacturing plants. Nevertheless, these plants typically have few links with other sectors of the domestic economy. For an analysis of the maquiladora program, see Carrillo (1989), Mendiola (1999), and Middlebrook and Zepeda (2003).

15 About 150 firms accounted for 54 percent of total exports in 2001 (Presidencia, 2001a, 31).

Table 7.10: Employment in Maquiladora and Large Manufacturing Plants in Mexico, 1987-2001

	Maquiladora [a]		Large Manufacturing [b]		
Year	No. of employees	Percent [c]	No. of Employees in 129 Industries [d]	No. of Employees in 205 Industries [e]	Percent [c]
1987	322,743	(25.4)	948,079		(74.6)
1994	600,585	30.1	809,373	1,393,884	69.9
1995	681,251	34.9	747,456	1,273,057	65.1
1996	799,347	37.8		1,314,066	62.2
2000	1,307,982	47.0		1,477,784	53.0
2001	1,081,526	43.3		1,416,043	56.7
			Number of Jobs Added		
Period	Number of Jobs Added	Annual Average Change (%)	129 Industries	205 Industries	Annual Average Change (%) [c]
1987-1994	277,842	9.3	-138,706		(-2.2)
1994-1995	80,666	13.4	-61,917	-120,827	-8.7
1996-2000	508,635	13.1		163,718	3.0
2000-2001	-226,456	63.6		-61,741	12.5

[a] Figures are collected from periodical census of registered maquiladora plants. [b] Figures are collected by INEGI's Monthly Employment Survey (EIM) from establishments accounting for about 80 percent of total production in the 6-digit in dustrial classification. The EIM excludes plants affiliated with the maquiladora program. During the period contained in this table, the sample-size was expanded twice, in 1990 and in 1994-95. Data are fully comparable from 1987 to 1994-95 and from 1994-95 to 2001, but not between these two periods. [c] Percent figures in brackets refer to maquiladora and 205 manufacturing industries; non-bracket figures refer to 129 industries. [d] Figures comparable between 1987 and 1994: 129 industries. [e] Figures comparable for 1994-2001: 205industries.

Source: Authors' calculations based on data from INEGI.

average rate of 20,000 jobs – 2 percent a year – over 1987-94, representing a total net loss of 139,000 jobs (Table 7.10).[16] At the same time, the creation of new jobs was concentrated in a small number of sectors – particularly export-oriented

16 Figures are based on INEGI's *Monthly Industrial Survey* (EIM). The EIM collects information from all fixed location establishments – except those associated with the maquiladora program – accounting for 80 percent of total production in the 6–digit industrial classification. These figures, therefore, generally differ from those provided by census data since the latter also includes information from maquiladora plants. INEGI has changed the sample size of the survey twice and, thus, the figures from these two sources are fully comparable only for the period 1987-94.

sectors – and firms. Indeed, only 29 of 129 sectors experienced some employment growth, adding a total of about 37,000 jobs between 1987 and 1994.[17] Moreover, just two sectors accounted for most of this increase in employment: automobile assembly and non-alcoholic beverages – the first one, an export oriented activity; the other, a domestically driven sector.

Overall employment trends in large plants worsened even further during the 1995 crisis; it is estimated that total employment in large plants suffered a loss close to 120,000 jobs, or 8-9 percent of the total, in 1994-95. The employment impact of the 1995 crisis was also felt by the formal private sector as shown by the Institute for Social Security (IMSS), losing the affiliation of more than 600,000 workers, or 6 percent of the total, in 1994-95 (Presidencia, 2001b, 178).

As the economy recovered in 1996, employment in large manufacturing firms began to increase once again, but the 40,000 jobs created in the first post-crisis year were not sufficient to compensate for the 120,000 lost in 1995. The recovery continued in the following year, and by 1998 total employment in large plants was already higher than in the 1994 pre-crisis year. Export markets played a critical role in the recovery of employment levels in 1996-98. Sectors such as automobiles (engines and electrical parts), computers, apparel and textiles, pharmaceuticals, and baked goods led the process of job-creation. This strong recovery of employment levels was, however, short-lived. As soon as the real value of the peso recovered to its pre-crisis levels, employment creation started to lose strength despite the continuous growth of non-maquila manufacturing exports. In the ensuing recession of 2001-02, large manufacturing plants once again experienced job loses estimated at more than 60,000.

In general, large manufacturing plants showed an impressive export record over the last 20 years, with some selective sectors also performing well – though not spectacularly – in regards to job creation. As a whole, however, large manufacturing plants contributed little to the solution of the crucial problem Mexico has been facing over the last 20 years: the pressing need to create sufficient 'good' jobs to meet the growing supply of urban labor.

Employment in the Maquiladora Sector The employment performance of the maquiladora industry contrasts greatly with that of large manufacturing plants. Indeed, over the last 10 to 15 years, the creation of most manufacturing employment has been concentrated in the maquiladora sector, located mostly in northern states. The maquiladora sector created 40,000 new jobs a year on average in the period 1983-94, and about 120,000 per annum over 1995-2000. The share of maquiladora employment in total manufacturing employment in fixed-location

17 These 29 sectors covered a wide range of activities. For a detailed discussion of employment trends over 1987-94, see Salas and Zepeda (2003).

establishments has continuously risen from 5 percent in 1980, to 14 percent in 1988, to 16 percent in 1993, and to 25 percent in 1998. Maquila plants were responsible for two-thirds of all new jobs created in manufacturing fixed-location establishments (excluding micro units) over the 1988-93 period; over 1993-98, they accounted for 85 percent of all new jobs created in this sector.

The total number of jobs in maquiladoras has risen continuously in the last 25 years from its 1975 level of 60,000 workers, almost doubling every five years to reach 420 thousand in 1990, and 1.3 million in 2000. The economic recession of 1995 had no negative impact on the number of jobs in maquiladora plants. On the contrary, the real devaluation of the peso strengthened the export potential of the maquiladora sector. In addition, the implementation of NAFTA opened up new export opportunities for the sector, particularly in the apparel industry, thus accelerating both exports and employment growth – the latter increasing by 17 percent in both 1996 and 1997. As the peso started to appreciate in real terms and the initial impact of NAFTA began to fade, both exports and employment annual growth rates slowed to about 12 percent in 1998-99. The 2000-01 U.S. recession further reduced the rate of employment growth to 9 percent in 2000 and, for the first time in many years, to a negative 17 percent in 2001.

The Export Promotion Strategy As noted above, Mexico's economic restructuring has been successful in several areas. Exports, for instance, have grown rapidly, particularly due to the expansion of manufacture sales abroad. Manufactures now represent the largest component of exports, with middle-range technology-intensive products predominant. But 20 years after trade liberalization, overall employment trends in the modern sector of the economy remain stagnant and the quality of jobs has not improved.

The contribution of the manufacturing export sector to job creation and, more generally, to the strengthening of the industrialization process and to the promotion of development in the broadest sense has remained a subject of heated debate (Dussel, 1997; Katz, 2001). Critics of economic liberalization have initially focused their argument against the maquiladora program, highlighting some of the most visible negative characteristics of this type of productive unit: low level of integration with the domestic economy, intensive use of mainly unskilled labor, low labor standards, and extensive use of low-paid female labor. Critics also point out that after 35 years of operation, 95 percent of the inputs used in the maquiladora sector are still imported. In addition, given that the export reorientation of large non-maquiladora manufacturing plants has implied the elimination of most backward linkages, critics argue that little will be gained by rising exports if this comes at the expense of reducing domestic production of final and intermediate goods.

The more enthusiastic supporters of trade liberalization argue that maquiladoras have gone through a real transformation, moving away from the typical sweatshop found earlier in the Mexican northern border. Indeed, the number of maquila plants in the modern sector – especially those producing auto parts and electronics – has increased continuously, and the average number of workers per plant has risen from about 200 workers in 1980 to 326 in 2000 (Salas and Zepeda, 2003). With respect to the new developments in the non-maquiladora manufacturing sector, defenders of trade liberalization argue that there is no justification for inefficient backward linkages and that, in any case, a low level of employment creation represents the inevitable cost of becoming competitive.

As both trade liberalization and frequent overvaluation of the peso have decreased the cost of imports, even traditionally well-integrated manufacturing plants are increasing their use of imported inputs, thus losing their backward linkages to other industrial sectors of the economy. At the same time, maquiladoras are slowly becoming more than mere assembly plants. Therefore, the once-clear distinction between these two types of productive units is vanishing: domestic firms are acquiring characteristics until recently present only in maquiladora-type arrangements while, at the same time, maquiladoras are losing some of their previous distinctive characteristics. The problem, however, is that the point of convergence is closer to the maquiladora-type of operation, which is more reliant on imported inputs and has little integration with the rest of the domestic economy. Therefore, the price Mexico had to pay to upgrade its production capacity and become competitive in international markets was, on the one hand, a loss of direct employment-generation capacity in its modern exporting sector, and on the other hand, a weakened capacity to create secondary employment – through larger backward linkages – in other productive sectors.

Have these results been inevitable in Mexico's attempt to increase its participation in global markets? We argue that the absence of a consistent and comprehensive development strategy during the period of economic reform is responsible for the poor social outcomes attained to date. International competitiveness of large exporting sectors has been achieved and maintained through increasing levels of investment, technological upgrading, and importing of capital and intermediate goods – at the cost, in many instances, of eliminating competing domestic producers. But this long restructuring process has not generated the conditions for a broader transformation of domestic producers into exporters, nor generated greater vertical integration in production. Successful exporters are either large foreign corporations or large domestic industrial groups formed during the import substitution industrialization era – that is, those productive units whose access to large financial resources, technology, raw materials and information has allowed them to successfully develop a strong competitive position in world markets (Dussel, 1997; Katz, 2001; Unger, 1993).[18]

18 This is the case of Monterrey's non-metal minerals (ceramics and glass) exports and of apparel and textile exports recently revived under the protection of NAFTA, and with a

Labor productivity has increased in export activities, sometimes rapidly; parenthetically, this can be considered a pre-condition for remaining competitive in international markets. The counterpart of this tendency has been a decrease in the employment elasticity of exports. Unfortunately, productivity growth has generally been restricted to those few activities directly involved in exports,[19] and thus the aggregate growth of productivity has not been impressive.[20] Lack of effective policies to improve the competitiveness of small and medium manufacturing firms has prevented the integration of these enterprises with the modern export sector and larger domestic producers; indeed, greater competitiveness would allow the small and medium enterprise (SME) sector either to attempt a more outward orientation or to become suppliers of larger domestic or foreign firms.[21]

Small and medium firms have been exposed to foreign competition with very little resources and support to enable them to succeed. Indeed, most SMEs do not have access to financial resources from banks; lack support for technological innovations and adaptation of technology; employ a poorly educated labor force with, at best, 6 to 8 years of formal education; have almost no resources available for job training; and have no effective institutional support to develop links with global markets. Nor has macroeconomic policy been of much help to the SME sector. Overvaluation of the domestic currency – as part of anti-inflationary policies but also as a way of attracting foreign capital – has been most damaging for small businesses. The absence of linkages between domestic producers and international market suppliers is further aggravated by the expansion of foreign investment, which usually brings with it its own network of suppliers and takes years to develop production links with local suppliers. By contrast, national export-oriented firms show a greater propensity to buy local inputs and establish strong links with local suppliers (Middlebrook and Zepeda, 2003, Ch. 1).

Poor employment performance in a country successful in gaining access to

---

strong presence of international investment. But, perhaps, the most remarkable cases are found in the auto and the electronic industries. A combination of old industrial sites, new facilities in the north, and a fast growing number of maquiladoras producing auto-parts, has catapulted Mexico into a prime producer in the highly internationalized auto industry. In the case of electronics, its rapid growth is explained by the global strategies of large international firms profiting from location advantages and export promotion programs in Mexico.

19 A recent study shows that Mexico's labor productivity increased relative to that of the U.S. over 1980-90 but decreased over the 1990-96 period; it also shows that labor productivity tends to improve only in export-oriented sectors (see Tables III.2, III.4 and III.7 in Katz, 2001).

20 Another recent study concludes that although Mexico's competitiveness in manufactures shows an upward trend in the first half of the 1990s, its growth pattern is not robust (Hernández, 2000).

21 For a discussion of the characteristics, challenges, and policy issues relevant to small firms, see Zepeda *et al.* (1999).

foreign markets reflects the inability of public policy to expand global economic opportunities. It also reflects the failure of social policy – for example education, training and health policies – to respond to the demands of a rapidly changing economy that requires rapid upgrading of its labor force – including those employed in smaller productive units. In the present environment, the link between enhanced productivity and improvements in employment conditions, and growth and poverty reduction, appears to have weakened significantly. Apparent also is an increasing inconsistency between the objectives of aggregate macroeconomic policy and their social impact.

Employment in the Informal Sector

With few employment opportunities in the formal sector and no system of unemployment protection in place, the expansion of the labor force translates into high levels of informality rather than high rates of unemployment. Thus, the national unemployment rate was only 3.8 percent in 1987 and as low as 2.3 percent in 2000, the latter year being one of rapid economic growth.[22] It must be noted that Mexican unemployment rates are low even within the Latin American and Caribbean context (Stallings and Peres, 2000, Table V-4). In contrast, informality has been consistently high and quite often on the rise. Informality is understood as employment in unregulated businesses, characterized by low productivity and low remuneration, lacking social security, and often enduring long working days; in short, it implies precarious forms of employment. The self-employed and workers in micro firms – those economic units with 5 or less employees – comprise the bulk of the informal sector.

Labor market informality increased from the mid-1980s to the mid-1990s (Table 7.11). The number of self-employed workers, for instance, increased during the years of economic restructuring from 15.2 percent of total workers in 1987 to 15.8 percent in 1994, and to 17.4 percent in 1996; similarly, the corresponding share of those working in micro enterprises increased from 20.6 percent in 1987 to 21.9 percent in 1994, and to 22.3 percent in 1996.[23] Employment in micro enterprises grew at an annual average rate of 3.3 percent over 1987-94, a significantly higher rate than the 1.6 percent recorded by large enterprises with more than 250 employees. During the economic crisis of the mid-1990s, employment in micro enterprises expanded at an annual average rate of 1.6

---

22 Only at the height of the 1995 crisis did the urban unemployment rate exceed 7 percent (7.5 percent in the second quarter and 8.8 percent in the third one).

23 Other measures of informality report even higher shares. Using the ILO's measure of informality – employment in micro enterprises, domestic services and independent workers – the share of informal employment in total non-agricultural urban employment increased during the years of economic restructuring from 55.5 percent in 1990 to 57 percent in 1994 (ILO, 2001).

Table 7.11: Urban Employment and Labor Income in Mexico; Selected Occupations; 1987, 1994, 1996, and 2000

	1987	1994	1996	2000
	Millions of Workers			
Total Occupation	10.3	11.9	12.0	14.2
	Percent in Total Occupation [a]			
Self-employed	15.2	15.8	17.4	15.9
Employees in micro business	20.6	21.9	22.3	18.6
Street vendors	4.1	3.0	4.5	3.7
Unpaid workers	4.7	4.6	4.8	3.2
Employees	78.7	79.8	78.1	78.7
Waged workers	69.2	68.2	66.3	69.3
Full time workers, all year	52.0	52.8	50.8	48.9
Employees in large business	33.0	31.7	30.7	34.0
	Average Monthly Income from Labor (1993 pesos)			
All Occupations	927	1,320	980	1,176
Self-employed	785	1,017	772	974
Employees in micro business	390	518	408	703
Street vendors	552	596	536	703
Employees	800	1,103	904	1,074
Waged workers	852	1,178	973	1,129
Full time workers, all year	991	1,386	1,039	1,196
Employees in large business	1,034	1,501	1,240	1,406

[a] Percent figures do not add to 100 since these are not self excluding categories; for example, some employees in micro businesses might also be classified as unpaid family workers.

Source: Own calculations based on micro data from Urban Employment Survey (INEGI) for a fully comparable sample of 16 cities 1987-2000.

percent, while employment in firms of all other sizes decreased. Clearly, employment in micro businesses was a way to compensate for the loss of employment elsewhere. As shown in Table 7.11, the employment shares of other precarious occupations, such as street vendors and unpaid workers, also increased during the crisis years.

The share of self-employed workers in total employment decreased during the years of rapid economic expansion in the second half of the 1990s, falling from 17.4 percent in 1996 to 15.9 percent in 2000. The shares of other forms of precarious employment also decreased during this period. Most important, not only did the share of micro enterprise workers in total employment fall over 1996-2000, but the actual number of workers employed in this type of productive units also decreased by 0.4 percent per annum in 16 major Mexican cities (Table 7.11). Unfortunately, this trend did not last long. The 2001 recession once again forced large segments of the labor force into precarious occupations. The data thus show that the long period of economic restructuring was characterized by a rising

Table 7.12: Income and Employment by Business Size in Mexico, 1987-2000

Year	Occupation by Business Size						
	1-5	6-15	16-100	101-250	250+	Other	All (Millions)
	Distribution of Workers (Percents)[a]						
1987	20.6	9.1	12.2	3.8	33.0	21.3	8.1
1994	21.9	9.0	13.5	3.7	31.7	20.2	9.5
1996	22.3	8.8	12.9	3.5	30.7	21.9	9.4
2000	18.6	8.4	14.1	3.6	34.0	21.3	11.2
	Average Monthly Income From Labor (1993 pesos)						
1987	390	715	871	960	1,034	---	800
1994	518	925	1,146	1,420	1,501	---	1,103
1996	408	772	985	1,096	1,240	---	904
2000	509	860	1,101	1,255	1,406	---	1,074
	Annual Change in Average Income (Percents)						
1987/94	4.7	4.2	4.5	6.8	6.4	---	5.4
1994/96	-10.6	-8.3	-7.0	-11.4	-8.7	---	-9.0
1996/00	6.2	2.9	2.9	3.6	3.3	---	4.7
1987/00	7.6	5.1	6.6	7.7	9.0	---	8.5

[a] Percent figures, except for rounding, should add to 100 by row.

Source: Authors' calculations based on micro data from INEGI's Urban Employment Surveys (EIM) for a fully comparable sample of 16 cities 1987-2000.

proportion of people moving into precarious occupations in Mexico. The modest improvement in employment conditions during the 1996-2000 fast-growth period proved unsustainable.

Occupation in the informal sector is characterized not only by low productivity, but also by lack of job security, long working days and low-income earnings. Wages and other forms of labor income in precarious occupations are low, and frequently follow a decreasing trend in real terms. Mean wages of self-employed workers, who represent about 15-17 percent of the workforce, are between three-quarters and two-thirds of mean wages in large firms. Street vendors report a level of income about half of that in large businesses. Effective wages for street vendors and the self-employed may be actually lower than reported, given that capital depreciation – as little as it may be – is often reported as part of labor income. Employees in micro firms comprise between one-fifth to one-quarter of all employees and their wages are also remarkably low – their 1987 levels were less than 40 percent of the wages earned by workers in large firms and about one-half of the wages in businesses with 6 to 15 employees (Table 7.12). By 1994, relative wages in micro firms had further decreased to one-third of those in large businesses, as wages in micro enterprises increased by 4.7 percent per annum over

Table 7.13: Income by Educational Level in Mexico, 1987-2000 [a]

	1987	1994	1996	2000
	Monthly Average Income by Educational Level [b]			
Incomplete primary school	665	750	523	655
Complete Primary school [c]	791	918	638	780
Secondary school [d]	859	1026	743	877
Middle-high school [e]	1046	1313	974	1106
University education	1563	2924	2094	2453
All	912	1296	966	1166
	Average Income Ratio of High to Low Education			
Secondary/Incomp. Primary	1.29	1.37	1.42	1.34
Secondary/Primary Complete	1.09	1.12	1.16	1.12
Middle/Incomplete Primary	1.57	1.75	1.86	1.69
Middle/Primary Complete	1.32	1.43	1.53	1.42
University/Incomp. Primary	2.35	3.90	4.00	3.75
University/Primary Complete	1.98	3.19	3.28	3.14

[a] Data refer to the second quarter of each year. [b] In 1993 peso. [c] It includes those with one additional year of technical education. [d] It includes those with technical degrees that require complete secondary education. [e] It includes those with degrees that require complete mid-high education certificate.

Source: Authors' calculations based on micro data from INEGI's Urban Employment Surveys (EIM) for a fully comparable sample of 16 cities 1987-2000.

1987-94 while those in large firms rose by 6.4 percent during this period.[24] The lowest relative wages of micro enterprises were recorded in 1996.

Wage Dispersion

A distinctive feature of the period of economic restructuring has been the tendency towards greater wage inequality. As in many other Latin American countries, rising wage dispersion in Mexico has taken the form of an increasing premium for education. Table 7.13 shows that wages of highly educated workers increased relative to those of workers with low education over 1987-96. Widening wage gaps by gender has become one of the main components of increasing wage inequality. Female wages relative to those of their male counterparts decreased over 1987-94 in four of the five educational categories considered in Table 7.14. Except for workers with university education, the 1995 crisis worsened this trend even further – female/male relative wages fell over 1994-96 for workers with incomplete primary education as well as for workers with basic and higher secondary education. During the 1996–2000 period of recovery, wage differential by gender

24 Rates of wage increases were clearly correlated with firm size. Wages in businesses with less than 100 employees grew by about 4 percent, whereas wages in businesses with more than 100 employees rose by about 6 percent per annum during this period.

Table 7.14: Relative Female to Male Income Ratio by Educational Level in Mexico, 1987-2000 [a]

Education	1987	1994	1996	2000
Incomplete primary	0.53	0.63	0.60	0.58
Complete Primary [b]	0.70	0.63	0.63	0.62
Secondary education [c]	0.91	0.86	0.84	0.81
Middle-high education [d]	0.85	0.79	0.73	0.75
University education	0.73	0.59	0.64	0.62
All	0.72	0.67	0.67	0.67

[a] Data refer to the second quarter of each year. [b] It includes those with one additional year of technical education. [c] It includes those with technical degrees that require complete secondary education. [d] It includes those with degrees that require complete middle-high education certificate.

Source: Authors' calculations based on micro data from INEGI's Urban Employment Surveys (EIM) for a fully comparable sample of 16 cities 1987-2000.

did not decrease, while wage differences by level of education experienced a slight reduction. Overall, relative wages of females in 2000 were lower than those in 1987.

The broad wage dispersion trend has been attributed to skill-biased technological change and increasing demand for skilled labor as a result of economic reforms and globalization.[25] Greater inequality has thus been perceived as the inevitable cost of modernization. However, there are reasons to believe that technological change and competitive market pressure are not fully responsible for rising wage inequality in Mexico. Indeed, had these two factors been responsible, increasing wage inequality should have occurred in the newly industrial sites along the northern border, where exports and foreign direct investment were concentrated (Feenestra and Hanson, 1994 and 1997). However, it is in the old industrial areas surrounding Mexico City and Monterrey that wage dispersion actually increased the most (Ghiara and Zepeda, 2001).[26]

More recently, however, attention has shifted towards other factors explaining greater wage inequality – i.e. the role of minimum wages and institutional factors. As suggested in the context of other Latin American countries (Maloney and Núñez, 2001; Morley, 2001), the reduction of real minimum wages, induced by stabilization policies and efforts to make labor markets more flexible, may be a

25 For example, Cragg and Epelbaum (1996) and Hernández *et al.* (2000) show that average wages across industries follow changes in productivity.

26 Incidentally, it would be quite difficult to fit widening male/female wage gaps, an important contributor to rising inequality, within the skill biased technological change type of argument.

contributing factor towards greater wage dispersion in Mexico as well (Fairris et al., 2001). Lower minimum wages were key to reducing inflationary expectations and, therefore, to providing macroeconomic stability throughout the period of adjustment.[27] In addition, reducing minimum wages in real terms was also seen as a way of eliminating 'rigidities' in the labor market, given the premise that their levels were artificially kept above market value.

Wage data generated over the last 20 years reveals the existence of multiple forces explaining wage dispersion in Mexico. In addition to the impact of technological change, institutional factors lie behind the observed increase in wage dispersion, two of the most important being unexplained wage differentials by gender, and the role of minimum wages in wage determination. Increasing wage dispersion in Mexico clearly reflects the negative social impact of economic reforms in a context of narrowly defined economic policies overly concerned with short-term objectives but inconsistent with longer-term development objectives. The wage dispersion also reflects faulty design of social policy unable to provide the basis for improvements in labor productivity or for a broad expansion of labor opportunities.

Final Remarks

The development process of the last 20 years has produced mixed results in the economies and societies of Latin America. The region was successful in reversing the large macroeconomic disequilibria of the early 1980s; prices are now fairly stable, fiscal deficits fluctuate within narrow margins, modest growth has resumed, and greater integration with the international economy has been achieved. However, important issues still challenge the successful restructuring of the economies of the region. As domestic markets become more integrated into the world economy, increasing international market volatility questions the ability of countries to maintain positive growth rates over time; international events in financial and product markets have had great destabilizing effects on the fragile Latin American economies in the 1990s.

Given this context of economic instability coupled with an absence of broad-based development policies, it comes as no surprise that the last 20 years have witnessed poor social outcomes in the region. Despite slight decreases in poverty rates, the incidence of poverty still remains high, and the absolute number of people living in poverty has increased as populations in the region have expanded.

---

27 In Mexico, representatives from the business sector, the largest unions, and the government would negotiate minimum wages every year as part of a social pact (*Pacto de Solidaridad*), which reflected the commitment of unions and the private sector to restrain their demands for higher wages and prices. The other key factor in these negotiations was the level of the exchange rate.

Although improving, other regional welfare indicators – for example education, health, and access to drinking water – still trail those attained in other countries with similar levels of development.

The underlying forces behind these trends are complex indeed, being affected by the dynamic interaction between domestic and international factors. We find disappointing the present lack of consistency between relatively successful economic stabilization policies and their unsatisfactory social impacts. In general, policy design in the region reflects little concern for the generation of virtuous circles of economic growth and human development.

Over the last 20 years, economic policy has been focused on maintaining macroeconomic stability, fast growth, and rapid integration with the international economy, regardless of the social cost of adjustment and structural change. At the same time, social policy has been mainly concerned with improving the administration of scarce resources and creating minimum safety nets to counter the negative social impact of economic policy. Less attention has been paid to long-entrenched social inequalities regarding education, health care, and housing. Less attention has also been paid to improving labor productivity and access to productive capital among large segments of society as ways of expanding their productive capacity and thus the broad-based growth potential of the economy.

Disarticulated economic and social policies are partly responsible for increasing polarization in Latin America. Growth opportunities from rapidly expanding export markets have been concentrated in a few modern sectors of the economy, or in sectors with strong foreign capital and few productive links with domestic markets other than the use of unskilled labor or natural resources. But the opportunities to generate virtuous growth circles by integrating smaller domestic producers into production chains linked to larger firms and markets have been wasted through poor sectoral policies, little or no strategic investment in human capital and endogenous knowledge and technology, and poor overall access to productive assets.

This chapter illustrates one particular aspect of this larger discussion in the context of Mexico: the poor employment performance of the fast-growing modern manufacturing sector. Because of poor integration with the rest of the economy, even rapid job creation in exporting sectors has failed to substantially improve overall employment outcomes. The fast growth of unskilled employment in labor-intensive plants has not been enough to compensate for lost employment opportunities in other sectors, nor to accommodate large annual increases in the workforce. In the absence of explicit industrial policies to create dynamic comparative advantages in priority sectors with large social impacts, export success stories have been limited to foreign firms and to a few large national industrial groups with access to investment, information, technology and foreign marketing networks.

Domestic producers with little access to finance capital and productive resources were left alone to confront import competition under difficult conditions: macroeconomic instability, shrinking domestic markets, frequent overvaluation of the domestic currency, high and fluctuating interest rates, and no strategic investment in research and development and in human capital development. Not surprisingly, productivity and technology gaps between leading firms and the rest of the economy have widened over the last 20 years, and large inequalities in the labor market – including overall wage dispersion – have emerged (Alarcón and Zepeda, 1998; Ghiara and Zepeda, 2001).

Industrial policy has not provided a timely response to the many challenges faced by deep industrial sector restructuring, limiting itself to implementing small, fragmented projects for medium and small firms. Most countries in the region have adopted explicit programs, sometimes large, to support small enterprises; judging from results, however, these efforts have been insufficient or misguided. The relevant literature on promoting small firms is extensive. International experiences have allowed us to learn much about factors explaining firms' success, but Latin America still lacks a strategic approach to policy design that would harmonize rapid changes in the economy with long-term development objectives. So far, policy design has been overly concerned with short-term, narrowly defined sectoral objectives which have failed to re-enforce positive links between large, medium and small firms, and between exporters and national producers of inputs. Most important, there has been little consistency between the objectives of economic and social policies, between the short- and the long-term objectives, between stability and growth, and between rising productivity and welfare improvement in a broad sense.

References

Alarcón D. and E. Zepeda (1998), 'Stabilization, Structural Adjustment, and Labour Market Performance after NAFTA: The Mexican Experience' in R. Anderson, T. Cohn, C. Day, M. Howlett and C. Murray (eds.), *Innovation Systems in a Global Context: the North American Experience*, McGill-Queen's University Press, Montreal.

Carrillo, J. (1989), 'Transformaciones en la Industria Maquiladora de Exportación: ¿Una Nueva Fase?' in B. González-Aréchiga and R. Barajas (eds.), *Las Maquiladoras: Ajuste Estructural y Desarrollo Regional*, COLEF-EBERT, Mexico City, pp. 37-54.

Clavijo, F. and S. Valdivieso (2000), 'Reformas Estructurales y Política Macroeconómica', In F. Clavijo (ed.), *Reformas Económicas en México, 1982-1999*, Fondo de Cultura Económica, Mexico City.

Cortés, F. (2000), *La Distribución del Ingreso en México en Épocas de Estabilización y Reforma Económica*, Centro de Investigaciones y Estudios Superiores en Antropología Social, Mexico City.

Cragg, M.I., and M. Epelbaum (1996), 'Why Has Wage Dispersion Grown in Mexico? Is It the Incidence of Reforms or the Growing Demand for Skills?', *Journal of Development Economics*, Vol. 51, No. 1 (July), pp. 99-116.

de Janvry, A. and E. Sadoulet (1995), 'Poverty Alleviation, Income Redistribution, and Growth during Adjustment', in N. Lustig (ed.), *Coping with Austerity: Poverty and Inequality in Latin America*, The Brookings Institution, Washington, D.C., pp. 101-145.

Dornbusch, R. and A. Werner (1994), 'Mexico: Stabilization, Reform, and No Growth', *Brookings Papers on Economic Activity*, No. 1, pp. 253-315.

Dussel, E. (1997), *La Economía de la Polarización*, Universidad Nacional Autónoma de México, Mexico City.

ECLAC (Economic Commission for Latin America and the Caribbean) (2002a), *Social Panorama of Latin America, 2001-2002*, ECLAC, Santiago.

ECLAC (Economic Commission for Latin America and the Caribbean) (2002b), *The Sustainability of Development in Latin America and the Caribbean: Challenges and Opportunities*, ECLAC Books No. 68, ECLAC, Santiago.

Edwards, S. (1997), 'The Mexican Peso Crisis: How Much Did We Know? When Did We Know It?', NBER Working Paper No. 6334, National Bureau of Economic Research.

Fairris, D., G. Popli, and E. Zepeda (2001), 'Minimum Wages and the Wage Structure in Mexico', paper presented at the international congress of the Latin American Studies Association (LASA), Washington, D.C. (September).

Feenestra, R.C. and G. Hanson (1994), 'Foreign Investment Outsourcing and Relative Wages', in Feenestra R., G. Grossman, and D. Irwin (eds.), *Political Economy of Trade Policy: Essays in Honor of Jagdish Bhagwati*, MIT Press, Cambridge, MA, pp. 89-127.

Feenestra, R.C. and G. Hanson (1997), 'Foreign Direct Investment and Relative Wages: Evidence from Mexico's Maquiladoras', *Journal of International Economics*, Vol. 42, No.3-4 (May), pp. 371-393.

Foster, J., J. Greer, E. Thorbecke (1984), 'A Class of Decomposable Poverty Measures', *Econometrica*, Vol. 52, No. 3 (May), pp. 761-66.

Ghiara, R. and E. Zepeda (2001), 'Relative Wages and Education Premium in Tijuana and Mexico City: 1987-1996', *Journal of Borderland Studies*, Vol. 16, No. 1 (Spring).

Hernández, E. (2000), *La Competitividad Industrial en México*, Universidad Autónoma Metropolitana/Plaza y Valdés, Mexico City.

Hernández, E., N. Garro and I. Llamas (2000), *Productividad y Mercado de Trabajo en México*, Universidad Autonóma Metropolitana/Plaza y Valdés, Mexico City.

Hernández, E. and J. Velázquez (2002), *Globalización, Desigualdad y Pobreza: Lecciones de la Experiencia Mexicana*, Universidad Autonóma Metropolitana/Plaza y Valdés, Mexico City.

ILO (Interntional Labor Office) (2001), *Panorama Laboral de América Latina*, International Labor Office, Geneva.

Katz, J. (2001), *Structural Reforms, Productivity and Technological Change in Latin America*. ECLAC Books No. 64, ECLAC, Santiago.

Krugman, P. (1995), 'Dutch Tulips and Emerging Markets', *Foreign Affairs*, Vol. 74, No. 4, pp. 28-44.

Londoño, J.L. and M. Székely (1997), 'Persistent Poverty and Excess Inequality: Latin America, 1970-1995', Working Paper No. 357, Inter-American Development Bank, Office of the Chief Economist.

Londoño, J.L. and M. Székely (1998), 'Sorpresas Distributivas después de una Década de Reformas: América Latina en los Noventa', *Pensamiento Iberoamericano: Revista de Economía Política*, Vol. 0, No. 0, Special Issue, pp. 195-242.

Maloney, W. and J. Núñez (2001), 'Measuring the Impact of Minimum Wages: Evidence from Latin America', Working Paper, The World Bank.

Mendiola, G. (1999), 'Las Empresas Maquiladoras de Exportación 1980-1995', in E. Dussel, M. Piore and C. Ruiz (eds.), *Pensar Globalmente y Actuar Regionalmente*, UNAM-EBERT, Mexico City, pp. 185-226.

Middlebrook, K. and E. Zepeda (eds.) (2003), *Confronting Development: Assessing Mexico's Economic and Social Policy Challenges*, Center for U.S.-Mexican Studies, University of California – San Diego and Stanford University Press, La Jolla and Stanford.

Molina, C., K. Mokate and N. Carcenac (2000), 'Indicadores Sociales y Económicos en América Latina y el Caribe', Instituto Interamericano para el Desarrollo Social (INDES), Inter-American Development Bank (IDB), mimeo.

Morley, S.A. (2001), *The Income Distribution Problem in Latin America and the Caribbean*, ECLAC Books No. 65, ECLAC, Santiago.

Morley, S.A., R. Machado, and S. Pettinato (1999), 'Indexes of Structural Reform in Latin America', Serie Reformas Económicas No. 12, ECLAC, Santiago.

Presidencia de la República (2001a), *Plan Nacional de Desarrollo, 2001-2006*, Presidencia de la República, Mexico City.

Presidencia de la República (2001b), *Informe de Gobierno 2001*, Presidencia de la República, Mexico City.

Ros, J. (1994), 'Mexico in the 1990s: A New Economic Miracle? Some Notes on the Economic and Policy Legacy of the 1980s', in M.L. Cook, K.J. Middlebrook, and J. Molinar Horcasitas (eds.), *The Politics of Economic Restructuring: State-Society Relations and Regime Change in Mexico*, Center for U.S.-Mexican Studies, University of California – San Diego, La Jolla.

Sachs, J., A. Tornell, and A. Velasco (1995), 'The Collapse of the Mexican Peso: What Have We Learned?', Working Papers Series No. 95-7, Center for International Affairs, Harvard University.

Salas, C. and E. Zepeda (2003), 'Employment and Wages: Enduring the Cost of Liberalization and Economic Reform', in K.J. Middlebrook and E. Zepeda (eds.), *Confronting Development: Asssessing Mexico's Economic and Social Policy Challenges*, Center for U.S.-Mexican Studies, University of California – San Diego and Stanford University Press, La Jolla and Stanford.

Stallings, B. and W. Peres (2000), *Crecimiento, Empleo y Equidad: El Impacto de las Reformas Económicas en América Latina y el Caribe*, ECLAC/Fondo de Cultura Económica, Santiago.

Unger, K. (1993), 'Productividad, Desarrollo Tecnológico y Competitividad Exportadora en la Industria Mexicana', *Economía Mexicana*, Vol. 2, No. 1 (January-June), pp. 183-237.

Weller, J. (2001), *Economic Reforms,Growth and Employment. Labour Markets in Latin America and the Caribbean*. ECLAC Books No. 66. Santiago: ECLAC.

Zepeda E., D. Alarcón and G. Félix (1999), 'Empleo, Competitividad y Apertura Económica: la Pequeña y Mediana Empresa en la Manufactura Mexicana 1985-1993', in E. Zepeda and D. Castro (eds.), *Restructuración Económica y Empleo en México*, Universidad Autónoma de Coahuila and Fundación Friedrich Ebert, Mexico City, pp. 16-62.

Chapter 8

Political Challenges to Equitable Development in Latin America[1]

Judith Teichman

Poverty, Inequality and Building Coalitions for Policy Change

Increased trade and investment flows – the core of globalization – has not ushered in sustained and equitable prosperity for most people of Latin America. The last twenty five years have witnessed recurrent economic crises, repeated attempts at stabilization under International Monetary Fund auspices, and World Bank participation in market liberalizing/structural adjustment reforms (trade liberalization, privatization and deregulation). Countries have struggled through the first stage of market reform, streamlining their states and opening their economies to foreign products and investment, only to face continuing economic difficulties and deepening social problems, particularly increases in inequality, rises in the level of poverty, and growing regional disparities. Indeed, in the years following the 1982 international debt crisis, Latin American countries have enjoyed only moderate growth, punctuated by economic crises of varying degrees of intensity.[2] The 1995 Mexican peso crisis, which rocked the other economies of the region, was followed by the 1997 Asian crisis, the 1999 Brazilian financial crisis and more recently, the 2001 Argentine crisis.

There is growing recognition that market reform produced important contingents of winners and losers. With the exception of Chile, where there was a sustained growth rate of more than 7.5 percent for over a decade until the Asian crisis hit (American Chamber of Commerce of Chile), poverty reduction has remained elusive. In Latin America, generally, the proportion of the population living in poverty rose from 41 to 46 percent while the proportion living in extreme poverty increased from 14 to 22 percent between 1980 and 1990 (Wilkie, 1999,

1 Some of the data in this chapter draws from in-depth interviews of key actors (government officials and business leaders) in Chile, Argentina and Mexico. In total, 80 interviews were carried out: 22 in Argentina, 24 in Chile, and 34 in the case of Mexico. As interviewees were promised confidentiality, informants will not be named.

2 With very few exceptions, rates of growth between 1990 and 1996 have been only moderate (ECLAC, 1997, 10).

431). Furthermore, while the incidence of poverty declined in the first half of the 1990s, it did not decline sufficiently to offset the increase of the 1980s (ECLAC, 1997, 14). Increases in unemployment have been a serious problem in some countries. In Argentina, for example, by 1995 unemployment had reached 18.5 percent, declining for a few years, and then spiraling to more than 20 percent by early 2002. Even in Chile, the tiger of the region, where important inroads have been made into poverty reduction, inequality has stubbornly persisted and unemployment rose from 6 percent in 1997 to 10.5 percent by 2001 (American Chamber of Commerce).[3]

Neither domestic market liberalizing elites, nor the multilateral lending institutions which were pressing so hard for market reform, attached much importance to the social implications of their reform agendas throughout the 1980s. However, concerns have shifted dramatically in recent years. The World Bank and the Inter-American Development Bank have now made poverty reduction the overriding objective of their corporate missions, while the International Monetary Fund now provides a Poverty Reduction and Growth Facility. The failure of market reforms to deliver equitable prosperity is also reflected in the growing disillusionment on the part of Latin American publics with market reforms.[4] Electoral campaigns in Argentina and Mexico in 1999 and 2000 involved calls for measures to address poverty, unemployment and the corrupt manner in which market reform, particularly privatization, had been carried out. The election of Luiz Inácio Lula da Silva in 2003, a Brazilian presidential candidate for whom poverty and hunger are major issues, has brought the social issue to the center stage of Brazilian politics. Even in Chile, where the achievement in poverty reduction has been substantial, there has been growing public criticism of what is regarded as the government's poor performance in the areas of employment and poverty reduction.[5]

As doubts about the efficacy of the original Washington consensus grow, a new consensus regarding policies required to achieve greater equality and the reduction of poverty is emerging. Even Latin American political leaders with a strong predisposition to the efficacy of the market have been forced to confront poverty

3 The Gini coefficient – an inequality index that increases from 0 to 1 as the distribution of income becomes more skewed – was 0.56 for Chile by the mid 1990s, as compared to 0.54 in 1983 and 0.50 in 1975 (World Bank, 1997, 215; Edwards and Cox Edwards, 1987, 167).

4 According to a recent public opinion survey of the region (*The Economist*, July 28-August 3, 2001, p. 38).

5 According to a public opinion survey carried out by the Centro de Estudios Públicos (*El Mercurio*, May 24, 2002, http://www.emol.com/noticias/detalle/detalle_diario.asp). With an increase in social spending which, by 1995, had reached 70 percent of total public spending, the proportion of poor of the total population in Chile had been reduced from 40 to 28 percent between 1990 and 1994 (Ministerio de Hacienda, 1995).

and inequality issues. The Mangabeira Group – an assemblage of Latin American intellectuals and politicians which includes market advocate Mexican president Vicente Fox – recommends a variety of policies to rectify the failure of the market model to bring about equitable distribution in income and wealth: the promotion of small and medium enterprise (key to employment and therefore to poverty reduction); an increase in social expenditures, funded by a reformed tax system (including progressive taxation on personal consumption, tax on assets and punishment of tax evaders); increased public investment in infrastructure; the termination of state protection of private cartels and monopolies; and the eradication of corruption and inefficiency in government.[6] These ideas reflect the serious concerns raised in the writings of ECLAC (1997) and elsewhere (e.g., Birdsall and de la Torre, 2000). Indeed, ECLAC (Economic Commission for Latin America and the Caribbean) has explicitly drawn attention to the fact that the big winners of market reform have been domestic conglomerates and transnational corporations able to modernize and obtain export markets, while small and medium companies were hurt by the process (ECLAC, 1997, 85). Moreover, while economic growth is necessary for poverty reduction, it has oftentimes not been sufficient in Latin America. Hence, there has been a call for mechanisms to protect the vulnerable during difficult economic times and to increase expenditure in such key areas as education since it is argued that such expenditures can in fact contribute to economic growth (Birdsall and de la Torre, 2000, 29). But for social expenditure to increase without causing fiscal disequilibrium, there must also be an expansion of the tax revenue and improvements in collection. Further, another consequence of market reform, monopolies in privatized sectors, can have substantial negative consequences for the distribution of income (Székely, 1998, 76) and therefore must be regulated. Finally, the targeting of state corruption and inefficiency is important because both of these promote inequality and waste resources, passing the costs onto the taxpayer and the consumer while facilitating further accumulation by the already wealthy.

While changes in the international economic order are a necessary condition for the alleviation of inequality and poverty in Latin America, such changes are not sufficient. This paper takes the position that domestic power structures and domestic policy initiatives are equally important. The argument presented in this chapter is that an effective program to reduce poverty and inequality requires that there be three types of domestic coalitions supportive of such a goal. Firstly, there must be a societal coalition; that is, a broad cross section of society (big, small and medium business, labor, middle sector groups, agriculturalists, grass roots organizations) that backs state pursuit of such an objective. State managers must maintain institutionalized links with, and draw their support from, this coalition. The policies necessary for the reduction of poverty and inequality cannot be

6 The Group was co-founded by Brazilian Harvard professor Roberto Mangabeira Unger and Jorge Castañeda, formerly Mexico's Minister of External Relations (*Latin American Weekly Report*, July 11, 2000, pp. 318-319).

expected to go forward if the state's social basis is a narrow one – an arrangement sometimes seen as a necessary aspect for the achievement of first stage reform (Waterbury, 1989, 40). If important societal groups oppose this policy goal, or do not value it as a national priority, and lobby in the direction of other priorities or block essential measures, chances of a program going forward are reduced considerably.

Secondly, there must be an electoral coalition calling for poverty reduction and greater equity. This requirement is distinct from a societal coalition; electoral coalitions may be fleeting but are necessary in order to get policy change on the agenda and bolster a program's legitimacy in demonstrating broad and diffuse public support. This means that, at the national level, at least one major presidential candidate will have such a policy goal as a major part of his/her platform. It means that this presidential candidate wins the elections as do a sufficient number of congressional candidates of the party, or of allied parties who also support this policy goal. The ideal of an electoral coalition assumes an electoral campaign in which poverty and equity are important issues, one in which key policies are advanced for their solution, and in which the electoral result signals broad public support for a solution to these problems. And finally, once assuming power, it must be possible to construct a third type of coalition – a governing coalition – that can propel programs forward and help secure their implementation. The notion of a governing coalition assumes that the president, his major cabinet appointees, especially those in the most important economic portfolios, members of Congress from the president's party or, if he lacks majority control, a sufficient number of members from opposition parties, support the policy goals of poverty reduction and equitable development as national priorities. Only if a governing coalition is present will programs not be blocked at the institutional level. The importance of all three types of coalitions stems from the reality that in Latin America electoral promises for policy change can be blocked at the institutional level or railroaded by powerful groups with privileged political access. In cases in which there is little party discipline, presidents cannot assume support just because congressmen are members of the same party. And in the absence of a broad societal coalition, there is the likelihood that powerful vested interests will be able to thwart policy change.

Even if such policy commitment in the form of the three types of coalitions outlined above should emerge, there is another requirement that is especially pertinent to the Latin American case. As Peter Evans observes, the links between state and society must be of a certain type for policy change to occur – they must be institutionalized links capable of inducing support, cooperation and compliance. Evans uses the term 'embeddedness' to refer to the ability of the state to remain autonomous, while sufficiently connected to the major social groups to successfully bring about policy change (Evans, 1992, 164). Such arrangements are especially important for policies to reduce poverty and inequality. Measures to break up monopolies, end tax evasion, reform the tax system in order to increase resources for social spending, support small and medium enterprise and end corruption, require a state not permeated nor unduly influenced by powerful private sector interests and one that is able to ensure the cooperation of all of those private sector interests affected by policy changes.

The construction of societal, electoral and governing coalitions favoring policies to reduce inequality and poverty along with sufficient 'embeddedness' to ensure that policy intentions are not corrupted, will not be easy to achieve. To accomplish such a feat would mean a substantial departure from the politics and policy making that characterizes most countries of the region. Indeed, the experience of market reform over the last two decades has exaggerated certain political features of the Latin American reality – features that present important challenges to policies conducive to equitable development and poverty alleviation.

Latin American Politics and the Political Legacy of the Market Reform Era

Although modeled after the U.S. political arrangements, Latin American political systems stand out for the high concentration of political power in the hands of the president. The constitutions of virtually all countries grant decree powers to the president. Although such powers are usually restricted in a variety of ways,[7] these powers have enormously strengthened the ability of presidents to take policy initiatives and keep policies from being altered by Congress. In a number of notable cases, decree powers were used to push through market reform measures by presidents who had run on vaguely populist platforms. In his 1989 electoral campaign, Peronist presidential candidate Carlos Menem had called for wage increases and a strong stand against the International Monetary Fund. Once in power, however, he changed his policy stand and, as the severity of the economic crisis increased, succeeded in securing congressional acceptance of two enabling laws which allowed him to privatize and reform the state through presidential decree.[8] This led to an unprecedented use of presidential decree powers between 1990 and 1994 (Blutman, 1994, 61). In Ecuador, between 1984 and 1985, 26 'urgent economic decrees' encompassed the core components of a neoliberal

7 In most cases, presidential decree powers can only be conferred by an explicit decision made by Congress, are confined to specific policy areas, usually must be later agreed to by Congress, and can be overturned or overridden by Congress (Shugart and Mainwaring, 1997, 44-45).

8 Because of the depth of the economic crisis, which saw inflation hit 4,000 percent in June of 1989, the Radical Party was anxious to have President-elect Carlos Menem assume office ahead of time. Hence, a deal was struck whereby Menem, by that time convinced that market reform was the only way to restore economic stability and propel future growth, agreed to assume power six months early in exchange for Radical Party congressional support for the two enabling laws (Teichman, 1997, 45).

reform program (Conaghan, 1994a, 276), while in 1985, Bolivia's market reform program, the New Economic Program, was put into effect through the passage of a single presidential decree (Conaghan, 1994b, 258).[9]

However, it is also true that formal constitutional powers have been exaggerated by other aspects of politics. The legacy of *caudillismo*, the Latin American form of patrimonialism, is probably the most important centralizing force. Caudillismo is personal power, power based not on institutions and laws, but on personal authority; it is authority which commands unquestioning loyalty from supporters. Personal authority places the president (or anyone who makes a claim to such authority) above the law and is one of the most important factors in what has been termed 'delegative democracy' in Latin America (O'Donnell, 1994). Caudillo authority has served to further concentrate powers in the hands of the president, propelling him to flout Congress and other institutions such as the judiciary. Former Argentine president Carlos Menem, for example, stacked the judiciary with loyalists to ensure that his use of emergency decree powers to pass his market reform program (which were of questionable constitutionality) would not be declared unconstitutional. He also put personal loyalists in key positions as interveners in public companies he wished to privatize – a move that corrupted and speeded up the privatization process. Similarly, in the case of Mexico, public companies were sold to close friends of President Carlos Salinas, while individual bankers negotiated rescue deals with the executive when the financial crisis hit in 1995 (Teichman, 2001). Caudillismo, or personal power, then, was integral to the market reform process; as such it concentrated power and selectively included in the process actors personally loyal to the president. It also inhibits the establishment of institutionalized links between the state and social actors.

Indeed, decree powers, and personal authority were used to insulate the architects of market reform programs, invariably technocrats, from outside meddling. The market reform process, insofar as it involved extensive policy dialogue with international financial institutions, particularly the IMF and the World Bank, strengthened the political clout of those intra state actors with whom it had continuous ongoing discussions. Usually these individuals, with graduate degrees from major U.S. universities, particularly in economics, were located in finance ministries and in central bank bureaucracies. In most of the large Latin American countries, the rise of technocrats to policy predominance was a key feature of the market reform process during the period (Centeno, 1997; Teichman, 1995; Centeno and Silva, 1998). Technocrats at the helm of finance ministries and

9 More recently some countries have taken measures to try to ensure that presidential power is placed under greater control, as occurred, for example, with the 1994 Argentine constitution (Jones, 1997) and the 1991 Colombian constitution (Shugart and Mainwaring, 1997). However, as I will argue below, such practices will not be eliminated by constitutional changes because personal power remains a key threat to accountability.

Central Banks remain, in most cases, the most important interlocutors between their countries and lenders for programs to address problems of poverty and inequality.

Another feature of Latin American politics is the weakness of political parties. Held together by personalistic leadership and clientelism, Latin American political parties have often not made issue-based appeals. Their promises are often vague, and leaders have few reservations about abandoning even these minimal commitments. While party weakness has been a long standing problem in the region, economic crises and the strain of carrying through politically difficult market reform agendas has eroded public support for, and trust in, traditional political parties. There is a wide range of variations on how and why political parties have lost legitimacy. In Peru, for example, public disillusionment was fed by traditional parties' failed attempts to stem the tide of economic crisis, producing instead astronomical inflation rates. In other cases, attempts at market reforms carried out by traditional parties are linked with increased unemployment, poverty and corruption (Ecuador, Bolivia, and Argentina). The push for market reform oftentimes signaled the exit of party militants from parties previously seen as populist (as occurred with the PRI in Mexico and the Peronist party in Argentina). Meanwhile, the concentration of power in the presidency and use of decree powers served to de-legitimize both parties and congresses. In the market reform era, parties were marginalized from the policy making process like never before as policy makers isolated economic policy from 'populist pressures' and 'special interests.' In some countries of the region (Ecuador, Bolivia), parties are very much detached from both public demands and from the societal organizations that make a legitimate claim to represent the interests of society. In these extreme cases, parties are incapable of establishing themselves as viable societal/state interlocutors.

The concentration of power in the presidency and the highly personalized nature of executive authority ensured the exclusion of a wide cross section of political actors from policy input – indeed there was often a conscious strategy of political exclusion in order to force through market reform measures. The weakness of parties, their clientelistic nature, and the low regard in which they are held, worsened as a consequence of both economic crisis and the failure of market reforms to bring sustained prosperity. In this context, parties may not be able to make an important contribution to the building of policy consensus on the need for measures to reduce inequality and poverty. 'Real' political struggle (and policy influence), as a consequence, often occurs outside of the institutions of electoral democracy. This is especially true for the political activities of the most powerful, for which market reform spelt enormously increased economic power and privileged and personalized policy influence. Below, I turn to an examination of this aspect of the market reform legacy – an aspect that presents perhaps the most serious challenge to policies to reduce inequality and poverty.

In those Latin American countries where market liberalizing reforms have been carried out with the greatest enthusiasm, assets became heavily concentrated in the hands of a few large conglomerates and their international allies. The commitment of Latin American private sector interests, in general, to market liberalizing measures was not, initially, enthusiastic. All members of the private sector, even the most powerful, were reticent about trade liberalization – and trade liberalization was pushed forward without prior consultation. Indeed, policy reformers faced considerable difficulties in finding private sector allies. Hence, once the difficult phase of trade liberalization was complete, market reformers opened personalized channels of policy influence to their countries' most powerful private sector interests in the belief that the active support of the private sector was key if greater dependence on market forces was to become a reality.

The most notable example of the concentration of assets stemming from privatization occurred during the first phase of the Chilean market reform (1975-1981). Unable to win much support for their ideas in the private sector generally, the designers of market reform – technocrats known as the Chicago boys – developed highly integrated, personal links with three powerful conglomerates: the Edwards group, BHC (Mortgage Bank of Chile) and Cruzat-Larraín. These powerful conglomerates were the beneficiaries of reform: they purchased the public companies put up for sale at bargain basement prices. By 1978, Cruzat-Larraín controlled 37 of Chile's 250 largest companies, while BHC controlled 25 (O'Brien and Roddick, 1983, 73). In the years to come, many technocrats shifted between top level positions within the state and executive level positions within these conglomerates, effectively blurring the distinction between government technocrat and conglomerate executive (Teichman, 2001, 68). While an attempt was made to disperse shares sold in public companies, wealth remained highly concentrated as domestic big business, now with foreign partners, bought up public firms during the next phase of privatization initiated in 1985. Access to economic policy makers privileged big business, involving a combination of personalized and institutionalized channels.

The Mexican market reform process also contributed to the increased economic and political clout of already powerful financial/industrial conglomerates. The most powerful industrial and financial interests – 37 businessmen controlling some 70 economic groups – were (and continue to be) represented by the Mexican Council of Businessmen (Consejo Mexicano de Hombres de Negocios, CMHN).[10] Throughout the market reform years of President Carlos Salinas (1989-1994), members of the CMHN maintained the most direct, immediate and personal access to cabinet ministers. And it was this type of access that was the most important avenue of policy influence. Although institutionalized mechanisms of representation and access were also present, they were dominated by big business

10 Indeed, the members of this organization have historically had direct personal access to the President and to members of the cabinet and this has been the primary means through which they have pressed their particular interest on the state (Camp, 1989, 171).

(Cockcroft, 1983, 208; Puga, 1984, 192). One of the most important channels of institutionalized access to policy for business during the Salinas administration was the Coordinating Committee for Commercial Export Business Organizations (COECE). It operated to guarantee big business input into the NAFTA negotiations (Luna, 1992, 16; Kleinberg, 1999, 127-151). Throughout the period, Salinas maintained top businessmen as policy advisers. Claudio X. González – a shareholder and member of the boards of directors of three of the country's biggest conglomerates, and a personal friend of Salinas – arranged Salinas' meetings with other conglomerate heads, acted as his advisor on foreign investment issues, and accompanied both Commerce Minister Serra Puche and José Córdoba – head of the office of the presidency – on official trips abroad. Purchasers of public companies, Carlos Cabal Peniche and Carlos Slim were both close to Salinas and both accompanied him on international tours. Big business provided financial support to the political leadership: it headed up Salinas' party fund raising committee, with top businessman Miguel Alemán serving as the PRI's finance secretary for the 1994 national elections. Enormous contributions were asked for by the PRI of its powerful business supporters and they usually complied.[11]

The access of the country's powerful businessmen to policy makers was paralleled by the favors they received. The owners of powerful conglomerates benefited from export promotion efforts that provided preferential treatment in the areas of credit and tax relief for the country's 100 biggest exporters (Heredia, 1996, 249). Furthermore, the most important privatized companies fell into the hands of the most important industrial/financial conglomerates; by 1992, the country's most important financial, industrial and service activities were in the hands of four conglomerates (Teichman, 1995, 187). It is widely believed that a number of privatizations, such as the privatization of the state telephone company (TELMEX), highways, and banks, were carried out in a highly discretionary fashion by the President and a few top officials, in a process that privileged the close business friends of the president (author's interviews with a businessman and two senior officials of the Federal Competition Commission).

In Mexico, big business' direct and personal access to policy makers was decisive in a number of policy decisions, e.g., the opening up of basic petrochemicals to private – including foreign – capital investment and privatization of the banking sector (author's interviews with three business executives). Moreover, pressure from big business was behind the decision to delay the opening up of the banking sector to foreign investors, in restricting competition in telecommunications following privatization, and in keeping foreigners out of the airlines.[12] Entrepreneurs wanting to buy state-owned banks and the conglomerate

---

11 The most notorious example of big business' campaign contributions occurred in 1993 when the country's top business leaders were each invited to pledge $25 million (U.S.) to the PRI's 1994 election campaign; public outcry resulted in a reduction of contributions to a third of a million each (Teichman, 1995, 256).

12 This contrasts with the Argentine case in which big business could not afford to buy

purchasers of the country's airlines and telecommunications firms demanded the restriction/ exclusion of foreign competitors and were able to get the agreement of technocrats on this because officials saw this concession as a means of obtaining higher prices for privatized companies (author's interviews with three senior government officials and two businessmen). Small and medium businesses, on the other hand, lacking both the personal contacts and institutional channels to the highest reaches of power, failed to reap any benefits from reform and were often highly critical of Salinas' market reforms. A plethora of local business organizations (in Nuevo Leon, Chihuahua, Jalisco) called upon the government to revise its economic model (Mizrahi, 1992, 19; *Proceso*, No. 966, May 8, 1995, p. 43; *ibid.*, No. 952, January 30, 1995, p. 14; *ibid.*, No. 988, October 9, 1995, p. 26).

In Argentina, as in Mexico, big business interests were already powerful prior to the onset of Carlos Menem's rapid reform program (1989-1995), having benefited from the previous military government's policies of contracting out state functions. Personalized access was paramount (and monopolized by big business) and institutionalized channels and the role of business associations were of even less importance than in Mexico. Under Menem, the owners and executives of the country's most powerful financial and industrial conglomerates had direct personal access to top policy makers and participated (even more fully than in the Mexican case) in policy development. Members of the Council of Argentine Business (CEA), the organization integrating the presidents of the country's 40 most powerful holding companies, had easy and immediate personal access to both Menem and the Economy Minister (author's interviews with two members of CEA). On the other hand, almost all entrepreneurial organizations were frustrated in their attempts to gain access to the highest reaches of political power between 1989 and 1995. Indeed, both business leaders and government officials interviewed agreed that entrepreneurial organizations and institutionalized channels were of little importance in allowing entrepreneurs access to important policy makers, especially the Minister of Economy. The official consultative mechanism, the Production Council, composed of representatives of business, labor and the government, was seen by both business leaders and government officials alike as 'window dressing' – a forum where, in general, the government would communicate policies it had already decided upon. When non CEA members did gain an audience with the Economy Minister, they claimed they were not listened to.

By far, however, the most excluded and angry businessmen were small and medium industrialists who claimed that they had absolutely no access to the highest reaches of political power. But even the leaders of the larger and more

---

public companies without foreign partners (also important was access to foreign technology so desperately needed by Argentina's decapitalized public companies) and so Argentine business were unlikely to attempt to keep foreigners out and if they tried, were less likely to meet with success.

powerful Argentine Industrial Union (UIA) claimed considerable difficulty in making their views known; its leaders expressed great reluctance at even broaching one of their greatest concerns: the issue of the negative impact of the fixed exchange rate on export competitiveness (author's interviews with two business leaders). Established in 1991 to control the country's hyperinflation, the Convertibility Plan pegged the peso to the U.S. dollar. But the government refused to budge on this issue, showing itself to be manifestly unsympathetic to the problems faced by industrialists when the Brazilian crisis hit in 1998 rendering Argentine exports even less competitive due to the Brazilian devaluation. Then Economy Minister Roque Fernández characterized the UIA's request for protection as coming from entrepreneurs 'who are trying to achieve through corporatism what they haven't achieved as businessmen.'

As in the Mexican case, Argentina's big conglomerates became the major beneficiaries of the market reform process. Big exporting firms benefited from tax breaks designed to stimulate exports with the consequence that by 1995, one half of the country's exports were accounted for by only 30 firms (*Latin America Weekly Report*, October 22, 1992, p. 3; *ibid.*, November 30, 1999, p. 558). But where big private sector firms benefited the most was in the privatization program. Indeed, the inordinate benefits stemming from privatization became a key part of the process of binding the private sector – especially the big industrialists who had been former state contractors – to the Menemista project and in ensuring enthusiastic entrepreneurial support for Menem. Public enterprise contractors, who had prospered under military rule, were strong opponents of privatization if it meant a reduction in business for them. Generosity toward the private sector, therefore, was key to the regime's ability to move forward rapidly not only in privatization, but in other areas of reform policy (author's interviews with four business leaders; Peralta Ramos, 1992, 103). A few domestic companies, mostly former government contractors, were part of consortia composed also of multinational banks and foreign companies which purchased public companies. (Schvarzer, 1995, 142; Azpiazu and Vispo, 1994, 54 and 138). Indeed, one analysis points out that the actual number of domestic firms participating in purchasing consortia is smaller than originally thought since there are numerous cases in which a particular enterprise participates in more than one consortium (Basualdo, 1994, 45). Moreover, potential purchasers were directly involved in the privatization process, and later, in regulatory policy. Both government officials and business leaders interviewed attested to the very close involvement of the private sector in the privatization process from gathering of information to the details of privatization decrees. Members of the private sector were involved in the development of tenders assuring them not only of winning the bids but of advantageous terms.[13] The government assumed the debts of the privatized firms

13 This sort of involvement, admitted to by a former top level official in the Ministry of Economy and two business leaders, was justified on the grounds that the technocratic team lacked the expertise to work out the details of a privatization program.

and companies were sold with less profitable activities removed and with their labor forces reduced (Felder, 1994, 58).

Politically, the conglomerates were closely linked to Menem. They made heavy campaign contributions to the Peronist party: officially the top six conglomerates are reported to have contributed $700,000 (U.S.) each to Menem's 1989 campaign, while Bunge and Born claims that its actual contribution was $3 million (U.S.). During his tenure as Economy Minister, Domingo Cavallo reportedly received a monthly stipend of $8,000 (U.S.) from the Fundación Mediterránea, a think-tank largely funded by the private sector (*Latin American Weekly Report*, July 8, 1993, p. 308; *ibid.*, November 26, 1992, p. 2). Numerous allegations and charges of corruption were brought against top level officials accused of taking kickbacks from the private sector.[14] In short, close personal ties between the executives of the country's big conglomerates and the political elite had produced a policy outcome which was both corrupt and inordinately beneficial to the country's powerful conglomerates.

At the same time as the owners and executives of powerful conglomerates have increased in power and influence, trade union power has been dramatically reduced – a key requirement of *labor flexibilization*, a process involving changes in labor policy and practice geared to reduce the cost of labor and render enterprises more internationally competitive. This process has been widely viewed in a positive light as trade union organizations (or, at least, their leaders) in Latin America were perceived as privileged and corrupt beneficiaries of the earlier import substitution phase. However, despite their questionable aspects, trade unions were among the few powerful corporate social/political actors capable of questioning national policy choices. Moreover, their rent seeking propensities were not more pronounced than those of the conglomerates which came to monopolize policy access in the market reform era.

In the process of restructuring state companies, it was usually necessary to implement large scale layoffs and change existing labor contracts in order to make companies more attractive for sale. In this process, violent repression of labor – involving the arrest and jailing of labor leaders – occurred, especially when the military was in power (Chile), but was also a feature of regimes with electoral processes, as occurred for example in Bolivia and Mexico (La Botz, 1991; Falabella, 1981). Moreover, the process of reform itself, once underway, served to weaken labor: as the numbers of workers declined so did trade union membership. Massive layoffs had a dampening effect on union militancy as those who were able to hang onto their jobs became increasingly fearful of losing them and sought ways

14 Charges were brought against the Minister of Public Works, Roberto Dromi, in 1991, against then president of the Banco de la Nación, Aldo Dadone, in 1996 and against Domingo Cavallo in 1996. Rumors and allegations circulated about Menem's involvement in corrupt practices culminating in his arrest in 2001 on charges of illegal arms dealings with Croatia and Ecuador.

to negotiate 'modernization.' Tactics of divide and rule, clientelistic and corporatist methods of political control also proved highly effective in quelling labor unrest and reducing its power (Teichman, 2001, 163). Labor movements in Latin America are now deeply fractured and enormously weaker than they once were – not well positioned to press the case for poverty reduction as a national priority.

Some observers place hope in the growing social and political strength of new social movements (Alvarez et al., 1998). Others note the fractured, relatively weak, and disparate nature of popular organizing (Zermeño, 1990; Oxhorn and Ducatenzeiler, 1999, 27 and 35), thereby suggesting that social movements may lack the political clout to force national leaders to view poverty and inequality as national priorities. Many social movements, emerging under authoritarian rule, played an important role in the struggle for democracy only to decline once the goal of electoral democracy had been achieved. Others, such as soup kitchens and food purchasing cooperatives, arose in response to the extreme economic hardships imposed by economic crisis and structural adjustment. Concerned primarily with issues of economic survival, such organizations do not necessarily involve themselves in national policy issues. In many cases, grass roots organizations have become linked to (or, have evolved into) non governmental organizations (NGO's), often with outside staff members and with outside funding sources. The increasing presence of NGOs, fulfilling service provision roles formerly provided by the state, does not necessarily signify pressure for improved social policies since such NGOs may seek to present themselves as 'non political' thereby keeping a distance from national political debates.

Nevertheless, NGOs have become critical of what they viewed to be the negative social impact of structural adjustment and have demanded a more concerted effort at poverty alleviation along with the involvement of civil society in multilateral lending programs (Nelson, 1997, 24). This pressure was key in the World Bank's move to a more participatory policy involving the consultation of civil society groups. However, it is important to note the limitations of the Bank's new thrust toward public involvement in policy development. Governments, such as that of Mexico, may be highly resistant to outside organizations being involved with domestic civil society groups (OED, 2001, 26). Furthermore, even if consultation is encouraged by the host government, it is largely confined to compensatory policies (social policies) and to infrastructural projects that impact upon populations and the environment, while openness and public scrutiny of structural adjustment programs is absent (Nelson, 1997, 43). Indeed, civil society organizations have had the greatest impact on policy in Mexico and Argentina in cases when they have been uninvited – a consequence of fierce resistance of societal groups to particular Bank initiatives (Fernández de Villegas and Adelson, 2000, 476). Meanwhile, the World Bank has resisted the involvement of the Argentine labor movement in policies affecting its interests, while involving NGOs whose representative credentials have been regarded as problematic (Acuña and

Tuozzo, 2000, 445; Tussie et al., 1997, 77).

But is it not just the representativeness of societal organizations invited to participate and the nature of the policies in which public consultation is allowed that is the problem. A process in which multilateral banks consult civil society is one which not only sidesteps democratic deliberative institutions but it is also one that fails to confront domestic political power inequalities. Indeed, it could be argued that the multilateral lending institutions, in directly consulting civil society, are assuming the rightful place of democratic government whose function it is to attempt to fairly aggregate competing societal interests and to be held accountable for performance. This is a role that most Latin American governments have not performed well (as evidenced by the process by which first stage reforms were carried out) and it is one that must be first learned and then practiced if a public policy process regarded by the public as legitimate is to emerge.

Finally, despite the decline in government resources, clientelist mechanisms of political manipulation and control of the poor have taken new forms in the market reform era. Social investment funds (SIFs) are the mechanisms by which the World Bank has sought to stimulate such targeted social programs. Since 1985, when these funds were first set up to mitigate the very devastating impact of harsh stabilization in Bolivia, they have been implemented in nearly every Latin American country that has carried out structural adjustment (ECLAC, 1997, 108). The SIFs have been designed to be administered by institutions responsible only to the presidency, independent of the state bureaucracy, an arrangement that has rendered them easy tools of political patronage (Stahl, 1996, 33). In most countries such poverty alleviation programs have also involved contributions by other lending agencies (such as the Inter-American Development Bank) and from home governments. Spending in these programs tends to be in short-term measures such as emergency employment and aid programs; therefore, such initiatives are unlikely to create productive employment. The most extensively documented case of the political use of targeted poverty alleviation programs is that of PRONASOL, Mexico's Solidarity Program which was put into place by market reformer, President Carlos Salinas, in 1989 (Dresser, 1994). PRONASOL and other similar programs at the time played an important role in the turn around for the PRI in the 1991 mid-term elections and in the federal election victory of the PRI in 1994. Salinas' successor in the Mexican presidency, Ernesto Zedillo, employed an even more targeted program, PROGRESA, which handed over money to women in extreme poverty provided that their children attend health clinics and school regularly. The manipulation of this program in rural areas to secure votes for the PRI was widely documented during the months leading up to the 2000 federal election (Global Exchange, 2000, 10). PROGRESA has been continued by current president Vicente Fox. In Peru, a Social Investment Fund was set up just in time for the upcoming referendum in 1993 on President Fujimori's new constitution, a constitution with anti democratic features such as a provision allowing the president to dissolve Congress at will, veto laws and promulgate laws by decree. Alberto Fujimori, like Carlos Salinas, appeared on television handing over cheques to poor communities for schools and other facilities, a tactic that reinforced the identification of poverty alleviation measures with the person of the president (Burt, 1996, 34).

The legacy of the market reform era, therefore, has been concentrated economic and political power and a weakening of those organizations (political parties and trade unions) which could act as a counterweight to powerful economic interests. New social movements and non governmental organizations are probably more independent of the state than popular organizations in the past, but they are fragmented. They are being consulted in the process of policy development by multilateral lending institutions but, as noted above, this process is limited and does not confront domestic power realities. The most important obstacle in building the necessary coalitional support to carry forward policies to address poverty and inequality is found in the growing disparity in political power and in the inequality of policy access. The following section explores some of the implications of this skewed policy influence and its implications for the policies needed to alleviate inequality and poverty.

Power and Powerlessness as Obstacles to the Reduction of Poverty and Inequality

Despite the wave of transitions from military rule to electoral democracy that has swept Latin America, policy access is profoundly undemocratic, with personalized channels accorded to the most powerful. Given the ability of the most powerful to change or block policy through non institutionalized channels, I argue that the establishment of all three types of coalitions – electoral, societal and governing – is a necessary condition of successful policy change. This section provides further evidence to substantiate this argument by examining recent attempts to address poverty and inequality. Chile is the closest to fulfilling the three required coalitional conditions and has the highest degree of 'embeddedness' in its state business relations. As noted earlier, Chile has been the most successful at reducing poverty. But even in this case, big business wielded enormous policy influence, especially during the governments of Patricio Alywin (1990-1994) and Eduardo Frei (1995-1999). It is also clear, as demonstrated by the Argentine case, that international factors continue to weigh heavily on domestic policy choices, strengthening conglomerates and blocking appropriate social policy initiatives.

The case of Chile under the Concertación government (1990-2000) illustrates a number of important aspects of the general argument being made here, e.g., that powerful private sector interests can have inordinate impact on policy even when there is an electoral coalition favoring social justice as a national priority. The Concertación – a political alliance in which the most important participants are the socialists and Christian Democrats – declared its support for the neoliberal model, but also its commitment to the rectification of that model's heavy social costs. However, the regime's aggressiveness on social issues had always to be tempered by its more important concern for business confidence, given that the private sector was fearful of a return to the statist policies of the pre-military years (Estrategia, 1994, 130). The strategy to maintain that confidence was to ensure the private sector ready access to the policy process, to pledge the maintenance of the key features of the neoliberal model, to heed business concerns about avoiding increases in public spending, and to afford the private sector increased investment opportunities through privatization (author's interviews with two senior Finance Ministry officials and three business leaders).

Secondly, the Chilean case illustrates the importance of a broadened coalition and 'embeddedness.' In contrast to our other two cases, a broad cross section of private sector interests was afforded access to key economic policy makers (especially the Minister of Finance) on a wide array of economic issues – although labor and rank and file party militants were excluded (Teichman, 2001, 186). Given that power is heavily concentrated in the presidency, access at the executive level was most important, although lobbying of Congress also occurred.[15] The institutionalized arrangements through which business associations participated in policy development were just as important as personal access. Working commissions on economic policy (Muñoz and Celedón, 1993, 128 and 131), the Foro de Producción,[16] and monthly meetings with the head of the Central Bank, all provided the private sector with regular opportunities to press its point of view. But personal access to top policy makers remained important. Notably, small and medium exporters, grouped together in an organization known as the Association of Manufactured Exports, claimed that access to top economic policy makers had never been better than under the Concertación government.[17] Indeed, the cordiality of business/government relations was reflected in the claim that business involvement in economic policy was greater under Concertación than it had ever been under military rule (author's interviews with two business leaders). Business, generally, had high praise for the economic policy of the 1990-2000 Concertación administrations.

15 Business lobbied Congress when support of the right wing legislators was required to defeat legislation it did not like. A forceful lobbying effort occurred against the 1995 proposal to reform the labor code, for example.

16 The Foro de Producción is a yearly conference where ideas on economic policy are exchanged. The CUT, the umbrella labor organization, was also invited to send representatives to the Foro but did not find it a useful arena in which to air its views and withdrew in 1996 (*La Epoca*, June 13, 1996, p. E1).

17 However, the most powerful business interests were still seen as having better access to top economic policy makers because they had personalized contacts (author's interview with a medium-sized exporter).

Indeed, policy makers under both Presidents Alywin and Frei readily acknowledged their openness to business leaders on all issues except generalized tariff reduction where consultation with 'affected business interests' would have blocked policy implementation. Business leaders maintained that their involvement in policy had pushed the government into privatization (of the ports and sanitary works) and had strengthened government commitment to negotiate bilateral trade agreements. Furthermore, the private sector's overriding concern for the public deficit served to bolster policy makers' cautiousness in social spending, no doubt part of the explanation as to why the government did not address social questions more aggressively. The private sector, in general, has opposed tax hikes, and it took a strong stand against the government's 1991 tax reform bill which aimed to raise funds in order to increase social spending. While social expenditure did come to account for a substantial portion of government expenditures during this period, its proportion of GDP did not increase after 1993 and remained below its 1970 level – despite the fact that the public treasury was in surplus until 1996 (Ministerio de Hacienda, 1995, 40).[18] The private sector also fiercely resisted attempts to expand labor rights and reform the country's highly flexible labor arrangements on the grounds that reform would make Chile uncompetitive (author's interviews with all business leaders; *El Mercurio Internacional*, July 15-21, 1995, p. 3; *Ibid.*, July 13-19, 1995, p. 4).[19]

The government of Ricardo Lagos, which took office in 2000, has shown greater resistance to the country's most powerful business interests along with openness to wider input from both Congress and labor in the policy process. Although Lagos took the Presidency by a narrow margin, it is clear that a broad cross section of the Chilean public supported addressing poverty and inequality. Indeed, the issues of jobs and poverty were raised by both himself and the opposition candidate. Upon taking office, Lagos pledged 'growth with equity,' promising measures to increase employment, reforms to bring about greater equity in the health care and educational systems, and labor reforms to provide greater security of employment among other things (*La Tercera*, January 21, 2001, p. 2). The president's ability to knit together a governing coalition to secure the passage of his reforms, however, has been an arduous one. This time, the government made a concerted effort to involve both business and trade unions in its labor reform bill through tripartite bargaining. Two attempts at reaching a consensus this way failed, however. There was also sharp disagreement within the ruling Concertación alliance over the extent of the labor reforms with a number of Concertación senators taking the position that the government's bill went too far. In the absence of a consensus on labor reform, the government sent the bill to Congress. Here, a

18 Social expenditures as a proportion of GDP reached 13.5 percent by 1995, while in 1970, the figure was 21.7 percent (Raczynski, 1995, 65).

19 Some minor changes were made to the labor code in 1991 requiring management to give a reason for dismissal, allowing for appeals before a labor tribunal, and requiring employers to pay compensation for wrongful dismissal.

number of modifications were made in the House of Deputies, on the initiative of a socialist party member, which provided labor greater protection.[20] And while the recalcitrant Concertación senators were brought on side, business was not. Its intensely negative reaction to the bill soured business-state relations for months to come (*La Tercera*, November 14, 2001). On health care reform, disagreements occurred among the Concertación parties on a variety of issues including the extent of union participation in the reforms, where funding should come from, and over the extent to which public sector health care should be strengthened *vis-à-vis* private care (*La Tercera*, September 24, 2001). Most of these issues have yet to be resolved. As with the labor reform, the health reform bill's stiffest opponents were the private sector; in this case, the companies that provided private health care viewed the government's bill as an attempt to dismantle the private health care system (*Estrategia*, April 10, 2002). In short, social policy under Lagos is a highly contested area. Both the labor and health reform bills lacked a societal consensus which included the private sector, raising the specter of declining business confidence. While the Lagos government may have reduced the privileged influence of big business to the policy process and provided greater access to other groups such as labor, it has failed to effectively link itself to business through embedded institutionalized channels that will maintain business confidence in the administration.

The government of Fernando de la Rúa, elected president of Argentina in 1999, illustrates the impact of economic crisis on domestic policy change and its role in strengthening the conglomerate/policy elite nexus. The election of the presidential candidate of the opposition Alianza (a multi party coalition including the Radical Party and FREPASO) reflected growing public pressure for a revised economic program to address the devastating social impact of market reform policies. The social basis of the new regime appeared to be considerably broader than the previous one; it had the support of a much wider array of private sector interests and across section of middle class and labor groups. With a new Economy Minister strongly supported by the majority of the private sector who had been excluded from political access during the past administration, the new government immediately announced an industrial policy geared to help small and medium business, an export incentive program, and in November 2000, a plan to promote investment, growth and employment by tax cuts (*El Cronista*, October 29, 1999; *Ibid.*, September 20, 1999; *Página 12*, July 12, 1999). The plans of the new government, however, ran headlong into a public deficit of $7 billion (U.S.) and the necessity, in the face of IMF demands, of making extensive budget cuts as the

20 The labor reform bill, given final approval in September 2001, among other things increased fines on businesses and compensations to workers for unjustified dismissals, lowered the number of workers required to establish a union, provided for inter-enterprise bargaining if business and labor agree, and mandated the rehiring of workers dismissed for union activities (*La Tercera*, September 13, 2001).

economy continued to stagnate. The strongest supporters of deficit reduction and of the Convertibility Plan continued to be the most powerful entrepreneurs grouped in the CEA, while the rest of the entrepreneurial sector demanded interventionist measures to protect industry and employment.

In March 2001, as the economic situation continued to deteriorate and as pressure from the international banking community, particularly the IMF intensified, President de la Rúa appointed Domingo Cavallo, the technocrat behind many market reforms and the architect of the Convertibility Plan, to the economy ministry. With Cavallo's appointment, the practice of highly selective, personalized access for big business returned. Shortly after his appointment, Cavallo summoned the country's 50 most important firms, most of them members of the CEA, to a meeting in the ministry of economy. Entrepreneurs appointed to the newly created 'Advisory Commission on Strategies for the Promotion of External Trade' were appointed as individuals (some allegedly 'amigos' of Cavallo), not in any capacity as leaders of entrepreneurial organizations (*Clarín*, April 16, 2001; *Ibid.* May 4, 2001; and *Ibid.* May 30, 2001).

But as the economic and political crisis deepened, growing social unrest produced the political demise of this latest exclusionary coalition involving Cavallo and the big conglomerates. The assumption of Eduardo Duhalde to the presidency probably indicates a broadened societal coalition, although not an electoral one. Given that Duhalde was chosen by Congress, his administration was in a better position to pull together a governing coalition than any other national figure. Now the big conglomerates of the CEA are excluded from the policy process. With the appointment of José Ignacio de Mendiguren – a prominent member of the business group (the Grupo Productivo) excluded from policy during the market reform years – as Minister of Production, and a former trade union House of Representatives candidate as Minister of Labor, those previously excluded from policy obtained the inside track. With this arrangement, which takes intensely polarized societal conflicts inside the state, economic policy, as in past Argentine history, is likely to attempt to punish political opponents and reward political supporters. On the one hand, the current Argentine situation illustrates the enormous constraints on policy by economic crisis – policies that might have addressed the social deficit have had to be abandoned. At the same time, it also reveals the role of politics in deepening that crisis and in rendering a solution more difficult. A broadened social basis without embeddedness is likely to take societal conflicts inside the state, endanger policy coherency and inhibit the ability of the state to enforce compliance on particular interests. This exaggerated state weakness has been a historical feature of the Argentine policy process. To a lesser degree, however, it has also been present in most other Latin American countries, causing the state apparatus to become highly politicized (Chalmers, 1977).

The Mexican case illustrates the resiliency of the conglomerate and policy elite alliance even in the face of an electoral defeat of the administration that had pushed through market reform, and it illustrates the ways in which powerful business interests and their foreign partners weigh in on social policy issues. When the PRI was ousted from the president's office in 2000 by presidential candidate Vicente Fox, an attempt was made to set a new policy agenda. But while the most important party of Fox's coalition, the rightist Popular Action Party, was very strongly pro-business, the Fox election campaign, having brought on board two leftist advisors, Jorge Castañeda and Adolfo Aguilar Zinzer, began to address such issues as poverty alleviation, support for small and medium enterprises, reform of the tax system, employment creation and an end to corruption. Fox, like de la Rúa, was also constrained by problems of the public deficit. But, perhaps more important has been the direct policy access accorded to many powerful members of the private sector who have received important government appointments. Like its predecessors, Fox's regime is a highly personalistic one and there is little evidence of an attempt to broaden the entrepreneurial basis of the state, or of institutionalizing state-business relations.

Powerful members of the private sector have been heavily represented among those closest to Fox and reflect the administration's firm commitment to continued market liberalization. Fox himself is a former Coca Cola executive. Roberto Hernández, the main shareholder in the country's largest bank, BANAMEX, and Justino Campean, a senior executive in the media giant Televisa, are leading members of the 'Amigos de Fox' movement. In addition, the private sector has now gained direct representation in the state – a situation comparable to Argentina and an important departure from past Mexican practice. An unprecedented number of cabinet appointments (nine) went to individuals with experience in the private sector – for example, Pedro Cerisola y Weber formerly the head of TELMEX in the federal district, and Fox's campaign manager, was appointed Minister of Communications and Transport; Ernesto Martens Rebelledo, a strong proponent of private investment in the energy sector and a former executive of Union Carbide, was given the Energy portfolio; the new Minister of Agriculture, Javier Usabiaga, is owner of an agricultural export company; and technocrat Francisco Gil Díaz, architect of Mexico's trade liberalization drive and later director general of Avantel, a subsidiary of the Banamex-Accival group, was appointed Finance Minister. Many other important government positions also went to businessmen.[21] While big business had nothing but praise for the Fox administration, the organizations representing small and medium enterprise were expressing the fear that the new government would privilege macro economic indicators (especially the fiscal deficit) over the well being of the population, the productive apparatus and the domestic market.

---

21 For a list of Fox's major government appointments (cabinet, directorships of major public companies and important positions) and descriptions of the appointees backgrounds, see *Reforma* (Mexico City), (no date given) www.reforma.com/flashes/nacional/gabinete_fox/; *La Jornada*, November 23, 2000; *Latin American Weekly Report*, February 20, 2001, p. 89; ISLA, February 2001, p. 74.

Nevertheless, upon assuming power, Fox's administration did make an effort in the direction of policies that would garner support from a wider cross section of the public. Indeed, by 2001, under growing political pressure, the new administration was promising higher spending on social welfare, health and education along with tax reform to raise money for these programs. But economic deterioration meant that the regime was going to have considerable difficulty obtaining the resources to carry out such proposed policies. By 2001, the Mexican economy was slowing down and markets were demanding that the fiscal balance be addressed.[22] Budget reduction was to come from, among other places, the support program for small and medium enterprise (ISLA, March 2001, pp. 38 and 39; *Latin American Weekly Report*, May 15, 2001, p. 221).

But business influence also played a key role in what would be possible during the Fox administration, as illustrated by the issue of tax reform – an issue which is a more pressing concern in Mexico than in some other Latin American cases, and essential to increased social spending.[23] Early in his election campaign, Fox had proposed a tax on wealth or property taxes (in Mexico this currently brings in only 0.3 percent of GDP as opposed to 3.2 percent in the U.S.) but this proposal met with stiff resistance from the private sector and was dropped. In its place, Fox then proposed to levy a 15 percent value-added tax (VAT) on all goods including food and medicine which had previously been exempt, a proposal which the private sector supported (*Mexico and NAFTA Report*, May 1, 2001, p. 8). While the administration dropped the extension of VAT to food and medicine in the face of congressional opposition, income tax was reduced from 42 to 35 percent. The combination of private sector resistance to increased taxes and the political impossibility of extending the VAT to food and medicine resulted in a reform that is expected to produce less than one half of the revenue originally anticipated from tax reform (*Mexico and NAFTA Report,* January 6, 2002, p. 1).

But Fox's solution to poverty relies more than anything on the market and it reflects the continuing policy influence of both market reform technocrats and big conglomerates. His grand scheme for poverty alleviation in southern Mexico (by far the poorest part of the country), the Plan Puebla Panama, envisions heavy investment in infrastructure (transportation) to encourage private investment in resource development (particularly electricity and natural gas), in agriculture, and in maquilas (export processing zones). The objective is to produce goods that will be export competitive. Supported by the Inter-American Development Bank, the scheme is being strongly encouraged by the U.S. given its desire for stable and secure sources of energy. The Plan is said to have arisen from the pen of one of the

22 The previous government had been under reporting its deficit situation such that by 2001 the fiscal deficit was expected to be 3.5 percent of GDP, not the earlier official estimate of 0.65 percent, making necessary a substantial budget cut.

23 Currently in Mexico, fiscal revenue represents just 11.6 percent of GDP, far below the 20 percent collected in Chile and Argentina; in the U.S. the figure is 30 percent of GDP (ISLA, January 2001, p. 1).

technocrats prominent in the previous administration, Santiago Levy, an economist and a former senior official in the finance ministry. In addition, the Plan has strong domestic supporters in the form of the country's internationalized conglomerates. The owner of Grupo Pulsar, Alfonso Reyes, for example, who is closely tied politically to Vicente Fox, is a strong supporter of the Plan. In the south, on the other hand, there is mounting popular resistance to the Plan: the Zapatistas have declared it an attack on popular culture, while civil society groups have contended that it will aggravate the social ills already present in the region, and have demanded programs to reduce social vulnerability (ISLA, March 2001, p. 41).

Public criticisms of Fox's personal links with the owners of the biggest conglomerates have been fueled by the fact that his government has made no attempt to carry out an investigation of the bank rescue operation carried out by the previous administration, and by the designation of eight entrepreneurs to accompany him on a trade mission to South America. The fact that three of these entrepreneurs were among those who had benefited from the highly questionable bank rescue operation of the previous administration triggered substantial criticism in the media and a promise by the government that henceforth the leaders of organizations representative of the business community rather than individual businessmen would be invited on such missions (*La Jornada*, August 4, 2000). As in Argentina, the big conglomerates are the strongest supporters of keeping down the public deficit, probably the administration's greatest concern at the moment (ISLA, March 2001, p. 21), but they also resist tax reform that would enhance the government's ability to address social needs.

Conclusion

While political power has always been distributed unequally in Latin America, economic crisis and the market reform programs believed necessary to enable Latin America to find prosperity and its place in the new global order, have increased the power of the already powerful and reduced the policy clout of civil society. The market reform years have witnessed increased power in the hands of powerful conglomerate executives, the growing fracturing and de-legitimization of political parties, new forms of clientelist political control of the poor, and the dismantling of trade union power. The big winners of market reform have been big domestic conglomerates and their foreign allies – those who were in the best position to take advantage of the new opportunities opened up by policy reform. Able to borrow on international financial markets, and take on foreign partners thereby gaining access to the latest technology, they were able to modernize and expand into export markets. But they also benefited from state largesse in the form of export incentives, and opportunities to buy into public companies either at bargain prices or with protected monopolies. The market reform era involved a narrow societal coalition comprised of technocrats, market reform politicians, and conglomerate executives.

A very important aspect of this political elite/conglomerate alliance was the highly personalized access of powerful private sector actors to the policy process. Conglomerate executives served as policy advisors, accompanied political leaders on foreign trade missions, and, in the admittedly extreme case of Argentina, were directly involved in the formation of privatization decrees. As a consequence, cronyism was the most notable feature of the market reform process, and was particularly marked in privatization. Informal and personalistic policy channels can impact heavily upon those policy initiatives that are either opposed or not seen as priority items by powerful private sector actors: they have the wherewithal to intervene at the highest level of political power to block policy change.

Hence, I have argued the importance of three types of coalitions as a necessary condition for domestic policies geared to the reduction of poverty and inequality. Taken together these coalitions would entail the empowerment of those excluded from policy *and* a commensurate reduction in the political power of the major beneficiaries of the market reform era. An electoral coalition is important in getting the social question onto the political agenda. In some cases, this is already occurring, although the commitment of political leaders may be suspect by members of the public for whom political parties are held in increasingly low regard. There must also be a governing coalition: with sufficient support in Congress and from the top levels of the political and state bureaucracies. But neither electoral nor governing coalitions will be sufficient. Power is highly centralized, and policy input heavily monopolized by the politically and economically powerful. Market reform technocrats are still present and remain important as the key interlocutors with multilateral lenders. And, parties are not effective avenues of policy input. Hence, an equity societal coalition actively supportive of a program to reduce poverty and inequality is key. It must be a coalition from which the government draws support and with whose members the regime is willing and able to establish institutionalized links – links able to ensure both cooperation and compliance. Such arrangements are especially important for the particular policies that would comprise a program to reduce inequality and poverty: increased tax revenue and collection to fund increased social spending, support for small and medium enterprise, and the regulation of monopolies. The biggest challenge, as illustrated by the Chilean case, is the incorporation of private sector interests, especially those which have been the major beneficiaries of market reform. Chile has been the most successful at reducing poverty although not inequality and it is the country that has most closely fulfilled the requisites defined here. It has had an electoral coalition favoring social justice and a governing coalition in the more limited sense of a policy/technocratic elite favoring increased social spending.[24] Its societal coalition

24 It should be noted that lack of control of the senate, due to the presence of appointed senators (a legacy of military rule) meant the absence of a true governing coalition for much of the period of Concertación rule. Increases in tax collection and changes in the

was certainly the broadest of the cases discussed here, in the sense of allowing for the opportunity for policy input from a broad array of business interests. But, the regime is only now taking tentative steps to include groups outside the private sector in policy development.

The political challenges of equitable development in Latin America are substantial; they involve a reduction in the policy influence of the extremely powerful winners of the last decades and an increase in policy access for those who have historically been disempowered as well as those whose influence has been reduced in more recent decades. While continued improvements in 'governance' issues (regulations, mechanisms of accountability) are important, they cannot, by themselves, address issues of informal policy access and exclusion. Hence, once an equity coalition emerges, the establishment and maintenance of regular and effective channels of policy access must become an essential part of the process.

References

Acuña, C.H. and M.F. Tuozzo (2000), 'Civil Society Participation in World Bank and Inter-American Development Bank Programs: The Case of Argentina', *Global Governance*, Vol. 6, No. 4, pp. 433-455.

Álvarez, S.E., E. Dagnino and A. Escobar (eds.) (1998), *Cultures of Politics and Politics of Cultures*, Westview, Boulder, CO.

American Chamber of Commerce of Chile. Santiago. http://amchamchile.cl/usa-chiledat.htm.

Azpiazu, D. and A. Vispo (1994), 'Algunos Enseñanzas de las Privatizaciones en Argentina', *Revista de CEPAL*, No. 54 (December), pp. 130-146.

Basualdo, E.M. (1994), 'El Impacto Económico y Social de la Privatizaciones', *Realidad Económica*, No. 123 (April 1-May 15), pp. 27-51.

Birdsall, N. and A. de la Torre (2000), *Washington Contentious. Economic Policy for Social Equity in Latin America*, Carnegie Endowment for International Peace and Inter-American Dialogue, Washington, D.C.

Blutman, G. (1994), 'Orden y Desorden en la Reforma del Estado Argentino (1989-1994)', *Ciclos*, Vol. 4, No. 7 (2nd semester), pp. 52-93.

Burt, J.-M. (1996), 'Local NGOs in Peru Devise an Alternative Anti-Poverty Program', *NACLA Report on the Americas*, No. 6 (May-June).

Camp, R.A. (1989), *Enterpreneurs and Politics in Twentieth Century Mexico*, Oxford University Press, New York.

Centeno, M.A. (1997), *Democracy within Reason*, The Pennsylvania State University Press, University Park, PA.

Centeno, M.A. and P. Silva (eds.) (1998), *The Politics of Expertise in Latin America*, St. Martin's Press, New York.

---

labor code demanded by the trade unions were blocked here. However, as noted in the earlier discussion of the Chilean case, there is evidence that, even without this institutional obstacle, business pressure may well have secured the same or a very similar outcome.

Chalmers, D. (1977), 'The Politicized State in Latin America', in James M. Malloy (ed.), *Authoritarianism and Corporatism in Latin America*, University of Pittsburgh Press, Pittsburgh.

Clarín (various dates), Buenos Aires. http://Clarín.com.

Cockcroft, J.D. (1983), *Class Formation, Capital Accumulation and the State*, Monthly Review, New York.

Conaghan, C.M. (1994a), 'Loose Parties, 'Floating Politicians,' and Institutional Stress: Presidentialism in Ecuador, 1979-88', in J.J. Linz and A. Valenzuela (eds.), *The Failure of Presidential Democracy*, Vol. 2, The Johns Hopkins University Press, Baltimore.

Conaghan, C.M. (1994b), 'Reconsidering Jeffrey Sachs and the Bolivian Economic Experiment', in P.W. Drake (ed.), *Money Doctors, Foreign Debt and Economic Reforms in Latin America from the 1890s to the Present*, Scholarly Resources Inc., Wilmington, Delaware.

Dresser, D. (1994), 'Bringing the Poor Back in: National Solidarity as a Strategy of Regime Legitimacy', in W.A. Cornelius, A.L. Craig and J. Barker (eds.), *Transforming State Society Relations in Mexico*, Centre for U.S.-Mexican Studies, University of California, San Diego.

ECLAC (United Nations Economic Commission for Latin America and the Caribbean) (1997), *The Equity Gap. Latin America, the Caribbean and the Social Summit*, ECLAC, Santiago.

Edwards, S. and Cox Edwards, A. (1987), *Monetarism and Liberalization. The Chilean Experiment*, Ballinger Publishing Co., Cambridge, MA.

El Cronista (various dates), Buenos Aires, http://cronista.com.

El Mercurio. Santiago, http://www.emol.com/noticias/detalle/detalle_diario.asp).

El Mercurio Internacional (various dates), Santiago.

Estrategia (1994), *El Gran Salto de Chile. La Historia Económica y Empresarial*, Publicaciones Editorial Gestión, Santiago.

Estrategia (April 10, 2000), http://www.estrategia.cl.

Evans, P. (1992), 'The State as Problem and Solution: Predation, Embedded Autonomy and Structural Change', in S. Haggard and R. R. Kaufman (eds.), *The Politics of Economic Adjustment*. Princeton, N.J.: Princeton University Press.

Falabella, G. (1981), 'Labour in Chile under the Junta, 1973-1979', Working Paper No. 4, Institute of Latin American Studies, University of London.

Felder, R. (1994), 'El Estado se Baja del Tren: La Política Ferrovaria del Gobierno Menemista. La Restructuración de los Ferrocarriles: Particularidades y Perspectivas', *Realidad Económica*, No. 123 (1 Abril-15 May), pp. 53-75.

Fernández de Villegas, M. and N. Adelson (2000), 'Civil Society Participation in World Bank and Inter-American Development Bank Programs: The Case of Mexico', *Global Governance*, Vol. 6, No. 4, pp. 473-491.

Global Exchange/Alianza Cívica International Delegation (2000), *Pre-electoral Conditions in Mexico 2000*, Global Exchange, San Francisco.

Heredia, B. (1996), *Contested State: The Politics of Trade Liberalization in Mexico*, unpublished Ph.D. thesis, Columbia University.

ISLA (Information Services on Latin America) (various dates), Oakland, California, http://isla.igc.org/.

Jones, M.P. (1997), 'Evaluating Argentina's Presidential Democracy, 1983-1995', in S. Mainwaring and M. Soberg Shugart (eds.), *Presidentialism and Democracy in Latin America*, Cambridge University Press, Cambridge, U.K.

Kleinberg, R.B. (1999), *Strategic Alliances and Other Deals. State Business Relations and Economic Reform in Mexico*, Carolina Academic Press, Durham, N.C.

La Botz, D. (1992), *Mask of Democracy, Labor Suppression in Mexico Today*, South End Press, Boston.

La Epoca (June 13, 1996), Santiago.

La Jornada (various dates), Mexico City, http://www.jornada.unam.mx.

La Tercera (various dates), Santiago, http://www.tercera.cl.

Latin American Weekly Report (various dates), http://www.latinnews.com.

Luna, M. (992) 'Las Asociaciones Empresariales Mexicanas y la Apertura Externa', paper presented at the XVII International Congress of the Latin American Studies Association (LASA), 24-27 September, Los Angeles.

Mexico and NAFTA Report (various dates), http://www.latinnews.com.

Ministerio de Hacienda (1995), *Estado de Avance de las Prioridades Planteadas al País el 29 de Agosto de 1994 por el Ministro de Hacienda*. Santiago: Ministerio de Hacienda.

Mizrahi, Y. (1992), 'Rebels Without a Cause? The Politics of Enterpreneurs in Chihuahua', paper presented at the XVII International Congress of the Latin American Studies Association (LASA), 24-27 September, Los Angeles.

Muñoz, O.G. and C. Celedón (1993), 'Chile en Transición: Estrategia Económica y Política', in J.A. Morales and G. McHahon (eds.), *La Política Económica en la Transición a la Democracia*, CIEPLAN, Santiago.

Nelson, P.J. (1997), 'Transparencia, Fiscalización y Participación', in D. Tussie (ed.), *El BID, el Banco Mundial y la Sociedad Civil: Nuevas Formas de Financiamiento Internacional*, FLACSO and Oficina de Publicaciones del CBC, Universidad de Buenos Aires, Buenos Aires.

O'Brien, P. and J. Roddick (1983), *Chile: The Pinochet Decade. The Rise and Fall of the Chicago Boys*, Latin American Bureau, London.

O'Donnell, G. (1994),. 'Delegative Democracy', *Journal of Democracy*, Vol. 5, No. 1, pp. 55-69.

OED (Operations Evaluation Department) (2001), *Mexico Country Assistance Evaluation*, The World Bank, Washington D.C.

Oxhorn, P. and G. Ducatenzeiler (1999), 'The Problematic Relationship Between Economic and Political Liberalization: Some Theoretical Considerations', in P. Oxhorn and P. Starr (eds.), *Markets and Democracy in Latin America: Conflict or Convergence?*, Lynne Rienner, Boulder, CO.

Página 12 (Buenos Aires), http://www.pagina12.com.ar.

Peralta Ramos, M. (1992), 'Economic Policy and Distributional Conflict among Business Groups in Argentina: From Alfonsín to Menem, 1983-1990', in E.C. Epstein (ed.), *The New Democracy. The Search for a Successful Formula*, Praeger, Westport.

Proceso (various dates), Mexico City. http://www.proceso.com.mx.

Puga E.C. (1984), 'Los Empresarios y la Política en México', in S.H. Cordero and R. Tirado (eds.), *Clases Dominantes y Estado de México*, UNAM, Mexico City.

Raczynski, D. (1995), 'Programs, Institutions and Resources: Chile', in D. Raczynski (ed.), *Strategies to Combat Poverty in Latin America*, Inter-American Development Bank and Johns Hopkins University Press, Washington, D.C.

Reforma (various dates), Mexico City. http://www.reforma.com/flashes/nacional/gabinete_fox.

Schvarzer, J. (1995), 'Grandes Grupos Económicos en la Argentina. Formas de Propiedad y Lógicas de Expansión', in P. Bustos (ed.), *Más Allá de la Estabilidad: Argentina en la Época de la Globalización y la Regionalización*, Fundación Fredrick Ebert, Buenos Aires.

Shugart, M.S. and S. Mainwaring (1997), 'Presidentialism and Democracy in Latin America: Rethinking the Terms of the Debate', in S. Mainwaring and M.S. Shugart (eds.), *Presidentialism and Democracy in Latin America*, Cambridge University Press, Cambridge U.K.

Stahl, K. (1996), 'Anti-Poverty Programs: Making Structural Adjustment More Palatable', NACLA Report on the Americas, No. 6 (May-June).

Székely, M. (1998), *The Economics of Poverty Inequality and Wealth Accumulation in Mexico*, St. Martin's Press, New York.

Teichman, J.A. (2001), *The Politics of Freeing Markets in Latin America: Chile Argentina and Mexico*, University of North Carolina Press, Chapel Hill.

Teichman, J.A. (1997), 'Mexico and Argentina: Economic Reform and Technocratic Decision Making', *Studies in Comparative International Development,* Vol. 32, No. 1 (Spring), pp. 31-55.

Teichman, J.A. (1995), *Privatization and Political Change in Mexico*, University of Pittsburgh Press, Pittsburgh.

The Economist (July 28-August 3, 2001), http://www.economist.com.

Tussie, D., M. Mendiburu, and P.I. Vásquez (1997), 'Los Nuevos Mandatos de los Bancos Multilaterales de Desarrollo: Su Aplicación en el Caso de Argentina', in D. Tussie (ed.), *El BID, el Banco Mundial y la Sociedad Civil: Nuevas Formas de Financiamiento Internacional*, FLACSO and Oficina de Publicaciones de CBC, Universidad de Buenos Aires, Buenos Aires.

Waterbury, J. (1989), 'The Management of Long Haul Economic Reform', in J. Nelson (ed.), *Fragile Coalitions: The Politics of Economic Adjustment*, Overseas Development Council, Washington, D.C.

Wilkie, J.W. (ed.) (1999), *Statistical Abstract of Latin America*, Vol. 35, UCLA Latin American Center Publications, Los Angeles.

World Bank (1997), *World Development Report 1997,* The World Bank, Washington, D.C.

Zermeño, S. (1990), 'Crisis, Neoliberalism and Disorder', in J. Foweraker and A.L. Craig (eds.), *Popular Movements and Political Change in Mexico*, Lynne Rienner, Boulder.

PART III

ECONOMIC REFORMS AND LABOR MARKETS

Chapter 9

The Impact of Liberalization and Globalization on Labor Market Policies in Latin America and the Caribbean[1]

Andrew Downes, Rafael Gómez, and Morley Gunderson

Introduction

The conventional emphasis of the impact of trade liberalization and globalization on labor markets is on the adjustment consequences pertaining to such outcomes as wages, employment and wage inequality. These direct impacts are important, but possibly more important is the *indirect* impact on social and labor market policies. Ironically, the demand for such policy initiatives may be increasing – to deal with the adjustment consequences of trade liberalization and economic integration – just at the same time as the ability of governments to supply such initiatives may be decreased by the forces of trade liberalization and globalization. This growing demand and decreasing supply of policy initiatives is creating a tension – albeit a healthy tension – that calls for creative initiatives in the policy-making process with respect to labor market issues. It also calls for a deeper understanding of the underlying causal mechanisms that link globalization and social policy, and the two-way interaction whereby social policies both affect and are affected by the globalization process.

The purpose of this chapter is to analyze this two-way interaction – the impact of social policy on the liberalization process, and the impact of liberalization on the social policy making process – in the context of labor markets in North America and, more particularly, in Latin America and the Caribbean basin. The analysis will focus on the conceptual level, using illustrative examples. The chapter begins with a discussion of the effects of social and labor market policy on the process of liberalization

1 Paper originally prepared for the conference in honor of Albert Berry, University of Toronto, April 19-20, 2002. We would like to thank all those participated in the conference and provided useful comments. We especially thank Gustavo Indart for his helpful comments and suggestions.

and globalization. It then turns to the effects of globalization on the social and labor market policy-making process, outlining the mechanisms whereby globalization affects labor market and social policy initiatives, and examining the necessary conditions for downward policy harmonization to take place.

The analysis is conducted in the broader context of both the deepening and widening of economic integration (Castro-Rea, 1996; Gunderson, 2001; Gómez and Gunderson, 2002) under liberalization and globalization. The deepening refers to the various dimensions of integration including trade liberalization, capital flows, foreign direct investment, labor and human capital mobility and technology transfer. The widening refers to the special aspect involving regional agreements such as NAFTA, MERCUSOR, the Andean Pact, CARICOM, and a possible all-encompassing Western Hemisphere agreement across North, Central, and South America, including the Caribbean Basin.

The labor market and social policy initiatives relevant to this context include a wide range of policies and programs:

- collective bargaining legislation that governs the establishment and conduct of bargaining;
- employment standards legislation in such areas as minimum wages, hours of work, advance notice and termination requirements;
- anti-discrimination and human rights legislation, including equal pay and equal employment opportunity initiatives;
- health and safety, and workers' compensation;
- income maintenance programs like unemployment insurance; and
- adjustment assistance programs in such areas as training, mobility, job search and labor market information.

Effects of Labor Policies on the Labor Adjustment Process

The effect of labor market and social policy initiatives on the labor adjustment process depends in large part on the nature of the policy initiative. In that vein, it is important to make a general distinction between active adjustment assistance and passive income maintenance programs (Gunderson and Riddell, 1995) and then move on to more specific labor policies.

Active Adjustment Assistance

Active adjustment assistance programs facilitate the workings of markets and encourage adjustment in the direction of basic market forces, often from declining sectors and regions to expanding ones. For that reason, such policies can deal with adjustment consequences on both the 'downside' (plant closings, layoffs, underemployment) in the declining sectors and regions as well as the 'upside' (labor shortages, job vacancies, skill bottlenecks) in expanding sectors and regions.

Active adjustment assistance policies generally include ones that both optimize and enhance the stock of human capital through such mechanisms as education, training, mobility, and job search. The provision of labor market information, for example, is an important component of that optimization process, especially as it can facilitate improvements in human capital quality by indicating the education and training needs and the location of job openings to facilitate job search and mobility.

With respect to human capital formation, a key issue is the appropriate role of the different stakeholders – employers, employees and their representatives, and governments – in the financing and provision of these programs. Governments run the risk of unnecessarily spending scarce resources on initiatives where the private parties themselves have an incentive to invest in human capital formation. This could lead to a displacement of private sector activity if, for example, governments were to support training programs that had been undertaken by employers in the first place. It could even lead to perverse results if, for example, government spending on elite higher-level education were to foster a brain drain of the very persons who could most help internal development.

In that vein, governments should *focus* their intervention on areas showing well-defined market failures in the provision of such adjustment assistance initiatives. That is, rather than asking 'What adjustment programs seem to foster competitiveness and the efficient allocation of labor?,' one should ask 'What are the well-defined market failures that inhibit the private parties themselves from undertaking adjustment initiatives that foster the efficient allocation of labor?' Research efforts should help identify those market failures.

It is well known, for example, that the private market fails to provide the socially optimal amount of labor market information – given that such information has public goods characteristics. The benefits are generally available to all users, with the use by one not detracting from the use by others; and it is not feasible to exclude non-payers from using the services. Obviously, private markets can and do exist in this area as evidenced by executive placement agencies. Nevertheless, the public goods nature of much of the information merits an important role for governments, certainly regarding the general workforce.

Similar issues apply in the well-known problem of poaching in the training business,[2] an issue generally applicable in a wide range of firms; indeed, such broad-based generic training is becoming increasingly important, given the market needs for

---

2 The issue of underinvestment in training in Latin America is emphasized in Berry (2001) and Berry and Méndez (1998). Possible market failures that can lead to underinvestment in training are discussed in Gunderson and Riddell (2001b).

flexibility and adaptability. Private firms may not have an incentive to pay for such training for their employees since they run the risk of losing their trained employees to firms that do not train but, simply, poach by offering a higher wage. In such circumstances, the firm that provides the training may incur double pay – paying both the training cost and the subsequent higher wage needed to retain the trained employee. Workers themselves have an obvious incentive to pay for such training – perhaps by working for a lower wage in return for the training – since they reap the benefits through the higher wage. However, they may be reluctant to pay for such training given the uncertainty about the returns from such an investment over which they have little control. Furthermore, they may not be able to borrow to finance otherwise profitable training because of liquidity constraints, which, when coupled with capital market imperfections, prevent the use of human capital as collateral to finance a loan – since banks cannot repossess the human capital in the event of a default.[3]

What is less emphasized is the potential market failure that can exist with respect to innovation in the area of developing efficient workplace and human resource practices within firms. Firms may not have sufficient incentive to innovate in this area of developing 'best-practices' since they would bear the full cost of such innovation, yet cannot reap the full returns since the successful ones would be quickly emulated by competitor firms and others. Innovating firms would have only some short-run advantage until competitors 'caught up.' The problem essentially arises because innovations in the workplace arena cannot be patented, unlike innovations in product markets. In such circumstances, private markets would yield less than a socially optimal amount of innovation with respect to workplace and human resource practices within firms, just as they would yield less than a socially optimal amount of innovation with respect to product development if patents did not exist. Even if a successful workplace innovation should occur, it would not be *diffused* optimally to other workplaces since the innovating firm would have a market incentive to hide the success, especially from competitors.[4]

These examples are meant to be illustrative of the possible market failures that can exist with respect to active adjustment assistance programs that could otherwise enhance productivity and competitiveness by 'greasing the wheels' of markets and facilitating adjustment in the direction of market forces. By focusing their intervention efforts in such areas of well-defined market failures, governments can ensure that their scarce resources are not dissipated and that their actions do not simply displace actions that would have occurred in the private market in any case.

---

3 As well, there is a moral hazard problem in that potential borrowers can influence the returns to their investment depending upon their subsequent work decisions.

4 There is also the question of the 'quality' of the innovation which, in terms of a workplace practice as opposed to a product, is difficult to measure and, therefore, replicate.

Passive Income Maintenance Programs

Passive income maintenance programs provide income support or insurance for those who are adversely affected by the adjustment consequences of liberalization and globalization. In contrast to active adjustment assistance programs, which facilitate and, indeed, encourage adjustment by providing assistance only if there is an adjustment in the direction of market forces, passive income maintenance programs can discourage adjustment in the direction of market forces by providing income support when there is no adjustment. They encourage the 'stay' option by supporting the stay decision; in effect, they blunt the market incentives to adjust.

By discouraging constant marginal adjustments – e.g., mobility of younger persons, or persons who are willing to move or change jobs – passive income maintenance programs can lead to a build-up of latent pressures that are likely to lead to more severe and costly *inframarginal* adjustments if the adjustment inevitably occurs. Such inframarginal adjustments can occur in such forms as mass layoffs or plant closings, affecting whole communities and older workers with families.

Passive income maintenance programs include unemployment insurance (Gunderson and Riddell, 2001a; Cortázar, 2001) and social assistance or welfare payments.[5] Government bailouts of failing firms – perhaps to save the jobs – can also be thought of as an indirect income maintenance program. Ironically, some of these programs, like unemployment insurance, can also discourage marginal adjustments in such areas as reduced hours or wage concessions as mechanisms to absorb negative demand shocks. This situation occurs because the income support is provided only in the event of the all-or-nothing unemployment event concentrated in the hands of a few, and not for more marginal adjustments to wages or hours spread over the firm's workforce. The same can apply to bailouts if they inhibit wage concessions, and hours reductions if a bailout is anticipated.

Safety Net to Reduce Resistance to Change

Even passive adjustment assistance programs that inhibit adjustment from declining to expanding sectors or regions can facilitate overall market adjustments by reducing resistance to otherwise efficient changes, such as those associated with globalization, trade liberalization, and technological change (Blank, 1994; Rodrik, 1997). In effect, they may provide a 'safety net' that makes workers more willing to accept change

5 Cortázar (2001) outlines negative effects of unemployment insurance (UI) in terms of increased unemployment and fraud through peoples' working in the underground economy while collecting UI. To alleviate these problems, he recommends mandatory UI savings accounts that the individual worker can draw on if unemployed. These would also replace the traditional high severance payments that are prominent in Latin America.

because of the insurance provided. As well, some programs like unemployment insurance may be used to finance efficient job search (Berry, 2001, 25). In essence, equity and efficiency need not clash – indeed, providing a degree of equity may facilitate efficient change. While passive income maintenance may provide a 'safety net,' active adjustment assistance programs can go one step further in fostering efficiency by providing a 'trampoline' effect, enabling those who are adversely affected to bounce back into the labor market.

The degree of employment security provided to Japanese workers through their lifetime employment system, for example, contributes to their willingness to accept – indeed embrace – technological and other changes that would otherwise jeopardize their jobs. In such circumstances, employees provide loyalty and commitment to their organization in return for the commitment given to them as employees. Such long-term employment prospects with the same firm also facilitated firms' investing in the training of their employees.

Quasi-Fixed Employment Costs[6]

Many labor policies can have a quasi-fixed cost component in that they increase the fixed costs associated with hiring a new employee. Such costs are not incurred if the incumbent employees work longer hours or more intensely, or if non-standard employees (limited-term contracts, subcontracting, self-employment, temporary help agencies and some part-time employees), who are not associated with such fixed costs, are utilized.

The fixed costs can arise for normal reasons associated with recruiting, hiring and training new employees. But they can also stem from legislative initiatives – common in Latin America – that increase the costs of terminating employees (e.g., advance notice, severance pay, and unjust dismissal claims). Such costs of terminating employees become quasi-fixed at the hiring stage since, in the decision to hire a new employee, employers factor in the cost the possibility of having to terminate that employee, thereby incurring these quasi-fixed costs. In such circumstances, in the face of demand expansions that may be uncertain, the employers may rationally be reluctant to hire new employees (Amadeo and Horton, 1997, 11). Instead, such employers expand the work-hours of their existing employees, even paying premium overtime; or they increase the intensity or the workload – creating, perhaps, stress and morale problems; or they use subcontracting or temporary help agencies – which can be expensive.

---

6 The following discussion makes reference only to those policies that discourage new hiring. In practice, however, certain policies which work in the opposite direction could accompany quasi-fixed costs, and, thus, mitigate the overall negative effect on job creation. These counterbalancing polices include such things as wage subsidies or differential payroll taxes for newly hired workers.

Quasi-fixed costs of hiring new employees may also arise if payroll taxes have a ceiling beyond which no further taxes are paid. This can be a common occurrence for unemployment insurance or workers' compensation or pension plans. If the payroll tax is simply a percentage of payroll or earnings, then the same amount of tax is paid whether the firm expands by hiring more workers or by working the existing workforce longer hours. However, if there is a ceiling beyond which no further tax is paid for an employee, then the firm has an incentive to work that employee longer hours – and not pay more payroll tax – rather than hire a new employee – and pay more payroll tax.

In effect, such legislated quasi-fixed costs of employment may bias the labor market adjustment process towards amortizing those quasi-fixed costs over longer hours and more intense working conditions for incumbent employees, and away from hiring new employees to meet demand expansions. This phenomenon may be increasing to the extent that these legislative quasi-fixed costs have increased, and to the extent that liberalization and globalization have increased the uncertainty over whether demand expansions are long-term. This scenario, in turn, can account for greater reliance on non-standard employment on the one hand, and longer hours and more work intensity of the core work force on the other hand, so as to absorb demand fluctuations. In effect, the more the existing workforce is protected by labor legislation, the greater the degree of bifurcation or polarization between the core workforce of the formal economy and the peripheral workforce of the informal economy.

Multiple Role of Wages in Serving Market and Social Objectives

Labor market policies often alter wages as an element of social policy. Minimum wages, for example, are designed in part to alleviate poverty and, somctimes, to provide an incentive for persons to voluntarily leave income maintenance programs for the higher market wage. 'Fair wage' legislation may require employers to pay a certain wage if they are bidding on government contracts. Wage control programs can be instituted by governments to control inflation. Equal-pay-for-equal-work laws can require that females be paid the same as males in similar jobs, or in the cases of pay equity and equal pay for work of equal value, that they be paid the same as in male jobs of equal value as determined by gender-neutral job evaluation systems.

All of these policy initiatives serve legitimate social purposes, and use wages as the mechanism for achieving those social objectives. As such, wages are called upon to serve various *social* purposes: alleviate poverty; provide 'fair wages' or 'living wages;' curb inflation; facilitate macroeconomic stability; and redress discrimination. Wages are also called upon to serve a variety of *market* functions: to allocate labor to its most efficient use; to encourage human capital formation by investing in education, training, job search and information; to reduce labor shortages; and to reward merit and encourage work effort. As well, wages often embody a *status* function both in society and in the workplace. In the case of efficiency wage premiums, wages may affect productivity as well as constitute a payment based on productivity. In such circumstances, when a single instrument or price – in this case the price of labor – is called upon to serve so many functions, it is not surprising that it may falter in achieving these objectives.

Altering the wage mechanism to curb poverty is particularly tenuous, given that poverty is largely an issue of the gap between family needs and family income. Wages relate only to the family income component, which depends upon the lifetime wages and employment of different family members as well as non-labor income. Using minimum wages to curb poverty, for example, is, at best, an exceedingly blunt instrument (Benjamin, 2001) since it affects the wages of only one family member, since their low wages may be a temporary phenomenon associated with being young, since they may be in a family of multiple earners, and since they may have high non-labor income. Furthermore, the measure may have perverse effects if it reduces the employability of the person (Riveros, 2001) or deters him or her from taking a low-wage job in return for training that may enhance future lifetime earnings.[7] In such circumstances, it may be best to allow the wage mechanism to serve its market functions in the hope that this will enhance productivity and reduce the need for social programs in the first place.

Importance of Internal Efficiency as a Precondition for External Competitiveness

In our more integrated and liberalized global economy, there is growing recognition that it is crucial that labor and social policies within a country – or region – enhance *internal* competitiveness as a precondition for the country's being *externally* competitive in the global marketplace (Gunderson, 2001). In essence, there is a growing premium on reducing the internal barriers to competitiveness within countries or regional trading blocks.

There are a variety of areas where this can be done in the labor policy arena. Harmonization of credentials and skills, or of trades or education standards, can facilitate the internal mobility of labor from declining sectors and regions to expanding ones within a country or region. This mobility can occur in the form of standardized credentials or mutual recognition of credentials, as well as by removing barriers created by unnecessary occupational licensing and certification, including residency requirements. Eliminating government procurement policies that give favoritism to local bidders fosters their efficiency and reduces the cost of providing public

7 In spite of the reasons for why minimum wages may be an exceedingly blunt instrument for reducing poverty, Morley (1995) and Lustig and McLeod (1997) find that minimum wage increases have been associated with reductions in poverty in Latin America.

infrastructures. Eliminating excessive public sector pay premiums can also save on the cost of providing public infrastructures and reduce any spillover effects that excessive public pay premiums may have on private sector wages, as well as the bifurcation that often exists between protected public sector jobs and private sector jobs. Governments getting their own 'house in order' can be an important precondition for expecting other employers to be competitive. Removing the internal tariff and non-tariff barriers to trade within a region can foster the internal efficiency and economies of scale that can enable the region to compete with other emerging trading blocks. Controversial privatization and deregulation policies, properly handled, can also foster internal efficiency. Providing labor market information that is broadly based across the country or regional trading block can foster internal mobility and efficiency.

Clearly, there is a wide range of labor market policies that can foster internal competitiveness within countries or regional trading blocks which, in turn, will facilitate external competitiveness against other countries or trading blocks. This scenario becomes crucial under globalization and increased trade liberalization.

Mechanisms Whereby Trade Liberalization and Globalization Affect Labor Market and Social Policies

The previous discussion focused on the effect that labor market and social policies can have on the competitiveness of a country and, hence, on its ability to compete in an increasingly integrated world under globalization and trade liberalization. This section focuses on the relationship in the other direction – the effect of globalization on a country's labor market and social policies. The emphasis is on outlining the various *mechanisms* whereby globalization affects a nation's labor market and social policy. This in turn will shed light on the key issue addressed in a subsequent section – whether the pressures will lead to the loss of the ability of nations to sustain their own independent labor and social policies, leading to downward harmonization to the lowest common denominator.

Inter-Jurisdictional Competition for Investment and the Associated Jobs

In a globalized environment with freer trade and capital mobility, countries will be under increased pressure to compete with other countries for business investment and the associated jobs. With reduced tariffs and reduced foreign ownership restrictions, employers can more easily locate their plants or outsource in different countries interconnected by sophisticated communication and transportation systems, and to export throughout the world. Financial capital is also more mobile under these conditions and quick to take advantage of arbitrage opportunities.

In such circumstances, countries are under more pressure to compete for that business investment and the associated jobs. One way to compete is to reduce costly regulations, including those associated with labor and social policies. In effect, at the political bargaining table where social and labor policies are negotiated, businesses – and especially multinationals – have more clout because of their more credible threat of relocating their investment (Langille, 1996).

In theory, this should lead to 'Tiebout-type' sorting (Tiebout, 1956) whereby individuals and firms locate partly on the basis of tax-expenditure 'packages' – including policy packages – that best match their preferences and needs. For example, firms that want minimal labor regulations but, perhaps, are willing to pay for public infrastructure would locate in jurisdictions that provide those tax-expenditure packages. In practice, of course, such markets are likely to be extremely 'thin' and not characterized by an infinite set of competitive buyers and sellers. Nevertheless, there will likely be some sorting along a spectrum ranging from low regulations and taxes with low public services and infrastructures to ones with more regulations and taxes in return for more public services and infrastructures.

In practice, of course, although developing-country officials have come to see foreign direct investment (FDI) as an essential part of their development strategies, only a few developing countries receive large amounts of FDI, or foreign investment for the purpose of controlling and operating a business. Over the five-year period before the Asian meltdown – the heyday of developing world FDI – ten countries received two-thirds of the FDI directed at all developing countries (Shatz and Venables, 2001). Many developing countries in South America face the same hurdles; though their leaders would like to attract investment, the countries remain unsuitable business locations or are unable to attract FDI for other reasons.[8]

Emulation of Best-Practices by Organizations and Policy Makers

The process of economic integration through trade liberalization and foreign investment increases interaction across countries. Such interaction in turn fosters the

---

8 Examples of this are the Andean countries – Bolivia, Colombia, Ecuador, Peru, and Venezuela – which, in 1991, decided to pursue a strategy of attracting multinational investment, with a firm commitment under the Andean Pact decisions 291 and 292. These decisions eliminated all government authorization requirements, replacing them with only simple registration by foreign investors, abolished divestiture requirements for foreign owners, and allowed the five countries full discretion in setting their own policies. The changes reversed years of highly restrictive policies toward foreign investors dating from the Andean Investment Code of 1971. These original policies were so restrictive that Chile abandoned the Pact in 1976 in order to liberalize its trade and investment rules. So far, however, the results of the liberalization have been mixed (Shatz, 2001).

emulation of 'best practices' across organizations (Chaykowski and Gunderson, 2001). Unfortunately, best *business* practices do not have to mean best *social* practices. In some cases, the two concepts may coincide. If, for example, health and safety or training practices are particularly effective in one country, they are more likely to be directly adopted by trading partners, or indirectly through the process of foreign direct investment. However, other practices that may be effective from a business standpoint, such as outsourcing to contractors who evade minimal labor standards, obviously may not advance social objectives.

The emulation of best practices across more integrated economies may also occur in the policy arena. Quite simply, the greater interaction that occurs across countries provides more information to policy makers on what works and what does not work in all phases of the policy process – design, implementation, and enforcement.

The increased integration that is fostered by trade liberalization and globalization can promote policy integration in a variety of areas pertaining to product standards, environmental standards, patent protection, intellectual property rights, common currency and common security concerns. In such circumstances, it is easier to foster the standardization of policy initiatives with respect to labor standards and labor policy initiatives.

Behavior of Multinationals

Multinationals are more prominent under trade liberalization and globalization and, hence, their behavior becomes an important mechanism affecting labor and social policy. In general, the wages and working conditions of multinationals in the host countries are better than the wages and working conditions of domestic employers; hence, multinationals reduce the need for labor and social policies to improve such wages and working conditions.[9]

This behavior of multinationals reflects a carry-over of their behavior in their home-base country where wages and working conditions are generally better than in the host country. More important, however, behavior reflects a concern for their brand name and public image in the global product market – an image that can be tarnished by *exposés* of bad working conditions. Generally, we think of the demand for labor as being a derived demand – derived from the demand for the products produced by firms and, hence, affected by the product market conditions under which products are sold. In the case of brand-name multinationals, the process also works in the other direction. The demand for the product is in part derived from the demand for labor

9 Evidence of multinationals providing better pay and working conditions than do domestic producers in the host countries is provided in Lim (1976), OECD (1999), and Jenkins (1990), although Forrest (1993) finds that multinationals in Guadalajara, Mexico, did not do so.

and, hence, affected by the labor market conditions under which the product is produced. Brand-name multinationals live by their image – hence they are also vulnerable to death by their image. This is recognized by social activists, who can threaten to discredit multinationals if they provide bad wages and working conditions.

In such circumstances, multinationals may try to distance themselves from the conditions under which products are produced by outsourcing to domestic producers who may be more willing to produce under 'sweatshop' conditions. Even here, however, multinationals can be vulnerable if those linkages are made public.

Although there is considerable controversy in this area, multinationals generally reduce the need for labor and social policy initiatives in developing countries by improving the wages and working conditions in the host countries. Furthermore, relative to lesser-known domestic producers, they are more vulnerable to enforcement pressures brought to bear by international NGOs (Klein, 1999). Globally, the net effect of multinationals on labor policy outcomes may therefore be neutral, as they tend to raise standards in less developed jurisdictions but reduce them in high standard jurisdictions through the threat effect highlighted earlier.

National Treatment Requirements in Trade Agreements

National treatment requirements in trade agreements can provide another mechanism through which trade liberalization affects domestic labor and social policies. Under such requirements, countries that impose regulations on imports are required to impose those same regulations on similar domestically produced products. The intent of such requirements is to inhibit such regulations on imports from being used as non-tariff barriers to trade.

Countervailing Duties for Social Programs that May Be Interpreted as Subsidies

Countervailing duties in trade agreements can be another mechanism through which trade liberalization affects domestic labor and social programs. Such duties can be imposed on imported goods if the imported goods are interpreted as embodying subsidies provided by the exporting country. The intent is that the countervailing duties imposed by the importing country would offset the cost reduction associated with the domestic subsidies of the exporting country and hence provide a 'level playing field' for domestic producers in the importing country.

To the extent that labor and social policies in the exporting country could be interpreted as providing an 'unfair subsidy' to exports, the threat of countervailing duties could put pressure to eliminate such policy initiatives. Establishing the 'subsidy' component of such exports is difficult, however, since many of the policy initiatives are paid out of general tax revenues. It would not be feasible to argue, for example, that the exports of a country embodied government education subsidies, in part because that component could not readily be determined and in part because the subsidies would come out of general tax revenues and, hence, involve higher tax costs.

Migration and Labor Mobility

To the extent that migration and labor mobility are enhanced by globalization and economic integration, such migration and mobility can have a complicated effect on labor and social policies. Since migration generally involves moving away from areas of low wages and poor working conditions towards areas of better economic opportunities, it can reduce the need for social policies in the economically depressed areas.

Migration, however, can also involve the 'best' individuals leaving an area, as in the case of the brain drain of the most motivated and talented persons – the very persons who could foster the development of the area they leave.[10] Such migration can be destabilizing, inducing a rapid decline in the region being depleted of workers and fostering pressure to provide social programs in that region.

Migration can also be propelled by offers of more generous social programs if there are no residency or other requirements to inhibit such opportunistic migration. In such circumstances, jurisdictions may be reluctant to provide such social programs since they would both serve as a 'magnet' for migrants, and repel taxpayers who would have to pay for them. Such a process would make it difficult for a progressive jurisdiction to sustain generous social programs.

Linkages that Are Necessary for Downward Harmonization

The previous discussion focused on the various *mechanisms* whereby globalization and economic integration affect a nation's labor market and social policy. This section focuses on whether this process would lead to the loss of the ability of nation states to sustain their own independent labor and social policies, and if so, whether there would be downward harmonization to the lowest common denominator.

In general, the mechanisms that were discussed were ones that would pressure countries to put more emphasis on the cost consequences of the labor market and social policies. Countries want costs low enough to attract capital and business investment and the jobs associated with that investment, and want to ensure that their policies are not considered subsidies to their exports or magnets for migrants. In that vein, the harmonization would generally be downwards towards the lowest common denominator – the country that imposes the least regulatory costs.

---

10 Discussion of such migration is provided in Myrdal (1957) and Gunderson (1996).

There are various linkages, however, that drive such downward harmonization of labor laws and policies (Gunderson, 1998a and 1999). Specifically, the laws must be enforced; the laws must impose a net cost to employers in that the costs must exceed the benefits; the costs cannot be shifted backwards or forwards; firms must respond to these costs in terms of their investment and plant location decisions; and countries must respond to this threat by adjusting their labor and social policies. Each of these linkages will be discussed in turn.

Policies Must Be Enforced

It is well known that labor policies that are 'on the books' may not be enforced, and there can be a huge gap between *de jure* and *de facto* in this area.[11] Laws may be passed to give a good appearance to the public and the international community, but they may not be enforced for various reasons. Strict enforcement of labor laws may discourage business investment, consume scarce government resources, and simply be too costly for some governments. Enforcement may also give governments some discretion to enforce in selective situations, but to not enforce in others. Not enforcing laws, however, can encourage disregard for laws in general, leading to obvious repercussions. Since enforcement is more difficult in the informal sector and for non-standard jobs, employment may shift to the uncovered informal sector and towards non-standard employment in response to legislative initiatives in the formal sectors.[12]

Laws and Policies Must Impose Net Costs to Employers

Even if labor laws are passed and enforced, they must be costly to employers if they are to discourage investment. While labor laws and policies are generally costly to employers, they can also yield benefits that can offset part of the costs. In essence, it is the net costs that will influence employer behavior.

Policies that require advance notice in the case of layoffs or plant closings can enable efficient job searches that can benefit other employers. Health and safety regulations can reduce costly accidents. Pension regulations can ensure the viability of employer-sponsored pensions. Anti-discrimination and human rights policies can enhance employee morale and reduce discord over diversity in the workplace. In a global marketplace, accommodating diversity can be 'good business,' given the diversity of the supplier and customer base.

---

11 For a discussion of the lack of enforcement in Mexico see Bensusán-Areous (1994).

12 This legislative-induced shift to the informal sector is discussed in Harrison and Leamer (1997), Lee (1997), Maskus (1997) and Portes (1990). The growth of non-standard employment in the U.S., Canada, and Mexico since the mid 1980s is documented in a recent report of the North American Agreement on Labor Co-operation (NAALC, 1997) and discussed in Roberts et al. (1996).

Other policies can provide a public infrastructure that facilitates competitiveness. This can be the case with human capital policies that support basic education, training, job search, and labor market information. Regulations on hours of work and overtime can reduce accidents and, perhaps, unemployment by 'sharing' the work.

Other labor and social policies can save on public and private expenditures elsewhere in the system, and hence, on the tax costs of providing such services. Health and safety regulations can reduce health-care expenditures. Advance warning legislation can save on unemployment insurance expenditures. Social policies in general can 'buy' social stability and save on the incredible social expenditures that arise from tensions between the 'haves' and the 'have nots' (Berry, 1997; Gindling and Berry, 1992).

Costs Cannot Be Shifted Backward or Forward

If labor policies impose costs on employers, the costs should not be shifted backward to employees or forward to consumers. In many cases, however, the costs can be shifted backwards to employees in the form of their accepting a lower wage in return for the benefit of the policy (Ehrenberg, 1994; Gunderson and Riddell, 1995). This can be the case, for example, with health and safety regulation that yields a safer workplace. It can also be the case with payroll taxes that are levied on employers for such programs as pensions, unemployment insurance and workers' compensation (Kesselman, 2001).

Shifting costs forward to customers in the form of higher product prices may be more difficult in a world of trade liberalization and global competition, where customers have alternative markets. Nevertheless, even if markets were lost because of cost shifting, this would be entirely appropriate if the higher cost of the regulation were to reflect the true social cost of producing the product. This can be the case, for example, with respect to health and safety regulation and payments for workers' compensation – the product price should reflect the true social cost of producing the product, including the social cost of workplace accidents and diseases.

Firms Must Respond to the Costs in Terms of Their Plant Location and Investment Decisions

Even if the labor laws are enforced and they impose net costs to employers, and if those costs cannot be shifted backward or forward, for such costs to lead to downward harmonization employers must respond to those costs by not locating plants or investments in countries that are associated with such costs. Unfortunately, there is very little evidence on the extent to which plant location and investment decisions are affected by such costs of labor regulations and social programs compared with other factors such as access to markets or resources, or transportation costs, or taxes or regulations in other areas (Gunderson, 1998b).[13]

The issue is further complicated by the fact that labor regulations are often associated with other factors that can *attract* investment, such as enforceable contracts, law-and-order, a public sector infrastructure, and established property rights. Employers may willingly accept some costly labor regulations when they are bundled with these other aspects, making countries attractive from a business perspective.[14]

Jurisdictions Must Compete for the Investment on the Basis of Reducing Regulations

Even if costly labor regulations deter business investment, for that deterrence to lead to downward harmonization of labor regulations and social policies, countries would have to compete for that business investment and the associated jobs by reducing their labor laws and social policies. They may do so, but they may not if they are willing to 'pay the price' of their policy initiatives by forgoing such investment. They may collectively not want to compete on the basis of what they consider as socially unacceptable labor and social standards. If adopting that option means lost trade and investment opportunities, that is the price worth paying for sustaining independent labor and social policies.

This collective decision could come from a democratic populace that willingly accepts, for example, a smaller economic pie that is more equitably shared. Or it could come from political elites who control a country and have more to gain by not having their economy open to globalization and foreign investment.

The Positive Side of Policy Harmonization

The previous discussion highlighted what is generally regarded as a negative effect of globalization and trade liberalization – it is more difficult for countries to maintain their independent labor market and social policies in the face of pressures for downward harmonization. As indicated, these pressures are likely to occur; however, there is also a positive aspect to such pressures.

---

13 The only reliable evidence we do have is based on the second-order effects of regulation-investment links, such as on output. For example, Rama (1995), based on data from 30 Latin American countries, finds that labor regulations such as minimum wages, severance pay or mandatory benefits tended not to have a negative effect on output growth.

14 Evidence that foreign direct investment is not attracted to countries of low labor standards is discussed in Stern (1999, 21).

First and foremost, the policies that are likely to dissipate are those that have no positive feedback effect on efficiency and competitiveness. As discussed, many of the policy initiatives do have such positive feedback effects, so such policies are likely to survive – indeed thrive – under globalization (Gunderson et al., 2001, 64). Furthermore, they are likely to be emulated and adopted as best practices by other countries once their positive effects become apparent, leading to the possibility of *upward* harmonization with respect to the policies.

In contrast, regulations that purely protect the rents of interest groups are most likely to dissipate since they are not efficiency-enhancing. It is the case that pressure from globalization and trade liberalization may stop governments from doing things they want to do, but it can also stop them from doing things they 'ought not to do.' In this vein, entering into that arena can be taken as a form of pre-commitment, whereby governments reduce the freedom they have in their policy-making process, compelling them to focus on efficiency-enhancing regulations.[15]

Governments can obviously still follow whatever policies they choose (Banting et al., 1997; Banting and Simeon, 1997) – whether those choices are driven by the general population or by elites who control the political process. The price or cost of those choices is now simply made more explicit in terms of their effect on investment and the jobs associated with that investment. The costs do not exist as items hidden behind tariff walls or devalued currencies.

Multiple equilibria are possible in the policy-making process just as they are in market processes. Some countries may provide an extensive public infrastructure in return for higher taxes and more extensive regulations, while others provide the opposite. These optimal combinations may also differ, depending upon a country's stage of development, and they may change as their impacts become more apparent. For example, a less developed country may try to compete in the global marketplace by providing a low-tax, low-regulatory environment to attract investment and jobs. If this process enhances growth and development, part of the increased wealth may be diverted to social programs and improved labor standards, especially if it is apparent that sharing in the gains ensures that the benefits will continue into the future (Cassela, 1996; Fields, 1995; Fields and Wan, 1989; Freeman, 1994; and Stern, 1999).

This rather rosy picture of a policy-making process constrained by market forces under globalization and trade liberalization is subject to an important caveat – a caveat that may be the Achilles Heel of the process. Pure equity-oriented distributional policy initiatives that have no positive feedback effect on efficiency will be difficult to sustain in this environment for reasons outlined earlier – they may serve as a magnet to attract recipients and repel those who would pay in the form of taxes or regulations. Yet such

15 This is analogous to the idea that the main rationale for NAFTA was not so much to get the direct benefits from free trade, but rather to 'lock in' the market oriented reforms that were occurring in Mexico (Prestowitz et al., 1991).

initiatives are entirely appropriate for governments – indeed, they may be the prime role for governments. Furthermore, the evidence suggests that the market-oriented changes associated with globalization, trade liberalization, and technological change are leading to increased labor market polarization (Berry, 1997 and 2001; Cline, 1997; Richardson, 1995; Wood, 1996; and Feenestra and Hanson, 1997).[16] In essence, the demand for policy initiatives to deal with the adjustment consequences of the market-oriented changes are increasing just at the same time as the ability of governments to provide those initiatives is being circumscribed by the same forces.

To the extent that these issues are beyond the purview of any one government, international responses are appropriate, but they will be difficult given the reluctance of governments to yield sovereignty in these areas. A wide range of international initiatives have been proposed, but all have associated problems. Labor standards can be imposed as part of trade agreements to restrict competition based on poor labor standards (Brown et al., 1996; Charnovitz, 1992; Erickson and Mitchell, 1996; Fields, 1995; Gunderson, 1999; and Maskus, 1997), but these are generally regarded by the developing countries as thinly disguised protectionism on the part of the developed countries that push for such standards (Bhagwati, 1994). Labor side accords,[17] such as the NAFTA accord, require trading partners to enforce their own internal labor regulations, but again, this is often regarded as a form of protectionism on the part of the more developed countries since they already tend to enforce their labor laws. They are also often thought of as largely a token, non-enforceable requirement, although they can provide the foundation for subsequent initiatives (Abbott, 1995). Corporate codes of conduct (Compa and Darricarrère, 1996; Blainpain, 2000) and multi-national 'best practice' guidelines (Blainpain, 2000; Gunter, 1992) can raise labor standards, but these are voluntary and may not tackle the worst practices from outsourcing to domestic producers. Consumer boycotts against products produced under 'sweatshop' conditions can be effective against brand-name products (Erickson and Mitchell, 1996), but these can be difficult to 'enforce' and they target only some producers. Social labels indicating the conditions under which the products were produced can enable consumers to make informed choices and make purchases based on what they perceive to be the social content of the product (Freeman, 1994). A more extensive form of international assistance would involve 'social funds' being transferred from wealthier countries to poorer countries that are part of trade pacts (as occurs in the European Union) to enable the poorer countries to harmonize their social policies upwards towards those of the wealthier countries (Sapir, 1996).

---

16 Feenestra and Hanson (1997) find that foreign direct investment by the U.S. in Mexico increased inequality in both countries by increasing the demand for skilled labor in Mexico and reducing the demand for unskilled labor in the U.S.

17 Aparicio-Valdez (1995) discusses such accords in Latin America and the Caribbean.

Each of these initiatives can have some effect on improving labor standards and social policy that otherwise may dissipate under globalization and trade liberalization. But they all have associated problems ranging from ineffectiveness to thinly disguised protectionism if they are effective. The hope, of course, is that the efficiency gains arising from globalization and trade liberalization will become more widespread across the population, perhaps assisted by active adjustment assistance programs. If this does not occur, then the policy challenge will be to deal with the increased difficulty of governments to sustain pure equity oriented policies – the old efficiency-equity trade-off simply in an international form.

References

Abbott, F. (1995), *Law and Policy of Regional Integration: The NAFTA and Western Hemispheric Integration in the World Trade Organization*, Kluwer Academic Publishers, Boston.

Amadeo, E. and S. Horton (1997), 'Labor Flexibility and Productivity: An Overview', in E. Amadeo and S. Horton (eds.), *Labor Productivity and Flexibility*, pp. 1-35, St. Martin's Press, New York.

Aparicio-Valdez, L. (1995), 'Hemispheric Integration and Labour Laws', *International Journal of Comparative Labour Law and Industrial Relations*, Vol. 11, No. 2, pp. 99-111.

Banting, K., G. Hoberg and R. Simeon (1997), 'Introduction', in K. Banting, G. Hoberg and R. Simeon (eds.), *Degrees of Freedom: Canada and the United States in a Changing World*, pp. 3-22, McGill-Queen's University Press, Montreal and Kingston.

Banting, K. and R. Simeon (1997), 'Changing Economies, Changing Societies', in K. Banting, G. Hoberg and R. Simeon (eds.), *Degrees of Freedom: Canada and the United States in a Changing World*, pp. 23-70, McGill-Queen's University Press, Montreal and Kingston.

Benjamin, D. (2001), 'Minimum Wages in Canada', in A. Berry (ed.), *Labor Market Policies in Canada and Latin America: Challenges of the New Millennium*, pp. 187-221, Kluwer Academic Publishers, Boston.

Bensusán-Areous, G. (1994), 'The Mexican Model of Labor Regulation and Competitive Strategies', in M. Cook and H. Katz (eds.), *Regional Integration and Industrial Relations in North America*, pp. 52-65, ILR Press, Ithaca, N.Y.

Berry, A. (1997), 'The Income Distribution Threat in Latin America', *Latin American Research Review*, Vol. 32, No. 2, pp. 3-40.

Berry, A. (2001), 'Dangers and Challenges: The New Context of Labor Market Policy in Latin America and in Canada', in A. Berry (ed.), *Labor Market Policies in Canada and Latin America: Challenges of the New Millennium*, pp. 1-50, Kluwer Academic Publishers, Boston.

Berry, A. and M.T. Méndez (1998), *Training in Latin America: Its Impact and Potential for Growth, Employment, Equity and Poverty Alleviation*, International Labour Office, Geneva.

Bhagwati, J. (1994), 'Fair Trade, Reciprocity and Harmonization: The New Challenge to the Theory and Policy of Free Trade', in A. Deardorf and R. Stern (eds.), *Analytical and Negotiating Issues in the Global Trading System*, pp. 547-98, University of Michigan Press, Ann Arbor.

Blank, R. (1994), *Social Protection Versus Economic Flexibility: Is There a Trade-Off?*, University of Chicago Press, Chicago.

Blainpain, R. (ed.) (2000), *Bulletin of Comparative Labour Relations: Special Issue on Multinational Enterprises and the Social Challenges of the XXI Century*, Vol. 37, Kluwer Law International, The Hague.

Brown, D., A. Deardorf and R. Stern (1996), 'International Labor Standards and Trade: a Theoretical Analysis', in J. Bhagwati and R. Hudec (eds.), *Fair Trade and Harmonization*, Vol. 1, pp. 227-80, MIT Press, Cambridge, MA.

Cassela, A. (1996), 'Free Trade and Evolving Standards', in J. Bhagwati and R. Hudec (eds.), *Fair Trade and Harmonization*, Vol. 1, pp. 119-56, MIT Press, Cambridge, MA.

Castro-Rea, J. (1996), 'Towards a Single North American Policy? The Effects of NAFTA on Mexican and Canadian Domestic Politics', in C. Paraskevopoulos, R. Grinspun and G. Eaton (eds.), *Economic Integration in the Americas*, pp. 88-102, Edward Elgar, Brookfield.

Charnovitz, S. (1992), 'Environmental and Labor Standards and Trade', *The World Economy*, Vol. 15, No. 2 (May), pp. 335–56.

Chaykowski, R. and M. Gunderson (2001), 'The Implications of Globalization for Labour and Labour Markets', in R. Chaykowski (ed.), *Globalization and the Canadian Economy: Implications for Labour Markets, Society and the State*, pp. 27-60, Queen's University School of Policy Studies, Kingston.

Cline, W. (1997), *Trade and Wage Inequality*, Institute for International Economics, Washington, D. C.

Compa, L. and T.A. Darricarrère (1996), 'Private Labor Rights Enforcement Through Corporate Codes of Conduct', in L. Compa and S. Diamond (eds.), *Human Rights, Labor Rights, and International Trade*, pp. 181-98, University of Pennsylvania Press, Philadelphia.

Cortázar, R. (2001), 'Unemployment Insurance Systems for Latin America', in A. Berry (ed.), *Labor Market Policies in Canada and Latin America: Challenges of the New Millennium*, pp. 97-108, Kluwer Academic Publishers, Boston.

Ehrenberg, R.E. (1994), *Labor Markets and Integrating National Economies*, Brookings Institution, Washington, D. C.

Erickson, C. and D. Mitchell (1996), 'Labour Standards in International Trade Agreements', *Labour Law Journal*, Vol. 47, No. 12, pp. 763-73.

Feenestra, R. and G. Hanson (1997), 'Foreign Direct Investment and Relative Wages: Evidence from Mexico's Maquiladoras', *Journal of International Economics*, Vol. 42, No. 3-4 (May), pp. 371-93.

Fields, G. (1995), *Trade and Labour Standards: A Review of the Issues*, Organization for Economic Cooperation and Development, Paris.

Fields, G. and H. Wan Jr. (1989), 'Wage Setting Institutions and Economic Growth', *World Development*, Vol. 17, No. 9 (September), pp. 1471-83.

Forrest, D. (1993), 'Relative Earnings of Permanent and Casual Employees in a Mexican City', *Journal of Economic Studies*, Vol. 20, No. 6, pp. 3-16.

Freeman, R. (1994), 'A Hard-Headed Look at Labour Standards', in W. Sengenberger and D. Campbell (eds.), *Creating Economic Opportunities: The Role of Labour Standards in Economic Restructuring*, pp. 79-92, International Labour Organization, Geneva.

Gindling, T. and A. Berry (1992), 'The Performance of the Labor Market During the Recession and Structural Adjustment: Costa Rica in the 1980s', *World Development*, Vol. 20, No. 11 (November), pp. 1599-616.

Gómez, R. and M. Gunderson (2002), 'The Integration of Labour Markets in North America', in G. Hoberg (ed.), *Capacity for Choice: Canada in the North American Economy*, University of Toronto Press, Toronto.

Gunderson, M. (1996), 'Regional Productivity and Income Convergence in Canada Under Increasing Economic Integration', *Canadian Journal of Regional Science*, Vol. 19, No. 1, pp. 1-24.

Gunderson, M. (1998a), 'Harmonization of Labour Policies under Trade Liberalization', *Relations Industrielles / Industrial Relations*, Vol. 53, No.1, pp. 24-52.

Gunderson, M. (1998b), 'Regional Impacts of Trade and Investment on Labour', *Canadian Journal of Regional Science*, Vol. 21, No. 2, pp. 187-226.

Gunderson, M. (1999), 'Labour Standards, Income Distribution and Trade', *Integration and Trade*, Vol. 3, No. 7, pp. 87-104.

Gunderson, M. (2001), 'North American Economic Integration and Globalization', in P. Grady and A. Sharpe (eds.), *The State of Economics in Canada: Fetschrift in Honour of David Slater*, pp. 355-77, Queen's University Press, Kingston.

Gunderson, M., A. Berry and C. Reynolds (2001), 'Canadian vs. American Labor Markets in a Context of Economic Integration and Structural Adjustment', in A. Berry (ed.), *Labor Market Policies in Canada and Latin America: Challenges of the New Millennium*, pp. 51-68, Kluwer Academic Publishers, Boston.

Gunderson, M. and C. Riddell (1995), 'Jobs, Labour Standards and Promoting Competitive Advantage: Canada's Policy Challenge', *Labour*, Vol. 9, pp. S125-48.

Gunderson, M. and C. Riddell (2001a), 'Unemployment Insurance: Lessons from Canada', in A. Berry (ed.), *Labor Market Policies in Canada and Latin America: Challenges of the New Millennium*, pp. 69-98, Kluwer Academic Publishers, Boston.

Gunderson, M. and C. Riddell (2001b), 'Training in Canada', in A. Berry (ed.), *Labor Market Policies in Canada and Latin America: Challenges of the New Millennium*, pp. 243-67, Kluwer Academic Publishers, Boston.

Gunter, H. (1992), 'The Tripartite Declaration of Principles concerning Multinational Enterprises and Social Policy', in R. Blainpain (ed.), *International Encyclopedia for Labour Law and Industrial Relations*, pp. 1-68, Kluwer Academic Publishers, London.

Harrison, A. and E. Leamer (1997), 'Labor Markets in Developing Countries: An Agenda for Research', *Journal of Labor Economics*, Vol. 15, No. 3 (July), pp. S1-19.

Jenkins, R. (1990), 'Comparing Foreign Subsidiaries and Local Firms in LDCs: Theoretical Issues and Empirical Evidence', *Journal of Development Studies*, Vol. 26, No. 2, pp. 205-28.

Kesselman, J. (2001), 'Payroll Taxes in the Finance of Social Security', in A. Berry (ed.), *Labor Market Policies in Canada and Latin America: Challenges of the New Millennium*, pp. 135-58, Kluwer Academic Publishers, Boston.

Klein, N. (1999), *No Logo*, Free Press, New York.

Langille, B. (1996), 'General Reflections on the Relationship of Trade and Labor (Or: Fair Trade is Free Trade's Destiny)', in J. Bhagwati and R. Hudec (eds.), *Fair Trade and Harmonization*, Vol. 2, pp. 231-66, MIT Press, Cambridge, MA.

Lee, E. (1997), 'Globalization and Labour Standards: A Review of the Issues', *International Labour Review*, Vol. 136, No. 2 (Summer), pp. 173-90.

Lim, D. (1976), 'Do Foreign Companies Pay Higher Wages Than Their Local Counterparts in Malaysian Manufacturing?' *Journal of Development Economics*, Vol. 4, No. 2, pp. 55-66.

Lustig, N. and D. McLeod (1997), 'Minimum Wages and Poverty in Developing Countries: A Cross-Section Analysis for Developing Countries', in S. Edwards and N. Lustig (eds.), *Labor Market Reform in Latin America: Combining Social Protection and Market Flexibility*, pp. 62-103, Brookings Institution, Washington, D.C.

Maskus, K. (1997), 'Should Core Labor Standards be Imposed Through International Trade Policy?', Working Paper No. 1817, The World Bank, Washington, D.C.

Morley, S. (1995), *Poverty and Inequality in Latin America: The Impact of Adjustment and Recovery in the 1980s*, Johns Hopkins University Press, Washington, D.C.

Myrdal, G. (1957), *Economic Theory and Underdeveloped Regions*, Duckworth, London.

NAALC (North American Agreement on Labor Cooperation) (1997), *North American Labor Markets: A Comparative Profile*, Commission for Labor Cooperation, Dallas.

OECD (Organization for Economic Co-Operation and Development) (1999), *Measuring Globalisation: The Role of Multinationals in OECD Countries*, OECD, Paris.

Portes, A. (1990), 'When More Can Be Less: Labor Standards, Development and the Informal Economy', in S. Herzenberger and J. Pérez-López (eds.), *Labor Standards and Development in the Global Economy*, U.S. Department of Labor, Washington, D.C.

Prestowitz Jr., C., R. Cohen, P. Morici and A. Tonelsm (1991), *The New North American Order*, Economic Strategy Institute, Washington, D.C.

Rama, M. (1995), 'Do Labour Market Policies and Institutions Matter: The Adjustment Experience in Latin America and the Caribbean', *Labour*, Vol. 9, pp. S243-68.

Richardson, D. (1995), 'Income Inequality and Trade', *Journal of Economic Perspectives*, Vol. 9, No. 3 (Summer), pp. 33-55.

Riveros, L. (2001), 'Minimum Wages in Latin America', in A. Berry (ed.), *Labor Market Policies in Canada and Latin America: Challenges of the New Millennium*, pp. 221-42, Kluwer Academic Publishers, Boston.

Roberts, K., D. Hyatt and P. Dorfman (1996), 'The Effect of Free Trade on Contingent Work in Michigan', in K. Roberts and M. Wilson (eds.), *Policy Choices: Free Trade Amongst NAFTA Nations*, pp. 235-60, Michigan State University Press, East Lansing, MI.

Rodrik, D. (1997), *Has Globalization Gone Too Far?*, Institute for International Economies, Washington, D.C.

Sapir, A. (1996), 'Free Trade and Evolving Standards', in J. Bhagwati and R. Hudec (eds.), *Fair Trade and Harmonization*, Vol. 1, MIT Press, Cambridge, MA.

Shatz, H.J. (2001), 'Expanding Foreign Direct Investment in the Andean Countries', CID Working Paper No. 64, Harvard University, Cambridge, MA.

Shatz, H.J. and A.J. Venables (2001), 'The Geography of International Investment', in G.L. Clark, M. Feldman and M.S. Gertler (eds.), *The Oxford Handbook of Economic Geography*, Oxford University Press, Oxford.

Stern, R. (1999), 'Labor Standards and International Trade', *Integration and Trade*, Vol. 3, No. 7-8 (January-August), pp. 15-38.

Tiebout, C.M. (1956), 'A Pure Theory of Local Public Expenditure', *Journal of Political Economy*, Vol. 64, No. 5 (October), pp. 416-24.

Wood, A. (1996), 'How Trade Hurt Unskilled Workers', *Journal of Economic Perspectives*, Vol. 9, No. , pp. 57-80.

Chapter 10

Causes of Rising Wage Inequality in the 1990s: Evidence from the Argentine Manufacturing Sector

Adriana Marshall

Introduction

In the 1990s the causes of rising wage inequality were at the center of two lines of studies: (i) those focusing on the employment and wage outcomes of trade liberalization, and (ii) those concerned with the wage effects of changes in labor institutions. Only rarely were these two perspectives combined as in Berry (1998), who highlighted the role of both economic processes and labor institutions in the determination of wage inequality, and ultimately, income distribution trends. Following the establishment of NAFTA, wage outcomes of trade liberalization in the U.S., Canada, and Mexico were the subject of numerous studies in the first half of the decade. Similar discussion extended to other countries embarking on trade liberalization, particularly in Latin America. The impacts of changes in union power, negotiation level, and minimum wages were, however, generally analyzed only in reference to OECD countries. In this chapter I will examine wage inequality trends in the Argentine manufacturing sector and their possible economic and institutional causes. This is a relevant case-study, given the far-reaching economic reforms implemented in this country in the early 1990s and their significant labor market implications. This process of reform included trade liberalization as well as important changes in wage setting institutions, for example, the state's withdrawal from the process of direct wage determination and the promotion of drastic modifications in bargaining structures.

The chapter is organized as follows. The analytical framework, presented in the next section, reviews the determinants of changes in the degree of wage inequality with the emphasis on changing skill requirements as a result, *inter alia*, of trade liberalization, and on trade union intervention. Next, evidence from Argentina during the 1990s is analyzed, focusing on manufacturing, the sector most directly affected by trade liberalization.[1] This analysis is divided into two parts. First, the impacts of trade liberalization and export expansion on the volume and structure of employment, as well as the changes that took place in trade union intervention and collective bargaining, are described. Then, trends in the degree of wage inequality across manufacturing industries and among skill and educational levels within manufacturing, as well as the incidence of employment trends and changes in the intervention of labor organizations in determining increasing wage inequality during the 1990s, are examined.[2]

Determinants of Changes in the Degree of Wage Inequality

Several factors, including some inter-related ones, help to explain the variations in the degree of wage inequality. General labor market trends, such as excess supply of or excess demand for labor, have traditionally been major determinants of such changes (OECD, 1966). An increase in the rate of unemployment is expected to widen the wage gap between protected workers and those more vulnerable to the pressure of excess labor, as well as between easily replaceable unskilled workers and those with greater skills. The increasing pressure of excess labor is not confined, however, to only the less protected segments of the labor force; indeed, though less vigorous, this pressure is eventually transmitted throughout the labor market (Marshall, 1980). Within the unionized sector, this differential pressure of unemployment implies that the more vulnerable the sector, the more drastically trade unions' bargaining power is curtailed.

The degree of wage inequality is also affected by employment trends, including changes in the skill and educational composition of labor demand in various industries, as well as in the supply-demand relationship in each skill and educational level resulting from technological progress. At the same time, the magnitude of inequality may be modified by institutional developments, such as changes in government policy, unions' roles, and collective bargaining dynamics. Here I will focus on the wage effects of changes both in the skill and educational composition of labor demand and in trade union intervention.

---

1 The period covered in this study ends in 2000, prior to the notorious 2001-2002 debacle of the Argentine economy.

2 Inequality also increased in the economy as a whole, to the detriment of the workers most exposed to increasing labor market competition (Marshall, 2001). It must be noted that wage inequality had also increased in previous periods, though less markedly (Marshall, 1980 and 1995).

Changes in Skill and Educational Requirements

Changes in the relative demand for different types and levels of skills as prompted by technological innovations – that, in Latin America, are generally associated with trade liberalization, with greater export orientation, and with direct foreign investment – may modify the skill premia by affecting the supply and demand relationship of each skill and educational level.[3] Moreover, differential changes in the skill mix within industries or firms could automatically translate into larger wage differentials across industries or firms. It must be noted that this impact differs from the previous one, although both may have been triggered by similar changes in skill requirements.

Two apparently competing – but complementary – hypotheses have been advanced in relation to the causes of increasing skill and educational wage differentials. These hypotheses have received considerable attention in the literature, including their application to Latin American countries (e.g., Hanson and Harrison, 1999; Robbins, 1994; Ghiara and Zepeda, 2001).[4] One hypothesis stresses the impact of international trade, particularly of trade liberalization in Latin America in the 1980s and 1990s. The other focuses on the effects of technological change on labor requirements, highlighting the bias in favor of highly skilled workers. It was initially argued that trade liberalization would modify wage differentials by generating changes in the distribution of employment. These changes would be detrimental to unskilled workers of advanced countries since their relative wages would decline as demand shifted to unskilled labor in low-wage countries. The perception consequently was that in low-wage countries – the typical example being the Asian countries – trade intensification would increase the relative wages of unskilled workers and thus contribute to the reduction in wage inequality (Ghose, 2000). At a later stage, the argument considered the distributional impact of trade liberalization on three different groups of countries: (i) advanced countries with an abundant supply of highly skilled labor; (ii) countries with an excess supply of unskilled labor; and (iii) countries with a surplus of labor of intermediate skills. According to this view, trade liberalization would raise inequality in the third group of countries as demand for unskilled labor fell as a result of greater trade with low-wage countries having largely unskilled workforces. As well, their specialization in the export of goods produced with intermediate skills would increase the demand for, and therefore the earnings of, workers with higher skills (Wood, 1997, cited in Singh and Dhumale, 2000). However, it has also been argued that evidence showing that the employment share and the relative wages of the more skilled workers rose in all industries and not only in export industries, giving support to the second

3 Educational levels, more easily identified in household surveys, are usually considered to indicate skill levels, but this is not necessarily correct since higher educational credentials may be demanded to fill jobs with more limited skill requirements.

4 Galiani and Sanguinetti (2000), Cristini (1999), and Frenkel and González Rozada (1999) examine some aspects of this debate with reference to the Argentine case.

hypothesis that rising wage inequality might have been triggered by the general introduction of technological change cited in Singh and Dhumale (2000). In Mexico, a country with a relative abundance of intermediate-skilled labor, increasing wage inequality among educational levels (Meza González, 1999) appears to be the result of technologically-induced demand shifts in favor of more skilled labor in modern industries having significant foreign investment (Ghiara and Zepeda, 2001). Like Mexico, Argentina also is placed in the group of countries not specializing in the production of low-wage goods.

Studies on the possible relative-wage impacts of potential changes in the demand for unskilled and skilled labor have been undertaken for countries experiencing economic growth and associated increases in employment. The effects of trade liberalization and the adoption of skilled-labor-biased technologies on manufacturing wage inequality may differ, however, according to both economic growth rates and employment-output elasticities. In turn, growth rates and employment-output elasticities are both affected, *inter alia*, by economic openings and the choice of technology. Moreover, wage inequality may be influenced by the degree of effective labor market competition – depending on unemployment rates and the existence of income maintenance programs for the unemployed – and by the nature of trade union intervention that might prevent the fall of unskilled wages. The analysis of the Argentine case must take into account these factors, particularly because of the negative employment effects of the intensification of international trade combined with the persistent appreciation of the domestic currency.

Trade Union Intervention

The international literature, particularly in the 1990s, has discussed the relationship between changes in labor institutions – unionization rates, union power, bargaining structures – and wage inequality. For example, it has been documented that lower degrees of unionization – in several countries, together with regulatory reforms detrimental to trade unions – have led to an exacerbation of wage inequality (e.g., Borland, 1996; Leslie and Pu, 1996; Machin, 1997). Although the wage effects of changes in the level of collective bargaining centralization within a country have not been thoroughly studied, cross-country comparative analyses have shown that wage inequality and degree of centralization of collective negotiation are inversely associated (e.g., Zweimuller and Barth, 1994; Marshall, 1999). Given this inverse relationship, it may be expected that a process of decentralization would result in greater wage inequality.[5] Indeed, decentralization from industry-wide to firm-level bargaining is expected to affect wage inequality among firms – according to size,

---

5 Barrett et al. (1999), however, point out the apparently paradoxical increase in wage inequality in Ireland within a context of highly centralized negotiation.

export orientation, etc. – within each industry, just as increasingly individualized negotiation is expected to aggravate inequality within the firms. In any case, extreme decentralization would eventually undermine trade union coordination and hinder the diffusion of wage increments among industries, thus increasing inter-industry wage dispersion.

While a consensus states that direct intervention in wage setting – a particular form of centralized wage determination – tends to reduce wage differentials (Marshall, 1999),[6] determining the impact of trade unions on wage inequality is more complex. On the one hand, it is argued that unions tend to homogenize wages among sectors covered by collective bargaining – across industries and among firms within each industry, as well as across skill levels within each firm or industry – by raising the rates at the low end while constraining the growth at the top.[7] On the other hand, labor organizations tend to preserve existing firm-industry wage differentials as changes in some firms and industries are rapidly followed by wage adjustments in others (Marshall, 1980). The generalized use of changes in the consumer price index (CPI) as the standard of reference for wage claims contributes to the homogeneity of wage increases across sectors covered by collective bargaining.[8] This index orients trade unions bargaining strategies, and in some countries, automatic wage adjustments governed by changes in the CPI are even included in collective agreements (Sylos-Labini, 1974; Marshall, 1980). When prices stop rising, this common standard for wage claims disappears and unions switch to other standards, such as productivity or profitability trends, which favor greater wage heterogeneity. On the other hand, it has been posited that unions generate persistent wage gaps between unionized and non-unionized sectors.

Evidence from Argentina

Both dispersion and inequality – as measured by the coefficient of variation and the Gini coefficient respectively – of manufacturing wages increased in Argentina during

6 Specific forms of state intervention in wage setting, such as introducing or raising the minimum wage, generally contribute to lower inequality – for instance, Fortin and Lemieux (1997) and Benjamin (2001) on the role of minimum wages in the U.S. and Canada respectively. Here I will not examine the role of the minimum wage in Argentina since it had little relevance in determining manufacturing wages over the period under consideration.

7 Saba Arbache (1999), however, finds that industry wage dispersion is magnified within the unionized sector in Brazil.

8 Ingram et al. (1999) find, with reference to Great Britain, a positive association between the rate of inflation and the use of the 'comparability' argument in wage bargaining.

Table 10.1: Trends and Inequality in Hourly Money Wages in Manufacturing in Argentina, and Consumer Price Index, 1990-2000

	(1)	(2)	(3)	(4)	(5)	(6)
1990	0.50	1.22	0.34 (.34)	...	...	1343.9
1991	...	...	0.25 (.24)	0.16	...	84.0
1992	0.33	0.11	0.24 (.23)	...	...	17.5
1993	0.35	0.13	0.25 (.23)	0.86	12.5	7.4
1994	0.35	0.12	0.24 (.22)	0.82	5.5	3.9
1995	0.35	0.24	0.26 (.23)	1.23	3.3	1.6
1996	0.34	0.25	0.29 (.25)	2.38	3.2	0.1
1997	0.37	0.25	0.36 (.31)	6.89	1.0	0.3
1998	0.36	0.24	0.35 (.31)	1.32	1.4	0.7
1999	0.37	0.28	0.35 (.31)	6.09	0.8	-1.8
2000	0.38	0.25	0.37 (.33)	2.00	1.8	-0.8

(1) Gini coefficient, EPH: overall inequality in manufacturing. (2) Coefficient of variation, EPH: wage dispersion in manufacturing. (3) Coefficient of variation, EI: wage dispersion in manufacturing; figures in parenthesis exclude the petroleum industry, outlier. (4) Coefficient of variation of wage increases, EI: dispersion of wage increases across industries. (5) Annual rate of change of manufacturing average wages. (6) Rate of change in consumer price index (CPI).

Sources: Author's calculations based on unpublished data from INDEC's Industrial Surveys (Encuesta Industrial - EI), 3-digit industries; INDEC's Household Surveys (Encuesta Permanente de Hogares - EPH), Buenos Aires-Cordoba-Rosario, wage earners with only one job working 30 hours or more per week, May; ECLAC (CPI).

the second half of the 1990s (Table 10.1).[9] Following the hypotheses discussed above, this increase is likely the result of several concomitant and inter-related factors. First, it could have resulted from the intensification of international trade because of domestic currency appreciation and subsequent productivity increases driven partly by technological innovation that precipitated both an employment restructuring in skills and a reduction in the level of employment. Trade liberalization preceded the sharp jump in unemployment and was one of its causes. As shown in Table 10.2, wage inequality, the unemployment rate, the import and export rates, and the employment share of the highly educated all increased in the second half of the 1990s, while manufacturing employment fell steadily throughout the decade.[10] Although the overall employment share of the highly educated expanded only slightly, as seen in the important differences across industries, this expansion could have contributed to some extent to the increase in wage dispersion and inequality. Second, the weakening of

9 In Argentina, inequality was higher in 1990 than in subsequent years because of differential wage adjustments to hyperinflation at the turn of the decade.

10 Henceforth only wage employment will be considered.

Table 10.2: Wage Inequality in Manufacturing and Selected Explanatory Variables in Argentina, 1991-95 and 1996-00

	(1)	(2)	(3)	(4)	(5)	(6)	(7)
1991-95	0.34	0.25 (0.23)	10.2	-3.5	5	42	27
1996-00	0.36	0.34 (0.30)	14.5	-3.0	6	52	35

(1) Gini coefficient of hourly money wages in manufacturing (Buenos Aires-Cordoba-Rosario), wage earners with only one job, working 30 hours or more per week, May, EPH; (2) Dispersion of hourly money wages, coefficient of variation across industries, EI, figures in parenthesis exclude the petroleum industry, outlier; (3) Average annual unemployment rate (%); (4) Annual average rate of change in employment (%); (5) Manufacturing employment share of workers with completed higher education (%); (6) Import ratio to manufacturing gross product (%); (7) Export ratio to manufacturing gross product (%).

Sources: Author's calculations based on INDEC's Industrial Survey (EI) and Household Surveys (EPH) and ECLAC's unpublished data.

trade union power and some substantial changes in the dynamics of collective negotiation may also help to explain the increase in wage dispersion and inequality.

Import and Export Growth with Appreciation of Domestic Currency: Impacts on Employment and the Demand for Skill

For the Argentine case, it is not possible to isolate the effects of trade liberalization from those of currency appreciation resulting from the fixed parity to the dollar established in 1991. Appreciation stimulated imports of both consumption and capital goods and, at the same time, restrained the expansion of manufacturing exports. The expansion of the manufacturing sector over the period 1991-98, interrupted only by the 1995 recession, was followed by a period of stagnation and later by a prolonged recession.[11] The combination of trade liberalization and currency appreciation contributed to the contraction of employment in the manufacturing sector at an annual average rate of almost 4 percent over the 1992-2000 period. This trend was shared by most industries. This reduction in manufacturing employment, at a time when employment opportunities in the other sectors were minimal and labor supply was expanding, led to a significant growth in open unemployment.

Manufacturing exports experienced a substantial growth during the 1990s (Bisang and Kosacoff, 1993; Kosacoff and Ramos, 2001) as the export rate – the ratio of manufacturing export to manufacturing gross product – increased from 22 percent in 1993 to more than 34 percent in 1999.[12] Although the export rate increased in most

11 According to data from the Industrial Survey of the National Institute of Statistics and Censuses (INDEC), real manufacturing output of firms with 10 or more workers expanded by an average of 3.2 percent per annum between 1990 and 2000.

12 Export and import ratios to manufacturing GDP and to gross production value (at 2- and 3-digit levels) reported in this chapter are derived from ECLAC's unpublished data, kindly provided by Bernardo Kosacoff and Adrián Ramos. Kosacoff and Ramos (2001) report that these ratios also increased between 1986 and 1993, particularly the import ratio.

manufacturing industries, by 1999 it had exceeded 30 percent in only 15 percent of them, or 7 of 47 industries, while it remained below the 10 percent level in 53 percent of all manufacturing industries. Export expansion did not, however, have a positive impact on employment levels, export industries actually showing a reduction in labor-absorption capacity. Indeed, the correlation coefficient between cross-industry export rates and annual average rates of employment variation during 1992-2000 was negative – although not statistically significant – but the correlation coefficient between export rates and annual average productivity growth rates was positive (Pearson = 0.37) – and statistically significant at 0.01.[13]

The marked growth in imports was, however, the main outcome of the economic openings of the early 1990s. The combination of a large reduction in tariff levels and the fixed parity of the peso to the U.S. dollar led to a sharp expansion in the import rate from 37 percent to 50 percent of manufacturing gross product between 1993 and 1999. This increase in imports was an additional factor fostering the restructuring of the manufacturing sector, with productivity advances in some sectors and declines in others, resulting in a detrimental impact on the level of employment. The correlation coefficient between import rates and cross-industry annual average rates of change in employment levels during1992-2000 was negative (Pearson = -0.42) and statistically significant at 0.01.[14]

The expansion of international trade was accompanied by significant increases in labor productivity, reducing the high dollar-cost of wages and improving competitiveness.[15] Labor productivity per hour rose markedly in 1991-1992 and then more slowly until the end of the decade, averaging an impressive annual increase of 6.4 percent between 1990 and 2000. Productivity growth was in part the result of the introduction of new technologies embedded in capital goods, mainly by firms with a high degree of foreign investment; indeed, the extent of the use of new technologies, apparently localized rather than generalized, is still a controversial issue (Kosacoff and Ramos, 2001; Bisang and Lugones, 2001; and Giosa, 2000). Work reorganization also contributed to improving productivity performance. This improvement prompted changes in the composition of employment in favor of highly skilled jobs, though the share of these jobs in total manufacturing employment continued to be relatively small. The expanding activities and occupations concerned mainly those not directly involved in production. The introduction of new techniques in administration, organization,

13 Author's estimates based on INDEC's Industrial Survey and ECLAC's unpublished data for 47 manufacturing industries. Import and export ratios to manufacturing gross production value are for 1999.

14 See footnote 13.

15 Unit labor costs fell by 30 percent between 1991 and 1997 as a result of productivity increases and payroll tax reductions (MTSS, 1997).

Table 10.3: Proportion of Manufacturing Sector Wage Earners with Completed Higher Education in Argentina, 1992-95 and 1996-00, Annual Averages, Percent

	1992-1995	1996-2000
Food/beverages/tobacco	2.8	5.9
Textiles/clothing/leather/footwear	2.6	3.1
Chemicals/petroleum/plastic/rubber	9.8	12.6
Metals/machinery/transport equip.	5.9	5.3
Total manufacturing	5.2	6.2

Source: Author's calculations based on data from INDEC's Household Surveys (EPH), Buenos Aires-Cordoba-Rosario, May.

distribution, and commercialization contributed to greater professionalization of related occupations, and to higher earning for those employed in these jobs. The share of professional occupations in total manufacturing employment rose from 1.1 percent in 1991 to 3.6 percent in 2000; within this range, the share of professional occupations directly involved in production rose from 0.2 percent to 0.7 percent over the same period. Participation in technical jobs also expanded from 6.8 percent of total manufacturing employment in 1991 to 9.5 percent in 2000, but again, the share of technical jobs directly involved in production grew significantly less – going from 1.4 to 1.7 percent. While the share of skilled production workers in manufacturing employment remained at about 45 percent during this period, the share of all skilled workers – including non-production workers – fell from 67 to 64 percent as a result of the externalization of some activities not directly involved in production; for example, the share of skilled administrative, accounting, and computing jobs declined. The share of unskilled workers in total manufacturing employment followed a similar downward trend, decreasing from 24 percent in 1991 to 21 percent in 2000.[16] In short, the composition of manufacturing employment changed in favor of professional and technical occupations, particularly in non-production areas, but showed loss in participation of skilled production workers.[17] It must be noted that the overall share of workers with higher education rose only slightly; however, this increase varied across industries but was more noticeable in the more modern sectors, some of which had a high export orientation, such as those associated with chemicals, petroleum, plastics and rubber, food and beverages, and tobacco (Table 10.3).[18]

16 Data are from INDEC's population census, 1991, and household survey, October, 2000, total urban areas.

17 Due to sample size and characteristics (Household Survey), it is not possible to obtain reliable estimates of over time changes in skill composition within industries.

18 Further industrial disaggregation is not possible because of the size of the sample (Household Surveys). The export rate is also high in other industries, such as the automobile industry included within 'metals, machinery, and transport equipment.'

In short, (i) the need to compete with imports and in the international market in a context of currency overvaluation led to a substantial improvement in productivity in some sectors and to factory closures or restructuring in others; (ii) this trend in turn led to a continuous decline in employment levels in the manufacturing sector, contributing to the expansion of unemployment; and (iii) the mechanisms that permitted the increase in productivity were also responsible for an increase in highly skilled jobs, mainly in modern industries with a high export orientation. These factors could have had an effect on wage inequality in the Argentine manufacturing sector in the 1990s.

Unionization and Changes in Collective Bargaining

In Argentina, wage rates set through collective negotiation apply – depending on bargaining levels – to all workers in the firm or sector regardless of whether they are unionized or not.[19] Although union membership does not affect individual wages, unionization rates in the firm or sector help to determine the degree of influence, representativeness, and mobilization capacity of labor organizations. In 1997 the unionization rate was 53 percent for all wage earners – excluding household services – and 59 percent in manufacturing, with substantial differences across industries.[20] Consistent with international trends, Argentina experienced a decline in the degree of unionization in manufacturing during the 1990s; this decline was not pronounced, however, going from an average of 66 percent in 1982-86 (Feldman, 1991) to 59 percent in 1997.[21] Unionization rates remained at relatively high levels across all industries during the 1990s, and thus, widespread loss of membership must be discarded as a possible explanation of any trade unions' loss of influence in collective negotiations during this period. Instead, any weakening in unions' bargaining power can likely be attributed to the extremely adverse labor market conditions prevailing since the mid-1990s.

---

19 In countries where collective agreements cover only unionized firms and workers, the impact of unionization on wage inequality may be assessed using household survey data, assuming a question about membership has been included in the questionnaire: wages of union and non-union workers may be compared after controlling for individual and occupational characteristics – e.g., Saba Arbache (1999) and Saba Arbache and Carneiro (1999) for Brazil, besides the many studies in the U.S., Canada, and Great Britain. A similar comparison is not possible, however, when collective agreements cover all workers as in Argentina.

20 Unionization rates exceeded 60 percent in the chemical-petroleum-rubber-plastic complex, and 57 percent in food, beverages, and tobacco industries. Even in low unionized industries such as textiles, clothing, and leather, the unionization rate was still quite considerable at 44 percent (author's estimates based on SIEMPRO, 1997).

21 These two estimates, the only ones available, come from different sources, and thus, comparisons must be made with caution.

Labor regulation was the subject of important changes in the 1990s, including the strong promotion of firm-level collective bargaining after 1991. To what extent did the new regulations affect collective negotiation and wage determination? In general, the new regulations did not lead to significant decentralization of the collective negotiation process in manufacturing industries, despite the fact that the unions' response involved some diversification of strategies and the gradual incorporation of firm-level bargaining. Indeed, 61 percent of almost 100 manufacturing trade unions still had exclusively industry-wide agreements in 1999, some of them negotiated prior to 1991 but still valid because of the prevailing rule that agreements are effective until formally replaced or modified. Moreover, 75 percent of those unions that had only industry-wide agreements prior to1992 continued in the same situation until 1999 by either not replacing them or negotiating new ones at the same level. Hence, the progress of the decentralization of bargaining in manufacturing was limited, even if decentralized negotiation became more common among the highly concentrated industries (Marshall and Perelman, 2002). It must be emphasized that informal bargaining at the enterprise level had always been practiced, particularly during times when collective negotiation was prohibited, and many unions continued the practice throughout the 1990s[22] with corresponding effects on wage inequality both within and across firms.

Institutional changes with the potential for contributing to the widening of wage differentials went, however, beyond changes in trade union power and levels of collective bargaining. The state's role in wage determination, for instance, was altered. Before 1990 the government had a strong homogenizing influence on wage increases (Marshall, 1980 and 1999), but it withdrew from the direct determination of wages after 1991. Since then, the government limited itself to setting general restrictions on wage increases, prohibiting wage indexation and mandating that sectoral wage increases should be backed by productivity increases – a condition that fostered greater wage heterogeneity.

The objectives guiding trade unions' bargaining also changed. Earlier, the inflation rate had become the standard of reference for wage claims in collective negotiation – an important mechanism that contributed to the uniformity of wage increases across industries (Marshall, 1980). This framework of reference gradually disappeared after the adoption of the 1991 Convertibility Plan and the implementation of other complementary reforms. Until 1992, wage bargaining had still been seeking to recover the purchasing power lost in the immediately preceding hyperinflation period, a loss that varied across sectors, but by the mid-1990s the consumer price index practically stabilized, and then even fell in 1999-2000 (Table 10.1). Consequently, trade unions shifted to other frameworks of reference for wage claims such as productivity trends or the general economic performance and profitability of firms and sectors. These two

22 The Unión Obrera Metalúrgica is a good example (Freytes Frey, 1999).

yardsticks – much more difficult to estimate than the CPI – had always played a role in collective negotiations, but now they became the only parameters available. This shift implied less coordination among unions and thus facilitated the fragmentation of collective negotiation. Bargaining outcomes were no longer expressed in changes in the basic wage rates – which, with few exceptions, did not increase after 1995 (MTSS, 1999) – but rather in gross earnings through the inclusion of differential benefits that provided further opportunity for wage differentiation.

Summarizing, it appears that declining unions' influence in wage determination – mainly as a result of negative labor market conditions – limited the expansion of decentralized collective bargaining, the disappearance of the shared standard for wage claims after price stabilization, and subsequently, the reduced coordination among unions in wage negotiations, all could have contributed to greater inter-industry dispersion of wage increments and, therefore, to rising wage inequality in Argentina.

Manufacturing Wages

Manufacturing wages increased at a declining rate in the 1990s, averaging 3.7 percent per annum in nominal terms and 2.3 percent in real terms over 1992-2000. As indicated above, wage inequality also increased during this period. However, the scarce available information does not allow us to apply a multivariate regression analysis – such as in MacPhail (2000) – to determine the degree of influence of several simultaneous factors affecting the level of wage inequality in the Argentine manufacturing sector. Therefore, alternative methods to determine the possible impact of each of these factors on the evolution of wage differentials must be used.

Table 10.1 shows that wage inequality across manufacturing industries started to rise after the 1995 recession – the Gini coefficient increasing from 0.35 in 1995 and 0.34 in 1996, to 0.38 in 2000. Wage dispersion also increased in the second half of the 1990s – the coefficient of variation increasing from 0.26 in 1995 to 0.37 in 2000. The dispersion of wage increases, however, started to rise early in the decade because of differential adjustments to the wage losses experienced during the hyperinflation period at the beginning of the 1980s – the corresponding coefficient of variation increasing from 0.16 in 1991 to 0.86 in 1993. In 1992-2000, the coefficient of variation of annual average wage changes in manufacturing industries was 0.70, showing a considerable widening of dispersion in the 1990s compared with the historical trend of less than 0.10 (Marshall, 1995).[23] Here, dispersion also increased sharply after 1995.

What factors contribute to explain the differential cross-industry evolution of

23 Note that the coefficient of variation of annual average wage changes (hourly wages, 3-digit industries, data from INDEC's Industrial Surveys) is not the same as the average of the annual coefficients of variation shown in Table 10.1.

Table 10.4: Explanatory Variables of Inter-Industry Differentials in Rates of Wage Change in Argentina, 1992-2000

A. Rates of wage change regressions	
Productivity growth[a]	0.122 (1.72)[e]
Export rate[b]	4.672 (2.08)[c]
R-squared	0.21
B. Rates of wage change, coefficients of association	
Pearson Coefficient	
Productivity growth[a]	0.36[d]
Export rate[b]	0.392[c]
Spearman Coefficient	
Productivity growth[a]	0.458 [c]
Export rate[b]	0.415 [c]

[a] Annual average rates of change of money wages per hour and of productivity corresponding to 47 industries; t statistics in parenthesis. [b] Export ratio to gross production value corresponding to 47 manufacturing industries; t statistics in parenthesis. [c] Significant at 0.01. [d] Significant at 0.05. [e] Significant at 0.09.

Sources: Author's calculations based on INDEC's Industrial Surveys (EI) and ECLAC's unpublished data.

wages in manufacturing? Results from both regression analyses and correlations – the less demanding Pearson and Spearman coefficients – suggest that wage increases were greater in industries with higher productivity growth rates and higher export rates than in other industries (Table 10.4). It must be noted that the positive association between productivity growth and export rates – productivity tends to increase faster in industries with greater export orientation – has to be taken into account when interpreting the results. These findings are consistent with the hypothesis – found to be applicable to different countries at different times – that the largest wage increases correspond to the most productive and profitable industries, meaning those having the greatest ability to pay. Moreover, the association between rates of change in wages and in productivity – also noted in previous periods in Argentina (Marshall, 1980) – was explicitly encouraged by the government. Contrary to ex-ante expectations, however, variables such as import rates or changes in output and employment do not appear to have had significant explanatory power regarding differentials in the evolution of wages across industries.[24] By contrast, results from an exploratory analysis suggest that the level at which collective bargaining was conducted – be it industry-wide, firm, or mixed – had some influence on wage change; in other words, wage increments were lower in more decentralized industries, the correlation coefficient being of the expected sign but not statistically significant.

24 The evolution of wages is not correlated with the trade balance coefficient either, as the latter is significantly correlated with the import rate.

But do productivity and export rate also help explain the increase in cross-industry differentials in rates of wage changes observed in the 1990s? The following conditions should have been met if these two variables were to help explain the increasing gap between rates of wage change across industries: (i) productivity growth rates should have become more unequal – but this trend has not occurred;[25] (ii) new export industries should have become noticeably distinct from existing ones – and this may indeed have happened; and (iii) standards such as increases in productivity or degree of success of export strategies should have guided unions' bargaining behavior to a much greater extent than in the past. As indicated above, the substitution of the common standard of reference given by increases in the CPI by productivity and profitability guidelines favored the adoption of more independent strategies among unions aiming to achieve different goals. Indeed, it was precisely when the CPI ceased to increase that the dispersion of wage changes across industries increased markedly, the coefficients of variation jumping from 0.56 for 1992-1995 to 2.10 for 1995-2000.[26] Although the decentralization of formal collective bargaining did not progress much in the 1990s, inter-union coordination has been undermined and trade unions affected differently by industry-specific sensitivity to excess labor pressures. The striking increase in the rate of unemployment after 1995 contributed to the creation of an adverse environment for unions' negotiations, particularly in industries intensive in the use of unskilled labor, with low profitability, and with little possibility of placing their output on international markets.

Differential changes in employment composition in terms of skill and education could have also contributed to the increase in wage inequality across manufacturing industries. As indicated above, the evidence suggests that the share of the highly skilled and educated workers increased relatively more in export industries (Table 10.3). However, since the share of workers with the highest educational level is small, being slightly above 10 percent even in these industries, its contribution to the aggravation of wage inequality between export and non-export industries is only marginal.[27] In manufacturing industries as a whole, skill and educational wage differentials increased – but only between the earnings of professionals and those of

---

25 The dispersion of cross-industry productivity increases in 1970-1990 seems to have been higher than in the 1990s (coefficients of variation; data from INDEC's Industrial Survey; 22 industries in both periods but different classifications).

26 Author's calculations based on data from INDEC's Industrial Survey (3-digit industries).

27 Greater disaggregation, not possible because of sample size and characteristics, could modify these results. Similarly, though the employment share of women expanded more significantly in some of those industries where relative wages declined, the lower wages paid to women had only a marginal impact on the sector's average wage (author's results based on simulation with data from INDEC's Household Surveys, Buenos Aires-Cordoba-Rosario, 1993 and 2000, May).

Table 10.5: Rate of Change of Wages According to Educational and Skill Levels in Argentina, 1992-2000, Annual Averages, Percent [a]

Education	
Primary	2.4
Secondary	2.3
University	7.2
Skill [b]	
Unskilled	4.0
Skilled	4.7
Professional	15.8

[a] Wage earners with only one job working 30 hours or more per week. Annual wages 1993-2000: average of figures from two surveys (May and October). [b] 1992-1997.

Sources: INDEC's Household Surveys (EPH), Buenos Aires-Cordoba-Rosario, May and October (1992: only May; 1996 October: Cordoba not included).

other workers.[28] Wage differentials between workers with primary education and those with secondary education, as well as between unskilled and skilled workers, showed almost no change (Table 10.5). It must be noted that the increase in the relative wage of the highly educated workers was taking place at a time when the unemployment rate for these workers was rising.[29] Nonetheless, the rate of unemployment increased much less for the highly educated than for the others – compared with the 1992 levels, the rate of unemployment in 2000 was 11 percent higher for those workers with primary education, 8 percent higher for those with secondary education, and 4 percent higher for those with university education (Marshall, 2001). Moreover, the widening of wage differentials was facilitated by professionals' earnings being negotiated individually, or through collective bargaining by their own separate unions. In any case, the behavior of educational and skill wage differentials differed among industries, such as export and non export industries – but this aspect is a topic that requires further research.[30]

28 The sample's size does not permit separate analyses for men and women, as normally found in the literature.

29 Barrett et al. (1999) point out a similar 'inconsistency' in the case of Ireland where the relative wages of the highly educated were rising while their supply was rapidly increasing.

30 Ghiara and Zepeda (2001), for example, conclude that in Mexico the increase in the wage gap between skill levels was localized in modern industries characterized by a high degree of foreign investment – those industries where the demand for skilled labor increased the most. In Argentina, as indicated above, the nature and size of the sample (Household Survey) precludes such a disaggregated analysis.

Conclusions

The nature of the available information precludes the use of multivariate regression analysis to determine the extent of the explanatory power of those factors affecting wage inequality in the Argentine manufacturing sector. Notwithstanding that fact, a separate examination of the potential explanatory role of each of these factors allows the following conclusions.

Inter-industry wage dispersion and inequality increased in the 1990s. Considering the manufacturing sector as a whole, the changes in labor requirements appear to have translated into a widening of the gap between the earnings of professionals and those of other manufacturing workers, even though the unemployment rate of professionals was increasing. This apparent paradox is explained by two factors: (i) the unemployment pressure on wages was relatively weaker in this labor segment, and (ii) professional workers tend to negotiate their wages independently of other wage earners. The increase in wage inequality across industries cannot be explained, however, by the observed changes in the composition of employment in the most advanced industries in favor of the highly skilled – which are associated with technological and organizational innovation driven in part by the intensification of international trade – given the marginal employment share of this group even in those industries.

Cross-industry differentials in the rate of variation of wages in 1992-2000 are not explained either by differentials in employment changes or by import pressure. On the contrary, wages appear to have increased the most in those industries with the highest export rates and largest productivity increases – two factors positively correlated. There is no evidence to support the claim that larger dispersion of wage increases was correlated with greater dispersion of productivity growth rates. Instead, greater dispersion of wage increases appears to have been fostered by price stabilization from the mid-1990s and by subsequent replacement of the shared standard in wage negotiations given by the inflation rate by productivity and profitability parameters intrinsically diverse across industries. Formal decentralized bargaining was far from being generalized in manufacturing, but the new economic and regulatory climate – including the very policies promoting bargaining decentralization and a stronger association between wage increases and productivity growth – that favored the development of more autonomous trade union strategies, contributed to the undermining of both inter-union coordination and diffusion of wage increases from one sector to another – incidentally, wage increases are obtained now exclusively by way of specific supplementary benefits instead of via wage rate raises. In addition, the high unemployment rates experienced since the mid-1990s weakened labor's bargaining power, particularly in non-export and less profitable industries, thus helping to explain the latter's lagging wages.

In summary, the main causes of the increase in wage inequality in the Argentine manufacturing sector appear to be, on the one hand, the unemployment trends and their impact on trade union power, and on the other hand, the changes in bargaining strategies triggered by price stabilization after a long-period of high inflation, as well as the reforms to labor regulation. The increase in the demand for highly skilled workers as a result of technological innovation, associated with the intensification of international trade, appears to have had a much smaller impact on wage inequality, the impact being restricted to the wage differential between the small segment of professionals and the other manufacturing workers. Further research will help to determine whether these economic and institutional causes of rising wage inequality are peculiar to Argentina or shared by other Latin American countries.

References

Barrett, A., T. Callan and B. Nolan (1999), 'Rising Wage Inequality, Returns to Education and Labor Market Institutions: Evidence from Ireland', *British Journal of Industrial Relations*, Vol. 37, No. 1 (March), pp. 77-100.

Benjamin, D. (2001), 'Minimum Wages in Canada', in A. Berry (ed.), *Labor Market Policies in Canada and Latin America: Challenges of the New Millennium*, Kluwer Academic Publishers, Boston, pp. 187-220.

Berry, A. (1998), 'Confronting the Income Distribution Threat in Latin America', in A. Berry (ed.), *Poverty, Economic Reform, and Income Distribution in Latin America*, Lynne Rienner, Boulder and London, pp. 9-41.

Bisang, R. and B. Kosacoff (1993), 'Las Exportaciones Industriales en una Economía en Transformación: Las Sorpresas del Caso Argentino', in B. Kosacoff et al. (eds.), *El Desafío de la Competitividad*, CEPAL/Alianza Editorial, Buenos Aires.

Bisang, R. and G. Lugones (2001), 'La Conducta Tecnológica de las Empresas Industriales Argentinas durante el Proceso de Apertura y Desregulación Económica', Annex in B. Kosacoff and A. Ramos, *Cambios Contemporáneos en la Estructura Industrial Argentina*, Universidad Nacional de Quilmes, Bernal, Argentina.

Borland, J. (1996), 'Union Effects on Earnings Dispersion in Australia, 1986-1994', *British Journal of Industrial Relations*, Vol. 34, No. 2 (June), pp. 237-48.

Cristini, M. (1999), 'Apertura Económica, Política Comercial y la Distribución del Ingreso:)Qué Aporta el Caso Argentino al Debate?', in FIEL (ed.), *La Distribución del Ingreso en la Argentina*, FIEL, Buenos Aires.

Feldman, S. (1991), 'Tendencias de la Sindicalización en Argentina', *Estudios del Trabajo*, No. 2, pp. 79-109.

Fortin, N.M. and T. Lemieux (1997), 'Institutional Changes and Rising Wage Inequality', *The Journal of Economic Perspectives*, Vol. 11, No. 2 (Spring), pp. 75-96.

Frenkel, R. and M. González Rozada (1999), 'Liberalización del Balance de Pagos: Efectos sobre el Crecimiento, el Empleo y los Ingresos en Argentina', Serie Documentos de Economía No. 11, Universidad de Palermo-CEDES, Buenos Aires.

Freytes Frey, A.C. (1999), 'Las Relaciones Laborales en la Actividad Sidero-Metalúrgica: Informalidad y Fragmentación', in A. Fernández and R. Bisio (eds.), *Política y Relaciones Laborales en la Transición Democrática Argentina*, Asociación Trabajo y Sociedad/Editorial Lumen, Buenos Aires.

Galiani, S. and P. Sanguinetti (2000), 'Wage Inequality and Trade Liberalization: Evidence from Argentina', Working Paper No. 11, Department of Economics, Universidad Torcuato di Tella, Buenos Aires.

Ghiara, R. and E. Zepeda (2001), 'Relative Wages and Education Premium in Tijuana: 1987-1996', *Journal of Borderland Studies*, Vol. 16, No. 1 (Spring), pp. 31-50.

Ghose, A.K. (2000), 'La Liberalización Comercial, el Empleo y la Desigualdad en el Mundo', *Revista Internacional del Trabajo*, Vol.119, No. 3.

Giosa, N. (2000), 'Neoliberalismo, Reestructuración Productiva y Empleo en la Argentina de los 90', Unpublished Masters Dissertation, Instituto de Economía, Universidad Estadual de Campinas, Sao Paulo.

Hanson, G. and A. Harrison (1999), 'Trade Liberalization and Wage Inequality in Mexico', *Industrial and Labor Relations Review*, Vol. 52 (January), No. 2, pp. 271-88.

ILO (International Labour Organization) (2000), *Panorama Laboral 2000,* Lima.

Ingram, P., J. Wadsworth and D. Brown (1999), 'Free to Choose? Dimensions of Private-sector Wage Determination, 1979-1994', *British Journal of Industrial Relations*, Vol. 37, No. 1, pp. 33-49.

Kosacoff, B. and A. Ramos (2001), *Cambios Contemporáneos en la Estructura Industrial Argentina*, Universidad Nacional de Quilmes, Bernal, Argentina.

Leslie, D. and Y. Pu (1996), 'What Caused Rising Earnings Inequality in Britain? Evidence from Time Series, 1970-1993', *British Journal of Industrial Relations*, Vol. 34, No. 1 (March), pp. 111-130.

Machin, S. (1997), 'The Decline of Labour Market Institutions and the Rise in Wage Inequality in Britain', *European Economic Review*, Vol. 41, No. 3-5 (April), pp. 647-57.

MacPhail, F. (2000), 'What Caused Earnings Inequality to Increase in Canada During the 1980s?', *Cambridge Journal of Economics*, Vol. 24, No. 2 (March), pp. 153-75.

Marshall, A. (1980), 'Labour Markets and Wage Growth: The Case of Argentina', *Cambridge Journal of Economics*, Vol. 4, No. 1 (January), pp. 37-60.

Marshall, A. (1995), 'Regímenes Institucionales de Determinación Salarial y Estructura de los Salarios, Argentina (1976-1993),' *Desarrollo Económico*, Vol. 35, No. 138 (July-September), pp. 275-288.

Marshall, A. (1999), 'Wage Determination Regimes and Pay Inequality: A Comparative Study of Latin American Countries', *International Review of Applied Economics*, Vol. 13, No. 1, pp. 23-39.

Marshall, A. (2001), '"Fuerzas del Mercado", Política Laboral y Sindicatos: Efectos sobre la Desigualdad Salarial', 5to. Congreso Nacional de Estudios del Trabajo, ASET, Buenos Aires (CD-Rom).

Marshall, A. and L. Perelman (2002), 'Estructura de la Negociación Colectiva en la Argentina:)Avanzó la Descentralización en los Años 90?', *Estudios del Trabajo*.

Meza González, L. (1999), 'Cambios en la Estructura Salarial de México en el Período 1988-1993 y el Aumento del Rendimiento de la Educación Superior', *El Trimestre Económico*, Vol. 66, No. 262.

MTSS (Ministerio de Trabajo y Seguridad Social) (1997), *Informe de Coyuntura Laboral*, Buenos Aires.

MTSS (Ministerio de Trabajo y Seguridad Social) (1999), *Revista de Trabajo*, Vol. 5, No. 13.

OECD (Organization of Economic Cooperation and Development) (1966), *Wages and Labour Mobility,* Paris.

Robbins, D.J. (1994), 'Earnings Dispersion in Chile after Trade Liberalization', Harvard University, mimeo.

Saba Arbache, J. (1999), 'Do Unions Always Decrease Wage Dispersion? The Case of Brazilian Manufacturing', *Journal of Labor Research*, Vol. 20, No. 3 (Summer), pp. 425-436.

Saba Arbache, J. and F.G. Carneiro (1999), 'Unions and Interindustry Wage Differentials', *World Development*, Vol. 27, No. 10 (October), pp. 1875-83.

SIEMPRO (Sistema de Información, Evaluación, y Monitoreo de Programas) (1997), *Encuesta de Desarrollo Social, Condiciones de Vida y Acceso a Programas y Servicios Sociales* (CD-Rom, September 2000), Buenos Aires.

Singh, A. and R. Dhumale (2000), 'Globalization, Technology, and Income Inequality', Working Paper No. 210, UNU/WIDER.

Sylos-Labini, P. (1974), *Trade Unions, Inflation and Productivity*, Saxon House-Lexington Books, London.

Wood, A. (1997), 'Openness and Wage Inequality in Developing Countries: The Latin American Challenge to East Asia Conventional Wisdom', *World Bank Economic Review*, Vol. 11, No. 1, pp. 33-57.

Zweimuller, J. and E. Barth (1994), 'Bargaining Structure, Wage Determination, and Wage Dispersion in Six OECD Countries', *KYKLOS*, Vol. 47, No. 1, pp. 81-93.

Chapter 11

The Impact of Minimum Wages on Wage Inequality and Employment in Costa Rica[1]

Fatma El-Hamidi and Katherine Terrell

Introduction

Minimum wage policies have always been controversial among economists and policy makers, and the debate on the issue has become more heated following the publication of a book on the topic by Card and Krueger (1995) and of related papers (e.g., Katz and Krueger, 1992; Card and Krueger, 1994). Supporters of minimum wages justify such policy as a way of improving the living conditions of the poor, unskilled, and unorganized workers. Critics emphasize the losses in efficiency associated with minimum wages, disqualifying this wage-floor as being inadequate for tackling inequality. They argue that in developing countries, minimum wages are the principal source of labor market segmentation and unemployment.

The traditional view, using the standard two-sector model that assumes a perfectly competitive labor market with a homogeneous and mobile labor force, is that an increase in the minimum wage reduces employment in the covered sector, creates unemployment, and has 'negative' spillover effects in the uncovered sector – meaning increasing employment there along with downward pressure on wages at the lower end of the distribution (Brown, 1999). Hence, increasing the minimum wage should increase income inequality in the uncovered sector and reduce it in the covered sector.

On the other hand, if minimum wages do not reduce employment in the covered sector, and hence, have no spillover effects – the outcome in a monopsonistic model of the labor market – changes in minimum wages will not

1 This paper benefited from comments and suggestions made by Charlie Brown, Richard Freeman and Gary Solon.

have an efficiency loss and may not affect wage inequality in the uncovered sector (Card and Krueger, 1995; Rebitzer and Taylor, 1995). If employment actually increases in the covered sector as a result of minimum wage increase and draws low-wage workers from the uncovered sector, then one might expect earnings inequality to fall in the uncovered sector. Prior to Card's and Krueger's (1994, 1995) and related research, which found a positive effect of minimum wage on employment in the U.S., monopsony was not a popular model of the labor market. Dickens et al. (1999, p.2) argue that monopsony may have been more common than we have traditionally believed from the one-company town examples: 'For example, in most labor markets employers that cut wages do not instantaneously lose all their workers, so the supply of labor to a firm is not perfectly elastic, and firms therefore posses some monopsony power… in the short and long run.'

This chapter examines the effects of changes in the minimum wage on earnings inequality and aggregate level of employment in Costa Rica's covered and uncovered sectors over the 1980-92 period. It also examines whether changes in the minimum wage lead to a reallocation of labor between the covered and uncovered sector.

A number of features about Costa Rica make it an interesting country for the analysis of minimum wages and inequality in the two sectors. First, a significant group of the country's workers – approximately one-fifth of the employed – are not covered by minimum wages; they are self-employed 'uncovered sector' workers.[2] Second, unlike most countries, Costa Rica has multiple minimum wages for various occupations and industries. In the 1970s and early 1980s, there were approximately 350 minimum wages, but in 1990 the number was reduced to approximately 80. Setting the minimum wage at different levels according to occupation and industry is not necessarily a more effective instrument than a single minimum for raising the wage floor and reducing wage inequality. However, the Costa Rican National Salary Council has taken the additional step of systematically raising the lowest minimum wages by a greater percentage than it raised the higher minimum wages over the 1980s and 1990s. Moreover, the Council did not allow minimum wages to erode over the 1980s, as was the case in most Latin American countries – especially in Ecuador, Mexico, and Peru. As shown in Figure 11.1, the plot of the *toughness* of minimum wages – where *toughness* is defined as the ratio between the lowest minimum wage in an industry and the average wage of covered workers in this industry – reveals that during 1980-1992, this ratio remained fairly stable and that the Costa Rican minimum wages had been relatively high – the median is 55 percent of the average wage – when compared with those of other countries in the region. Hence, one would expect from the manner in which minimum wages are designed and changed over time that minimum wages would

2 In this chapter, the uncovered sector comprises the self-employed workers only, therefore, we use the terms 'uncovered sector' and 'self-employed' interchangeably.

Figure 11.1: Minimum Wage/Average Wage Ratio ("Toughness") by Industry in Costa Rica, 1980-1992

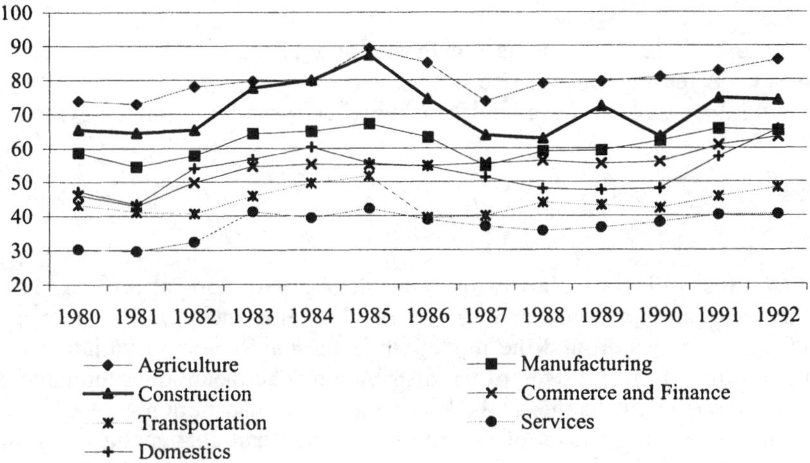

Source: Authors' estimates using data from the 1980-1992 annual Household Survey of Employment and Unemployment and various issues of the *Gazeta,* both provided by the Ministry of Labor and Social Security.

reduce inequality among Costa Rican workers in the covered sector. Their impact on the uncovered sector depends on whether the labor market is competitive or monopsonistic.

Method

Inequality

There are many ways to measure wage inequality, and we have used three widely accepted measures.

First, the coefficient of variation is expressed as

$$CV = \frac{\sigma_x}{\overline{Y}} = \frac{\sqrt{\sum_{i=1}^{n} (Y_i - \overline{Y})^2 / n}}{\overline{Y}} \qquad (1)$$

where Y_i is the earnings or wage of person i in the population, n is the number of people in the population, and $\overline{Y}$ is the mean wage in the population.

The second indicator we use is the most common measure of wage inequality –

the Gini coefficient:

$$G = 1 + 1/n - 2/n^2\overline{Y}\ [Y_1 + 2Y_2 + 3Y_3 + ... + nY_n] \qquad (2)$$

where n and $\overline{Y}$ are the same as previously, and Y_1, $2Y_2$, ...nY_n are the individual incomes in decreasing order of size.

The third measure we have selected is the Theil mean logarithmic deviation:[3]

$$\mathrm{T} = (1/n)\sum_{i=1}^{n} \log\left(Y_i/\overline{Y}\right) \qquad (3)$$

The measures differ in their sensitivity to income variations at different levels of the distribution. For equidistant transfers, the Gini index is considered more sensitive to changes around the mode, while the coefficient of variation is more sensitive to transfers at the top of the distribution. The mean logarithmic deviation is more responsive to changes at the lower end of the distribution.

To test whether the level of the minimum wage and changes in the minimum wage affect wage dispersion in the covered and the uncovered sectors, we estimate the following equation separately for the covered and uncovered sectors:

$$\ln D_{it} = \alpha_o + \alpha_1\, (MW_i/W_i)_t + \sum_{i=1}^{7}\beta_i I_i + \sum_{t=1}^{13}\gamma_t T_t + \mu \qquad (4)$$

where

- $i = 1 \ldots 7$ relates to each industry,[4] and $t = 1 \ldots 13$ to years (1980–1992);
- D_{it} is a measure of hourly wage dispersion within an industry and sector in each of the 13 years;
- MW_i/W_i is the lowest average hourly minimum wage set by the government for each industry divided by the average hourly wage in each industry. This variable captures the toughness of the minimum wage;
- I_i is an industry-specific dummy, with domestics as the base; and
- T_t is a dummy for the year for the period 1980-1992.

Industry and time dummies are added as controls for industry and time fixed effects, such as changes in aggregate output and shocks over time. We also test whether the impact of the minimum wage is non-linear – with a quadratic specification – and whether the minimum wage has a lagged effect, using a one-year lag.

---

3 For further definitions see Coulter et al. (1992).

4 The seven industrial sectors are: agriculture, manufacturing, construction, transportation, commerce and finance, services and domestics. Domestic servants were singled out because they are a large group (about 10 percent) of the work force.

Figure 11.2: Three Measures of Inequality in Costa Rica, Total Population, 1976-1992

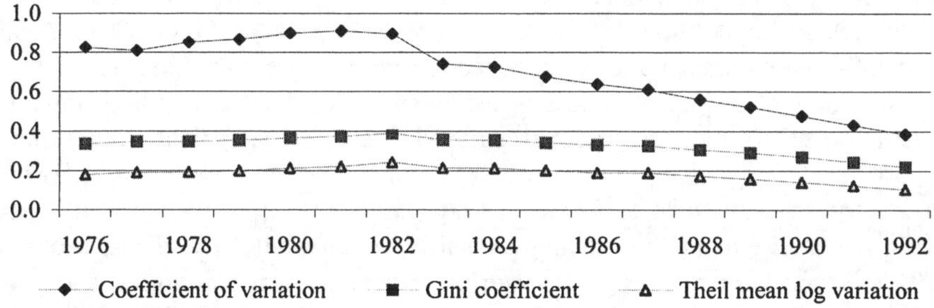

Source: See Figure 11.1.

Employment Effects

To estimate the employment effect of the minimum wage, we estimate separate regressions for the covered and uncovered sector workers using two different measures as dependent variable: a) the log of the number of workers employed, by industry and year, and b) the total number of hours worked in an average week, also by industry and year. These measures allow us to learn about the reallocation over time of workers and the hours worked across industries. We also examine whether there is a reallocation of labor within an industry between covered and uncovered employment as the toughness of minimum wages rises. For this, we use the percentage of workers in the covered sector in each industry – and year – as a dependent variable. All three of these measures are regressed on various specifications of the toughness measure, with industry and time as fixed effects.

Data

The analysis is based on aggregated data from the Costa Rican Annual Household Survey of Employment and Unemployment (HSEU), published by the Ministry of Labor and Social Security. The minimum wage data were taken from an unpublished table from the Ministry of Labor and Social Security, given to us by Orlando García (Director, Salary Division), and from the minimum wage laws published in the *Gazeta* (the official record of the Legislature).[5] Because it was not

5 The specific categories used from the minimum wage laws for each broad category are: for agriculture 'peones' (in Chapter I of the legislation), for manufacturing 'trabajadores del proceso' (in Chapter II), for electricity and other utilities 'trabajadores del proceso' (in Chapter V), for construction 'peones' (in Chapter IV), for commerce 'trabajadores en otras actividades comerciales' or 'peones' (in Chapter VI), for transportation and

Figure 11.3: Three Measures of Inequality in Uncovered (Self-Employed) and Covered Sectors in Costa Rica, 1976-1992

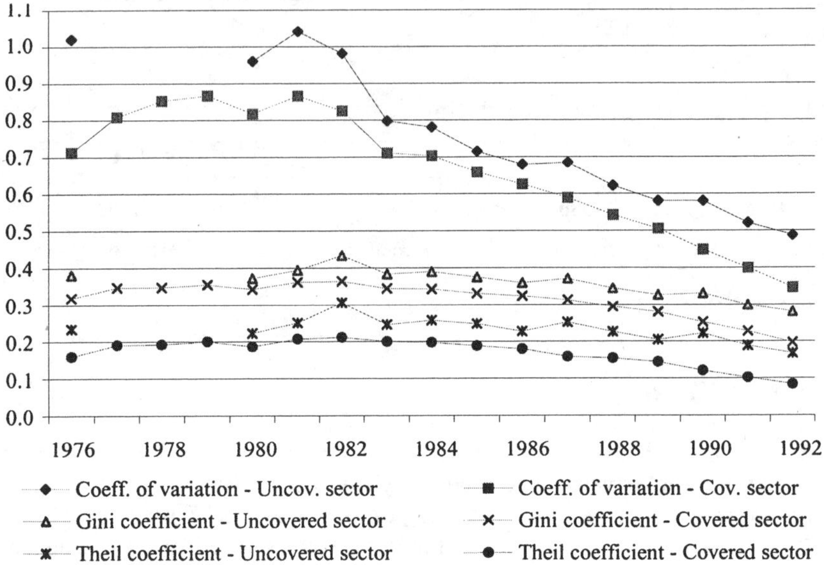

Source: See Figure 11.1.

possible to match the occupational codes in the HSEU with those in the *Gazeta*, we have selected as our benchmark the lowest minimum wage in each one-digit industrial sector. The toughness measure used in our analysis is plotted in Figure 11.1. In the regression analysis, we could not use the data from the 1976-1979 household surveys because no questions were asked to distinguish self-employment from other forms of employment in 1977-79.

Findings

Trend of the Wage Inequality (1976–1992)

In Figure 11.2 we present plots of the three measures of inequality in the hourly labor earnings of all workers. In Figure 11.3 we plot these measures for the covered and uncovered workers. The plots reveal the following patterns:

---

communication 'transporte por agua y otros trabajadores' (in Chapter VII), domestic servants 'servicio doméstico' or 'servidores domésticos' (in Chapter VIII), other services 'otros servicios' (in Chapter VIII).

Table 11.1: Effect of the Minimum Wage on Wage Dispersion in Costa Rica, Covered and Uncovered (Self-Employed) Sectors, 1976-1992

	Covered Sector	Uncovered Sector
Panel A: Log of coefficient of variation		
Toughness	-0.015	-0.0039
	(0.015)	(0.0158)
Toughness-square	0.00008	0.00005
	(0.00010)	(0.00011)
Time Dummies	Yes	Yes
Industry dummies	Yes	Yes
Adjusted R-square	0.80	0.77
Panel B: Log of Gini		
Toughness	-0.0315 [a]	-0.015
	(0.013)	(0.013)
Toughness-square	0.0002 [b]	0.0001
	(0.0001)	(0.0001)
Time Dummies	Yes	Yes
Industry dummies	Yes	Yes
Adjusted R-square	0.73	0.79
Panel C: Theil mean log deviation		
Toughness	-0.055 [b]	-0.034
	(0.025)	(0.031)
Toughness-square	0.00034 [c]	0.00029
	(0.00018)	(0.00022)
Time Dummies	Yes	Yes
Industry Dummies	Yes	Yes
Adjusted R-square	0.69	0.60
No. of Observations	91	91

[a] Significant at the 1% level; [b] significant at the 5% level; [c] significant at the 10% level.

Source: See Figure 11.1.

a) Earnings inequality for the whole population fell during 1982–1992. This is the case for all three measures of inequality, but the decline is most dramatic in the coefficient of variation. (Inequality was high in 1981-1982, coinciding with high inflation.)

b) The hourly earnings of covered workers are distributed more equally than those of the uncovered sector in every year.

c) The level of earnings inequality fell in the covered sector more than in the uncovered sector. An examination of the Gini for the covered and uncovered workers in each of the seven industries indicates the same overall declining pattern, but a more erratic pattern among the industries in 1981 and 1982, when inflation was high. Furthermore, the relative level of inequality among the industries is not consistent across the covered and uncovered sectors.

Table 11.2: Impact of Changes in the Toughness of the Minimum Wage on Inequality, Employment and Hours Worked in Costa Rica

	Range of Toughness Measure		
	Lowest (30%)	Median (55.5%)	Highest (89%)
Gini	-0.0195	-0.0093	0.0041
Theil	-0.0346	-0.0173	0.00552
Total employment	0.0106	0.0346	-0.0059
Covered Sector Employment	0.0127	0.0556	-0.0038
Hours worked covered sector	0.0037	0.00141	-0.0016
Hours worked uncovered sector	0.1210	0.00343	-.0.0080

Source: See Figure 11.1.

Inequality Results

The results from estimating equation (4) with the three measures of wage dispersion are presented in Table 11.1. Panel A contains the coefficients from the regression using the log of the coefficient of variation as the dependent variable, Panel B contains the findings using the log of Gini, and Panel C presents the results for the Theil mean log deviation measure.

The main finding is striking: up to a point, an increase in the industry-specific minimum wage relative to industry average wages reduces wage inequality in the covered sector when inequality is measured with the log of Gini and the Theil mean log deviation. However, it has no effect on the covered sector when measured with the log of coefficient of variation. The toughness measure has no impact on the earnings inequality of the self-employed in all three regressions. The effect on the covered sector is non-linear, and it is decreasing at a decreasing rate.[6]

As seen in Table 11.2, at the lowest level of toughness we find in the data, 30 percent, a 1 percent point increase in the toughness measure reduces inequality by 2 to 3 percent, depending on which measure is used. A unit increase at the median level of toughness, or 55.5 percent, reduces inequality between 0.9 and 1.7 percent, but at the highest level of toughness, or 89 percent, a 1 percent point increase actually increases inequality – but only by 0.4 to 0.6 percent. Hence, as long as the minimum wage is not set 'too high,' it reduces inequality.[7] One explanation offered for this is that enforcement is even less stringent when the minimum is high.

---

6 Tests for other specifications of the equation indicated that neither the coefficients for the linear toughness specification nor those for the lagged toughness specification were not significantly different from zero for either sector.

7 The turning point is when minimum wages were about 79-81 percent of the average wage in the industry.

Employment

Contrary to the traditional view, we find that, up to a point, minimum wage increases are associated with increases in the level of total and covered sector employment (Table 11.3, Panel A). We find no statistically significant correlation between the toughness of the minimum wage and the number of self-employed. The relationship between the minimum wage toughness measure and the level of employment is non-linear for both total and covered sector: an increase in the toughness of the minimum wage increases employment at a decreasing rate.[8] As seen in Table 11.2 total employment rises by 1.1 percent and covered sector employment by 1.3 percent when the toughness measure rises from 30 to 31 percent. The employment effect is positive until the toughness measure reaches between 68 and 75 percent for total employment and covered sector employment, respectively. At that point, further increases in the minimum wage reduce employment. At the highest level of toughness observed in Costa Rica over this period, a 1 percentage point increase lowers total employment by 0.6 percent and covered sector employment by 0.4 percent.

These findings may be interpreted as supporting the monopsonistic model, which predicts that increases in minimum wages can increase employment to the point where the marginal cost (in the absence of the minimum wage) is equal to the marginal revenue. Any increases above that point force the employer to be on his or her demand curve. However, it is difficult to imagine that the labor market for unskilled workers as a whole would function as in the monopsonistic model. Hence, another plausible interpretation of these findings is that they support the traditional model of the labor market for less skilled workers and the monopsonistic or efficiency wage models for the skilled workers. In particular, industries that use unskilled labor and pay low wages have a high ratio of minimum to actual wage, that is, high toughness. Firms in these industries face an elastic supply of labor; a rise in minimum wage forces these firms to move up their demand for labor curves and lay off workers. This is consistent with the negative employment effect documented in Table 11.2 and Table 11.3, Panel A. On the other hand, industries that employ relatively more skilled labor – and where capital intensity may be higher – have a low ratio of the minimum to the average wage, that is, low toughness. These are also the industries that are likely to face an upward-sloping supply curve of labor or where employers may pay efficiency wages to attract and keep skilled workers. In these industries, an increase in the minimum wage is expected to raise employment under the monopsonistic or efficiency wage scenario. This is consistent with the positive effect of increasing minimum wage on employment found for these industries in Table 11.2 and Table 11.3, Panel A.[9]

---

8 The coefficient on toughness was not significant either in the linear specification or the lagged specification (when the lagged term was entered in addition to the current term).

9 Note that in the monopsonistic model a rise in the minimum wage results in an increase in employment as the firm moves rightward along the supply curve of labor. The positive effect will of course be reversed when one reaches the point of intersection of labor supply

Table 11.3: Effect of the Minimum Wage on Employment and Number of Hours Worked in Costa Rica; Covered and Uncovered (Self-Employed) Sectors, 1976-1992

Panel A: Impact on log of employment			
	Total Employment	Covered Sector	Uncovered Sector
Toughness	0.0190 [c]	0.0211 [c]	0.0160
	(0.011)	(0.0118)	(0.190)
Toughness-square	-0.00014 [c]	-0.00014 [c]	-0.00018
	(0.00007)	(0.00009)	(0.00014)
Time Dummies	Yes	Yes	Yes
Industry dummies	Yes	Yes	Yes
Adjusted R-square	0.97	0.97	0.97
Panel B: Impact on log of numbers of hours worked			
	Total Economy	Covered Sector	Uncovered Sector
Toughness	0.0055	0.0064 [c]	0.0223 [b]
	(0.0035)	(0.0035)	(0.0091)
Toughness-square	-0.00004	-0.000045 [c]	-0.000017 [b]
	(0.00003)	(0.000025)	(0.000066)
Time dummies	Yes	Yes	Yes
Industry dummies	Yes	Yes	Yes
Constant	3.503 [a]	3.508 [a]	2.835 [a]
	(0.132)	(0.130)	(0.334)
Adjusted R-square	0.80	0.80	0.79
Panel C: Impact on relative level of employment in covered sector			
	(1)	(2)	(3)
Toughness	0.019 [d]	0.0018	0.0018
	(0.012)	(0.0035)	(0.0037
Toughness-square		0.000000034	0.000000589
		(0.000025)	(0.00003
Lag toughness			0.0029 [b]
			(0.0012)
Time dummies	Yes	Yes	Yes
Industry dummies	Yes	Yes	Yes
Constant	4.32 [a]	4.33 [a]	4.25 [a]
	(0.06)	(0.12)	(0.12)
Adjusted R-square	0.89	0.89	0.90
No. of observations	91	91	91

[a] Significant at the 1% level. [b] Significant at the 5% level. [c] Significant at the 10% level.
[d] P = 0.113.

Source: See Figure 11.1.

Our empirical estimates are hence consistent with the view that the minimum wage increases assist in reallocating labor from the 'traditional' to the 'modern' sector in the spirit of the Lewis model. The high-wage modern-sector firms would not raise

and demand and further wage increases will result in a backward movement along the employer's demand curve.

wages and employment unless induced to do so by the minimum wage increase. The low-wage traditional-sector firms, in turn, release labor that migrates to the expanding high-wage modern sector. The concept is appealing, but it should be fine-tuned to better explain skill compatibility between the two sectors.

Regarding the impact of minimum wages on the number of hours worked in an average week, we find that up to a point, increases in hours worked are positively correlated with the toughness of the minimum wage in both the covered and uncovered sector (Table 11.3, Panel B). Moreover, the impact is much greater – and more significant – among the self-employed workers. Whereas at the lowest toughness level a 1 percent point increase in toughness increases number of hours worked by covered sector workers by 0.4 percent, it increases the number of hours worked in self-employment by 1.2 percent (Table 11.2). Hence, although the number of self-employed workers does not change with changes in the minimum wage relative to average wage, the number of hours of the self-employed does change. As with the impact on employment, once the minimum wage toughness reaches 66 to 71 percent of the average wage in the industry, the number of hours worked in the covered sectors begins to fall, and at the highest level it falls by 0.2 percent in the covered sector and 0.8 percent among the self employed. Tests for longer-term effects show that the estimated coefficients on the toughness variable lagged one year are not significant when entered with the current measure of toughness.

Reallocation of Workers between the Covered and Uncovered Sector, within an Industry

Our analysis of the allocation of workers between the covered and uncovered sectors within an industry indicates that as minimum wages rise relative to average wages in an industry, the percentage of workers in the covered sector will rise (Table 11.3, Panel C). The short-run impact is marginally statistically significant (with P value of 0.113) and indicates a linear effect of 0.19 percent increase in the percentage of covered sector workers. This of course relates to the findings in Table 11.1, where increases in the toughness of the minimum wage increase the number of covered sector workers – up to a point – but seem to leave the number of self employed unchanged. However, we also find that the coefficient on the lagged value of toughness is significant – at the 5 percent level – and indicates that a 1 percent point increase in toughness in one year will raise the number of workers in the covered sector by 0.29 percent in the following year. Hence, the redistribution of labor from the uncovered to the covered sector within each industry, brought about by increases in the minimum wage, is both significant and long-term, countering the traditional view that increases in the minimum wage enlarge the uncovered sector.

Summary and Conclusions

The purpose of this paper is to test whether the Costa Rican government is reaching its goal of reducing wage inequality without simultaneously reducing significantly the level of employment in the covered sector by means of a complicated minimum wage policy. We also examine the redistributive effects of the minimum wage between the covered and the uncovered (self-employed) sectors.

Costa Rica has a complex system of minimum wages that are industry- and occupation-specific. Over the 1980s and 1990s, the government has been systematically raising the lowest minimum wages by a higher percentage than the higher ones. We show that minimum wages in Costa Rica have been maintained at relatively high levels with respect to average wages – the median is 55.5 percent over this period. Moreover, unlike the case in most Latin America countries, this ratio has risen in the 1980s compared with in the 1970s. We find a declining trend in overall inequality – using three measures – during 1980-1992. We also find that the level of wage inequality among covered sector workers is lower than among the uncovered sector workers. Finally, inequality has declined more rapidly in the covered sector than it has in the uncovered sector.

Regression analysis reveals that at the median, a unit increase in the minimum wage relative to the average wage in the industry is associated with: a) a reduction in wage inequality in the covered sector of between 0.9 percent (based on the Gini coefficient), and 1.7 percent (based on the Theil mean logarithmic deviation), and no effect on earnings inequality among the self-employed (using all measures); b) an increase in the level of covered sector employment by 0.56 percent and total employment by 0.35 percent, but has no effect on the number of self-employed; c) an increase in the average number of hours worked per week by 0.14 percent in the covered sector and 0.34 percent in the uncovered sector; and d) a rise of 0.29 percent in the number of covered sector workers within an industry one year after the minimum wage is increased. Hence, the Costa Rican government indeed appears to be accomplishing its goal, and its policy appears to be assisting the reallocation of workers from the self-employed, or uncovered, sector to the covered sectors, countering the traditional view.

From a theoretical perspective, these findings run counter to the traditional competitive two-sector models of the minimum wage. We interpret these findings as supporting the monopsonistic and efficiency wage models of the labor market in those industries where the ratio of the minimum wage to the average wage (*toughness*) is low, but supports the traditional models in those industries where toughness is high. Hence, workers in traditional industries with low average wages are losing jobs, whereas workers in more modern industries with high average wages are gaining jobs. Given that we found overall employment to have increased, minimum wages could be interpreted as assisting the reallocation of labor from the traditional to the more modern sectors.

References

Bell, L. (1997), 'The Impact of Minimum Wages in Mexico and Colombia', *Journal of Labor Economics*, Vol. 15, No. 3 (July), pp. S102-34.

Brown, C. (1999), 'Minimum Wages, Employment, and the Distribution of Income', in O. Ashenfelter and D. Card (eds.), *Handbook of Labor Economics*, Vol. 3, North-Holland, New York.

Card, D. and A.B. Krueger (1994), 'Minimum Wages and Employment: A study of the Fast-Food Industry in New Jersey and Pennsylvania', *American Economic Review*. Vol. 84, No. 3 (June), pp. 772-93.

Card, D. and A.B. Krueger (1995), *Myth and Measurement: The New Economics of the Minimum Wage*, Princeton University Press, Princeton, N.J.

Coulter, F.A.E., F.A. Cowell and S.P. Jenkins (1992), 'Differences in Needs and Assessment of Income Distribution', *Bulletin of Economic Research*, Vol. 44, No. 2 (April), pp. 77-124.

de Villarreal, N.S. and R.S. Breach (1988), 'Evaluation of the impact of Minimum Wages on the Mexican Economy', in ILO (ed.), *Assessing the Impact of Statutory Minimum Wages in Developing Countries: Four Country Studies*, International Labour Organization, Geneva.

Dickens, R., S. Machin and A. Manning (1999), 'The Effects of Minimum Wages on Employment: Theory and Evidence from Britain', *Journal of Labor Economics,* Vol. 17, No. 1 (January), pp.1-22.

Freeman, R.B. (1996), 'The Minimum Wage as a Redistributive Tool', *The Economic Journal,* Vol. 106, No. 436, pp. 639-649.

Katz, L. and A. Krueger (1992), 'The Effect of the Minimum Wage on the Fast Food Industry', *Industrial and Labor Relations Review,* Vol. 46, No.1 (October), pp. 6-21.

Machin, S. and A. Manning (1994), 'The Effects of Minimum Wages on Wage Dispersion and Employment', *Industrial and Labor Relations Review,* Vol. 47, No. 2 (January), pp. 319-29.

Rebitzer, J. and L. Taylor (1995), 'The Consequences of Minimum Wage Laws Some: New Theoretical Ideas', *Journal of Public Economics*, Vol. 56, No. 2 (February), pp. 245-55.

SATEP-ILO (South African Team for Employment Promotion - International Labour Organization) (1988), 'Minimum Wage Fixing in Botswana: Implications for Employment and Income Distribution', in ILO (ed.), *Assessing the Impact of Statutory Minimum Wages in Developing Countries: Four Country Studies*, International Labour Organization, Geneva.

Chapter 12

European Social Protection: What is to be Learned for Latin America?[1]

François Bourguignon

Introduction

The high macroeconomic volatility observed in Latin American countries during the last 20 years, and its associated economic and social costs have brought social insurance to the forefront of the current debate about policy reforms needed in the region. Truly effective safety nets would indeed yield several major benefits. First, they would shield the poor and the vulnerable against macroeconomic shocks and help prevent inefficient disruptions in long-run pro-poor strategies. Second, the availability of such instruments might free governments from the permanent 'income distribution threat,' as lucidly stressed by Berry (1997a, 1997b, and 1998), thereby increasing the credibility and efficiency of macroeconomic management in periods of crisis. Third, by providing diversified income or employment insurance in normal times, the measures would ease asset accumulation and possibly promote rewarding – if risky – projects among the poor. As such, they might be seen as part of long-run growth strategies.

The experience of Western European countries, where large-scale social insurance has developed since the Great Depression, is encouraging, because social insurance has contributed there to a drastic reduction in poverty, vulnerability and inequality. Although these countries differ from one another in the systems they use, nearly all individuals now find themselves well protected against the main risks to their economic wellbeing: income losses, health problems, handicaps, old age, divorce or separation, widowhood, etc. Although these insurance systems were gradually built in times of prosperity when the risks were essentially

1 This paper was prepared for the conference and festschrifts in honor of Albert Berry, Toronto, April 19-20, 2002. It partly draws on a presentation made at the Annual World Bank Conference on Development Economics, Paris, June 26-28, 2000.

idiosyncratic and therefore diversifiable, it is remarkable that they did not break down when macroeconomic volatility became more pronounced after the early 1980s, or when large-scale unemployment hit Europe.

Does this mean that Latin American countries should simply follow a similar path in social insurance policy? Many countries there today enjoy the level of real GDP per capita that Europeans enjoyed in the 1930s,[2] precisely when the development of social insurance started to acquire some momentum. Thus, the question addressed in this chapter is, 'Should Latin American countries now consider engaging in mass social insurance?'

Asking whether social insurance should be developed in Latin American countries at a time when voices loudly call for downsizing the Welfare State in industrial countries may seem ironic. However, the two groups of countries are very different. At present, social protection represents, on average, up to 3 or 4 percent of GDP in Latin America whereas it may reach 25 to 30 percent in industrial countries, the latter proportion perhaps excessive according to some observers.

In any case, developing countries can learn lessons from Western Europe's experience with social insurance and safety nets, and this chapter intends to focus on these lessons. It tries to identify the main features of social protection in industrial countries – the achievements as well as the direct and indirect costs of protection. It then examines the relevance of the main protective instruments available to Latin American countries.

The chapter is organized as follows. The next section presents some general remarks on the demand for social insurance that will be relevant when evaluating existing systems or those proposed to be erected. The following section is then devoted to the experience of industrial countries in the field of social protection. This is followed by a section focusing on the implications of this analysis for Latin America, and concludes with a brief review of recent major social developments in several Latin American countries, particularly the significance of the *Progresa/Oportunidades* program in Mexico.

Individual Demand for Social Insurance and Public Response: General Considerations

Many risks may affect individual or family economic achievements. Income risks include those linked to employment, such as problems affecting employers, or employee bad health and old age. For the self-employed, risks include changes in labor income due to changing economic conditions, as well as climate effects in the agricultural sector. For dependent persons, the income risk includes separation

2 That is, around $5,000 ppp-adjusted 1990 U.S. dollars.

– as when the main breadwinner leaves the family. But risks also arise on the consumption side, such as in changes in consumer needs caused by an increase in the number of children, or the caring for elderly parents, or unexpected expenses for illness and funerals.

In all cases, consumption needs generally exceed spending income. Three types of response to the problem are possible: (a) the gap between income and needs is covered by available savings, possibly by the sale of physical assets; (b) the gap is covered by formal or informal borrowing, that is, by future savings; or (c) consumption spending is reduced, starting with the least essential items, but often also with expenditures on intangible assets such as child education. Of course, solutions (a) and (b) assume that saleable assets have been accumulated and that borrowing is possible, solutions that may be out of reach for the very poor – who have no savings – and for those who have suffered recurrent economic hardships. But these liquidity constraints are also likely to affect many non-poor households.[3]

Liquidity constraints not only curtail people's optimal spending over time, but may also adversely affect people's future opportunities as a result of sub-optimal-consumption-induced ill-health or poor education. Recent literature on the link between growth and inequality highlights the more structural aspects of these constraints – the inefficiency they impose on investment allocation. Here, however, the focus is on inefficiencies arising from the inability to cope with unexpected fluctuations in economic conditions.[4]

Precautionary savings, which avert situations of liquidity constraints in cases of adverse economic shocks, constitute a self-insurance mechanism that substitutes for market insurance. Although self-insurance is likely less efficient and often more costly than any available market insurance, the latter is not always available, or is too costly, and thus self-insurance – even if partial – becomes the only available option.

Demand for social insurance arises when market insurance or its substitutes are not available, or when the average individual cannot afford them. Private companies do not insure risks strongly correlated among individuals and, hence, difficult to diversify – as with unemployment in periods of economic recessions; as well, it may be difficult to establish private contracts compatible with existing informational asymmetries. For instance, income guarantee schemes, like unemployment insurance or the multiple forms of social assistance, may require the intervention of a discretionary public authority to define who should qualify for benefits. However, individuals who cannot afford market insurance require subsidizing of their insurance premia, not the substituting of market insurance by

3 Frankenberg et al. (2002) offer an excellent empirical analysis of these responses in the context of the Indonesian crisis of the late 1990s.

4 On the growth/inequality literature, see Aghion, Caroli and García-Peñalosa (1999). For a more concise view and the relationship between inequality and macroeconomic volatility, see Aghion, Banerjee and Piketty (1999).

alternative schemes. The notion of social insurance is quite different in the latter case.

Excluding for the moment altruistic or political economy considerations, there are several economic reasons why this demand for social insurance is likely to be satisfied by the public sector, two of them important. First, as mentioned above, some people are forced to rely on self-insurance; their being unable to do so generates inefficiencies which society as a whole must remedy. Second, the drop in private expenditure in the case of a person's sudden loss of income may have collective implications. For instance, it may be important for public health that all individual illnesses be correctly treated. Likewise, overall economic growth, as well as the functioning of a society, may require that all children attend school regularly even if their parents are suffering great economic hardship.

It follows, then, that social insurance must respond to various motives and may appear under various forms. First, it may be a pure *market insurance* scheme run by the public sector, often with some implicit or explicit subsidizing of individuals in particular situations; but even then, the public sector might function differently from the private. For instance, old age insurance tends to be pay-as-you-go (PYG) when run by the public sector, but to rely on capitalization when privately run. Second, *social insurance* may be the only insurance device available whenever moral hazard or adverse selection prevents the private sector from functioning adequately, as is the case of most unemployment insurances. Third, social insurance may actually be *social assistance*, in which case benefits distributed as income support are balanced by the general budget rather than by prior contribution or insurance premiums.

Social insurance may also be provided indirectly through risk-preventing state regulation or intervention. Indeed, many public interventions in good and factor markets aim at protecting the income of some specific social groups. Setting minimum agricultural prices, controlling the price of some utilities, imposing a minimum wage, regulating the labor market so as to make lay-offs costly and infrequent all are ways of reducing the income-risk of agents. As such, *market regulation* should be considered as part of the social insurance system, or as imperfect substitute to true social insurance instruments, even though it is generally difficult to evaluate precisely who benefits from or pays for them, and how much they cost.

Social protection is costly, whatever its form and whether or not it is a perfect substitute for market insurance. Competitive market insurance schemes are such that the premium covers the expected loss and the operating costs. But social insurance differs in many aspects. First, as mentioned, it tends to concentrate on risks where information asymmetries may increase the expected loss through moral hazard or adverse selection. Second, it covers individual risks that are sometimes highly correlated – as with unemployment in a recession – and that are therefore not diversifiable. Third, it suffers a loss when it subsidizes the poor – who are privately uninsured. This implies that social protection cannot be financed by actuarially fair contributions and, therefore, must be financed out of the general budget, or through specific taxes.

But those taxes are generally levied on people independent of their exposure to the risks covered; therefore, there is normally some redistribution across individuals in any social protection system, often giving rise to confusion in the literature between the concepts of social protection and redistribution. This problem does not exist with private insurance, which simply redistributes from an individual in one circumstance to the same individual in another. Identifying the actual redistribution behind social insurance schemes is difficult; it generally involves not only a direct transfer from taxpayers to beneficiaries but also distortions caused by both the taxes and the distributed benefits, affecting various social or income groups differently. The difficulty is still greater for 'non-insurance social insurance' instruments, like market regulation.

In summary, social insurance is a substitute for market mechanisms that are not economically viable or that tend to exclude part of the population. Because it cannot operate as standard market insurance where everybody pays a premium equal to his or her expected loss, social insurance redistributes from taxpayers in general to individuals at social risk. This redistribution entails social benefits and costs – benefits that arise from gains in efficiency and a more cohesive society; costs that arise from the distortions generated both through taxes and benefits. Additional distortion costs arise when non-insurance social insurance instruments are taken into account.

Social Insurance in Industrial Countries

Brief History

The history of social insurance in industrial countries divides itself naturally into three periods: 1) the infant stage from the end of the 19th century until the 1930s, when basic instruments were developed; 2) the maturation into comprehensive systems from the 1930s to the end of the 1970s; and 3) subsequent attempts at reforming these systems, motivated by their increasing burdens. At the same time, the structure of the social protection system in terms of the four basic components defined above – that is, straight market insurance, social assistance, social insurance strictly speaking, and market regulation – has changed continuously, but in directions and at speeds that differed across countries.

The infant stage is marked by two events: first, the creation by Otto von Bismark of a compulsory state-run, earnings-based worker insurance system in the

1880s; and second, the enacting of the 1911 National Insurance Act in Britain.[5] Bismark's state-insurance corresponds to the case where social insurance may be seen as a perfect substitute for private market insurance. Its 'social' nature was limited to the fact that it was run by the state rather than private companies, that it was compulsory for some groups of workers, and that it was subsidized so as to provide the appropriate incentive for workers to indeed collectively accumulate savings to cover their old age, their disability, their sick leave, and their funeral. The incentive for employers to contribute to this system was the fear of the mounting socialist movement.[6] With time, this worker- or earnings-related insurance spread to other countries in continental Europe and to Britain. The 1911 National Insurance Act may be seen as a combination of social assistance through an adaptation or extension of traditional poor-laws and worker insurance schemes in the German style. But it also included a true social insurance instrument – unemployment insurance – making it the precursor of modern social insurance systems.

Available social insurance instruments at the infant stage were limited in scope but also in their coverage and effectiveness. Only a limited proportion of wage-workers were actually insured – and often, for tiny amounts. Farmers or self-employed in the non-farm sector generally were not covered, a situation analogous to that in many Latin American countries today.

The golden age of social insurance starts either after the Great Depression or after World War II – depending on the country being considered, the landmarks being the U.S. Social Security Act in 1935, the Beveridge report in 1941 in the U.K., and various major 'social security' laws in continental Europe passed just after the war.[7] These laws consolidated and extended existing instruments, achieving comprehensive social insurance systems aimed at universal coverage and benefits significantly larger than in previous systems. Each of these new social protection schemes included a variety of instruments: *worker insurance* – that is, old age, health, disability; *social insurance* under the form of unemployment insurance and various types of family allowances financed by labor taxes; *social assistance*; and, most important in continental Europe, *market regulation*. These ingredients were initially combined in different proportions in the various countries, worker insurance in the Bismarck tradition being still dominant in continental Europe and, in the U.K., social assistance in the Beveridge tradition being dominant. With time, however, some deformation of the initial systems took

5 For a thorough historical analysis of the beginning of social security systems in Germany and Britain, see Ritter (1983). For a more recent historical analysis of social security and its various components in developed countries, see Gordon (1988).

6 At least initially, since it is likely that, in the absence of minimum wage legislation, employers' contributions were progressively passed on to workers.

7 It must be stressed that 'social security' in Europe generally includes health and disability insurance and not only pensions as in the U.S.

Table 12.1: Social Protection Instruments by Type of Risk in Industrial Countries

Instruments	Type of Risk (1)	(2)	(3)	(4)	(5)	(6)	(7)
			Substitutes to Market Insurance				
Pensions	X						
Disability benefits			X	X			
Occupational injury and disease			X				
Sickness benefit			X				
Survivors		X					
Health	X	X	X	X			
			Social Insurance				
Unemployment					X		
Active labor market programs					X		
			Family Benefits				
Children allowance						X	X
Family support						X	X
Lone parents						X	X
Maternity and parental leaves							X
Day care							X
Housing benefits						X	X
Low income	X	X	X		X	X	X
Market regulation			X		X	X	
Labor-market regulation					X	X	

(1) Old age (employment related); (2) Old age (other); (3) Health risk (employment related); (4) Health risk (other); (5) Unemployment; (6) Income; (7) Family.

Source: Author's elaboration.

place, and some convergence appeared across countries. Most noticeable has been the evolution in continental Europe, where 30 years of unprecedented growth has permitted a rapid extension of existing systems to initially uncovered groups, a substantial increase in the social assistance function under the form of means-tested family benefits, and an extension of market regulation.

In view of the pace of economic growth in the post-war period, such an expansion of the social security system has not been overly costly. The cost became more apparent in the second half of the 1970s when growth started to decelerate and both inflation and unemployment started to increase. Population aging was also emerging as a threat to old-age PYG pension schemes, leading some observers and policy makers to doubt that the established social protection systems were sustainable in the long-run. Two types of reactions then developed: in some countries, a roll-back or significant reforming of existing systems was set into motion; in others, partial reforms were implemented, the rising cost of social protection being met simply by higher taxes on the economy. As of today, however, the share of social protection expenditures in GDP has not fallen substantially in the first set of countries, whereas in the second set of countries, the recent increase will likely be offset by the reforms presently being debated.

The recent evolution of social protection in Western Europe is thus close to a status quo, though its structure has somewhat changed. In particular, unemployment insurance has become less generous nearly everywhere, making it necessary in some countries to create instruments to deal with the problem of long-term unemployment, such as increasing social assistance to the destitute. Note, however, that the public debate that started 20 years ago about the future of the Welfare State is not yet finished, so it would be a mistake to suppose the present situation represents a steady-state condition. Institutions like social protection embody considerable natural inertia, and actual changes may be slow to materialize.

The Anatomy of Present Social Protection Systems

Over time, social protection systems in industrial countries have grown huge and more complex. The complexity comes from two sources: 1) the number of social instruments, and 2) the need to adapt these instruments to the types of populations they cover. In the list of expenditures given by the OECD social expenditure database used in the tables that follow, more than 200 entries appear for France, Sweden, and the U.K. Despite the complexity, however, the various types of risk singled out in the previous section and the corresponding types of instruments appear clearly.

Table 12.1 classifies risks into five categories: old age, health, employment, income, and family. For the first two items, an additional distinction is made according to whether the risk bearer is employed or not. Instruments are classified first into two groups according to whether they are more or less close substitutes of market insurance or clearly belong to social insurance or assistance. They are then broken down by functions that, in many countries, correspond also to institutions responsible for the management of these instruments. These various instruments are mapped into the various types of risk. Close substitutes to market insurance instruments cover employment-related old age and health risks. Pure social insurance instruments tend to cover employment, income, and family risks. But the mapping is not perfect. Because of the variety of individual situations, some instruments cover various types of risk. Thus, low-income instruments may actually cover the income risk of potentially active persons – for instance, people who left the labor force after losing their right to unemployment benefits – as well as old-age risks for individuals whose working career was too short to qualify them for full retirement benefits.

This complexity and diversity makes the analysis of national social protection systems difficult, and international comparisons hazardous. To provide more insight into the diversity in the architecture of existing social protection systems, Table 12.2 compares the importance of the previous instruments for countries

Table 12.2: Social Protection Expenditures and Their Financing, Selected Countries, 1995

Expenditures	Sweden	France	Germany	U.K.	U.S.
Old age	*9.0*	*12.3*	*10.9*	*7.3*	*6.4*
Old age	8.2	10.4	10.3	6.5	5.4
Survivors	0.8	1.9	0.6	0.8	1.0
Health	*9.9*	*10.0*	*10.1*	*8.7*	*7.5*
Disability, sickness and other occupational injury benefits	4.0	2.0	2.0	3.0	1.2
Health (other)	5.9	8.0	8.1	5.7	6.3
Labor market related risks	*4.7*	*3.1*	*3.8*	*1.4*	*0.6*
Unemployment	2.3	1.8	2.4	0.9	0.4
Active Labor Market Programs	2.4	1.3	1.4	0.5	0.2
Family benefits	*6.0*	*4.1*	*2.8*	*4.6*	*1.2*
Child allowances and family support	4.2	2.6	2.0	2.4	0.6
Housing benefits	1.2	0.9	0.2	1.9	---
Low income	0.6	0.6	0.6	0.3	0.6
Other	*3.4*	*0.6*	*0.4*	*0.5*	*0.2*
Total	*33.0*	*30.1*	*28.0*	*22.5*	*15.8*
Financing					
Social Security Contributions	16.9	22.7	20.4	6.3	8.6
Taxes	34.4	22.0	22.9	28.5	21.8
Total mandatory Social Security Contributions and Taxes	*51.3*	*44.7*	*43.3*	*34.8*	*30.4*
Social protection expenditures financed on taxes	16.1	7.4	7.6	16.2	7.2
Taxes used for other public expenditures	18.3	18.3	15.3	12.3	14.6

Source: Author's calculations based on OECD social expenditure database (1980-96) and OECD National Accounts.

thought to be at an extreme in the range of some general philosophy of social protection. Thus, Sweden is representative of Nordic European countries with the most advanced welfare system, whereas the U.S. represents those with the least. Other countries would fall in the mid-range, but France and Germany may be considered as typical of the Bismarckian tradition in continental Europe, whereas the U.K. illustrates the Beveridgian legacy.[8]

Table 12.2 clearly shows the importance of the GDP share of social protection expenditures in most countries. While it is well known that such expenditures for Scandinavia have been large, the 33 percent of GDP value is somewhat astonishing. In the U.S. the expenditures are much lower at 16 percent of GDP, but

8 Japan would also be an interesting example, but available statistics are downward-biased by the fact that a large part of social expenditure falls under the responsibility of employers and local governments.

even that is substantial compared with the 5 percent or less that is normal for developing countries.[9]

The table also demonstrates the large variation across countries of (a) the total relative size of the social protection system, (b) the structure of that system in terms of instruments, and (c) the way the system is financed. But these differences are often somewhat artificial, as, for example, in the case of pensions. The pension system in Sweden, France and Germany is mostly publicly operated and is included in the first two rows of the table. Yet part of this system is fully comparable with privately operated systems in the U.K. or the U.S. Retirees in a PYG system receive, basically, the actuarial return on their accumulated social-security savings minus an amount equivalent to the discrepancy between a public PYG and a privately funded system. Formally, only that difference should appear as part of the social insurance cost in Table 12.2. In other words, a public pension system may be loosely considered as the combination of an actuarially neutral market system with some intended or unintended redistribution across various groups of agents at various times.[10] A meaningful comparison between countries with different systems should ideally separate out the common component of all systems and leave only what is truly different. This suggests that effective differences among the countries appearing in Table 12.2, in terms of the importance of social protection for old age, are less important than they appear. For instance, the contribution of employers to private pension funds in the U.K. – that is, the private counterpart of public pension systems in continental Europe – amounts to 3.1 percent of GDP, yielding a total figure for pensions close to that observed in the two continental European countries. Likewise, in the U.S, employer pension contributions amount to 7.5 percent of GDP.

The same argument can be made for health expenditures when comparing the U.S., where a large part of health insurance is private, with the other countries. However, the financing of health insurance creates an important difference; in many countries financing is done through the tax system, so paying for the insurance is divorced, so to speak, from the receiving of benefits. When compared with a market insurance system like that in the U.S., European health insurance systems thus include a double dimension: on the one hand, they indeed offer the same services as market insurance; on the other, as tax systems are roughly proportional, European insurance systems redistribute a substantial part of income by raising contributions proportional to income and providing benefits roughly equal, ex-ante, for all.[11]

9 According to OECD data, for instance, it was 3.8 percent in Mexico and 7.1 percent in Turkey in 1995.

10 For an analysis of the conditions under which a public PYG pension system may replicate the operations of a funded system, see Hassler and Lindbeck (1999).

11 It must be noted that the issue of non-compulsory health insurance in the U.S. is completely ignored.

Unemployment insurance is another source of asymmetry across countries. In view of present differences in the prevalence of that risk, it is not surprising to find more being spent on that item in continental Europe than in other countries, a fact reflecting more the aggregate or macroeconomic nature of that particular risk than the structure of social insurance systems. However, the cost of unemployment insurance shown in Table 12.2 is not proportional to national unemployment rates, whether based on unemployment benefits *stricto sensu* or on active labor market programs. This lack of proportionality shows that unemployment benefits are generally more generous in continental Europe than elsewhere. On the other hand, the importance of Active Labor Market Programs suggests that, without market interventions like employment subsidies, early retirement schemes, retraining, etc., European rates of unemployment would be higher than what is observed. That item may thus be considered as a direct substitute for unemployment benefits.

No such differences in the relative importance of private and public insurance schemes, or in the size of unemployment, can be invoked to explain the large discrepancies found for family benefits. Because of this, the differences may be more significant and more indicative of true variations in social protection across countries. In this respect, the breakdown in Table 12.2 is somewhat misleading, since it suggests that only a small proportion of family benefits are covering the low-income risk. Indeed, programs covered by that data are those that explicitly guarantee a minimum income to individuals and families, or extensions of such programs, like the EITC (Earned Income Tax Credit) system in the U.S., or the WFTC (Working Family Tax Credit) system in the U.K. But a large part of housing benefits, children's allowances, and other family support are explicitly means-tested; therefore, they can be considered as covering low-income risks in addition to family risks related, for instance, to the number of children or to single-parent situations.

Two last remarks on social protection systems are of relevance. First, it is interesting that the Bismarck/Beveridge distinction still appears clearly when comparing the structure of social protection across countries, as shown in the expenditures and financing sections of Table 12.2. The expenditures section shows the relative weight of family benefits – the Beveridgian bias – in comparison with old age and health insurance – the Bismarckian bias. Interestingly, the financing section shows that France's or Germany's social protection expenditures are predominantly financed out of social security contributions based on earnings, but those of the U.K. are predominantly financed from taxes. This evidence suggests that history is persistent, an important point for Latin American policy makers in the field of social protection. Second, note that the social protection intended through market regulation – and in particular, labor market regulation – is absent from Table 12.2. That no comparable quantified information is available on the cost of these policies does not mean those costs are negligible.

In sum, any large differences in social protection systems across industrial countries are likely associated with differences in institutions, in particular, the relative importance given to market and public insurance mechanisms. Yet substantial differences remain, even in comparisons limited to the social assistance, that is, insurance of low-income and family risks. Also, public coverage of market-insurable risks generally adds a redistributive dimension to market insurance – possibly at the expense of some economic efficiency. The redistribution that takes place through tax-financed health insurance, for instance, may be quite substantial.[12] Through that redistribution, public insurance schemes which are substitutes for market insurance may sometimes add to the coverage of low-income risk by reducing the cost borne by those at the bottom of the income scale.

The Performance of Existing Systems

The preceding discussion suggests how difficult it can be to evaluate rigorously the performance of social protection systems. A counterfactual analysis is really needed, showing the situation of individuals or families at a given time, or throughout their life, and when facing various contingencies without existing public insurance systems. Such analyses of low-income risks were made in several countries, generally as part of comprehensive studies of income redistribution. This section focuses on this aspect of social protection, but also deals with the other components of the system.

A natural inertia pervades all national pension systems since a specific pension regime could hardly be interrupted if there were still some people contributing to or benefiting from it. As a result, many systems, or their public component, have developed over time a high level of specificity and complexity that reflects their history, often making it difficult to draw a balance of the welfare gains permitted by public and private pension systems in a given country.

The literature emphasizes the difference between privately funded systems and public PYG systems (Falkingham and Harding, 1996; Falkingham and Hills, 1995; Brunner, 1996; Nelissen, 1998; Belan and Pestieau, 1999). One method of comparison is to simulate on the basis of 'typical careers' all the contributions a person makes during his or her life and how much he or she receives at retirement under alternative systems, making assumptions about the key parameters of the calculation – interest rate, productivity and age-related earnings growth, subjective time discount rate, etc. More ambitious general equilibrium 'representative' agent models have also been devised to compare privately funded vs. public PYG pension schemes. However, the conclusions from this research are not clear-cut. If,

12 In most European countries, the health system may be conceived as a linear tax system where a proportional 12-percent income tax is used to finance a universal lump-sum transfer equivalent to 12 percent of the average household income. This is potentially much more redistributive than the income tax and other redistributive instruments used in most countries.

under some conditions, the superiority of funded market systems with homogeneous agents is established, the switch from one system to another necessarily involves some redistribution across agents in a steady state, whereas intergenerational redistribution takes place on the transition path towards that steady state. This redistribution bars unambiguous comparisons between the two systems.

The debate about the role of public and private actors also affects health insurance, but differently from the ways discussed above. During the post-war period, considerable progress has been made in most industrial countries to establish the quasi-universality of health insurance – the U.S. remaining the sole industrial country without a National Health Insurance system. With that exception, and on the basis of coverage, the performance of existing systems seems satisfactory. However, the rapid rise in public health expenditures has led some countries to revise their policy by trying to regulate the prices of service-providers and escalating cost–recovery measures, with exemptions for low-income persons. This latter evolution is equivalent to reducing the coverage of public health insurance and, thus, offering more opportunities to private insurers. The debate continues on how much of that evolution is inherent in public health insurance systems themselves and how much is due to increased demand fostered by rapid technological progress in that field, or to the pressure of service-providers (Diamond, 1992).

Judging the performance of unemployment insurance cannot really be isolated from judging that of low-income social insurance. Indeed, incomplete unemployment coverage means that some individuals without a job cannot claim unemployment benefits. With the rise of unemployment, such a situation occurred frequently in Europe in the 1980s. For example, the long-run unemployed in France and Germany lost their right to unemployment benefits; young people who lacked experience did not qualify for unemployment benefit; and women wanting to return to work were unable to find work. In some instances, minimum-income-guarantee schemes have been set up to respond to these situations. Therefore, the performance of the unemployment and low-income insurance systems are to be judged together by considering the risk of a person's income falling below an unacceptable level. In effect, efficient safety nets have evolved in most countries to prevent people's income from falling below the poverty line.[13]

A convincing proof of the effectiveness of safety nets in continental Europe is found in the remarkable stability of the distribution of disposable incomes in most countries hit by the 1980 surge in unemployment rates. An increase in the number of unemployed is normally accompanied by a drop in the income shares of the

---

13 Of course, one may wonder whether data based on standard household surveys include the most vulnerable part of the population and, in particular, the homeless; the situation is not clear. There is anecdotal evidence in several countries that homeless may receive social assistance payments (Paugam, 1999).

Table 12.3: Effect of Family Benefits and Low Income Insurance Schemes on the Bottom Quintile of the Population, Selected European Countries, Percents, 1994

	(1)	(2)	(3)	(4)
Belgium	7.4	28.3	34.6	3.8
France	6.7	37.2	32.7	5.9
Germany	4.8	40.7	56.1	5.9
Ireland	4.4	40.2	80.1	8.1
U.K.	3.9	54.9	82.7	5.4

(1) Bottom quintile's share of total of total household primary income; (2) Bottom quintile's share of family benefits and income maintenance transfers; (3) Bottom quintile's percentage change in income due to transfers; (4) Family benefits and income maintenance transfers as a percentage of household income.

Source: Bourguignon (1998).

bottom household deciles.[14] The observed stability in the distribution of disposable incomes as unemployment rates increased from about 7-8 percent to about 13-14 percent in a number of countries means social insurance mechanisms indeed protected the poor (Atkinson et al., 1995).

Table 12.3 reveals the performance of selected European countries in redistributing income to the poorest quintile. Because the transfers being considered cover family benefits which may be universal – for instance, child allowances in some countries – as well as means-tested benefits and minimum-income-guarantee programs, the targeting of these transfers is not perfect. Yet the targeting is rather strong: in all countries, the bottom quintile receives a much higher share of these social transfers than does the rest of the population – twice as much in the case of France and Germany, more than twice for the U.K. Of course, targeting would be perfect if the analysis were restricted to means-tested instruments. Thus, cross-national differences in Table 12.3 reflect the proportion of transfers that are means-tested as well as the correlation of non means-tested family benefits with income. Given the overall size of the transfers, however, the effect of transfers on the income of the poor is quite substantial, raising the latter by 30 percent in France and Belgium and by more than 80 percent in the U.K.[15] In

14 This is obvious in the case where unemployment means that household market income falls to zero. However, unemployment does not necessarily have this implication when it hurts only one person in a household with multiple earners.

15 In fact, these figures are somewhat ambiguous because the concept of primary income may differ across countries. For instance, primary income is defined here as including old age pension as well as unemployment benefits. This ambiguity is a problem, since income maintenance programs for long-run unemployed are included in unemployment benefits in Belgium but not in France or Germany. Likewise, some minimum pension schemes are included in pension payments in some countries but are considered a transfer in others.

absolute terms, the average net transfer per adult-equivalent to the bottom quintile amounted to approximately 15 percent of the mean household income per adult-equivalent in the whole population, something like $3,000 U.S. per annum, in several countries.

Little has so far been said of the tax system and its role in social protection. Income tax is of little consideration to people in the lower income range because they pay no income tax – that is, that part of the tax system is truly progressive. But the argument here resembles that for the funding of public health care: if benefits do not change when both income and tax payments fall, then the whole system is effectively providing low income insurance.[16] Evaluating social protection systems solely on the basis of their social insurance component could, thus, lead to under-estimating the overall social gains – regardless of the strength of social insurance. A more comprehensive evaluation must also take tax funding into consideration.

The Efficiency Costs of Social Protection

The gains from social protection systems must be balanced against the indirect costs they may introduce by distorting the price and incentive systems. For instance, means-tested benefits introduce high implicit marginal tax rates that may discourage labor supply; public PYG pension systems may involve a loss in savings compared with funded private systems; or taxes and social security contributions that finance social protection systems may be seen as disincentives to savings and employment and, therefore, detrimental to economic activity and growth. The literature on this subject is extensive. What follows highlights the main issues, emphasizing those of relevance to Latin America.

Income maintenance programs that guarantee a minimum income level may significantly reduce labor supply incentives – as is the case when means-tests imply effective marginal tax rates close to 100 percent. If a poor family manages to increase its gross income from labor, such as through longer working hours or a better-paying job, it may, in turn, lose some of its benefits. If the increase in gross income is small, and the budget curve flat, then it may not be of interest to such a family to garner the higher income. And even if the income increase is large enough to produce a definite increase in disposable income, that increase may indeed not compensate for the disutility of more work or effort.

Empirical evidence on the importance of these disincentives is not always conclusive because of the difficulty of observing the true earning capacity of inactive individuals. Indeed, it is difficult to determine whether people who opt for long-term unemployment benefits do so because of their income-leisure preferences, because they might engage in 'moonlighting' activities, or because

16 The idea of considering the progressivity of the income tax schedule as an insurance mechanism dates to Varian (1980).

they truly cannot find work in the formal sector – a more likely possibility under minimum wage and other labor market regulations. Econometric techniques do not permit us to clearly identify these aspects of the labor supply decision except, perhaps, in quasi-natural experiments – as when a significant reform is introduced to the social protection system (Blundell, 1995; Blundell et al., 1998). The lesson to be drawn from the extensive literature is that the elasticity of the labor supply, with respect to the marginal disposable wage, is positive, and that it is greater in some instances than in others – for example, for married women vs. men, and for workforce participation vs. hours worked. This, in turn, raises concerns about the effect of labor supply disincentives on social protection schemes, and also suspicion that social insurance may in some instances result in 'poverty traps.'

Consequently, reforms have been implemented in various countries – and are being considered in others – in an attempt to correct for that potentially negative effect by increasing the slope of the lower part of the budget curve, especially between total inactivity and full-time employment. Such is the objective of measures like the earned income tax credit (EITC) in the U.S., the working family tax credit (WFTC) in the U.K., and more recently, the employment premium (PPE) in France; in these schemes, a negative income tax is received by individuals who work a minimum number of hours and earn less than some gross income floor. Studies suggest that these reforms significantly increased the participation rate of the targeted population without increasing income risk (Bird, 1996; Eissa and Liebman, 1995).

When evaluating the adverse effects of social protection systems on the labor market, analysts tend to focus on the systems' distorting effects on labor demand rather than on labor supply. Because minimum-income-guarantee schemes will likely not be introduced in Latin America in the short- or medium-run – if only because of the administrative cost of measuring actual income – the demand side may also be more relevant there.

Several countries have voiced concern that the financing of social protection might increase labor costs and, therefore, lower the employment rate, an issue important to countries with some minimum wage legislation and strong labor market regulations. With minimum wages enforced, any increase in social contributions and labor taxes needed to finance the social protection system would result in higher real labor cost at the bottom of the skill-scale. Higher in the skill-scale, this increase would be borne by employees whose take-home salary would fall by an amount similar to the rise in social contributions. At the bottom of the scale, however, such 'pass-through' is impossible because of the guaranteed minimum take-home pay – any change in the level of social contributions being then borne by employers. In several continental European countries, the combination of increased mandatory contributions – often aimed at balancing increasing pension and health insurance expenses – and minimum wage legislation resulted in a strong increase in the cost of unskilled labor, a cost blamed, in turn, for the surge in unemployment. Given the negative employment impact of mandatory contributions at the lower end of the skill-scale, since the beginning of the 1990s the European Commission has recommended the reduction of employers' social security contributions on low-wage labor so as to increase the demand for unskilled workers – in effect, progressively tying social contributions to wage levels.

This evolution is interesting. On the one hand, it shows that long-run unemployment may be as much a problem of labor supply as of labor demand. In both cases, the social protection system worsens the situation: on the supply side, income insurance devices discourage workers; on the demand side, a higher minimum labor cost implies fewer people are 'employable.' On the other hand, the preceding argument suggests that it is the combination of higher mandatory contributions and market regulation that generates this efficiency cost in the financing of social protection. It is likely that, without minimum wage legislation, no such adverse employment effects would be observed; instead, a continuous fall would likely occur in the take-home wage of people at the bottom of the wage ladder, the compensation being a better insurance coverage of health, unemployment and old age benefits. Such a system represents more closely a mandatory insurance scheme, its only social dimension being found in any redistribution implicit in compensation payments to formal sector workers, or in situations when part of the contributions are channeled to the benefit of non-insured workers employed in the informal sector. This is the perspective that best examines the present role of social protection in Latin America.

The preceding argument is also applicable to other types of labor-market regulation and, indeed, to all government interventions in the market place. A key issue in the current debate about the cost of social protection systems focuses on the evaluation of a perhaps more efficient alternative: the introduction of pure income insurance devices and the simultaneous elimination of all types of government market intervention, particularly in labor markets and in financial markets – that is, in relation to pensions. However, the *a priori* consideration of this alternative as being more efficient would be the same as assuming that all markets function perfectly and that competitive insurers can insure all risks. Such may not be the outcome, however; interventions may be justified independently of redistribution or social insurance objectives, whereas private insurers cannot cover some risks.

The preceding statement is not intended to defend all types of government interventions or advocate the status quo in countries where social protection combines with many such interventions. Social protection has a cost in terms of price distortions and lost incentives. The preceding argument merely suggests that quantifying that cost is impractical because of the difficulty of defining the correct counterfactual approach. Not surprisingly, the debate about the Welfare State has been inconclusive, and although it has pointed to desirable reforms, particularly in cases of notoriously high social protection costs, the debate has not led to a consensus among analysts about substantially downsizing it. This fact may also explain why the overall level of social protection and social expenditures has not significantly fallen in any industrial country during the last 20 years.

The following points summarize this review of the characteristics of social protection systems in industrial countries: 1) large, mostly historic, variations exist across countries concerning *the role of the public sector in market insurable risks* – in particular, old age and health. The difference lies not only in the identity of the insurer but also in the insurance mechanisms themselves – that is, PYG vs. funded pension systems, or free public health care vs. standard insurance. 2) Public intervention in these sectors generally means *substantial income redistribution* driven by the insurance system and its financing. It has been suggested that it is that redistribution that renders public coverage of old age and health risks truly *social* insurance rather than a straight substitute for market, actuarially neutral, mechanisms. 3) Unemployment insurance and active labor market programs aimed at 'preventing' unemployment represent in continental Europe a significant share of social protection expenditures and GDP, expenditures that are somewhat *cyclical* as well as structural. 4) The structural component of unemployment insurance is influenced by the existence of 'non-insurance' insurance instruments, corresponding to various types of *labor market regulations* aimed, presumably, at preventing employment-related risks. 5) Although the remaining social insurance represents a small share of GDP, it exhibits a *highly effective coverage of low income and family risks because of powerful targeting*. In most countries, instantaneous redistribution to low income households through these instruments is significant. 6) Social protection instruments give rise to distortions and, thus, may generate substantial *indirect costs* that are difficult to quantify. Several countries are taking steps to re-establish individual incentives threatened by existing systems. But an important proportion of indirect costs arise from the interaction between social protection and its financing on the one hand, and different forms of *market regulation* on the other.

Lessons for Latin American Countries

Given this panorama of the industrial countries, where do Latin American countries stand today in terms of social protection? Far from advanced – in terms both of the volume of social expenditures relative to GDP, and of the structure of expenditures and the risks covered. Indeed, this section suggests that, with a few exceptions, current social protection in the Latin American region resembles that in pre-World War II European countries. The question therefore becomes whether comparable development paths can and should be followed, and with what new instruments.

The difference in the aggregate relative importance of social protection between industrial countries and Latin America is impressive. Table 12.4 – the Latin American counterpart for Table 12.2 – indicates that social expenditures were, on average, 13 percent of GDP by 1998-89, a figure that includes public spending on education – not in contrast to the data for the industrial countries. That item was not included in social 'risks' covered by 'social protection' because public spending on education more closely resembles a publicly provided (private) service, possibly with some social objectives, than coverage of a well-identified risk.[17] In any case, using the same definition of social expenditures leads to differences larger than the straight comparison of the total row of Table 12.2 and the total column of Table 12.4: including public spending in education would be equivalent to adding approximately five percent of GDP for industrial countries, excluding it would lead to subtracting four percent for the Latin American region. Using the latter definition, social expenditures would represent less than 10 percent of the region's GDP compared with a range of from 16 percent in the U.S. to over 30 percent in continental Europe. Note, however, that the trend is increasing – social spending increased by almost 3 percent of GDP in the 1990s.

Of course, the preceding share of expenses exhibits considerable variation across Latin America, ranging from only five percent or less in Honduras, Paraguay and Peru to around 15 percent for Argentina, Brazil, Chile and Uruguay. However, as with the situation in industrial countries, not all expenditures contribute to social protection in the same proportion. In particular, the reason for considering old age insurance coverage as different from social assistance coverage is still stronger for Latin America than for industrial countries. Social security coverage in Latin American countries is usually limited to wage workers in the formal sector of the economy, so the implicit redistribution stressed in public pension systems of industrial countries favors the more disadvantaged in that sector – and not necessarily the poorest among the old.[18] The same may apply to some public expenditures on health care, but the problem may be less serious because a larger proportion of these expenditures is non-contributive. Applying these corrections increases the difference between industrial and Latin American countries, while decreasing country-differences among the latter. What was considered 'pure' social insurance represented between six and ten percent of GDP in European countries, compared with 4.3 percent average across Latin America

17 In the presence of compulsory schooling provided by the private sector, this could be considered as some kind of risk associated with children. However, there are many other reasons for the public sector to invest in schooling infrastructure.

18 Bourguignon et al. (2002) found pensions to be one of the main causes of Brazil's excess inequality over the U.S. Also note that in various instances of financial difficulties of pension systems in the region, the redistribution has even gone from the poorest households – generally not concerned with pensions – to the middle and upper middle class.

Table 12.4: Social Expenditures as Percent of GDP, Selected Latin American Countries, 1990-91 and 1998-99

	Education		Health		Pensions		Housing and social assist.		Total		Total without education		Total w/o educ. and pensions	
	1990-91	1998-99	1990-91	1998-99	1990-91	1998-99	1990-91	1998-99	1990-91	1998-99	1990-91	1998-99	1990-91	1998-99
Argentina	3.5	4.7	4.3	4.6	6.8	8.7	3.0	2.5	17.7	20.5	14.2	15.8	7.3	7.1
Brazil	4.5	3.9	4.5	3.4	5.5	11.5	3.6	2.2	18.1	21.0	13.6	17.1	8.1	5.6
Chile	3.1	3.9	2.7	2.8	5,1	7.5	2.1	1.8	13.0	16.0	9.9	12.1	4.8	4.6
Colombia	2.6	4.7	2.0	4.1	2.6	5.2	0.8	1.0	8.0	15.0	5.4	10.3	2.8	5.1
Costa Rica	3.9	4.4	4.9	4.9	4.6	5.8	2.2	1.7	15.7	16.8	11.8	12.4	7.2	6.6
Guatemala	1.3	2.3	0.7	1.3	0.6	0.9	0.9	1.7	3.4	6.2	2.1	3.9	1.6	3.0
Honduras	4.4	4.1	2.2	2.0	0.0	0.0	1.3	1.3	7.9	7.4	3.5	3.3	3.5	3.3
Mexico	2.1	3.8	2.6	2.1	1.1	2.3	0.7	0.9	6.5	9.1	4.4	5.3	3.3	3.0
Nicaragua	4.8	5.7	3.8	4.4	0.0	0.0	2.2	2.6	10.8	12.7	6.0	7.0	6.0	7.0
Panama	4.8	6.0	5.8	6.7	6.0	5.4	2.0	1.3	18.6	19.4	13.8	13.4	7.8	8.0
Paraguay	1.4	3.7	0.5	1.1	1.1	2.6	0.1	0.1	3.1	7.4	1.7	3.7	0.6	1.2
Peru	1.1	2.2	0.7	1.3	1.2	2.8	0.3	0.5	3.3	6.8	2.2	4.6	1.0	1.8
Dominican Rep.	1.6	2.8	1.0	1.5	0.6	0.8	1.1	1.5	4.3	6.6	2.7	3.8	2.2	3.0
Uruguay	4.2	3.2	5.1	2.8	6.5	16.3	1.0	0.5	16.8	22.8	12.6	19.6	6.1	3.3
Venezuela	3.6	3.8	1.5	1.3	2.6	2.6	1.3	0.8	9.0	8.6	5.4	4.8	2.8	2.2
Arithmetic mean	3.1	3.9	2.8	3.0	3.0	4.8	1.5	1.4	10.4	13.1	7,.3	9.1	4.3	4.3

Source: Author's calculations based on data from ECLAC (2001).

Table 12.5: Distributive Effect of Social Expenditures, Selected Latin American Countries, 1999 (Share of Poorest 40 Percent on Social Expenditure)

Country	Percentage of total household income	Transfer of social expenditure: Health		Housing and social assist.		Total		Total transfer with social security and education	
		(1)	(2)	(1)	(2)	(1)	(2)	(1)	(2)
Argentina	13.9	55.3	23.3	38.5	7.5	51.2	30.8	38.6	70.6
Bolivia	12.1	29.9	4.9	18.9	4.5	24.7	9.4	43.9	62.2
Brazil	13.3	58.0	18.1	57.7	21.1	57.8	39.1	55.9	118.9
Chile	11.9	54.1	16.2	64.9	13.2	59.0	29.5	32.0	54.5
Colombia	12.6	37.3	15.6	n.a.	n.a.	n.a.	n.a.	46.0	79.8
Costa Rica	16.7	51.3	32.0	n.a.	n.a.	n.a.	n.a.	36.4	64.8
Uruguay	18.0	54.8	16.1	31.3	1.2	53.1	17.3	37.2	66.4

(1) Transfer to the 40% poorest households as percentage of total social expenditure.
(2) Transfer to the 40% poorest households as percentage of their primary income.

Source: Author's calculations based on data from ECLAC (2000).

in the 1990s.

The small size of social expenditures in Latin America as a proportion of GDP and the tendency there to concentrate on sectors where expenditures are not very redistributive is often reinforced by the limited growth in those expenditures. The first rows of Table 12.5 show the impact of health, housing, and social assistance spending on the income of the poorest 40 percent of the population in several Latin American countries. Spending is modest, most of it occurring in health care rather than social assistance. In effect, expenditures on the poorest barely exceed the poor's share of the population – and sometimes do not even meet it. Both health expenditures and social assistance achieve greater redistribution toward the poorest in industrial countries.

The effect of redistribution on the income of the poor in Latin America is more pronounced when we include both education and social security expenditures in the analysis – see the last columns of Table 12.5. However, the redistributive power is limited because often the poorest 40 percent get less than 40 percent of the expenditures – rarely do they get more. Furthermore, including education and social security in redistribution – as done in Table 12.5 and in many studies on redistribution – is an artificial approach. As well, the fact that spending on education is not really 'social protection' expenditure means it does not provide income redistribution for current working-age cohorts but for workers of the future, a feature that makes the expenses much different from spending on social assistance or health care.[19] Concerning pensions, on the other hand, standard redistribution analysis on current incomes of the type reported in Table 12.5 ignores previous pension contributions by pensioners during their lifetime and

19 Although preventive care would have much the same function.

excludes pension payments from their primary income. Much different would be the outcome were one to adopt an inter-temporal view, by which pension systems correspond to the periodic redistribution of one's very own income to oneself, and different as well were we to take into account present contributions to the pension system and the way the deficit is financed.

In summary, compared with industrial countries, Latin America sees little redistribution of income and therefore little social insurance. But what does such a comparison mean considering that the two sets of countries are at different stages of economic development, have different needs, and function differently? The comparison should be made, perhaps, between the Latin America of today and the industrial countries of pre-World War II, when these countries' economic development was similar to that of Latin America now. The question then becomes whether Latin America should follow roughly the same path of social protection- and institution-building that Europe has followed since the war, or bypass intermediate stages and aim at different objectives.

An analogy can be drawn between the present state of social protection in Latin America and that in Europe before World War II, making it clear that the process of economic development is the driving force. Two features are important in this respect: 1) the proportion of the labor force not covered by formal wage-labor contract is still high in many countries of the region, and 2) the administrative capacity to measure income is limited. The first feature explains why social protection instruments, now practically universal in industrial countries, cover only part of the population, as was the case in pre-World War II Europe. The second feature explains the difficulty in developing social insurance instruments tied to the current welfare of households – that is, means-testing – and making the tax system truly progressive.

Although it would be unrealistic to consider all Latin American countries identical, the features described are apparent in the structure of social protection in most countries in the region. Pension systems, with variable weights given to the public and private sectors, cover wage workers in some sectors and in firms greater than a minimum size.[20] Health insurance systems feature much the same types of contribution and coverage, although coverage of the poor varies from free to greatly subsidized. The development of contributive unemployment insurance is constrained by the difficulty of assuring the unemployed status of beneficiaries, given existing employment opportunities in the informal sector. Unemployment risks are, thus, covered indirectly through severance payment or forced savings legislation in formal employment. Also, the labor market is often strongly regulated to protect employment and promote 'equity' and some kind of income

20 Less than 30 percent of the economically active population contributes to pensions in Argentina, Brazil and Mexico. In Chile, where the pension system is probably the most developed, 100 percent of the active population is actually 'registered' in the system, but only 50 percent contributes to it.

insurance through minimum wage legislation. Finally, given the difficulty of determining actual income, social assistance goes through limited transfers in kind. Targeting is imprecise, often relying on geographical criteria or even on structural indicators of poverty, although transitory poverty should also be a concern.

This structure of social protection in Latin America is probably similar to that of continental Europe in the 1920s and 30s, social protection being then more advanced in the U.K. because of the National Insurance Act. The favorable economic conditions in Europe during the first three decades of the post-war period permitted drastic modification of the structure of social protection towards the level of development already described. In Latin America likewise, it is expected that economic development will eventually increase the share of formal employment and the capacity to control incomes as transactions escalate through financial intermediaries accountable to the fiscal authority. Although only education and pensions were usually emphasized, the evolution of social expenditures during the 1990s shows that such a tendency exists. But will this evolution trigger the development of effective universal social protection similar to that in industrial countries today? And what path should such an evolution follow? And what are the alternatives to such an evolution?

Development of an effective social protection system is not always an automatic sub-product of economic development. In industrial countries, universal social protection developed vigorously as a response to social demands that sprung from the tragedies of the Great Depression and the war, and was affordable as a result of fast economic growth. Although the macroeconomic volatility of the past two decades in Latin America has increased the demand for social protection, the slow economic growth there does not permit the construction of a social protection system. Moreover, inequalities in several countries may reduce the demand for universal protection. The middle class is likely satisfied with social protection being limited to the formal sector, with little help for the poor. The paradox is that there is a growing presumption among economists and policy makers that existing inequalities and poor social protection are contributing to slow economic growth and to the persistence of inequalities – and therefore, to the delay in developing social protection. Perhaps this vicious circle will stimulate social protection initiatives.

Assuming a consensus has been reached on the need to accelerate the development of social protection, the question arises concerning the structure of that system and the opportunity of replicating or adapting the various systems presently observed in industrial countries. As shown by the recent trend towards reforms in the region, this question has already been debated in the case of pensions and health insurance. Indeed, there was no need to wait until the coverage of existing systems had significantly increased to discover that some instruments or some combination of them might not suit the Latin American economic environment. From that point of view, most of the present debate about the *future* of pensions and health insurance in industrial countries is also of some relevance to Latin American countries. The debate about the efficiency – and equity – cost of financing social protection in the presence of labor-market regulations, like minimum wage or employment protection, and more generally about what was called 'non-insurance' protection instruments, is also important (Heckman and Pagés, 2000). Likewise, the issue of disincentives associated with social assistance may gain relevance as means-tested cash transfers begin to develop.

Conclusion

The recent policy initiatives undertaken in Latin America point to both an increasing demand for social protection and a capacity to respond to that demand through instruments adapted to existing constraints. These initiatives herald, perhaps, a genuine structural change in redistribution policy in the region.

The *Trabajar* program in Argentina is an example; this program offers an alternative to unemployment insurance. Responding to high unemployment with low-wage employment programs is by no means an innovation, however; the tactic has been often used to tackle crises and is a common strategy in Maharashtra state, India (Ravallion and Datt, 1995). More original, however, is to regard such a program as a long-term strategy to deal with unemployment risk rather than as a transitory response to a crisis. Indeed, other countries in Latin America may well start to implement a similar program – as has Colombia. However, with the recent crisis in Argentina, the *Trabajar* program has been unable to deal adequately with the sudden mass unemployment problem there. Even if practical obstacles had been overcome, budget constraints would not have permitted extension of the program to deal adequately with acute unemployment.

A second example is provided by the *Progresa* program in rural Mexico (Behrman et al., 2001; Gertler, 2000) – recently extended to *Oportunidades*. This program consists of cash transfers to poor families identified on the basis of, for example, land ownership, demographic composition, housing, and parents' education. These transfers differ from guaranteed income schemes already discussed. On the one hand, eligibility criteria refer to permanent rather than transitory income, so *Progresa* is not a true income insurance device. On the other hand, a distinctive feature of these transfers is the condition that children of the affected families be sent to school and undergo regular medical examinations. From that perspective, *Progresa* achieves two goals: on a permanent basis, it provides parents an incentive to invest in their children's' future; and on a transitory basis, it insures that children attend school even when their family is undergoing financial hardship – although a hardship buffered by the cash transfer. In other words, the insurance provided by *Progresa* constitutes insurance of children in poor families – an original initiative being followed in Brazil,

Colombia, and Ecuador.

This program was recently extended to some urban areas in Mexico and launched at the federal level in Brazil – an important development because it means that cash transfers have appeared as a significant component of the redistribution system in Latin America. While they represent only a small share of GDP now, their strategic targeting has likely achieved much more than ever before. Furthermore, their size will likely expand significantly in the future.

These two examples – and the echo they have had in the region – suggest a strengthening of the belief that redistribution and social protection are important components of a development strategy. This development increases the urgency to design instruments well adapted to the structural characteristics of the region.

References

Aghion, P., E. Caroli and C. García-Peñalosa (1999), 'Inequality and Economic Growth: The Perspective of the New Growth Theories.' *Journal of Economic Literature*, Vol. 37, No. 4 (December), pp. 1615-60.

Aghion, P., A. Banerjee and T. Piketty (1999), 'Dualism and Macroeconomic Volatility', *Quarterly Journal of Economics*, Vol. 114, No. 4 (November), pp. 1359-97.

Atkinson, A., L. Rainwater and T. Smeeding (1995), 'Income Distribution in European Countries', Working Paper No. 9535, Department of Applied Economics, University of Cambridge.

Behrman, J., P. Sengupta, and P. Todd (2001), 'Progressing through PROGRESA: An Impact Assessment of a School Subsidy Experiment', PIER Working Paper 01-033, Penn Institute for Economic Research, University of Pennsylvania.

Belan, P. and P. Pestieau (1999), 'Privatizing Social Security: A Critical Assessment', *Geneva Papers on Risk and Insurance: Issues and Practice*, Vol. 24, No. 1 (January), pp. 114-30.

Berry, A. (ed.) (1998), *Poverty, Economic Reform and Income Distribution in Latin America*, Lynne Rienner, Boulder, CO.

Berry, A. (1997a), 'The Income Distribution Threat in Latin America', *Latin American Research Review*, Vol. 32, No. 2 (Spring), pp. 3-40.

Berry, A. (1997b), 'Poverty Policy in Latin America during the 1980s', *Review of Income and Wealth*, Vol. 43, No. 1 (March), pp. 119-29.

Bird, E. (1996), 'Repairing the Safety Net: Is the EITC the Right Patch?', *Journal of Policy Analysis and Management*, Vol. 15, No. 1 (Winter), pp. 1-31.

Blundell, R. (1995), 'Tax Policy Reform: Why We Need Microeconomics', *Fiscal Studies*, Vol. 16, No. 3 (August), pp. 106-25.

Blundell, R., A. Duncan and C. Meghir (1998), 'Estimating Labor Supply Responses Using Tax Reforms', *Econometrica*, Vol. 66, No. 4 (July), pp. 827-61.

Bourguignon, F. (1998), 'Redistribution and Development', invited lecture, Congress of the International Institute of Public Finance, Cordoba, Argentina (August).

Bourguignon, F., F. Ferreira and P. Leite (2002), 'Beyond Oaxaca-Blinder: Accounting for International Differences in Income Distribution', Working Paper No. 2828, World Bank, Washington, D.C.

Brunner, J. (1996), 'Transition from a Pay-As-You-Go to a Fully Funded Pension System: The Case of Differing Individuals and Intragenerational Fairness', *Journal of Public Economics*, Vol. 60, No. 1 (April), pp. 131-46.

ECLAC (Economic Commission for Latin America and the Caribbean) (2000), *Equity, Development and Citizenship*, ECLAC, Santiago.

ECLAC (Economic Commission for Latin America and the Caribbean) (2001), *Social Panorama of Latin America, 2000-2001*, ECLAC, Santiago.

Diamond, P. (1992), 'Organizing the Health Insurance Market', *Econometrica*, Vol. 60, No. 6 (November), pp. 1233-54.

Eissa, N. and J. Liebman (1995), 'Labor Supply Response to the Earned Income Tax Credit', NBER Working Paper No. 5158, National Bureau of Economic Research, Cambridge, MA.

Falkingham, J. and J. Hills (1995), 'Redistribution between People or across the Life Cycle?', in J. Falkingham and J. Hills (eds.), *The Dynamic of Welfare: The Welfare State and the Life Cycle*, Prentice Hall/Harvester Wheatsheaf, New York, pp. 137-49.

Falkingham, J. and A. Harding (1996), 'Poverty Alleviation vs. Social Insurance Systems: A Comparison of Lifetime Redistribution', *Contributions to Economic Analysis*, Vol. 232, pp. 233-66.

Frankenberg, E., J.P. Smith, J. Strauss, and D. Thomas (2002), 'Economic Shocks, Wealth and Welfare', paper presented at the IMF conference on Macroeconomics and Poverty Reduction, Washington, D.C. (March 14-15).

Gertler, P. (2000), *The Impact of PROGRESA on Health*, Final Report, International Food Policy Research Institute, Washington, D.C.

Gordon, M. (1988), *Social Security Policies in Industrial Countries*, Cambridge University Press, Cambridge, U.K.

Hassler, J. and A. Lindbeck (1999), 'Can and Should a Pay-as-You-Go Pension System Mimic a Funded System?', Institute for International Economic Studies, Stockholm, mimeo.

Heckman, J. and C. Pagés (2000), 'The Cost of Job Security Regulation: Evidence from Latin American Labor Markets', Working Paper No. 40, Research department, Inter-American Development Bank, Washington, D.C.

Nelissen, J. (1998), 'Annual versus Lifetime Income Redistribution by Social Security', *Journal of Public Economics*, Vol. 68, No. 2 (June), pp. 223-49.

Paugam, S. (ed.) (1999), *L'Europe Face à la Pauvreté: Les Expériences Nationales de Revenu Minimum*, La Documentation Française, Paris.

Ravallion, M. and G. Datt (1995), 'Is Targeting through a Work Requirement Efficient? Some Evidence from Rural India', in D. van de Walle and K. Nead (eds.), *Public Spending and the Poor: Theory and Evidence*, John Hopkins Press, Baltimore.

Ritter, G. (1983), *Social Welfare in Germany and Britain: Origins and Development*, Berg, Dover, N.H.

Varian, H. (1980), 'Redistributive Taxation as Social Insurance', *Journal of Public Economics*, Vol. 14, No. 1 (August), pp. 49-68.

Index